Introduction to Social Administration in Britain

Muriel Brown

Lecturer in Social Administration
London School of Economics
and Political Science

Hutchinson of London

Hutchinson & Co (Publishers) Ltd
3 Fitzroy Square, London W1

London Melbourne Sydney Auckland
Wellington Johannesburg and agencies
throughout the world

First published 1969
2nd edition 1971
Reprinted 1974
3rd edition 1976
© Muriel Brown 1969, 1971 and 1976

Printed in Great Britain by The Anchor Press Ltd
and bound by Wm Brendon & Son Ltd
both of Tiptree, Essex

ISBN 0 09 125960 6 cased
ISBN 0 09 125961 4 paper

Contents

Preface to the third edition

It is tempting to conclude the second revision of material first put
together in 1968 with the cliché that the more things change the
more they stay the same. There has undoubtedly been change and
as much of it as possible is reported here. Not only has the social
services field had an abundance of Acts of Parliament, White
Papers and Reports in the last few years, but it has also had
reorganization. In personal social services, local government and
the national health service major administrative change has been
imposed, while important developments in policy and subtle
changes in emphasis and attitude have continued to occur in all
the social services. Moreover the academic aspect of social
administration has not remained static: research on social problems
and provisions is constantly being reported on and the theoretical
contours of the subject are continually revised and redefined. But
despite these changes the difficulties and dilemmas remain remarkably constant. Gloomy economic prospects still dominate the
social policy scene, social services providers are preoccupied with
problems of resources and the old debate about how far services
should be subject to market forces and how far they should be
provided freely and universally is still going on. Old complaints
about poverty, slum housing, educational inequality, the lack
of a family policy and so forth, are still being validly put forward.
In one sense there is a depressing sameness about both the criticism of
the Welfare State and about the solutions offered to deal with them.
In another sense the subject continues to shift and develop, calling
for new skills and new approaches to our understanding of social
affairs. I continue to hope that a general introduction has some
place for new students of social administration who wish to make a
start somewhere. I also hope that it encourages them to pursue the
subject. For whether it changes or whether it stays the same, the
territory of social administration is likely to prove worth exploring.

Muriel Brown
London School of Economics and Political Science
November 1975

Preface to the first edition

The aim of this book is to convey something of the meaning, content and excitement of the study of social administration to those who do not yet know what the term means. It is very much an introduction to the subject and so it is directed to what I hope is a fairly wide range of people who for various reasons do want to know what social administration means. It should be of use to undergraduates in social science faculties who are about to embark on a course in social administration or who are wondering whether to do so. The original concept of the book was, in fact, derived from lectures I gave to first-year students who were studying basic social sciences and intending to go on to a full study of social administration. The lectures, and this book, were planned to give them some idea of the scope of their chosen subject and also some understanding of why they were starting their university studies with courses in economics, sociology, government, etc, instead of getting straight into social administration itself. But the book is also directed to students on courses leading to social work qualifications at colleges of further education, and to voluntary workers, supplementary benefits officers, local government officers, teachers, and so on, who attend short courses or evening classes on the social services and need some simple introductory reading. It is also for all the people, whether students in a formal sense or not, who simply want to know more about the social problems of this country and the services we have developed to cope with them, and who want to start with a relatively short account.

One or two points about the book's scope must be mentioned. Most of the descriptions of social services and legislation refer to the position in England and Wales. In general the position in Scotland is similar, but there are some important differences. There are, on the whole, few statistics, because these change too rapidly to warrant inclusion in a textbook of this kind. But reference is made in the text to official publications, Annual Reports and so on, from which up-to-date information can be obtained. Where figures are given they usually refer to the position in 1967, but their main purpose is to give some indication of proportion rather than precise data.

Not all the main areas of social problems and policies are covered here and I want to mention the two major omissions: the social issues of employment are not discussed in Part One on basic provision, although they clearly form a very important area of need and policy; and the problem of offenders against the law is left out of the second part of the book on the special need groups. There are several reasons for these omissions but the main one is the simple one of lack of space. These topics are, however, well covered in other books of which I would mention two: A. F. Young's *Social Services in British Industry* and D. J. West's *The Young Offender*. Both are recent and very readable.

Those are major omissions of whole topics. Clearly there are innumerable other omissions (and simplifications) in this book, again mainly because it is trying to be a brief and simple introduction to a very complicated subject. The suggestions for further reading at the ends of chapters are given as some compensation for the brevity of my treatment of many important issues.

It is impossible for me to make precise acknowledgements to the many people who have helped me to produce this book: the debt is too enormous and widespread. To the writers of many books I am indebted for inspiration and information. To the people who have talked to me about their problems or their work in the social services I am indebted for the greater insight they have afforded me. Above all, I am indebted to my one-time teachers at the Social Administration Department of the London School of Economics and very, very deeply indeed to my colleagues, past and present, at the Department of Social Administration here at Manchester University. They have given me the encouragement, constructive criticism and practical help I needed, as well as most of my knowledge, and I am sincerely grateful.

Muriel Brown
University of Manchester
1969

Part One
Introduction and basic issues

1 Some definitions of the subject

Social Administration is not an easy field to define. At a superficial level it means a study of the social services. A social service is usually defined as a service provided by the State whose object is the improvement of the welfare of the individual. To distinguish social services from public services and utilities, this element of individual welfare is always stressed. The provision of roads and motorways is a vital public service which benefits the whole community. The provision of retirement pensions benefits the individual in a highly particular manner: he does not share collectively in the benefit but receives it personally for his peculiar use. This concept of collective provision to meet individual need is the hallmark of a social service. Social administration starts with a definition of social services and a description of them. But as an academic discipline it has proceeded from this starting point to take the definitions deeper and ask fundamental questions about the services: what needs are they trying to meet; why do the needs arise; on what grounds, political, moral, economic, does society base its attempts to meet need; how effective are its policies and indeed what are our criteria for effectiveness in this context?

The list of questions is endless and can lead the enquirer into many and diverse fields of interest, but for convenience it is possible to group them into two main areas of study. First one can say social administration is concerned with social problems and second it is concerned with the ways in which society responds to those problems.

Social problems are problems which affect not just the individual but the society in which he lives. They arise from individual human needs which are common to all members of society. Some needs are obvious like the need for food and clothing and housing; some are more conceptual and sophisticated like the need for dignity and status; some are powerful and intangible like the need for love and affection. These common human needs are largely met by personal and family action: individuals work for their living, find accommodation, establish friendship, obtain care, security and a sense of purpose within family and social groups. But when the needs are not met they give rise to problems which society as a whole increasingly tries to tackle. The basic need to subsist leads to the social problem of poverty if family and individuals are unable to meet the need themselves. The common need for shelter is the basis of the housing problem. Society does not, of course, always recognize or accept that individual needs give rise to *social* problems. Society can leave the individual and the family to cope with such things as poverty and unemployment and loneliness, or it can see that collective action is taken to deal with them. The scope of social action itself in part determines what we mean by social problems. Poverty and crime are readily accepted as social problems because their effect on society as a whole is so marked that action is taken to deal with them. Loneliness amongst the aged or child neglect can exist yet not be perceived as social problems if society has neither the will nor the means to tackle them. This is partly because poverty and crime are generally perceived as more threatening to society than loneliness or child neglect and it is important to appreciate that society responds to problems as much out of concern for the maintenance of order as out of altruistic interest in the welfare of the individual. It is fascinating to probe into why certain social facts become 'social problems' at different times in a society's development, and no one theory of social progress or social control is adequate as an explanation of these changes in perception. But while there can be no universal agreement on what constitutes or causes a social need or a social problem it should be possible to agree on what is generally regarded, at a given time, in a given society, as appropriate under such a heading. And on this commonsense basis the study of social administration usually proceeds.

It is not possible to give a once and for all, agreed definition of social problems, or to make a list of them, and this is one of the reasons of course why it is not easy to give an agreed definition of social administration either. But whatever are generally accepted as social problems, together with the concept of human needs that underlies them, must be the first area of study for the social administration student. The second area of study is of the ways in which society organizes itself to meet the needs and cope with the problems. This is a study of social policy and it involves an understanding of the development of social policy, of the legislation which makes it explicit, of the government machinery and administrative procedures concerned with social provision, of the role of voluntary action, the recruitment and professionalization of staff and the problems of financing the social services. Like the area of social problems the subject matter of social policy is not a fixed territory. As society defines more and more problems social action is extended into new areas. Moreover new perspectives on old problems and provisions can reveal that social policy is perhaps more pervasive than was sometimes thought and many economic policies or even foreign policies have social implications that must not be overlooked. An example of this is the growth of interest by students of social policy in the field of taxation. Fiscal policies are not simply a question of money raising but may involve a recognition of, for example, the needs of the family, to such a practical extent that they must be regarded as much as a social policy as an economic intervention. But the focus, or at least the starting point, of the social administration student's concern with social policy will be the social services, which provide the most tangible evidence of social action. Consideration is given to the process of establishing social services; to the numerous factors which determine their development or modify their operation; the economic and philosophical principles that underlie them and, increasingly, to attempt to evaluate their performance and measure their effectiveness.

If we define social administration as this two-fold concern with social problems and with social response and policy, then clearly it is a subject which must borrow heavily from the basic social sciences. In order to study a problem one must examine it from many different angles asking questions about size and prevalence, causation and effect. Then one must look at it from sociological, psychological and statistical viewpoints in order to arrive eventually at a reasonable and rounded perception of the whole. Obviously in order to do so one needs to have some understanding of the different disciplines concerned with the study of society.

Let us take one example of a current social problem – old age. How do we know this is a problem? To some extent we know from commonsense and observation that many old people are unhappy that old age can bring a wearisome degree of financial insecurity, a frustrating sense of physical dependency. Most of us have theories or views about the problem of old age – that, for example, the old are neglected by their families, that pensions are not adequate, that there should be more old people's homes etc. But to take effective action to deal with the problem, to reduce as far as possible the threat of old age, we need to have proper understanding of the situation. To start off with, we need to look at it statistically to find out how many old people there are, how old they are, what proportion of the total population they represent, whether the proportion is rising or falling. Sociology helps us to understand how old people fit into society, what attitudes prevail towards them, how and with whom they live, what their changing role in society is. It is no less important to consider the problem from a psychological viewpoint: what does it *feel* like to be old, how does a person adjust to giving up work, to leaving his home, what are the hopes, the needs, the fears, the compensation of ageing? A study of history can throw further light on the problem: one can find out how the problem has appeared in different times and how and why attitudes and policies have changed. The economics of old age are yet a further important dimension of the problem.

Finally when we study social policy and social action, the response of society to its problems, we need to base our study on some understanding of politics, of public administration, of finance etc. In order to understand what factors contribute to the formation of social policy we need some grasp of political and economic history, we need to know something of the complexities of the legislative process and of the intricacies of local administration. To turn again to the example of old age we need to know more than simply what services there are, but how such services, for example sheltered housing or pensions, are administered and financed, how effectively they are run, what is the balance between central departments and local authorities in the making of decisions regarding services, and so on. And we need to examine some of the moral assumptions that underlie our social action and the validity of the social theories on which our policies are based.

Social administration, then, is an eclectic field of study. It takes such facts and methods and ideas from the basic social sciences as are relevant and applies them to the understanding and solution of social problems. The major academic disciplines that underlie this applied knowledge are sociology, economics, statistics, politics, history, public administration, psychology and moral and social philosophy. Other subjects and fields of interest are relevant and in future years might emerge into greater prominence as our understanding of their contribution to social administration deepens, for example, a study of the legal system and the relationship between law and social policy is currently being explored. But at the moment the main basic disciplines are those first listed. Obviously the student of social administration cannot be an expert in all these fields before turning to his final area of study. He will therefore attempt to understand a little of what is relevant from all these diverse and interrelated fields and probably gain his most thorough grounding in sociology, politics, public administration and social economics. In many cases the student of social administration has specialized in one particular field and must well regard himself primarily as an historian or a sociologist or an economist. When he turns to the study of social problems and social action he will approach it from his specialized standpoint. So the economist will deal with problems of of old age or housing and the policies we have towards them primarily in economic terms, while the sociologist will take a sociological view. The different views are all valid and all part of our steadily deepening understanding of the subject.

Another way of appreciating the meaning of social administration is to accept that the social services cannot possibly be studied in a vacuum. They can only be understood by reference to the problems they are trying to tackle and in the context of the overall political, economic and social structure of the country. This is so obvious that it is almost overlooked, but in fact even the most avowedly straightforward description of the social services will tend to include references to history, to the economic situation, to political factors and so on. This is because without such references the description would not only be rather dull but inexplicable. Whether we acknowledge it or not our social services are based on certain social and economic facts about the distribution of income, the concentrations of population, the kinship patterns in urban communities, etc. It is clear then that in order really to understand the services we must look closely at these facts and try to understand the way in which our society works, the factors which influence the availability of resources and the beliefs and traditions which have shaped our peculiar response to social problems. So once again we must have recourse to the basic social sciences if we are to appreciate and understand the problems and the policies of our society.

A simple description of the social services of this or any other country would not remain useful for very long, because it would become out of date in a very few years. Social policy is continually developing and the structure and methods of the social services change. This is yet another reason why the term social administration implies so much more than a straightforward picture of the major social services. Because once it had been recognized that social services are an integral part of society and that society itself must be studied in some detail if they are to be understood, it is easily accepted that the services will constantly be changing. Society itself changes all the time. Social needs, the recognition and definition of social problems and the resources available for social policies all change. Social administration by its very approach to the subject acknowledges the dynamic nature of the process. It is essentially concerned with changing needs and developing response.

I think it would be useful at this point to offer a lengthy quotation which helps to provide a clear focus for much of what has been discussed so far. This is a definition of social administration written in 1966 by Kathleen Jones, Professor of Social Administration at the University of York.* It outlines precisely and imaginatively the scope of the subject.

Social Administration is a term which has changed its meaning. Originally, it meant simply teaching about what the social services actually do, mainly for the benefit of intending social workers. The rapid development of the social service since 1948 had led to the emergence of many issues of academic study with much wider implications. The study of housing, for instance, is no longer only a question of re-housing individual families from the slums, but of population distribution and movement, industrial location, physical communications, and systems of regional or local government. The study of the health services is not only a question of how individual sick people are cared for, but of deploying scarce resources in skill, money and accommodation to produce the best results for the health of the whole population. In these and other fields, social administration draws on economics – what can we afford? How can resources best be utilized?; on politics – who makes the decisions? who should make them, and on what grounds?; on philosophy – what do we mean by the good life and the good society?; and on sociology – what is our society like, and how does it function as a whole?

Social administration is problem centred. It starts from the problem end of sociology, which some sociologists call social pathology; but while sociology is concerned only with the identification and description of social problem areas (suicide, crime, poverty and so on) social administration is concerned with action. It proceeds from social pathology to social legislation and social policy, continues to the study of executive action (what is actually done by administrators, and social workers and others – which may not be the same as what is laid on the statute book) and ends in consumer research: how the services affect the ordinary citizen in need.

*Taken from *The Compassionate Society*, Seraph Books, SPCK, 1966.

In the next chapters some of the major social problems and policies in contemporary Britain will be examined. First we will look at what may be termed the basic social services, those which try to deal with a basic universal need, with a problem in which everyone is to some extent involved. The most obvious problem areas are poverty, sickness, housing and the need for education and we have major services which have developed in response to these, such as income maintenance and the health service. The personal social services are still largely a response to special minority needs but since they have recently moved towards a position of greater relevance to the needs of the whole community their contribution to social welfare will be examined in the first part along with the other major, fuctionally organized social services. In the second part of the book a somewhat different approach is taken with the examination of the special needs of certain minority groups and the description of the special provision made to meet these needs, both within and outside of the basic services. The groups will be deprived children, old people, the disabled and the mentally disordered. Clearly in neither section is the coverage exhaustive. Other basic problems and services could be examined, problems of employment for example; and other groups could have their needs and relevant policies and provisions detailed, ethnic minorities or single parent families for example. The areas here chosen for examination at an introductory level are simply those generally accepted as the major social services and the most obvious special need groups. Admittedly arbitrary boundaries have been drawn in order to keep the book a tolerable length. In the final part of the book some basic administrative and financial issues are examined and some trends and aspects of social policy discussed.

As this is simply a short introduction to the subject of social administration there will not be space for much detail or depth. But it is hoped that insofar as each chapter provides merely a descriptive account of present social problems and services, the reader will himself realize the shortcomings of this. When the description alone is unsatisfactory the wider objects of social administration can be recalled and the need for deeper analysis and more sophisticated application of the relevant social sciences should become both evident and imperative. Social administration is, in a sense, an approach rather than a subject, and it is this approach which it is hoped will be conveyed through the following chapters. The approach is to look first at social problems, in terms of their causes, dimensions and trends, and then to analyse society's response, through the examination of social action, and to apply to this two-fold task the knowledge, skills and theories of the basic, well-established social sciences.

2 Poverty and social security

The problem of poverty

Poverty is perhaps the most fundamental social problem because the need to survive and therefore have the means to survive is universal. Absolute poverty means the condition in which it is not possible to obtain the basic necessities of life. In Britain today mass poverty of this kind does not exist although it is all too prevalent in many parts of the world. But relative poverty remains a major problem and there is increasing evidence that for some individuals and minority groups absolute poverty is still a real threat if not an actual torment. Relative poverty means basically that some people are poorer than others. This is almost bound to exist unless the whole basis of society and indeed of human nature were to be radically altered, and it is not necessarily a problem. The problem arises when the difference between the richest and the poorest becomes too great. What is meant by 'too great' in this context is very much open to argument, but a simple explanation would be that the gap between rich and poor is too great when the poor, while not actually starving or homeless, are nevertheless unable to enjoy many of the goods and services which others take for granted. This, then, depends on what is regarded as the normal standard of living for a particular society. If most people not only have enough to eat and somewhere to live but also have money for entertainments and travel, luxury goods and drinks and fashionable clothing then the minority who are merely subsisting are justly considered to be, in relative terms, in poverty. And poverty involves much more than lack of money, although that is still a fundamental aspect of it. People who live in slums and have to make use of inadequate, ill-equipped schools and overcrowded, obsolete hospitals are poor even if they have money in their pockets. People whose physical, emotional and intellectual growth has been stunted by poor conditions have been deprived of opportunities for personal fulfilment which no subsequent material comfort can make amends for.

It is obvious that it is very hard to obtain a satisfactory definition of poverty. The concept of poverty is widely debated and is regarded as a problem that society ought to tackle, but it is hard to obtain a consensus of opinion on what actually constitutes poverty in our present day society. Consequently it is difficult to find out the nature and extent of poverty although such findings should be the basis of an effective social policy to deal with the problem.

In attempting to define poverty various standards can be used. One of the simplest to grasp, although not necessarily simple to work out in detail, is the physiological standard. Roughly this means that a person is considered to be in poverty if he lacks the resources to obtain enough food, clothing, warmth and shelter to maintain a tolerable standard of physical health and efficiency. This standard is a reasonably scientific one in that such things as nutritional requirements can be worked out precisely and data can be collected on the cost and availability of the necessary items, in order to produce figures of what income is required to maintain a person in physical efficiency. A physiological definition of poverty is one which permits relatively easy translation into cash terms. This makes it possible to carry out the measurement of poverty on a large scale. A poverty line is drawn, being the minimal amount of money needed to keep a person out of poverty, and the numbers of people who fall below this line can then be counted. This technique of measuring poverty was first used effectively in Britain around the turn of the century in the pioneering surveys conducted by Booth and Rowntree. At that time the information they obtained indicated that, by their rather stringent standards, over one quarter of the population was living in poverty.

Definitions of poverty in physiological terms can be relatively clear cut and enable precise quantitative assessment of the problem to be made, but they are hardly adequate for a society which has an average standard of living that is well above mere subsistence level. In any relatively affluent society it is necessary to define poverty by a social standard, that is, to define what society considers is or is not a reasonable minimum standard of living. This standard is reflected in what society is prepared to provide to keep people in a minimal state of health and decency. It will depend on a variety of factors such as the wealth of the society, the average standard of living, the numbers in need, the sense of community and prevailing attitudes and ideologies. It is essentially less precise than a basic physical standard but rather more relevant in comparatively wealthy societies. To arrive at a social definition of poverty it is necessary to decide what aspects of a complex pattern of consumption should be regarded as essential. For example, is it essential to have food that is varied and palatable as well as nutritionally adequate? Is it necessary to have clothing that is clean, which means having spare clothing and money for laundry and dry cleaning facilities, or is it enough just to be warmly clothed? Is it necessary to watch television, catch a bus rather than walk, buy newspapers, use cosmetics, stand a round of drinks? At what point does society maintain that a person who lacks resources for these and other goods and services is in poverty? Clearly it is hard to give precise answers to such questions and equally clearly they must be asked. We cannot tackle the problem of poverty until we define it and we must try to do so by reference to the standards of living prevailing in society, by deciding what mode of living is or is not acceptable to society.

A further yardstick of poverty is a subjective one that is, those people are counted poor who *feel* poor. This personal standard will, of course, vary enormously between individuals according to their expectations and accustomed living patterns. It is not, therefore, much use in calculating a poverty line, but nevertheless the concept of felt poverty must not be ignored. Recent research has tended to concentrate on whole groups of people whose life styles are substantially poorer than those of the rest of society: the old and single-parent families are examples of groups with a high risk of poverty. Yet another approach is to look at geographical areas in which the concentration of poor conditions adds up to a definition of poverty or urban deprivation.

Other ways of defining poverty are possible: the above examples are intended primarily to indicate something of the complexity of the problem. The importance of acceptable definitions is that they allow poverty to be measured and that is obviously a first step to understanding and dealing with the problem. The most common way of measuring poverty today is to use an income based 'poverty line' and ascertain the numbers below it. The level of income taken which is put on a sliding scale according to age, numbers of dependants, etc, is usually enough to raise people above the bare physical subsistence standard with some further allowance for what is vaguely deemed a socially acceptable standard of living. But very large variables in the cost of basic necessities, particularly housing, makes simple *per capita* income surveys of limited use in obtaining an accurate measure of the numbers in poverty. At the moment, definition and exact measurement of poverty are rarely attempted partly because of the practical difficulties involved and partly because of a widespread belief that the first is self evident and the second would lead to few findings of any significance. But this is really to shirk a very important problem.

Another aspect of the poverty issue which is of tremendous importance is understanding something of the causes. This is perhaps a more feasible approach than that of obtaining precise measurements of extent, and investigations into why people are poor have yielded some pretty clear results. The first major cause of poverty is insufficient earnings either because wage levels are too low, or because families are too large in relation to earnings. Low wages can be the consequence of a general exploitation of labour or low productivity etc, or in the case of a particular individual they can be the consequence of a lack of skill and training which causes a person to take low-paid employment. The second major cause of poverty is loss or interruption of income due to temporary or permanent inability to work for such reasons as sickness, unemployment, disablement, maternity or retirement. At any given time the pattern of poverty causation is likely to vary according to the prevailing social and economic conditions. When the first surveys were conducted the major causes of poverty were found to be low wages and large families. Surveys in the 1930s indicated that unemployment was a major cause of poverty. Recent research has shown that in the 1960s and 1970s the main causes of poverty are old age, chronic sickness, large families and single-parent families, with low pay still an important factor of poverty causation.

One concept which is useful in understanding poverty is that of the poverty cycle. That is, that people tend to experience poverty in childhood, rise above it when they grow up and start earning, fall back into poverty when they marry and start a family, rise above it again when the family grows up and contributes to the household expenses and sink finally into poverty again when the family leaves and they enter retirement and old age. This concept is important in showing where help must be concentrated if poverty is to be tackled. It also indicates that many more people experience poverty than the proportion who are found to be poor at the actual time of a survey, and that they tend to experience it at particularly vulnerable points of their lives. A further important consideration about poverty is the distinction made between primary and secondary poverty. This was first drawn by Rowntree in his original survey, already mentioned, and at that time it could be seen quite clearly: primary poverty was a condition in which a person lacked the resources to maintain himself in physical efficiency, which was the stringent physiological definition of poverty being used. Secondary poverty existed if a person had the resources but used part of them on goods or services, wasteful or useful, which were not strictly contributing to the 'maintenance of physical efficiency', and thereby fell into poverty by that definition. Today, when more generous standards of poverty tend to be used, the distinction is less clear but is still valid. Even though a modern 'poverty line' would be higher than bare subsistence it would not be likely to include an allowance for such things as cigarettes or dry-cleaning charges. So a person who used up part of a very low income or allowance on such things would have to go short on food or fuel or fail to pay the rent, and this would constitute a form of secondary poverty. Indeed some people just manage their finances badly and spend money unwisely and therefore have to go short of essentials even though they appear to have adequate resources. So the idea of secondary poverty is still relevant although, because it involves a good many value judgements about the way people spend their money and order their lives, it must be used with considerable caution.

Most attempts to find a working definition of poverty tend to be focussed on the cash aspect of being poor. That is they involve measuring the cash resources an individual or family commands and relating the amounts obtained to a poverty line drawn in monetary terms. This is understandable because, as we have already noted, money is crucial in our society and this approach does facilitate the measurement of poverty. But increasing attention is being directed to other aspects of deprivation and attempts are being made to quantify housing standards and the level of amenities enjoyed by different groups of people. It is increasingly accepted that poverty of environment and education are strongly linked to poverty of monetary resources. A poor background still tends to mean poor prospects for most children a fact now acknowledged by current concern over the 'cycle of deprivation'.

Further aspects of deprivation which are now considered under the heading of poverty include such things as the relative lack of political power enjoyed by some groups of society, and the poverty of social relationships suffered by some people. But at the same time as the concept of poverty is being steadily broadened out from its earlier preoccupation with cash, the study of this central element of poverty has itself become more penetrating. Measurement of income now tries to take account of all the ways an individual or family, over time, ensures command over the use of resources. This means that income must be seen to comprise not only current cash receipts from wages, salaries, dividends, interest, pensions, benefits and so forth, but also capital assets, occupational benefits and benefits in kind from social services, or from relatives and friends. Only by such a comprehensive approach to income can we begin to determine how far individuals or groups are in any meaningful sense richer or poorer than one another.

It can be seen that poverty remains difficult to define or measure but it is being discussed with increasing sophistication by social scientists. Leaving aside the problems of conceptualization for a moment it is worth remembering that for some people poverty is an experience that is too real to require any definition. Let us consider, very briefly and simply, the effects poverty has on those who experience it. Obviously a condition of absolute poverty can lead to starvation and death, but what affect does living around the present poverty line have on the families and individuals who are dwelling in this situation? Clearly if a person has just enough to live on and no more he must be very careful in managing his income. The housewife must buy cheaply and make do and mend with such things as clothes and resist the temptation, or the demands of children, to spend money on luxuries or toys. The poor live in constant anxiety, worried that their precarious budget won't work out, that they will be overtaken by debt or eviction. They live in constant humiliation as they observe the cheerful affluence of those around them and have to get by with secondhand goods, with restricted opportunities for a show of generosity or hospitality, with the clamour of children who don't understand why they can't have the things which their friends enjoy. Frequently the poor suffer from malnutrition and even hunger, their actual life expectancy will be lower than average, their living conditions are likely to be squalid and overcrowded. The response to these ills is often deep despair, an erosion of self respect, a deterioration of family relationships. In short, poverty means a good deal of physical and mental suffering for those who experience it and it involves the risk of permanent damage to health and well-being and to a person's chances of personal development and happiness.

The effects of poverty on the community as a whole are no less striking and damaging than they are on individuals. Poverty leads to other social problems such as sickness, not necessarily as a direct cause but as an exacerbating factor. For example, the poor are unable to give their children the attention they require and the care they need and so the problems of the deprived and delinquent child are closely associated with poverty. Poverty leads to slums which are an eyesore and a health hazard. It breeds unrest and discontent and even violence where it is co-existent with great affluence and is a growing symptom of grave social injustice. Poverty means a waste of valuable human resources as it stunts the full physical, intellectual and emotional growth of those who suffer it, and that can only be a tragic loss for the whole society.

Social security: different approaches

The social policy needed to deal with problems as complex as poverty cover a wide front. It must aim to raise the level of real wages, improve general standards of health and education, maintain full employment and raise productivity. It must also cope with the immediate financial needs of the individual and attempt to obtain a just distribution of such things as educational opportunity. That part of the policy which is concerned directly with maintaining income, primarily when people are unable to work, and thereby securing them against falling into poverty in the narrow but important sense of being short of money, is known as the social security system. It is with this aspect of the total response to the problem of poverty that the remainder of the chapter will primarily be involved. For the social security system, in addition to having a lengthy history, is undoubtedly one of the major social services in this country and it deserves considerable critical attention.

The most obvious way for a society to deal with straightforward financial difficulties is to accept responsibility for meeting the need of any of its members who fall below a certain defined level. If a substantial section of the community lives at a bare subsistence level then the assistance offered by the community must itself be at a very low level and offered to the totally destitute. This is because it is generally accepted that state assistance cannot be so generous, relative to the prevailing living standards, that people are attracted to it from paid work. This is often referred to as the principle of 'less eligibility' because it was enunciated clearly in this country with the passing of the Poor Law Amendment Act of 1834 in the statement that the condition of the recipient of relief 'shall not be made really or apparently so eligible as the situation of the independent labourer of the lowest class'.* It is still considered basically unjust that a man should obtain more money by state assistance than by working for it. Fortunately once the community lives at a reasonably high standard of living then help for the poor can be offered at a level beneath the general standard but somewhat above bare subsistence. So less eligibility in the nineteenth century meant the workhouse with its punitive regime and social stigma because it was impossible otherwise to offer relief below the lowest prevailing levels. Today, however, it simply means a definitely meagre existence, which contrasts sharply with the standards of the rest of a fairly affluent consumer society and probably with the previous situation of the people whom misfortune forces on to assistance. This change reflects the changing interpretation of poverty from the notion of absolute destitution to that of substantial relative deprivation.

State assistance to relieve poverty has always tended to carry some stigma, as it is only available on test of need and the desire to maintain the principle of less eligibility means that it tends to acquire a reputation for the systematic degradation of its recipients. Moreover it is usually seen as 'charity' in the sense that the better off are taxed to help the poor. It can be the sole source of income for some people or it can be provided to bridge the gap between a person's resources and his needs. Assistance can be provided as cash, by regular allowances or occasional lump sums for use as the recipients determine; or as grants for specific purposes such as clothing; or in kind, as free school meals, for example; or as specific rebates or allowances, as in the rate rebate scheme. But all forms of assistance are selective, that is, they operate through some kind of means test.

An alternative approach to income maintenance is that of state or national insurance. This is based on mutual aid, rather than 'charity' and has been generally regarded as a more acceptable basis for income maintenance than selective assistance as it aims to prevent people becoming destitute rather than to assist them once they are. The insurance idea, put quite simply, is that everybody who is working pays a small amount each week into a fund and then they can claim a weekly benefit in the event of their being unable to work because of sickness or unemployment or any other contingency against which the scheme ensures them. Eventually they can claim a retirement pension for which they will have, in a sense, saved during their working life. In an insurance scheme the contributors

*Report of the 1832 Commission on the Poor Law.

are protected against poverty but also against the humiliation of a means test as their benefit is their due entitlement regardless of any resources they may have. Insurance means a pooling of risks and a horizontal redistribution of income from those who are well to those who are sick and from those who are working to those who are unemployed as compared to the vertical, rich to poor, redistribution of assistance methods of poverty relief. It also involves a redistribution of income over the individual's life, saving in good times to help out in hard times. Poverty caused by loss or interruption of normal earnings can be prevented by this method of social security. Investigations into the causes of poverty have shown that loss of income because of inability to work is a major problem. If the main risks of loss of income are determined then the population can be insured against them. These risks are usually, unemployment, sickness, disability and, for women, maternity and widowhood. Retirement is not in the same sense a risk, but it involves a loss of income and can be insured for likewise. If a basic minimum income is assured when a person suffers any of the contingencies which cause loss or interruption of earnings, there should not be any need to have recourse to assistance. Clearly this approach does not help those, such as the congenitally disabled, who never have an income to lose. Nor does it help those who deviate from average, anticipated life styles, such as the deserted wife. It is essentially an approach geared to the average needs of the normal working population as society interprets these at any given time.

A further method of tackling poverty and maintaining income is to pay, from general taxation, a universal benefit in respect of any of the known common causes of poverty, such as old age. In other words to pay a pension not just to those old people who lack resources as in the case of assistance schemes, nor just to those who have paid contribution to entitle themselves to it, but to everyone over a certain age. This method, sometimes referred to as a demogrant, avoids the stigma and disincentive of a means test and the complexity and restrictions of any insurance scheme but it is obviously a costly method. It can be applied to any category of persons such as the disabled or dependent children.

The British Social Security System

The problem of income maintenance can be tackled by any one or any combination of the strategies briefly outlined above: assistance to those who prove their need; insurance against loss of income from a variety of causes; and universal payments to certain categories of persons likely to be in financial need. In present day Britain the social security system makes use of all three approaches and a variety of methods. It has a National Insurance Scheme to cover the major risks of loss or interruption of earnings, including retirement; a universal Family Allowance Scheme to direct extra resources to those responsible for the maintenance of children, and a major assistance scheme, known as Supplementary Benefits, for those who are not covered adequately, or at all, by the insurance scheme. These schemes were set up more or less in their present form shortly after the Second World War. They followed recommendations contained in the Beveridge Report, *Social Insurance and Allied Services*, which was published in 1942, although their origins lie much further back in our social history. Basically they indicated that for most causes of interrupted earnings the working population would earn its own cover through insurance. For those outside of insurance a safety net of assistance would keep people at a basic subsistence level. There was some redistribution towards dependent children, but not a clear family policy, just a relatively modest allowance towards the costs of second and subsequent children.

Since these schemes were established there have been various additions and modifications. After numerous developments in the insurance scheme the Social Security Act of 1973 changed the system fairly radically but still further changes are about to be implemented. An attendance allowance for severely disabled people has been added and a variety of selective assistance measures have been introduced, most notably the Family Income Supplement and rent and rate rebates and allowances. Despite these changes there is still much anxiety about the present social security system and much discussion of alternatives and improvements, such as tax credits or payments to single-parent families. The next sections will describe the present system then look briefly at some of its problems and some proposals for change in this complex field.

Central adminstration   The main income maintenance schemes are administered by the Department of Health and Social Security under the Secretary of State for Social Services. The DHSS was established in 1968, bringing together the previously separate Ministries of Health and Social Security. The Supplementary Benefit Scheme is administered by the DHSS but has a separate, appointed body, the

Supplementary Benefits Commission responsible for supplementary benefits policy. The staff, offices and administration of insurance and assistance are combined. The DHSS is also responsible for War Pensions. It has overall concern for all levels of administration and has a network of local and regional offices which try to ensure that this highly individual social service does not become too remote from the needs it exists to serve.

National Insurance   The central feature of the present social security system is the national insurance scheme. This was established in 1946 but has been substantially altered and developed over the years. The 1973 Social Security Act, as amended in 1974, replaced all previous legislation and established an earnings related basic insurance scheme which became operative in April 1975.

The idea of national insurance is to *prevent* people from falling into poverty when they are unable to earn. The contributions employees pay afford cover against sickness, including chronic invalidity, unemployment, disablement through accident or disease arising from work, and retirement. The scheme assumes that most men will marry and support a family, so their contributions cover for benefits for dependent wives and children and cover against their wives' risk of widowhood. Cover also includes orphans' allowances and lump-sum payments for maternity and on death. Married women have traditionally been treated as dependent on their husbands but working women who pay a full rate of insurance have their own rights to benefit including a maternity benefit when they interrupt employment to have a child. The scheme is financed partly by regular weekly contributions paid by employees and employers, and partly by the State through taxation. Contributions include a token payment towards the cost of the national health service and payment to the Redundancy Fund. Since national insurance is highly complicated and it has an alarming number of rules, classifications, categories and conditions, only a bare outline of its main provisions can be given here.

Contributions are in four classes related to four main categories of insured persons. Class 1 contributions are paid by the average worker who is in full-time contracted employment. This contribution is earnings related and consists of a percentage of weekly earnings between £11 and £69. The primary contribution, paid by the employed earner, is $5\frac{1}{2}$ per cent of relevant earnings. The secondary contribution, paid by the employer, is $8\frac{1}{2}$ per cent of relevant earnings.

Class 2 contributions are flat rate payable by self-employed earners. These are currently £2.41 per week for a man and £2.10 for a woman.* Class 3 contributions are payable by the non-employed and are £1.90 per week. Class 4 contributions are payable in respect of profits or gains of a trade or profession and are 8 per cent between £1600 and £3600 per annum.

Contributions entitle people to a wide range of benefits but these mostly depend on contribution record and on class of contribution paid. Class 1 contributors are eligible for all benefits. Short-term benefits are unemployment and sickness benefit and maternity allowance. These have provision for earnings related supplements, where relevant, for up to six months and all benefits have increases payable in respect of adult or child dependants. Short term benefits are currently payable at the rate of £11.10 per week for a single person plus £7.80 for a married woman, £6.90 for an adult dependant, £3.50 for a first child and £2.00 for second or subsequent children. Unemployment and sickness benefit is not payable for the first three days off work. Unemployment benefit is payable for 312 days after which entitlement ceases and only begins again after the insured person has been employed for at least thirteen weeks. Sickness benefit is payable for up to 168 days after which a person is entitled to invalidity benefit. Maternity allowance is payable to fully insured working women for eighteen weeks beginning the 11th week before the expected week of confinement. Maternity grant is a single payment, on the insurance of a woman or her husband, payable on the birth of a child. It is currently £25.

Retirement pensions, widows' benefits and invalidity benefits are paid at a higher rate of £13.30 per week for a single person or £21.20 for a married couple with £5.65 payable for the first child and £5.00 a week for second and subsequent children. Invalidity allowances are paid in addition to benefits, depending on the age at onset of disability and these are continued in retirement. The rates vary from £2.80, where disability began before age thirty-five, to £0.85. Retirement pensions are payable to men over sixty-five and women over sixty. The weekly rate can be increased by deferring retirement. Those who retire but do part-time work will now be able to earn up to £20 per week before losing entitlement to their full pension. Those over the age of eighty are entitled to a small age addition to pension. All old people are now entitled to pensions, even if they

*Contribution and benefit rates quoted here are as from November 1975. Up-to-date rates can be checked at local offices of the DHSS.

were not insurance contributors, but the minority who were never covered have a smaller pension payable. Death grant is a fixed sum paid on the death of an insured person or close relative of an insured person. It is variable according to age and is currently £30 for an adult. Widows' benefits are payable to all widows for up to twenty-six weeks after the death of a husband and thereafter as widowed mothers' allowance, if the widow has dependent children, or widows' pension if she is older. Widows' benefits are not payable if the widow remarries or is she is cohabiting with a man as his wife. Guardian's allowances are payable in respect of orphaned children of insured persons. Attendance allowances are payable with no contribution conditions to a person who is so severely disabled, physically or mentally, that he requires frequent attention or supervision either by day or through the night. Claims for this allowance are decided by the Attendance Allowance Board. Current rates are £7.10 per week or £10.60 per week for more serious disability involving both day and night attendance.

Under the Industrial Injuries Scheme, Class 1 contributors can claim when they are injured at work or disabled by a prescribed industrial disease. Injury benefit is not dependent on the number of contributions paid and it applies even to those not paying earnings-related contributions. Injury benefit is payable at the rate of £13.85 a week for up to twenty-six weeks. Disablement benefit is a pension or gratuity for any disablement which remains when injury benefit stops. This varies according to the degree of disability, being £21.80 a week for a 100 per cent disablement, and it can be supplemented by extra benefits such as constant attendance allowance, or special hardship allowance, where necessary.

These are the main national insurance provisions but the exact detail of entitlement for different benefits and allowances is very complex. The scale of insurance is now considerable. Just over ten million people were national insurance beneficiaries in 1973. Over eight million of these were retirement pensioners or widows over sixty. The next single largest category was persons receiving sickness and invalidity benefit, which on average amounted to over a million. Taking a count on a single day in 1973, 197 000 persons were in receipt of unemployment benefit. The other categories such as widowed mothers and those in receipt of maternity allowances made up the total. The full cost of the national insurance scheme is now quite considerable. In 1973 it amounted to over £4000 million and the levels of benefit have substantially increased since then.

B

Supplementary Benefits The Beveridge Plan for national insurance was a bold one particularly in its emphasis on universality, i.e. all persons contributing regardless of their income level, and one comprehensive risk coverage. It was overtaken by economic and social changes and to some extent it failed right from the start to provide the real social security it promised. Nevertheless it remains the basis of our present system. Yet however effective an insurance scheme is, it can never hope to cover everyone in society but only those who are able to be consistent contributors. Those who are too old when a scheme is introduced, those who outrun their entitlement to benefit or, like deserted wives, lose it, and those who cannot work must all look for help elsewhere. Some scheme of financial assistance is always necessary as a safety net to catch the variety of cases who cannot for an equal variety of reasons rely on insurance. In 1948 the National Assistance Act provided this safety net with the setting up of the National Assistance Board. This provided not only a safety net for those outside of insurance but increasingly an additional support to national insurance beneficiaries when they had no resources other than their pensions and allowances. For this reason the NAB changed its name in 1966 to the Supplementary Benefits Commission and responsibility for insurance and assistance was merged into social security.

The Supplementary Benefits Commission pays benefits as of right and without any contributions to people whose incomes, whether from other benefits or private resources, are below a level of requirements laid down by Parliament. Anyone over sixteen who is not in full-time work is entitled to benefit if their resources are less than their requirements. In computing resources certain amounts of income from capital or disability pensions, for example, and up to £4 a week of earnings, can be disregarded. In computing requirements the scale rate is taken for a single householder or a couple, plus amounts for dependent children which vary according to age, plus the actual cost of rent and any discretionary payments towards special expenses such as diets. There are two scale rates, for short-term claimants and long-term claimants, the latter including all pensioners. The current rates are £10.90 for a single person and £17.75 for a couple on short-term benefit and £13.95 and £21.55 for long-term claimants. Payments for dependent children vary according to age ranging from £3.10 for a child under five to £5.60 for one between thirteen and fifteen years old. Payment of supplementary pensions and allowances is normally through order books at the post office and a combined retirement pension and supplementary benefit pension book can be obtained. For the unemployed payment is made at an employment exchange. People on supplementary benefit are entitled to exemption from certain other charges, those for prescriptions and school meals, for example.

Supplementary benefits were paid to a total of 2,675,000 people in 1973. In addition to the regular weekly payments the SBC makes numerous single payments for exceptional needs. The majority of claimants, over 1.8 million, were old people most of whom were also retirement pensioners. Roughly 250,000 claimants were unemployed and of these 10,000 had their allowances reduced under the, now abandoned, wage stop. The sick and disabled accounted for 280 000 claimants and women with dependent children 228000 claimants. The total cost of supplementary benefits in 1973 was £730 millions.

Other social security measures Family allowances were first introduced in 1945. They are payable to all families with children in respect of the second or subsequent child under school leaving age or in full-time education or training under the age of nineteen. The current weekly rate is £1.50 per child. Family allowances are a universal benefit payable to any family regardless of income level and financed out of general taxation. Their aim is to reduce the poverty in families which may be caused by the impossibility of stretching one wage to cover a variable number of dependants. They are of most importance to families of low-wage earners but have been paid universally as a general recognition of the importance of family responsibility at all income levels. A similar recognition is implicit in the tax system which makes allowances for dependent children but includes the first child who is still left out of the family allowance scheme (although plans have been announced to include all first children from 1977). Family allowances were paid to 4 365000 families in 1973 at a cost of £359 million. This was only 6.3 per cent of the total social security budget so it can be seen that family allowances are afforded a low priority at present as a means of combating family poverty.

Partly as a result of the low rates of universal family allowances several families have fallen into poverty, i.e. below official supplementary benefit levels, while being supported by a wage earner. Since supplementary benefit cannot be paid to those in full-time work while an extension and substantial increase of family allowances was not politically acceptable, a further selective family benefit was introduced in 1971. The Family Income Supplement is payable to families whose normal gross weekly income is less than amounts prescribed by Parliament. The prescribed amounts are £31.50 per week for a family with one child plus £3.50 per week for each additional child. Anyone, including a single person, with at least one dependent child can claim if he or she is in full-time work. The amount payable is half the difference between the family's income and the prescribed income up to a maximum of £5 a week for families with one child and 50 pence per week for each additional child. Those who are entitled to FIS are automatically entitled to free school meals, prescriptions, etc. Those who wish to claim must furnish evidence of their earnings and, if eligible, they receive books of weekly orders. In 1973, 106 000 families received the supplement which cost £15 million. Take-up of FIS remains low despite extensive advertising. It is estimated that only 50 per cent of families who are eligible for some supplement actually claim it, partly because of the claims procedure and partly because the amounts involved are often small.

A further task undertaken by the Department of Health and Social Security is the administration of war pensions. These are payable to persons disabled as a result of war service, including civilian casualties of the 1939–45 war, or service in the Armed Forces since 1945, and to the widows, parents and other dependants of those who have died as a result of such service. In addition to the cash pensions and allowances, the Ministry also provides a welfare service for war pensioners.

The main social security provision is through the DHSS, as outlined above, but mention must be made of the numerous benefits which are now available through the local authorities. The most important of these are rent and rate rebates and allowances. Rate rebates are available where an applicant, either owner-occupier or tenant, has an income of less than a certain amount. Tenants of council housing can claim rent rebates which are deducted at source and tenants of private lettings can apply for a rent allowance calculated according to means and family responsibility. Local authorities can also provide certain education benefits on test of need, such as free school meals and clothing allowances. People on low incomes can also obtain free legal advice and assistance and, if necessary, legal aid for court proceedings.

Difficulties and dilemmas in social security

Social security is highly complicated and costly. Its primary aim is to eradicate poverty but, inevitably, in trying to establish some degree of social justice by redistribution of income it raises more difficult issues. The present system, as the previous sections have indicated, is widely criticized both in terms of its primary aim and of its wider implications. The criticisms are founded on facts as well as on convictions. The substance of the criticisms are first, that the present system has failed to keep some people out of primary poverty, and second, that where people are kept above the official poverty line they are kept at a mere subsistence level which is itself regarded in an affluent society as constituting poverty. The first criticism is that the basic aim of a social security system is not being realized. The second is more concerned with issues of social justice than of primary poverty.

Allegations that some people were living in primary poverty, that is their resources were less than was allowed by the official poverty line (the standard-rate allowance plus actual rent provided by the Supplementary Benefits Commission) were met with surprise by a nation accustomed to believing that want had been abolished. Research in 1965, however, revealed that some people, amongst old people, the chronic sick and members of large families, were actually living below the official basic minimum.* The independent research findings were substantiated by two official enquiries.† That on retirement pensioners revealed that of the six and a half million people currently claiming retirement pensions about 800000 were provisionally entitled to assistance but were not receiving it. Of these it was estimated that about 300000 would have absolutely no resources other than their retirement pensions and would therefore be living in extreme poverty. This survey did not calculate the numbers of people who were neither on assistance nor claiming pensions who might be in poverty, but it was likely that a similar number of non-pensioners might be in need also. These facts were very disturbing, confirming as they did the suspicions of many social workers and researchers who had noted individual examples of extreme

---

* See Brian Abel-Smith and Peter Townsend, 'The Poor and the Poorest'. *Occasional Papers in Social Administration* No 17, 1965.

† See *Financial and other Circumstances of Retirement Pensioners,* Ministry of Pensions and National Insurance (1966), and *Circumstances of Families,* Ministry of Social Security (1967), for further details.

hardship among the old. Action was taken in 1966 by the creation of
a Ministry of Social Security and the renaming of assistance 'supplementary benefits'. These changes were accompanied by a determined
campaign to advertise a person's entitlement to a reasonable living
standard and encourage old people to claim their rights. These
moves were implemented because the official survey had revealed
that the two main reasons why people failed to claim assistance were
ignorance of their entitlement and pride which rejected assistance
as charity.

The second survey was on families and it also produced disturbing
results: that nearly half a million families, containing up to about one
and a quarter million children, had resources amounting to less
than the then current supplementary benefit rates would have
afforded. Families were living below the official poverty line because
the fathers were in full-time work and could not be assisted, or
because the father was on assistance but subject to the wage stop
which reduced his allowance below his normal earnings. Others at
risk included fatherless families and those on insurance benefits not
claiming assistance. The basic reason why these families, whether
in work or on assistance, were in poverty was the inadequacy of
family allowances. These had fallen in value, relatively, and they
failed to meet the additional costs of keeping a child. The answer to
family poverty seemed at first glance simple: considerable increases
in family allowances were needed. But as allowances are paid to all
families the necessary increases would have proved very costly. As
the country was trying to keep down the rising level of public
expenditure this solution was therefore not acceptable and a variety
of selective measures was introduced instead.

Since this 'rediscovery' of poverty in the 1960s, anxiety has
increased not abated, because despite many additions and modifications to the social security system there is still evidence of disturbing levels of poverty in Britain. On the basis of the *Family Expenditure Survey*, at December 1972 it was estimated that there were still
980000 people over pensionable age not claiming a supplementary
pension whose incomes were below the supplementary benefit level.
There were also 800000 people under pensionable age living below
supplemetary benefit levels. Current estimates are of roughly two
million people living below subsistence level. Meanwhile there is
still concern that the level of subsistence itself is low in relation to
average living standards. Although benefit rates have risen substantially they remain highly vulnerable to inflation which has been

increasing alarmingly. Moreover the complexity of the social security system is such that many people probably fail to get their full welfare rights from it and in order to obtain even a part of the help available, a humiliating and bewildering succession of means tests must be undergone. There can certainly be no room for complacency, therefore, in contemplating the present income maintenance scene.

The two major problems remain those of family poverty and the financing of retirement, although others, such as inadequate provision for the disabled, continue to cause concern. The discovery of family poverty led to the foundation of the Child Poverty Action Group in 1965. CPAG has now acted as a pressure group in this field for ten years exposing the plight of families, encouraging a welfare rights approach and putting forward proposals to improve the situation. Basically the relatively low level of family allowances and their non-coverage of the first child remains at the heart of the problem. CPAG has long campaigned for an effective family policy based on family allowances and this approach is supported by much informed opinion. But the trend since 1965 has been towards greater selectivity in social security so assistance has been relied on, together with means-tested benefits such as FIS, rather than an improved universal service. This approach claims to concentrate help on those who need it, but there is evidence both that it fails to do this, because of low take up of means-tested benefits, and that it can only do so at the cost of the humiliation of clients. Although supplementary benefits can be claimed as a right there is still a strong odour of reluctant charity about many local social security offices' treatment of claimants. The use of discretion in making extra payments has led to underpayment of many clients and the wage stop and the cohabitation rule, whereby a woman loses benefit if living with a man as his wife, have been applied too rigorously and unfairly. This is partly the consequence of the SBC having to carry an immense burden of work in supplementary insurance benefits. Working under constant pressure is not conducive to the provision of a truly humane and flexible service. Unpleasantness to supplementary benefit claimants is also the consequence of unfavourable public opinion which is ever fearful of its funds being misused by welfare scroungers. The low take up of many means-tested benefits is frequently the direct result of unpleasant practices designed to put people off rather than to encourage them to apply. The fact that more benefits can be obtained when clients are supported in their claims by welfare rights workers indicates that clients on their own are too humiliated or confused to persist in applications.

Much of this depressing picture is the consequence of reliance on a variety of selective means-tested services rather than universal services. This reliance continues for the present but various proposals have been made to improve the situation in the future. The most imporant of these are: proposals for tax credits, a child benefit scheme and provision for single-parent families. In 1972 the government published a discussion paper, *Proposals for a Tax-Credit System*. This proposed a form of income maintenance which would operate through the tax system. Tax allowances would be replaced by tax credits which could be set against tax assessed at a standard rate of 30 per cent. If the tax assessed exceeded the credit due a tax would be payable of the amount of the excess. If the tax liability was less than the tax credit no tax would be payable and instead an additional payment would be made. This would replace both child tax-allowances, which primarily help the higher paid, and family allowances and would supersede FIS. The scheme would cover all in work and all insurance beneficiaries so it would help the elderly pensioner as well as the low paid family but not those on supplementary benefits.

There was much discussion of the tax credit system but a change in government led to the proposals being dropped. The tax credit idea was essentially selective, since it would have resulted in payments being made only to low-income families although it was hoped that by using the tax system the selectivity would be rendered easy and non-humiliating. In August 1975 a Child Benefit Act was passed providing for the extension of renamed family allowances to the first child in single-parent families from 1976 and subsequently to all first children. This does not appear to herald the radical development in child-endowment policy which was hoped for although it does at least extend the scope of a universal scheme for child benefits. But evidence that in a European context Britain lacks an adequate family policy might influence the politicians to move more positively in this direction in the future.

The particular needs of one-parent families were studied by a committee from 1969 to 1974. The committee's conclusions, known as the Finer Report*, were an impressive account of the problems faced by one-parent families and included numerous recommendations for an improvement in their relatively disadvantaged position

*Report of the Committee on One-Parent Families, Cmnd 5629, 1974.

in society. Amongst the practical recommendations the most important one was for the introduction of a new non-contributory benefit, the Guaranteed Maintenance Allowance. The GMA would involve a fairly substantial payment to single parents, plus an allowance for each child, according to means. GMA would be enough to remove single-parent families from reliance on supplementary benefits and give single parents a clear option to work or not. This specific proposal was not accepted by the government but some help for one-parent families was promised. The announcement in 1975 of the payment of family allowance to the first child in single-parent families from 1976, a year ahead of the promised extension of the scheme to all first children, was a small gesture of positive discrimination towards this group as was the 1975 increase in single parents' tax allowances. It remains to be seen whether any more substantial measures will be introduced.

The failure to develop an effective family policy in Britain has resulted both in a serious problem of poverty among families and in a confusing proliferation of measures to help the poorest families. While it is clearly necessary that the poorest are helped it would appear that special programmes to help *only* poor families or certain groups of families do not work well. Policies to support *all* families, financially and in other areas of social provision, are more likely to be successful and acceptable and it is hoped such policies will be developed soon.

The other major social security problem concerns the aged. The immediate problem is that of today's pensioners and their risk of poverty. The changeover from assistance to supplementary benefit was a response to the official discovery of the plight of old people who would not claim their rights. But far too many old people are still not prepared to claim supplementary pensions. Higher rates of pension have been introduced and benefits are now to be uprated each year in line with increases in the cost of living. But assistance rates remain higher than insurance rates so substantial numbers of old people will continue to need supplementary pensions and more effort needs to be made to ensure a high take up.

The higher social security benefit rates introduced from April 1975 were a welcome improvement but they still left the beneficiary financially well below the average worker. To avoid this severe drop in income especially in retirement, efforts have been made to develop a wage related rather than flat-rate insurance system. The first modification of the original system was the introduction of graduated pension in 1959. These were grafted onto the basic scheme and allowed contributors to opt out of payment if they were covered by a suitable occupational pension scheme. The wage related idea was extended in 1966 to contributions and benefits for sickness, unemployment and other short-term benefits. Today the idea of wage related insurance is generally accepted and changes in the system are accordingly being implemented but in a rather confusing fashion. Alternative schemes for earnings related pensions were produced by successive governments. In 1971 the Conservative Government's White Paper, *Strategy for Pensions**, was produced. This recommended a basic flat-rate state pension financed by graduated contributions and then either a suitable earnings related occupational pension or a 'state reserve' pension. There was much criticism of the state reserve scheme on the grounds that it would afford very inferior cover for the lower wage earners and that it would be out of line with European experience. The proposals became law by the Social Security Act of 1973 but before they became operative a change of government took place. The Labour Government put an amending Act through Parliament in 1974 which meant that the basic scheme proposed in the 1973 Act (as described in the earlier section), became effective from 1975, but the state reserve scheme was scrapped. A White Paper, *Better Pensions*, was produced in 1974† and a Pensions Bill went before Parliament in the spring of 1975 to become effective by 1977–8. The new scheme for *Better Pensions* is based on the existing basic insurance scheme and the aim is to provide adequate wage related cover in retirement, widowhood or chronic ill-health. Contributions will be wholly earnings related and the scheme will, like its predecessor, operate in partnership with occupational pension schemes. One important innovation is that the new scheme will apply equally to men and women contributors. Women will no longer be dependent on men for their pensions, reflecting the much greater involvement of women in work in recent years. In future married women will pay full contributions for long-term benefits but may contract out of short term benefits. Those who are in suitable occupational pension schemes can contract out of part of the state cover and will pay, therefore, a reduced contribution. For the majority, pensions will be based on the earnings on which contri-

*Cmnd 4755. *Strategy for Pensions: The Future Development of State and Occupational Provision.*

†Cmnd 5713. *Better Pensions. Fully Protected Against Inflation. Proposals for a New Pensions Scheme.*

butions have been paid in the individual's best twenty years. The weekly pension will be a base-level pension and a quarter of earnings between the base level and a ceiling of seven times that amount. No one will get less than the base level pension whatever their contributions and all pensions include this element so the scheme is particularly advantageous to those on low incomes. The scheme will mature in twenty years and all pensions will be guaranteed against inflation because past earnings will be revalued in line with the average earnings of the year of retirement. After retirement the base level element of the pension will be maintained in its relationship with current earning levels while the remainder will be protected against price increases.

These proposals are complex but they should ensure that both men and women, either by state cover alone or by state insurance plus occupational cover, will have earnings related pensions, fully guaranteed against inflation, which will afford security in retirement or widowhood or chronic invalidity. Security means an end to dependence on supplementary benefits and an end to a catastrophic drop in income after retirement. This has long been an aim of social policy and it is hoped that the proposed system will be implemented and will prove effective for many years ahead.

It can be seen that we have a bewildering range of social security provisions and these are still muddled and ineffective in respect of families and under process of radical revision in respect of the long term dependency of old age and invalidity. There is less talk nowadays of abandoning insurance or relying on comprehensive negative income tax solutions to the problems of income maintenance. It is now generally accepted that there is no simple solution to the problems of poverty and no easy replacement for our complex, apparently contradictory, social security system. Any change is difficult because of the vested interests of long-established schemes, the range and diversity of the needs it is trying to meet, and the confusion which abounds over its real aims. Inevitably when we examine the income maintenance field our primary concern with absolute poverty moves on into an attempt to tackle relative deprivation and ends up trying to decide what is meant by social justice. We are increasingly aware that the state's social security system should not be viewed in isolation from fiscal and occupational welfare measures or, indeed, from the general distribution of rewards in our society; that lack of cash resources is only one aspect of poverty and our reforming policy must embrace the concomitant evils of bad housing or lack of education; that the machinery of social security reflects attitudes and values prevailing in society and can be used to achieve considerable redistribution of income or to underline a callous or patronizing rejection of dependent groups. In attempting to overhaul the social security system, we must look, therefore, not only at strategies but at aims. This brings us back, remorselessly, to the initial question of what we mean by poverty. In searching for a definition we must, quite properly, raise even more fundamental questions about the whole structure and values of our society even as we simultaneously struggle to comprehend the economic, administrative, and straightforwardly human implications of tedious social security techniques.

Sugestions for further reading

Atkinson, A. B., *Poverty in Britain and the Reform of Social Security* (Cambridge University Press, 1969).

Bull, David (Ed.), *Family Poverty* (Duckworth, 1971).

Coates, K. & Silburn, R., *Poverty: the Forgotten Englishman* (Penguin, 1970).

Field, Frank, *Unequal Britain* (Arrow Books, 1974).

Kincaid, J. C., *Poverty and Equality in Britain* (Penguin, 1973).

George, V., *Social Security: Beveridge and After* (RKP, 1968).

Marsden, D., *Mothers Alone* (Penguin, 1969).

Rodgers, B. N., *Comparative Social Administration* (Allen & Unwin, 1968).

Rodgers, Brian, *The Battle Against Poverty* (RKP, 1968).

Townsend, P. (Ed.), *The Concept of Poverty* (Heinemann, 1968).

Wynn, M., *Family Policy* (Penguin, 1970).

Young, M. (Ed.), *Poverty Report 1975* (Temple, 1975).

3 The health services

The problem of sickness

Sickness is a major social problem and a universal one. Mankind is afflicted by numerous diseases, fatal, permanently crippling or merely trivial, which are a constant threat to survival and prosperity. To the individual, sickness is not only a source of immediate suffering in terms of pain, discomfort and dislocation of routine, it is also a source of anxiety, for it can be fatal, and can lead to all the agony of bereavement by premature death; it can also chronically disable, and result in poverty and hardship. It is a problem to the country as a whole, since widespread epidemic and endemic disease can decimate the population and poor standards of physical fitness will lead to low productivity. Moreover sickness can cause poverty, the break-up of families, the destruction of community life and generally can hold up social and economic progress. It is hardly surprising then, that sickness is widely recognized as a social problem and that efforts are made to combat and prevent it. The preservation of health and the improvement of general standards of fitness are goals common to both individuals and nations.

The problem of sickness and ill-health is many sided. It is in part a biological problem: man has to fight to survive and overcome the diseases which threaten survival by developing his medical skill and knowledge. But it is also a sociological problem because many of the factors which promote, encourage and even cause sickness are directly concerned with the way people behave and the environment in which they operate. It is increasingly accepted nowadays that sickness is as much a social as a medical problem, that the conditions in which people live and work influence their health as much as the existence of actual disease organisms, and that emotional and behavioural factors are important in the aetiology of many illnesses. As the more basic threats to life are controlled by medical science new hazards emerge, which are the consequences of the stresses of complex urban civilizations. So, for example, we can control the spread of fatal epidemic diseases by vaccination programmes but we have to cope with the consequences of increasing numbers of road accidents and a higher incidence of mental illness. Thus the pattern of sickness and ill-health changes, reflecting not only advances in medical science but also the changing habits and conditions of people. The interrelationship of biological, environmental, behavioural and psychological factors in the causation of sickness is now accepted. It is even more apparent that sociological and biological determinants are interdependent when one looks at the concept of good health rather than sickness. This has been defined by the World Health Organization as a 'state of complete physical, mental and social well-being' which is a strikingly positive concept, involving much more than the absence of sickness, and certainly much more than a mere biological fitness.

One important consequence of the complex nature of sickness is that the policy to deal with it must cover a very wide front. The environment must be made as safe as possible in order to control the incidence and spread of disease and the hazards of contaminated air, noxious industrial processes and the risk of accidents. Diagnostic and treatment facilities must be made readily available so that people who are ill or suffer accidents can receive care and treatment and be cured and rehabilitated. Adequate numbers of doctors, nurses and professional, technical and other ancillary workers, such as pharmacists, laboratory technicians and radiographers, must be recruited, trained and effectively deployed. Health education is necessary so that individuals, organizations and the community at large know how to reduce the risks of contracting diseases, how to ensure maximum resistance to sickness and how to promote health. And efforts must constantly be made to understand the relationships between the biological, environmental, behavioural and psychological factors in sickness in order better to coordinate health and other social policies.

Contemporary Britain is by many standards a 'healthy' society but this does not reduce the demand for medical and related services, in fact in some ways it has the reverse effect. For example, one way of comparing health standards is to look at mortality rates and at life expectancy in different countries. Britain has reasonably low mortality rates and high life expectancy* but one consequence of this is that there is a high proportion of old people in our society and they need more medical care than those in the middle age groups.

*Life expectancy at birth in 1971 was 68.6 years for males and 74.9 years for females.

It is difficult to measure or describe concisely the morbidity of a country. Most of the statistics we have relate to the use of medical care facilities which might only approximate to the actual incidence and prevalence of sickness. National insurance records can show the reasons for absence from work for certified sickness but this only relates to the working population. The Registrar General collects and publishes information on standard mortality rates but not on general morbidity although some general information is now collected from the Government's General Household Survey. Some statistics expose the distribution of sickness by class and region others by age and sex but most morbidity studies relate to a particular disease or medical problem, such as lung cancer or venereal disease, and provide detailed information about such specific problems only. Some trends in morbidity are reasonably clear such as an increase in fatal heart disease and lung cancer and a reduction in infectious diseases like tuberculosis but it is virtually impossible to generalize about the state of the country's health. The detailed picture is fascinating and also very instructive and it is certainly abundantly clear from what statistics we have that patterns and trends in sickness are strongly and sometimes disturbingly related to environmental and social factors.

The provision of medical care is not, of course, only related to morbidity although treatment of sickness is always a first necessity. Concern with prevention of disease and the promotion of health has meant that such things as the maternity services, mass screening, vaccination and a full range of medical rehabilitation facilities form an increasingly important part of the health services.

It is clear that vigorous and comprehensive social policy is required to ensure provision of all the public and personal health services necessary to combat sickness and promote health. As our understanding of sickness develops we modify the structure of our response to it. Once it was accepted that environmental services were fundamental to any effective attack on disease we introduced public health measures which were collectively provided and financed. Gradually the role of the state has widened from its initial concern with basic sanitation to involvement in all aspects of treatment and care. The progress of medicine as a science and technology has necessitated the development of large organizations to provide the resources necessary for training and specialization. Such organizations cannot easily be sustained by private entrepreneurial concerns and an extension of the collective approach, already established in public environmental health, has steadily taken place. Moreover, as we gradually understood the connection between environmental conditions and personal health we recognized the importance of linking preventative treatment approaches administratively.

It is now acknowledged that a high degree of medical skill will not by itself solve the problem of sickness unless it can be backed by supportive services of prevention and care and made readily available when and where it is needed. This necessitates a complex administration and massive public finance. Likewise high standards of care which reach only a small section of the population will not ensure a healthy nation so it is necessary to try to spread facilities equitably by class and by area and to organize them on a national basis in order to encourage this.

While sickness remains a personal problem for the individual who is ill and needs appropriate care and treatment, it is now clearly seen as a public problem also, the solution to which must lie in collective action on a wide front. At the same time the promotion of health, although now a complex technological process involving increasingly specialized and diversified groups of professionals and experts, must ultimately remain the concern and responsibility of individuals. In the next section an attempt will be made to describe in simple terms the complex structure of health provision which has evolved to meet the dynamic and the paradoxical problems that sickness presents to society.

Health services in Britain

In Britain the response to the problem of sickness has been the creation of the National Health Service which has comprehensive concern for all aspects of medical care and public and environmental health. Different aspects of health care developed in voluntary and statutory hands in a variety of ways, but by the 1946 National Health Service Act they were all brought together into one major social service. Prior to 1946 primary care through the general practitioner was mostly on a private practice basis except that National Health Insurance gave some workers access to it through the panel system. Hospitals were provided by local authorities, either as poor law infirmaries, public health hospitals or mental hospitals, or they were run on a voluntary basis; in which case they varied from large, well-supported and prestigious teaching hospitals to small specialist clinics and rural cottage hospitals. Finally, local authorities, in addition to running hospitals, had wide responsibilities for environmental and preventive health services and they operated domiciliary maternity, mental health and school health services.

Within these different settings medicine had developed both scientifically and professionally at a great pace. Scientific development meant increasing specialization amongst doctors and the growth of teaching and research facilities on a large and costly scale. It also meant the growth of numerous professions ancillary to medicine as the scope of medical technology increased. As the potential of medical science had grown, so inevitably had its costs. The State had intervened increasingly in the health sphere, and it has steadily accepted a growing responsibility for the direct financing of health care. But in 1946 the various branches of medical care were in considerable administrative and financial chaos and this was proving detrimental to the quality of treatment offered and especially to the effectiveness of prevention. In many cases two services with two standards of provision were operated, side by side, for public and private use. Medical care was inequitably distributed in two ways: geographically, because some areas, notably the South-East, had far higher doctor–patient ratios than others, and also by socio-economic status, because medical care was distributed more according to a person's ability to pay for it than according to his clinical need. Moreover, many of the voluntary hospitals were desperately short of funds and had to offer poor quality care, while the standards of local authorities provision varied enormously. So although medicine as a science was maintaining good progress, the financing and administration of health care was badly in need of a coherent rational organization.

The 1946 National Health Service Act aimed to provide this. It created a service that was comprehensive in its scope and universal in its coverage. The aim was to remove all financial and organizational barriers between the doctors and their patients. The Minister of Health was given responsibility 'to provide the establishment in England and Wales of a comprehensive health service designed to secure improvements in the physical and mental health of the people and the prevention, diagnosis and treatment of illness, and for that purpose to provide and secure the effective provision of services'. The State was to finance the health service largely through general taxation so that medical care would be free to the individual at the point of use. The administrative structure devised was a complicated tripartite one reflecting professional and administrative differences existing prior to 1946. The hospitals were 'nationalized' and they and the specialist services operating from them were administered, under the Minister of Health, by a two tier structure of regional hospital boards and hospital management committees. The general practitioners continued to operate fairly independently but were under contract to local executive councils. This structure was the outcome of a compromise between competing political and professional interests, and it was far from completely satisfactory. Nevertheless it worked, not without problems, but reasonably effectively for a good twenty years before real efforts were made to amend it. Likewise, the financial basis of the health service has remained largely unchanged although there has been mounting criticism from within and without of gross under-financing which has recently reached crisis proportions.

Administrative organization

The tripartite structure of the British health service has been criticized almost since the inception of the NHS in 1946. It was obviously difficult to maintain continuity of care for patients when different authorities were concerned with different aspects of provision. The three branches of the system were not only separate but they were administered by different kinds of authority. Hospitals, the most expensive and most visible part of the service, were planned by fifteen large regional bodies with members directly appointed by the Secretary of State. Day-to-day management was in the hands of 330 hospital management committees whose membership was again by appointment. Hospitals were financed directly from the central Department of Health and Social Security. Local authorities on the other hand, with elected members, remained responsible for a wide range of services in the community including preventive health service and domiciliary maternity services. Money for these services had to come through the local government financial machinery and the medical officer of health had to compete with other chief officers, from education or social services or housing for example, in bidding for resources. General practitioners remained on a semi-independent contractual basis separately administered by the 134 local executive councils, with separate funds.

Clearly this variety and number of responsible bodies was an obstacle to effective joint planning of services. It was difficult to ensure coordination and flexible use of resources and communication and cooperation was particularly difficult between hospital doctors and general practitioners. Some services such as the geriatric hospitals, and some patient groups such as the chronic sick were very badly served. The unfair and uneven distribution of resources was widely attributed to the absence of a clearly defined unitary authority for purposes of planning, and the need to establish priorities. As the necessity for joint planning became more apparent the pressure for an integrated service intensified. Various proposals for change were made including some fairly radical ones from the medical profession itself notably in the Porritt Report, *A Review of the Medical Services in Great Britain*, published in 1962. In 1968 the first Green Paper on *The Administrative Structure of the Medical and Related Services in England & Wales* was published. After comment and discussion a further Green Paper, *The Future Structure of the National Health Service*, was published in 1970. This advocated a unified system under the control of about ninety area health authorities. The detailed proposals were considerably modified after a change of government in 1970 but the broad principle of integration was retained. A White Paper, *National Health Reorganization: England**, appeared in 1972, the changes became law in 1973 and came into operation on 1 April 1974 at the same time as the reorganization of local government.†

The new structure of the NHS

Central responsibility, as before, lies with the Secretary of State for Social Services and the Department of Health and Social Security. The DHSS is advised by the Central Health Service Council and several standing advisory committees which advise on particular areas such as nursing and maternity services. It is intended to continue the advisory service at different levels of management so that there will also be advisory machinery at regional and area levels. The object of this extensive advisory service is two-fold – to help the members of the health authorities in their decision making and to ensure that the health professions exercise some say in the planning and operation of the NHS.

Under the DHSS the whole range of services that comprise the NHS – hospitals, family practitioner and community services – are

*Cmnd 5055. Proposals for health care in Scotland, Wales and N. Ireland were made separately, but on the same principles.
†Local Government Reorganization is described in chapter 11.

administered and managed by a complicated mix of appointed bodies and professional staff. This complexity arises out of attempts to reconcile the need for central coordinated planning of services with the need for effective management by those with professional clinical responsibility for the actual provision of services. A detailed management study* was made for the working of NHS by an inter-professional group which advocated as its theme 'maximum delegation downwards matched by accountability upwards'. The need to allow some consumer say in the running of the health services was also taken into account and relationships with other social services, particularly in local government, were considered.

The diagram attempts to summarize the new structure in England. Under the DHSS fourteen Regional Health Authorities have been established. Their members are appointed by the Secretary of State and include businessmen, lawyers and members of the medical profession who are knowledgeable about the needs of the region. They will keep close contact with the universities and teaching hospitals of the region. The RHAs have overall responsibility for planning services in their regions in the light of central government policy and regional needs. They have some powers for directly undertaking major building works and they are initially to be responsible for the appointment of senior medical staff, but their main function is to plan, and then allocate resources accordingly to the second tier bodies, the Area Health Authorities.

There are ninety AHAs in England and these are also appointed bodies with the chairman appointed by the Secretary of State, some members by the matching local authority and the rest by the RHA. AHAs are coterminous with the new local authority areas. Both the RHAs and the AHAs have teams of administrative and professional staff to assist them to discharge their functions and the AHA is the major employing authority for most of the health service staff. Senior officers include the area administrator, the area medical officer, the nursing officer and the treasurer. The AHA is responsible for the development and operation of the health services of its area. It does not, however, have direct control of the development of the GP services but has to establish a Family Practitioner Committee, which has a separate budget, so this aspect of medical care still remains rather isolated. The rest of the hospital and community services come under the AHAs' direct concern and it is

*DHSS: *Management Arrangements for the Reorganized National Health Service* 1972.

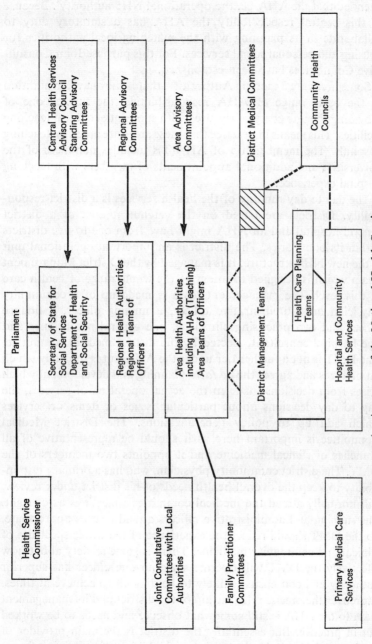

An Anatomy of the National Health Service

intended that the AHA be 'the operational NHS authority'. Because of this central responsibility the AHA has a statutory duty to collaborate in its planning with the matching local authorities for housing and personal social services. For this purpose Joint Consultative Committees have been established.

Some areas are Teaching Authorities, that is they have, in addition to the basic range of AHA responsibilities, the further one of providing the university of the area with substantial clinical teaching facilities. This means in practice that these areas are based on teaching hospitals. The membership of AHA(T)s includes nominees of the universities and additional appointments of members with teaching hospital experience.

The day to day running of the health services is a district responsibility. Districts are based on the catchment area of a district general hospital and an AHA might have from one to five districts within its boundaries. The district is an important operational unit in the new NHS structure. It is managed by the District Management Team which is designed to integrate the whole range of health care at this level. The management team is made up of a community physician and administrative officer, a nursing officer, a finance officer and two practising clinicians, one general practitioner and one hospital consultant, elected by the district medical committee. The DMT is not a further tier under the AHA but is the body which rationalizes and agrees the *de facto* planning and development which arises from decisions made in the actual operation of services, the day to day decisions about particular issues or items or services which add up to policy generalizations. The District Medical Committee is important here as it should be representative of all branches of clinical medicine and it appoints two members of the DMT. The district community physician, who has a primary responsibility to keep the overall health needs of his district under review, will normally attend the medical committee's meetings as of right. The nursing and administrative officers attend also as appropriate. So the DMT should reflect the experience of the whole spectrum of clinical and community medicine. There is some anxiety about how effectively the DMT will operate since no one officer has superior authority and consensus is likely to be difficult to achieve at times. Moreover the precise relationship of the district and its management team to the AHA is still somewhat obscure and needs to be worked out in practice. But essentially the district is the main provider of services, of hospitals, maternity and child welfare clinics, home nursing, school health services and the like, while the Area Health Authority monitors this provision.

In addition to DMTs each district will have Health Care Planning Teams, normally led by a clinician, to consider the development of services and assess the needs of groups such as old people or the chronic sick. These teams will not have a management function but will simply pool information and ideas, drawing upon interested personnel from outside the health service as well as from within. Voluntary bodies as well as local authority services will be represented on these teams which will concern themselves with a wide range of problems and provisions.

Finally at district level there is a system of Community Health Councils which aim to involve the community as the consumer in the provision of health care. Each district has a community health council consisting of about thirty members, half of the members being local government appointments the remainder chosen by the AHA and RHA from relevant voluntary bodies and interested persons. It is intended to establish a national body to advise and assist the councils. The CHCs have power to obtain information about the health services of their district and they can inspect health premises, including hospitals. They have close links with the DMT and contact with the AHA and it is intended that they be consulted before any major decisions affecting the health services of the district are made, especially any that might involve hospital closures. They publish an annual report which should comment on the health service provision from the consumer point of view. The councils each have a secretary and a budget from the RHS. Under new proposals in a White Paper, *Democracy in the National Health Service*, published in 1974, their role is to be increased to include the election of some members to the AHA in order to increase local democratic participation in health services planning.

The community health councils aim to involve the consumer positively in the provision of health care. But consumer complaints can also be voiced directly to the Health Services Commissioner. The commissioner does not investigate complaints until the health authority concerned has investigated and replied to the complainant and only if the complainant then remains dissatisfied. This extension of the ombudsman principle is an important acknowledgement of consumer rights in the sensitive area of health care.

The reorganization of the NHS took place in 1974 and it proved a considerable upheaval. For many people within the service it appeared to be a deliberate disorganization as existing administrative procedures came to an end and new ones had difficulty in establishing themselves. Inevitably the objectives of change tend to be overshadowed for a while by the turmoil it produces and in 1974 there was much anxiety about what had been achieved by so much upheaval. It is difficult to assess achievements at such an early stage and it is perhaps better to reassess the objectives of reorganization. The prime objective was to improve the quality of service. It was definitely felt that the quality of care available under the NHS could be improved by better management of existing resources. It was especially held that better services could be obtained for the weaker groups such as the chronic sick and mentally handicapped. There is clearly a growing need for forward planning of services which should benefit from the greater central control and unified administration which the new health service offers. Moreover health services depend on, and interact with, welfare services and housing and therefore planning must operate in a collaborative way and involve local government as well as the health services for which the reorganized service provides.

Finally the aim of reorganization was to create an effective community health service. It was agreed that the hospital sector had for too long dominated the health scene and community services had lagged in development and prestige. This was proving detrimental to the preventive aspect of health services since epidemiological studies have shown the importance of social and environmental factors in sickness. No one aspect of medical care – primary care from general practitioners, community health care or specialist hospital treatment – could be effective on its own and it was considered vital to integrate them and develop an integrated approach to the community's health needs.

Criticism of reorganization has been made on several grounds: that it has concentrated on an over-theoretical management approach and produced a structure that is both unwieldy and at times obscure and contradictory, that it is undemocratic and leaves too much power in the hands of the professionals and that it has failed to achieve an integrated service.

It would be a hard task to establish as complex a management structure as that of the NHS in a new area of service. In a service with long traditions of disparate operation and planning, strict hierarchy and clinical autonomy it is likely to prove an impossible task at least for some years so there is currently much chaos and confusion. Some compromise between old and new styles of administration will evolve as the reorganized service gets into its stride but there is a real fear of over-bureaucratization in the new structure. Inevitably with such a complex blueprint, different patterns of administration are emerging in different areas. In some places the district with its practical managerial responsibility appears as the key organizational level. In others the new area health authorities are establishing the dominance of the area level. It is difficult to generalize and this is probably a hopeful sign. Diversity of practice should help to overcome the criticism of too much theory but it does remain a valid one.

It is fair to say that reorganization strengthened central government control and in some ways it lessened the democratic element in the NHS. There were some arguments for putting the health services into local government which is responsible for other, interdependent services, but this was not acceptable to the medical profession and so unification meant the removal of the community health services from local government control. But the hospital sector and the general practitioner services were already outside democratic control and at least the creation of community health councils offers some chance of a consumer having a say in the development of services in the new structure. Moreover the appointment of the ombudsman should help to make criticism both heard and constructive. But the democratic input does remain slight and it is hoped that the benefits of planning and coordination outweigh this disadvantage. The professionals, basically the doctors, have retained a considerable say in health service management especially at district level but this should be more effectively balanced in the new structure by the creation of the area authorities which can monitor district performance and rationalize provision. Real integration cannot be said to have been achieved as the primary medical care services remain isolated and the hospitals still dominate at district level. But although integration is only partial there is room for the development of a more comprehensive and community based approach to health care. Changes take time and administrative reorganization can only facilitate, not order, changes in medical care delivery.

Finance of the NHS

Some people, especially professionals within the health service, have been heard to argue that the shortcomings of the NHS were not administrative but financial. It is certainly true that however good an organization is it cannot function effectively without adequate resources and this is something which it is hard to determine let alone provide for a national health service. There has been a reluctance in Britain to provide enough money for health services partly through fear of insatiable demand, partly because of suspicion over the effectiveness of some costly methods of treatment and partly out of grudging refusal to accept the urgency of the needs of some of the weaker and less glamorous groups of long-stay patients. Discussions about finances have for many years centred on arguments about whether or not the health service should be free to the user and financed out of general taxation or whether a private sector should be encouraged. These arguments have been fierce and have detracted attention from more important issues. Health services are labour intensive and extremely vulnerable to the effects of inflation. Costs are, therefore, rising steeply yet the proportion of GNP spent on health in Britain remains relatively low. There is an urgent need for more money in the health services and relatively little of this comes or is likely to come from the private sector. Those areas of health provision in greatest need of more resources are those least likely to attract private finance so the bulk of resources must continue to come from the Exchequer. Health services do compete with other services for their resources so if they are to receive greater priority, especially in times of economic difficulty, then they must justify their use of resources on one method of treatment or care as opposed to another, and match provisions more equitably to needs.

The hospital service

Nearly two thirds of the NHS costs go on hospital provision. The NHS runs around 2800 hospitals with over half a million beds. The hospital service provides a full range of hospital care including, for example, psychiatric hospitals, maternity units, convalescent homes and rehabilitation centres as well as the big general and teaching hospitals. The national ratio of beds is 9.8 per thousand of the population and these are broadly divided as 3.7 acute, 4.0 psychiatric, 1.3 geriatric and chronic sick and 0.5 maternity. At the hospitals all the appropriate medical, nursing, administrative and ancillary staff are available. There are a vast number of different hospital occupations from the senior medical staff through laboratory technicians and social workers to domestics. About 26 000 medical personnel work

at hospitals and over 300000 nurses with 40000 professional technical staff such as radiographers and 240000 ancillary staff. Patients
are mostly referred to hospital by their general practitioners. They
may be admitted for treatment or dealt with as outpatients. Consultant specialists are appointed in all branches of an increasingly
complex medical field. They head the hierarchy of medical staff that
service the hospitals on the wards and in the clinics but in many
cases they also practise in their consultative capacity outside the
hospitals. Both hospital and specialist services are free to the patient,
those who wish can pay for additional amenities or the full cost of
treatment. The existence of 'pay beds' within the NHS has recently
aroused bitter controversy. It is argued that people with money can
pay to jump the queue but do not pay the full economic cost of
treatment and this is unjust in a basically free health service. Others
argue that the private sector brings extra resources to the health
service and people should be encouraged to pay if they wish. It is
undoubtedly true that the private patient is a source of income for
some consultants and any ban on private practice by NHS employees
would result in large and costly pay demands by medical personnel.
It would also anger many senior staff, and for these reasons the anomaly will probably continue for the forseeable future unless political
pressure to end it overrules caution. Efforts are being made to separate the public and private provision more effectively by phasing out
paybeds from NHS hospitals but consultants are likely to retain
some freedom to do private practice. The controversy has revealed
deep divisions of opinion between the medical profession and the
government over professional freedom and the problem of resources
in the NHS, and an effective compromise needs to be reached on
this issue.

The hospital services are large and complicated. As medicine
develops it produces more specialists, more techniques and skills,
and consequently it requires more space and more ancillary staff. As
standards rise more people can be treated for conditions that once
were considered hopeless. Patterns of hospital usage change. For
example, there are now fewer TB patients and acute surgical and
psychiatric cases have a more rapid turnover than before the war but
there are also more long-stay geriatric beds and more maternity beds
needed. Accordingly hospitals very easily become both obsolete and
overcrowded. This is very strikingly so in Britain where half of the
hospitals date from the nineteenth century and lack space for laboratories, elaborate operating theatres, occupational therapy units,

etc, as well as being often in poor structural condition with inadequate sanitary and heating arrangements. So there is a need for more and up-to-date hospital accommodation even though overall bed demand has not risen. A further problem presented by hospital provision has been the uneven distribution of hospital resources. Some areas are well endowed, others grossly neglected since historical accident determined the location of many of today's large hospitals. This was one of the reasons why the National Health Service was created – so that there could be some overall planning of hospital provision. But in its early years little was spent on hospital building. It was only in 1961 that the Minister of Health asked the Regional Boards to plan really large-scale expansion of their hospital services. In 1962 the Hospital Plan was published embodying their programmes for the next decade. In addition to a general acceleration of building plans attempts were made to reorganize the pattern of hospital provision and provide a rational basis for planning. Accordingly estimates were made of the number of beds that would be required in any area for the different sorts of cases – acute surgical, maternity, psychiatric, etc. With these estimates, calculated from the relevant demographic data on population size and age structure, etc, and recommended ratios of bed provision to population for the various categories of patient, it was possible to make more rational plans for provision to meet the likely demand. Moreover, it was possible to think about the organization of hospital facilities in terms of suitable size of units, scope of services, and so on. The plan therefore introduced the concept of the district general hospital. Instead of haphazard provision of hospitals it was decided that for every 100000–150000 of population there should be a district general hospital of 600–800 beds. This would be located near the centre of the population which it was designed to service and it would provide, in addition to the ordinary specialities, a full range of diagnostic and treatment facilities for in- and outpatients and would include a maternity unit, a short-stay psychiatric unit, isolation facilities and geriatric care. More specialist facilities such as radio therapy, neurosurgery, etc, would require larger catchment areas and so would only be located at some hospitals. It was anticipated that as the new district general hospitals developed to meet most of the bed-demand, some of the existing smaller hospitals would be closed down or be used as annexes for maternity or geriatric cases only.

Clearly this plan for hospital provision involved massive building projects and considerable reorganization. It was hardly surprising that some parts of it proved highly controversial. The capital expense of it, and the difficulties of finding sites for such vast new premises as are required by a modern hospital, have meant that progress has not been as rapid as had been hoped, and there has been some modification of the original plans, including the retention in many cases of the small cottage hospitals. But a considerable amount of new building and remodelling is under way as the hospital plan revisions show, and the prospects for the hospital service are certainly good, even though the present situation is not satisfactory. Buildings are not, of course, the only or even the most important part of hospital provision: staff are vital and there are constant problems in obtaining enough medical, nursing and ancillary staff at the required standards. Junior hospital posts are filled largely by doctors from overseas and there is a growing anxiety at our over-reliance on foreign medical staff. This is especially problematic in the long-stay hospitals. Nursing shortages are no less acute in some sectors of hospital provision. The need to keep demand for staff continuously under review, and to adjust recruitment and training programmes, pay and prospects accordingly, is an urgent one if the hospital service is to maintain and improve its quality.

Primary medical care

For most people the main contact with the NHS is through their general practitioner. There are about 24000 GPs, with a further 1000 assistants, working for the health service. GPs have frequent contact with patients often over a considerable period of time, and they have an important preventive as well as diagnostic and curative role to play in medical care. All members of the community are registered with a general practitioner and he is the usual first point of contact with health problems. He deals with all minor complaints and chronic conditions and is responsible for referral to hospital and specialist services where necessary. It is therefore important that general practitioners have a high level of diagnostic skill and technique available and a considerable degree of rapport with their patients. The general practitioner's role has changed radically during recent decades, particularly since the creation of the NHS. He used to be very much an independent entrepreneur, running his own practice and providing a wide range of medical services for his patients. As medicine has become increasingly scientific and more specialized the family doctor has of necessity become more dependent on others. He must refer to specialists much more frequently and make use of the services of pathology laboratories and X-ray departments, for example, to aid his diagnosis. In many ways the general practitioner feels that he himself can do less than formerly for his patients since he must often refer them to the hospitals' more specialized care. Many have found this change an unhappy one, and feel dissatisfied with what they consider is a reduced role. But in some ways the range of work of the general practitioner has widened with, for example, the development of modern drugs which make possible the treatment of quite serious complaints without recourse to hospitalization. His role in social and preventive medicine is also being increasingly recognized. Some general practitioners have responded well to the change of role and adapted themselves accordingly. Group practices are becoming more frequent and some groups are able to offer a degree of specialized care, different doctors being predominantly responsible for work with children, old people, mental health problems, etc. Others have experimented with purpose-built premises offering accommodation for not only the group of doctors but some technical, nursing and social work assistance in addition to the usual secretarial help. The advantages of group practices are that they permit the doctors to organize their work better, enabling them to have time off instead of being permanently on call; they offer a more stimulating environment to the doctors; and they make possible the use of relatively expensive equipment and ancillary staff. Since the establishment of the NHS a central committee, the Medical Practices Committee, has worked with the local executive councils and, since 1974, with the Family Practitioner Committees to ensure an even distribution of primary medical care facilities across the country. The Committee monitors the spread of general practice and has powers to forbid the setting up of new practices in areas it considers to be adequately covered.

Despite these new ideas there continues to be a shortage of good general practitioners, some areas being especially deprived. It has been suggested that the two main reasons for this are the relatively low status of family doctors compared to hospital doctors and the problem of remuneration. The status problem is largely the consequence of the developments in medicine which have shifted the emphasis in medical care on to the hospital and consultant specialist side. General practitioners have been regarded as non-specialists in a profession tending increasingly to specialization of interest and skill. Recently it has been suggested that general practice should itself be regarded as a specialist field, and appropriate training provided for doctors after their basic training which takes place, of course, predominantly in a hospital setting. The Royal Commission on Medical Education which reported in April 1968 went even further than this and made far-reaching proposals for the reorganization of the whole field of training. Once these are implemented all young doctors including prospective GPs will, after their initial five year course, have to undergo a further five years' supervised training in hospitals, health centres, etc. This will consist of three years of general professional training followed by two of specialized work as either assistant principals in general practice or junior hospital specialists. After this the young doctors will become either principals in general practice or hospital specialists. A further suggestion for improving both the status of the GP and making his job more interesting is to involve him in the work of the hospitals and some experiments are under way on such lines. The remuneration issue itself is not divorced from the status problem. Not only high status but potentially high financial rewards are attached to the senior hospital posts whereas the GP is in a job with a fairly steady level of pay but slight career or advancement prospects. Payment of GPs was established on a per capita fee basis, that is according to the number of patients rather than the amount or quality of work done. This method, therefore, is regarded as failing to reward the more industrious or ambitious doctor. Attempts have been made to improve this financial position in recent pay settlements which should make possible the financial recognition of extra effort and qualification. In 1966 a settlement known as the 'Doctors' Charter' firmly established the link between remuneration and quality of service. This, together with more opportunity for work in group practices or health centres, has encouraged more young doctors to opt for a career in this important branch of medical care, and the future of general practice seems reasonably well assured today.

The general practitioner services are provided on an independent contractor basis and the GPs enter into contracts with the family practitioner committee set up by the AHA. Like its predecessor, the Executive Council, the FPC has thirty members, half of them appointed by the professions involved and the remainder by the AHA and local authority. The FPC contracts not only with GPs but also with dental practitioners, pharmaceutical services and ophthalmic services. The general dental service aims to provide adequate dental services including all conservative dentistry. Each person can choose his own dentist and attend for the necessary treatment. Unlike the GP service, which is entirely free, dental treatment is provided on payment of part of the cost up to a maximum payment of £10 per course of treatment, with special charges for dentures. Young people and expectant and nursing mothers are exempted from charges. About 12000 dentists work as independent contractors and a further 800–900 work in dental hospitals which are responsible for training dentists as well as developing knowledge and skill in dentistry and tackling the more complex dental problems referred by outside dentists.

The provision of pharmaceutical services in the community is a responsibility of the FPC which makes the necessary arrangements with local registered pharmacists. Prescriptions are made out by doctors for such drugs, dressings or appliances as are required and these are dispensed by the pharmacist who then recovers the costs. The patient now has to pay a charge of 20p per item for his prescription but children, old people, expectant mothers, certain categories of chronic sick and people on low incomes are exempted from the charge. There is continued controversy over prescription charges which are regarded by many as an anomaly in a free health service and by others as a necessary check on abuse. The drug bill is a large and growing one and this causes much anxiety. Prescription charges only cover about one quarter of the actual cost of each item and are not recovered from those categories of people who make most use of drugs. Proposals for a graduated charge related to the cost of the drug were made in 1971 but not implemented due to administrative difficulties and the unpopularity of the idea which was felt to reintroduce the financial barrier between patient and doctor which the NHS was designed to remove. Nevertheless, despite the emotion aroused by the 'tax on sickness', charges do appear to restrain the demand for drugs and are therefore likely to remain. A further way to reduce the drug bill would be to reduce the profit of the drug companies and efforts have been made to do this. Intervention in this sphere causes enormous political controversy however. Perhaps the most hopeful way of cutting back or restraining the growth of the drug bill would be to reorientate primary medical care more towards prevention than treatment. Both patients and doctors are at times over enthusiastic about drugs and much education is needed to inculcate more positive attitudes towards health and reduce dependence on drugs. This is particularly important in the case of 'mood effecting' drugs such as tranquillizers and sedatives, which are now very widely prescribed for conditions of anxiety and insomnia, and that of antibiotics which again are prescribed with increasing frequency and insufficient discrimination.

Ophthalmic services have, like the dental and pharmaceutical services, a local professional committee which appoints members to the family practitioner committee. The local committees draw up lists of qualified practitioners who can freely test sight and make up glasses where necessary. Charges are made for lenses and frames approved by the health service or the patient can pay the full costs and enjoy a choice from a wider range of type and style of glasses.

Community health services

Before reorganization in 1974, public and domiciliary health services were in the hands of the local authorities which appointed a medical officer of health to be responsible for a wide range of duties under the NHS Act and the Public Health Act. In the recognized health service community health becomes one of the major responsibilities of the new unified organization with doctors and administrators from hospital and public health working together. The role of the community physician, the new specialism that has been created by reorganization, will be in assessment, evaluation and planning. The community physicians, at both area and district level, will study the health needs of the community and plan to meet them. They will be particularly concerned with developing preventive health services so they will plan and organize health education and health visiting, screening and vaccination programmes, maternity and child welfare clinics, family planning and school health services. They will have a major responsibility for liaison with the local authority especially over the basic public health duties which are remaining with local government, the drainage, sewage, refuse disposal and other sanitary services. They will also cooperate with personal social services departments so that health and social needs can be dealt with together where possible. For many groups of patients such as the mentally ill and the chronic sick the need for care is as great as the need for treatment. The local authority has responsibility for care, both residential and in a person's own home, and the importance of cooperation between health and social services cannot be overstated. It is one of the aims of reorganization to achieve better collaboration between health and local government in all these areas.

C

The scope of community health services is quite considerable. The maternity and child welfare services are well established and comprehensive. Their aim is the reduction of maternal and infant mortality and the improvement of the health of children. Ante-natal, post-natal and infant welfare clinics are established in all districts, run by AHA staff and local general practitioners. At ante-natal clinics mothers can obtain medical checks, relaxation classes and instruction on labour and the feeding and care of small babies. This service is available for mothers awaiting home confinements and those who expect to have their babies in hospital obtain a similar service there. Post-natal care is offered to all and involves visits by midwives, health visitors and, if required, domestic helpers. Mothers are then encouraged to bring their children to infant welfare clinics where routine medical inspection, general advice, regular weighing, etc, is made available and vaccination and immunization programmes carried out. Welfare foods, that is subsidized milk preparations and vitamin supplies, are on sale at the clinics. Health visitors continue to make such domiciliary visits as are necessary to offer advice on health and hygiene, child rearing and general family problems.

Under section 28 of the National Health Service Act the health authorities have power to make arrangements for the prevention of illness and the care and after care of persons suffering from illness. Under this section a wide range of services are provided such as sick-room equipment, chiropody, laundry services and physiotherapy classes. The home nursing service is a crucial part of the community health provision. The aged are the principle beneficaries of this traditionally important service which is a great help to old people seeking to live independently in their own homes.

The school health service is an important part of community health care. Medical inspection and treatment of school children is one of the oldest public health services pre-dating the NHS by many years. Even today, when all children should be registered with a general practitioner and receive whatever medical care they need, it has an important part to play in preventive medicine. Children are regularly inspected by a school doctor and nurse, usually a health visitor. Parents are encouraged to attend and discuss with the doctor any health problems the child may have. Action can be taken to remedy any defects. Vaccination and other prophylactic measures can be carried out, and specialist services, such as speech therapy or child guidance, can be brought into play if necessary. Not only do individual children benefit from these regular checks and many, who would otherwise be neglected, receive some medical attention, but also the process of inspection monitors the collective health of school children. Trends in diseases or defects such as malnutrition or hearing problems can be noted and acted upon in the community and important epidemiological information obtained.

Health education is a vital aspect of a community health service but it has not been well developed in the past. Many personnel, especially the doctors, both those in general practice and those in clinics, and the health visitors, are actively but informally involved in educating people about their health. But health education, if it is to be successful, can involve the alteration of behaviour patterns both in individuals and the community, which is no easy task. In order to promote better health education a council was set up in 1968. The Health Education Council has central responsibility for advising AHAs on priorities and helping with the mounting of campaigns especially through the provision of educational material, and it promotes research in this area. At area level, health education specialists are appointed who can concentrate on this work with audio-visual aid staff to assist. They must work closely with social services and education departments as well as with their health service colleagues. At a time when it can be asserted that more and more disease is self-induced by bad behaviour patterns the importance of health education cannot be overstated and it is to be hoped that it will receive greater priority in the reorganized health service as a vital adjunct to a genuinely community oriented medicine.

Another aspect of health care that has been somewhat neglected by the NHS until recently is family planning. Contraception has remained such a controversial subject that the major developments in specialized provision have been through voluntary organizations, especially the Family Planning Association, albeit often working in partnership with local health authorities. It is expected that the AHAs will henceforth play a more positive part in this field as recognition of the importance of planned parenthood and population control becomes more widespread.

There has been much hope for the development of a community oriented health service through the medium of health centres. When the NHS was first established in 1948 local authorities had power to establish health centres which could bring together the work of the family practitioner services and local clinics. In the event very few have been established partly because of lack of resources, partly because of reluctance of general practitioners to move from established practices. It is thought by some practitioners that really effective health centres could not only serve to bring together doctors, dentists, community nurses and social workers to work in a team situation but could act as a focus for health education and truly preventive medicine. Much could be done by way of advice on diet and physical fitness, and the provision of occupational and physical therapy for rehabilitation and prevention, to swing the emphasis away from disease and over to health. Lack of such development is clearly a depressing sign of the acute shortages of resources suffered by the NHS in recent years.

Environmental health

Outside the new health service but a crucial basis to it, lie the environmental services provided by the local authorities. These include the provision of good water supplies and such services as sewerage, street paving and cleaning and the removal of refuse. A further task is the detection and control of statutory nuisances as defined by the Public Health Act of 1936 and current regulations concerning the control of air pollution. Steps are taken to protect the community from disease through provision for notification of infectious diseases and such measures for isolation and disinfection as are deemed necessary. Special regulations concern seaport and airport health control. Acts regulating the production and sale of food and drugs have to be enforced and control of slaughter houses carried out. The local sanitary authority is also responsible for pest control. Under various Acts local authorities also provide public baths, swimming baths, playing fields and recreation grounds, either directly or by grant aiding voluntary organizations, and all these measures contribute towards the community's health.

The full list of environmental health-care measures is very long. Sanitary inspection and control has a lengthy history and has emphatically proved its fundamental importance in any health programme. The mass of regulations and resultant inspections, reports, licences and registrations provide the unglamorous but vital basis to the nation's health programme.

The National Health Service meets the bulk of the nation's demand for medical care and together with the public environmental health services it goes far to prevent and treat sickness and improve the health and physique of the people. The service is comprehensive in scope but other medical services are available outside the NHS.

Doctors may practise privately and numerous clinics and nursing homes are run privately and for these services patients pay. Industry often offers limited medical care to its employees and several institutions offer their own medical services, such as the student health centres, but these services are usually limited in scope and designed to dovetail into the main NHS provision.

Health is a complicated field and it is inevitable that the services designed to maintain and promote it will have considerable financial and organizational problems to face. Shortage of resources remains a major difficulty in all aspects of medical care hence the perennial suggestions for a shift away from the present system, where care is largely free at the point of use, towards more payment by patients for the services they obtain. But the arguments in favour of collective provision and financing of health care are overwhelming from a medical as well as a social point of view. The full cost of medical care nowadays is too high and always too unpredictable for the individual to meet it and there is no intrinsic reason why expenditure on a collective basis should not be appropriately raised to offer the necessary standards of care. Good preventive medicine especially requires that there be early and easy access to medical facilities for all the population. Ultimately it is a question of priorities and the nation must be made more aware of the political decisions involved in the allocation of resources to health and other social services so that it can decide what quality of health care it wants.

The reorganization of the NHS has been a recent major upheaval which has left many people uncertain of what has been gained and what has been lost by change. Administrative change alone cannot solve all the problems involved in delivering medical care but it can help. The administrative structure is the framework within which the changing patterns of demand for medical care are matched to the changing resources of medical knowledge, expertise and equipment in order to ensure the maintenance of a high standard of health service. Not only standards of care but the distribution of resources according to area, class and population group are issues of current crucial concern. The search for better management and for more effective and equitable planning of medical resources must continue, despite the chaos and anxiety it can produce, until we are satisfied that we have the best and fairest health service possible.

Suggestions for further reading

Brown, R. G. S., *The Changing National Health Service* (RKP, 1974).

Cartwright, A., *Human Relations & Hospital Care* (RKP, 1964).

Cartwright, A., *Patients and their Doctors* (RKP, 1967).

Cochrane, A. L., *Effectiveness and Efficiency: Random Reflections on the Health Service* (Nuffield, 1972).

Dalzell-Ward, A. J., *A Textbook of Health Education* (Tavistock, 1975).

Forsyth, G., *Doctors and State Medicine* (Pitman Medical, 1960).

Illych, I., *Medical Nemesis* (Calder & Boyars, 1974).

Lindsey, A., *Socialized Medicine in England and Wales* (Oxford University Press, 1962).

Logan, R. F. (*et al.*), *Dynamics of Medical Care* (London School of Hygiene and Tropical Medicine, 1972).

McLachlan, G. (Ed.), *Problems and Progress in Medical Care,* Series 1–7, 1964–1972, *Challenges for Change* (Nuffield, 1971).

Malleson, A., *Need Your Doctor be so Useless?* (Allen and Unwin, 1973).

Rowbottom, R., *Hospital Organization* (Heinemann, 1973).

Stevens, R., *Medical Practice in Modern Britain* (Yale University Press, 1966).

Watkin, B., *Documents on Health and Social Services* (Methuen, 1975).

4 Education

The problem

The formal education system exists to meet the need of individuals to obtain the information and skills necessary to live full, satisfying and capable lives and also the need of society to have a responsible and productive population. When society is a modern, industrialized democracy, as Britain is today, these basic needs are considerably sharpened. A democratic society needs a people who are literate, reasonably well-informed about domestic and foreign affairs, able to exercise their democratic rights in a responsible manner and to participate at a variety of levels in the process of government. An industrialized society demands a skilled population and the scientists, technologists, technicians and business administrators necessary to keep industrial development moving and compete effectively with foreign competition. As we have become more generally civilized, humane and cultured, we have increased the need for more doctors, social workers, teachers, artists, etc. In other words the more complex and advanced the social, political and economic organization of the country becomes the greater is the need for a well-educated people. And as this complexity, and the resultant specialization and differentiation of role, continues, the need for a more advanced education becomes increasingly important to the individual if he is really to use his capacities to the full, and find his place in modern society. Education is the key to success in most walks of life today. Without basic literacy and general knowledge people don't know their way around, they don't know their rights or duties, cannot obtain jobs or command recognition or respect. Without training they cannot so easily advance in their careers or obtain good positions, or earn money and status. Without education people are unable to make full use of the growing amount of leisure that higher productivity brings nor can they benefit from cultural opportunities or develop their personalities and interests widely. Lack of education can result in problems of sickness and mental health and inadequate methods of child care, thus leading to much personal unhappiness and frustration which might be perpetuated through generations,

Education is clearly vital and more education on both higher levels and on a more broad and socially relevant basis is increasingly necessary as society progresses. A good deal of education is, of course, an informal process. People learn about life, about themselves, all their lives. Children learn from parents, from older children and from their own observation and experience. But formal education in literacy, in skills, in appreciation of culture and use of leisure is obviously necessary if learning is to be rapid and integrated, and this has been long recognized. Formal education used to be a voluntary and private concern, but now, although both of these elements are still present, it is primarily a statutory service. When the state first entered the educational scene during the early nineteenth century it was concerned with elementary education – that is with reading, writing and arithmetic, together with religious instruction. This was because the need for a literate population became urgent with the coming of democracy, industry and urbanization. As industry grew more competitive, by the end of the century the need for skilled workers increased and there was a corresponding development of vocational training in technical colleges and central technical schools. Secondary education and higher education were at that time the preserve of a privileged minority consisting of the wealthy who could finance their own education and the exceptionally bright who won scholarships. But gradually the statutory provision widened to bring secondary and higher education within the reach of more and more individuals as the need to make use of the potential talent and capacity throughout the population became more apparent. Today the statutory system is concerned with the whole range of educational facilities as it acknowledges both the need for more and better educated people and the right of people to education.

An effective education system should be constantly adapting to the social and economic changes within society. It should be highly sensitive to these changes and able quickly to reflect them by developing the training most suitable for individuals and the output of skills most needed by the country at any given time. Education is, of course, itself a powerful instrument of social change which can do a great deal to advance or retard developments in the pattern of life and work of any society. So there is also much room for discussion on the philosophy of education as well as on its more practical aims and the effectiveness of its methods.

Unfortunately the education system tends to lag behind many changes of emphasis in the organization and structure of society.

For example, it was slow to reflect in its curricula and the extent of provision an increasing emphasis upon science and technology in industry, politics, war etc, and consequently many individuals have finished their formal education lacking the necessary skills and information for success in a technological age while the country has experienced a grave shortage of certain kinds of scientists, technologists, and technicians. Similarly, higher productivity has resulted in greatly increased leisure for all classes, but there has not been a rapid enough development of education for leisure so that far too many people constantly and passively require entertaining instead of being able to use some of their free time in a creative and satisfying way. Even more subtly, changes in Britain's social structure and international role have not been reflected adequately in her education system. We still tend to have an élitist system, concentrating on the production of a handful of top people rather than on maximizing the potential of the bulk of the population. We still tend to emphasize qualities more suitable for imperial control than competitive business management. That the system dates, and lags behind the very changes it should be in the van of, is partly because education very easily acquires powerful traditions which can frustrate changes in its aims and organization. These are reinforced by the natural human reluctance of the current adult population – among them Her Majesty's Inspectors (HMIs), the education officers, teachers, and so on, who are now responsible for the system – to admit that there is anything wrong with the system which was a vital formative influence on them: to do so is tantamount to criticizing themselves as products of the system. But clearly there are no absolutes in education, no right or wrong systems. The aim should be a system capable of changing with society and sometimes itself capable of contributing to change. So it should essentially be flexible and dynamic. One of the major problems of the British system is the pervasion of a heavy nostalgia for the old ways which precludes a more objective assessment of contemporary educational needs.

The present system

The education system is largely administered by central and local government. At central government level the Department of Education and Science, working for the Secretary of State for Education, is responsible for national educational policy. It is concerned with the whole range of educational provision from nursery schools to higher education. Two central Advisory Councils for Education, one for England and one for Wales, advise the Department on educational policy. They have been responsible for the production of several important reports in recent years, such as the Newsom Report of 1963, entitled *Half our Future*, which was concerned with the secondary education of children of average and below average ability. There is also a central inspectorate, which is nominally an independent service under the crown rather than a ministerial body, in the hope that this will ensure standards are maintained without undue political control of education. HMIs aim to advise and encourage schools and ensure some uniformity of standards throughout the country. They visit and report on schools and colleges but see their role more as one of positive advice and support giving than one of rigid investigation. At local level the local authorities have considerable responsibility for education. They are actual providers of the services, they build the schools and employ the teachers and carry out all the duties laid down by the 1944 Education Act. Following local government reorganisation there are now 104 Local Education Authorities. These are the thirty-nine counties of England and eight of Wales and the thirty-six metropolitan districts of the major conurbations together with the Inner London Education Authority and the twenty Greater London borough authorities.

The 1944 Education Act, often referred to as the Butler Act, since it was under Lord Butler's presidency of the then Board of Education that it was passed, is the legislative basis of the present state system of education. It provides for three stages of education: primary, secondary and further. Primary and secondary education are available free and are compulsory between the ages of five and sixteen. The majority of schools are provided and run directly by the local education authorities but voluntary bodies, mostly religious, also provide premises as assisted schools at which running costs, mostly teachers' salaries, are met by the local authority. Direct grant schools are independent of the LEAs, but until the mid 1970s they received financial assistance direct from the central department. Private schools, confusingly known as public schools, are financed independently, largely by fees charged for attendance, and they remain outside the state system except that some are registered as efficient by the central department.

Nursery education LEAs can provide education for children from the age of two but have only provided it for a small minority to date. The importance of nursery education has long been recognized but it has never been given much priority. Educationally the pre-primary school years are very important. This is when children can get used to the idea of school gradually. They have the opportunity to meet and mix with other children and so enhance their social and emotional development. Their intellectual ability, especially in language and creativity, is also stimulated and their physical development aided. Nursery education prepares a child for primary education and is particularly valuable for the child from a home where, for a variety of reasons, he may receive little effective encouragement or preparation for schooling. It is also of considerable benefit to mothers if their young children can attend nursery schools as it releases them for part of the day either for work or for giving more attention to younger children. For all these reasons an extension of nursery schooling has been urged for many years but the number of places has remained small until the late 1960s. As part of the urban aid programme* local authorities were then encouraged to provide more nursery schools, especially for children in deprived areas, and some development took place. In 1972 a White Paper, *Education: A Framework for Expansion*, outlined the government's proposal to make, over a ten-year period, nursery schooling available without charge to all children aged three and four whose parents wished them to benefit from it. As a result of this a start has begun on the expansion of nursery education. Most of the recent development has been in the growth of nursery classes attached to primary schools and this is still regarded as the appropriate alternative to pursue in the next ten years. The nursery schooling will largely be provided on a part time basis with provision for a minority of children to attend full time.

The development of nursery education is long overdue both on social and educational grounds. The present position is that only about 15 per cent of the child population aged three and four are receiving nursery education and this includes many four-year-olds who have started primary school reception classes early. Since the urban programme began, relatively more places have been provided for children who suffer the multiple deprivations of living in the decaying areas of large cities. For these children, many of whom are additionally handicapped by poverty, and come from large, often

*See page 229 for further details.

immigrant families, nursery education is surely vital and it is depressing that still so few have the chance of it now. The neglect of this area of provision by the State has led to considerable development of private and voluntary activity. The most important and dramatic example of this has been the growth of the pre-school playgroup movement. Playgroups exist to provide the social benefits and often the educational benefits of nursery education in an informal setting. Many groups began on a neighbourhood basis mostly using the mothers of the children concerned to staff the groups on a part time rota and using a variety of make-shift premises. In 1961 the Pre-school Playgroups Association was formed to aid and encourage the spread of groups most of which can now obtain grants for equipment and accommodation from the local authority. The future of these groups is now uncertain in view of state plans to expand nursery education. Playgroups have been criticized for their predominantly middle-class character but they have played a vital part in developing awareness of the needs, both of children and of their mothers, and in showing what can be done by involving people in the organization and running of the services they need and want. It is hoped that the experience and good will of the playgroup workers can be utilized in the expansion of more formal public provision in the next few years.

Primary education Primary schooling is currently provided for children in two stages, infants from five to seven years and juniors aged seven to eleven. All children receive a primary education, many beginning before the age of five. The emphasis throughout primary education is on development, activity and experience rather than on the acquisition of facts. There is a real attempt to involve the children in the learning process rather than to dictate to them. Primary schools are fairly small, the majority of the present number, something under 27000 schools, catering for around one to two hundred children. Numerous experiments in educational method are under way, especially in new methods of learning to read and in the 'new maths'. At their best Britain's primary schools are very fine, stimulating, flexible and humane, offering an excellent opportunity to the child of developing his confidence and capacities and awakening his interest in learning. But the best is not always available. For too often the aims of primary schooling are frustrated by inadequate premises, lack of suitable equipment and a shortage of teachers which leads to over-large classes and high staff turnover.

In 1967 the Central Advisory Council for Education (England) produced a report on primary schools having been invited in 1963 'to consider primary education in all its aspects, and the transition to secondary education'. This report, the Plowden Report, made some very important recommendations and gave a detailed analysis of the existing situation. It pointed clearly to the fact that some schools were falling well below acceptable standards both in material and in educational terms. Among its suggestions were some for improving relationships between schools and parents and the development of schools which were more integrated with the communities they served. Most importantly it recommended a national policy of 'positive discrimination'. This involved the designation of Educational Priority Areas being areas where general social conditions were poor. The Plowden analysis of existing schools had shown to some extent that poor areas had 'poor schools'. The new policy was to bring the schools of poor areas up to the level of the best, in part to compensate the children for their social deprivation. To this end they were to be given extra books and equipment, priority in building and improvement plans, and encouragement to attract and retain good teachers by offering an additional payment at EPA schools. Numbers in classes were to be limited and teachers' aides recruited to provide more adult contact with the children.

The Plowden policy was a new departure insisting that equality of opportunity in education could only be achieved if there was positive discrimination in favour of the most under-privileged. Some efforts have been made to implement its recommendations. The expansion of nursery education with priority for deprived areas has tentatively begun. Educational priority schools have received some extra help and recent proposals for new building, and as a substantial programme for the replacement of unsatisfactory premises initiated in 1972–73, have further emphasized the need to shift educational building resources towards the primary schools. Teacher training and recruitment has been reviewed and attempts made to improve links between schools and colleges of education. And generally there has been a good deal of interest and discussion focussed on primary education. Arising out of the Plowden Report a small programme of action research began in 1968 to experiment in ways in which an educational priority policy could best be implemented and evaluate its results. The research team, led by A. H. Halsey, were concerned to link their study of the practical difficulties and methods of compensatory schooling with the broader aims of education and more especially the place of educational policy in the context of wider social and economic problems. Their findings have been published in 1972 as *Educational Priority: EPA Problems and Policies*. As with the Plowden Report itself it is difficult to summarize the report's findings because the issues involved are so complex. But at a simple level the Halsey Report endorsed the validity of an educational priority area approach, emphasized the value of a pre-school education, and claimed that it was possible to improve the links between home, school and work towards the creation of community schools. The educational priority approach will continue and, hopefully, not only should many primary schools be substantially improved in a material sense in the next few years, but also efforts will be made to adapt and improve their teaching and learning so that it becomes more relevant and meaningful to the children they serve.

Secondary education Secondary education is provided for children of eleven to nineteen years. After the 1944 Education Act the tripartite system prevailed in secondary education, that is children were sorted out, usually by the now notorious eleven plus examination, for grammar, technical or modern schools. This system was partly the natural outcome of the historical development of secondary education, which at first was only available to the minority of very able or relatively well-to-do children. In part, also, it was the consequence of the belief that different children required different kinds of education reflecting their wide variation in aptitude and ability. Not all children, it was felt, would want or benefit from the traditional grammar school education and an alternative, but not necessarily inferior, pattern should be developed in the new 'modern' secondary schools. In the event, roughly 25 per cent of children have received an 'academic education', mostly in grammar schools, since the 1944 Act. This in practice has tended to mean an emphasis on book learning and training for the examinations which give access to higher education, currently ordinary and advanced levels of the General Certificate of Education. A wide range of subjects are taught and as many pupils as possible encouraged to obtain some GCE qualifications and stay on for specialized sixth-form work well beyond the minimum school-leaving age. For some children technical schools offered a less academic and more vocationally oriented education still with some emphasis on study for examination. For the remaining 75 per cent secondary modern schools aimed to provide a good general education usually up to the school-leaving age, with little or no interest in examinations, until the Certificate of Secondary Education was introduced in 1965 to give secondary modern school children some chance of leaving with formal assessment. These schools have varied enormously in character and quality. At best some real attempts have been made to provide a rich educational experience for the child of average and below average ability. Courses have been made as stimulating and as socially relevant as possible. But some schools, especially those in inadequate premises, have tended to become little more than minding places where children have waited apathetically or sullenly for release to the adult world of work. Increasingly it has been realized that much of secondary modern education has failed to develop the capacities and potential of many pupils and the whole concept of the tripartite selective system of secondary education has been powerfully attacked and partially replaced.

The tripartite selective system was criticized on several grounds, some of them educational and others social. Over the years doubts have grown about the accuracy and fairness of the actual selection, since it has proved very difficult to measure innate rather than acquired ability. Clearly a child's background, particularly as regards parental attitudes towards education, and the quality of his primary schooling, were influencing the selection. Surveys tended to show that the selection of pupils for grammar schools was biased in favour of the middle class child of a small family from a good area. Moreover the percentage of places available to children for grammar schooling varied widely over the country so that geography rather than ability could determine a child's type of schooling. The concept of the late-developer became generally accepted: the idea that some children would not demonstrate their full potential at the age of eleven however fair the test. On social grounds it was argued that the division of children into different kinds of schools exacerbated class differences. On psychological grounds it was claimed that the failure of children at the age of eleven to reach the grammar school entrance standard could thwart their further intellectual development and encourage anti-social attitudes. Undoubtedly the fair concept of different schools for different types of children had been turned, by many people, into a strong division between good schools for the clever and successful, and dumping grounds for the failures and rejects. Despite the actual quality of the education

offered, many secondary modern schools were perceived as inferior
to grammar schools and many pupils, and their parents, therefore
sensed failure rather than sensible selection when allocated to them.
But the main and overwhelming argument put forward was that the
existing system, because of the discouraging effect it has on many
children and the inferior academic opportunity it offered them,
failed to make good use of the nation's resources of ability and the
country could not afford this wastage. Far too many children were
leaving school at the minimum school leaving age or well before
they had reached the level of education their ability warranted, and
most, though not all, of this wastage was from the secondary
modern schools.

There were strong arguments on the other side, however, defend-
ing the existing tripartite system. Many people felt that the alternative system of comprehensives would produce schools that would
be too large and impersonal, that the brightest children would be
held back and the dullest make no greater progress. It was held that,
if teaching was to be possible at all, streaming would be necessary
and this would be as socially and psychologically damaging as
selection for different schools. Much of the opposition was inevitably
based on prejudice rather than facts about comprehensive schooling
since experience of it was limited. But a telling and practical argument
undoubtedly lay in the vast expense that would be involved in
reorganization, particularly when other education priorities, such
as the raising of the school-leaving age, were being canvassed. Also,
in many areas the sheer physical difficulties of utilizing the existing
pattern of school building along different lines were very daunting.
But the main argument against reorganization was focussed on the
folly of destroying what was good in the existing system for the sake
of a rather intangible idea of educational equality. To many people,
the prospect of the end of the separate identity of the grammar
schools, some of them with centuries of tradition, and high academic
standards, has seemed one of wanton destructiveness. Others
have felt that the best of the modern schools would be sacrificed
in comprehensives dominated by grammar school practices and
aspirations.

The debate over comprehensive or selective education became a
party political issue and different governments have urged different
solutions on the local education authorities. For several years there
have been experiments with different systems but in 1965 all LEAs
were asked to submit schemes to the Department of Education and

Science for the reorganization of their secondary education on comprehensive lines. Most have now done so and non-selective secondary schools are becoming the norm for secondary as for primary education although a surprising number of authorities have managed to retain some degree of selectivity and a grammar school education, if necessary provided privately, is still highly sought after by many parents.

The great tragedy of this battle over secondary school reorganization is that so much of it has been fought out on political, emotional or financial grounds while the real educational issues have been neglected. The organization of a secondary school system is important, but more important is the content and quality of the education provided within it. And there have been grave reservations about this, in particular about its suitability, at academic and at general levels, for children of the present technological, leisured and rapidly changing age. Two important reports have been issued by the Central Advisory Council for Education (England) relevant to this issue. The first, the Crowther Report, published in 1959, was concerned with the education of children aged fifteen to eighteen and it recommended the raising of the school-leaving age, more technological education, proper courses for modern school pupils leading to an external examination and the creation of county colleges for sixth-form pupils. It also canvassed the concept of 'minority time', for the grammar school children, in particular, to ensure the literacy of scientists and the numeracy of arts specialists, urged the development of strong youth service, and made suggestions for the improvement of technical education.

The Crowther Report contained a wealth of material about the background changes in population structure, social and economic needs, etc, as well as much information and advice on how to make the education system more relevant to the society and age group it was designed to serve. Unfortunately not all its recommendations have been taken up, at least with the necessary vigour. A rather similar fate awaited the Newsom Report, *Half our Future*, which pointed out that the children concerned would in time constitute half the country's citizens, workers, parents, etc, and they deserved, accordingly, rather more attention than the existing system gave them. Apart from many detailed recommendations, the Newsom Report was important in stating authoritatively that 'there is much unrealized talent, especially among boys and girls whose potential is masked by inadequate powers of speech and the limitations of home background. Unsuitable programmes and teaching methods may aggravate their difficulties . . . the country cannot afford this wastage, humanly or economically speaking.'

Among its many suggestions for improving the situation were, once again, the raising of the school-leaving age, research into teaching techniques to help backward children, particularly those with linguistic handicaps, development of audio-visual and improved curricula to make subjects more relevant and interesting to the pupils.

In 1972 the school-leaving age was raised to sixteen. As indicated this has been advocated for many years and strongly recommended by the reports of the Central Advisory Council but it has not been an unequivocal success. By the time it was implemented many secondary schools had been dominated by the selective/comprehensive battle for several years and far too little attention had been paid to the development of curricula suitable for non-academic adolescents. Many of the new comprehensive schools are very large and impersonal, others are still coping with unsuitable collections of old buildings. Most importantly, too many schools lack staff who understand the objectives of a comprehensive approach. Many teachers are baffled and threatened by reluctant school children who can see little to gain from prolonging their education and many would prefer to concentrate attention on the more academic. As a result secondary education in general and comprehensive schools in particular have been having a difficult time in recent years. Some improvements have been made to teaching methods and curricula and some schools have attempted to provide a broad and relevant education for their pupils. But many are still dominated by outmoded concepts, values and regulations and as a result truancy levels are high, especially amongst the older children, and discipline problems loom large within the schools. There is clearly a need for much experiment and thought about the meaning of secondary education and some renewal of faith in its importance and value for all children.

Private education plays a part in all aspects of education but it is perhaps most obviously seen as a challenging alternative to state provision in the secondary area. There are currently just under 6000 state secondary schools and a further 446 independent and 269 assisted schools. As disillusion with the state system has increased, with many parents angry at the ending of the separate local grammar schools or worried about the problems of the new comprehensives.

interest in the private sector has increased. There has also been much support for the direct grant schools which have frequently provided a grammar alternative when comprehensive schemes have been implemented by the local education authorities.

Both private schooling, especially that provided by the prestigious public schools, and direct grant schooling have been heavily attacked for their role in perpetuating an educational élite. The persistence of segregated schools alongside comprehensives tends to cream off some of the more able and academically motivated children. This has made it difficult for the comprehensive school to compete effectively, in terms of proving academic standards, with the segregated system it has only partially replaced. The hold of the public schools in particular over recruitment to key positions in the country's social, political and economic institutions is an extremely tenacious and disquieting one. The public schools accentuate the unequal distribution of rewards and privileges in our society and to many people appear incompatible with democracy.

In 1965 a Public Schools Commission was set up to consider ways in which the public schools could be integrated with the state system. The first report of the commission in 1968 recommended the creation of a Boarding School Corporation to supervise this integration. The second report in 1970 recommended an end to direct grant status and fee-paying schools. Both reports have aroused much controversy but nothing has as yet been done to alter the position of independent schools radically. An end to direct grants to certain selective schools was announced in 1975. This provoked considerable opposition both from those who wished to save the schools as fine traditional grammar schools, and those who feared that such action would result in a strengthening of the independent sector in secondary schooling rather than a reinforcement of the comprehensive ideal.

Further education Turning now to further education, the third arm of the statutory LEA system, this term covers an extraordinarily wide field from the big city polytechnics to the local evening institute. 'Education' here is broadly interpreted to cover the vocational, cultural, social and recreational needs of everyone over school-leaving age who is not in full time secondary or higher education. The main concern of further education in terms of resources devoted to it, is vocational training, mostly of a technical nature. The main fields of study are technology: in engineering, building, etc, commerce and social studies, art and design, service trades: such as catering, and GCE overlap courses. These studies are catered for in a variety of technical colleges, art colleges, colleges of commerce, etc. A programme of expansion and reorganization from 1957 to 1962 graded colleges according to the level of courses offered and the type of qualification that could be obtained by students, and began the deliberate process of concentrating higher level studies in fewer colleges serving wider areas. Colleges were accordingly designated local technical colleges, area colleges and regional colleges. At the top of the pyramid were a few colleges of advanced technology but these were soon given independent university status. The next step of reorganization was to convert the regional centres into polytechnics, which offer advanced courses in a variety of fields, often as a result of combining colleges of technology, commerce and art into single polytechnics. This policy of concentration was made explicit in a White Paper *A Plan for Polytechnics and other Colleges*, published in 1966, which provided for higher education in the further education system. Henceforth, as an alternative to a much greater expansion of the universities, polytechnics have offered degree level work and opportunities for research while maintaining to some extent their technological bias and links with industry, commerce and the professions. This development, offering as it does an alternative opportunity for higher education outside the universities, resulted in there now being a binary system in higher education, a situation which many educationalists find disturbing. But it has indubitably led to a concentration of resources on polytechnics and rapid growth in buildings, staff and student number and scope of courses.

The courses provided at local technical colleges and area colleges are mostly on a part-time basis, taking students on day release or evenings or, nowadays, on block release from employment. Many of the courses are expected to dovetail the practical training provided by industry in order to provide fully trained craftsmen, technicians and skilled workers. On the industrial side the 1964 Industrial Training Act was designed to improve the training offered by the traditional apprenticeship system and put it on a more equitable and uniform basis. Industrial training boards now operate for most industries to bring together the employers and the education authorities and ensure that adequate training is provided. On the technical college side the courses offered lead to a bewildering variety of qualifications such as the City and Guilds Craft Examinations and the Ordinary and Higher National Certificates. For degree level work the Council for National Academic Awards was created but this work is now concentrated in the polytechnics. The Haslegrave Report of the Committee on Technicians' Courses and Examinations, issued in 1969, has made recommendations which have led to the establishment of Councils for Technician and Business Education which aim to keep the courses and examinations relevant to the vocational needs they serve. These include a variety of careers in industry and commerce so the range of work done, both in terms of subject matter and level attained, is astonishingly large. Technical education contributes enormously both to the nation's demand for skilled personnel and the individual's need to obtain education and training to the level he wants and desires. But much development could still take place to ensure that more young people, especially girls, had the opportunity to benefit from further education.

On the cultural and recreational side of further education LEAs provide day and evening classes in a huge number of fields from pottery to musical appreciation. Many LEAs have adult education colleges offering short-term residential courses on a variety of subjects. Further education is also responsible for the statutory youth service. Most LEAs have a youth officer and provide a network of clubs, outdoor pursuits centres and the like. In 1960 the Albemarle Report on the Youth Service was published which recommended that the youth service, as part of education, be considerably expanded and developed. The Youth Service Development Council was established to foster discussion and monitor progress and considerable experimentation took place in the following decade. Particular efforts have been made to reach the young people who were not interested in the traditional clubs and formal youth organizations. Detached youth workers have been appointed in many areas and informal coffee bars and centres opened. Much of the experimental work has been undertaken by voluntary organizations, encouraged and grant aided by the LEAs.

The development council examined the future of the youth service in a report published in 1969. Entitled *Youth and Community Work in the Seventies* the report recommended that the youth service became increasingly community oriented. For the older age group especially, it was felt that the work should be flexible and involve young people themselves more directly in running their own organizations and projects. More contact should be made with local agencies, firms and trade unions and more use made of existing facilities especially educational ones. The hope was that youth

workers could help young people to take a more involved and participating part in the development of their society. No formal action
has been taken on the report and the council itself was wound up
but the trend throughout the country has been for youth workers
to move out into the community wherever possible.

Special education   A further important responsibility of the LEAs
under the 1944 Education Act is the provision of special education.
This is provided for children who are handicapped and may be educated in special residential or day schools or in special classes within
existing schools. Some schooling is also provided in hospitals for
school-age children there and a peripatetic service is available for
children bedridden in their own homes. Special education has to be
provide for the following groups: children who are blind, partially
sighted, deaf, partially hearing, epileptic, physically handicapped,
delicate, emotionally maladjusted, educationally sub-normal, those
who have speech defects and, since 1971, mentally handicapped
children. Many of the special schools, particularly the residential
schools, are provided in fact by voluntary organizations and the
LEAs pay to send their children to them.

By far the largest category of pupils requiring special education
is the educationally sub-normal. For these children and for the
maladjusted children there is difficulty in finding enough places in the
schools. The relative newness of responsibility for the mentally
handicapped, who were previously looked after by local health
departments in junior training centres, means that there is a need
for development of schools for this group. For other groups the
provision appears to be adequate. But there is some controversy
over the manner in which provision is made. Some educationalists
argue that all children should, where possible, be brought up in the
same schools and that to segregate the handicapped child is to add
social difficulties to the sensory or emotional ones he already
possesses. Moreover, many children suffer from having to go to
boarding schools as it is usually uneconomical to provide day schools
for small numbers and there is a limit to the amount of daily travelling the child can be expected to cope with. If they can attend their
local schools they can remain in their own homes. There is, therefore,
some movement towards making this kind of provision available,
but at the same time, there is a tendency to provide ever more
specialized schooling for different groups. For example, schools
are being provided for spastics or for spina bifida children. And

within certain categories, eg blind children, special provision has been made for the brighter children capable of benefiting from a more academic education. Most of these specialized schools are provided by voluntary organizations which argue that the very particular needs of the groups they cater for demand completely specialized provision.

Clearly there can be no hard and fast ruling on this question and the needs of different groups must be met in a flexible manner after carefully balancing the pros and cons of segregated or integrated schooling. What undoubtedly is needed is more provision of specialized teacher-training courses so that staff are available with additional qualifications to teach the handicapped child. Courses are provided, especially for teachers of the blind, the deaf and the maladjusted child, but the output is not nearly great enough. More attention should also be given to the questions of vocational training and the transition from school to work which present particular problems for the handicapped school leaver. Handicapped pupils remain at school at least until the minimum age of sixteen but of course much of their time is taken up with overcoming their disabilities rather than on general learning, so many need even more time before they can benefit from vocational courses. Some colleges offering pre-vocational courses are now available but more needs to be done in this field. On the placement side the links with youth employment officers are being improved but the need here is for continuous assessment during the school career rather than a final discussion at school-leaving age. For some severely handicapped pupils the possibility of liaison with local welfare authorities providing occupational and social welfare services for the handicapped is to be encouraged.

Other local education authority responsibilities Youth employment services have not been solely an LEA responsibility, until 1974. Before that date they could be provided by the Department of Employment and Productivity. The service is an important one in helping to ease the transition from school to work, which is particucularly hard for the average or below average child who is not moving on clearly to further or higher education. The youth employment officer has access to reports on the child's ability, health and character and he discusses each child's future with him and with his parents. Account is taken of ability, temperament, interests, etc, and the availability of local employment, and recommendations are made regarding the most suitable line for the child to follow. If desired, help is made with actual placement and follow-up help and general guidance is now available to all people using the education system, whatever their age.

Schools, especially primary schools, have had a long tradition of concern over the health and welfare of children. The school health service provided medical and dental examination for all school children, before health care was more generally available. The service was operated by the local health authorities after 1948 although it retained a separate administrative identity. It is now one of the responsibilities of the Area Health Authorities to ensure that the schools are provided with facilities for examination and health education. Regular check-ups can play an important part in preventive medicine especially if adequate treatment facilities are made available and parents are kept closely informed of their children's medical and dental state.

Some education authorities run child guidance clinics for the special treatment of emotionally disturbed children. In other areas this facility is provided by the health authority. Child guidance clinics operate on a team basis with help offered, by psychiatrists, social workers, psychologists and therapists, to both parents and children in the handling of problems of maladjustment. The school psychological service provides facilities for assessment of children with learning difficulties; speech therapy clinics are also available to help children with speech defects. The provision of such special facilities varies considerably in different authorities. In large cities there tends to be a greater range of specialist services for children with problems than exists in rural areas. For some problems, such as dyslexia, provision of help is very slight and uneven and can often depend on whether individual teachers, psychologists or parents have taken an interest and urged action.

Some general welfare facilities are provided by schools such as school meals, milk in infant schools, and special transport facilities. Despite rising standards of living it is still the case that a significant number of children cannot make the best use of such education as is offered to them because of family poverty. To alleviate this a small amount of help is available, for example, free school meals, clothing grants and maintenance grants for helping with the costs of keeping children on at school beyond the minimum school-leaving age. Unfortunately such selective benefits are not as well used as they should be partly because of the complexity of means tests and partly because of the stigma which is attached to receipt of such services as free meals. Even where these services are made use of there are many activities at schools: outings, holidays, extra lessons and such like which increasingly form part of the total education provision, for which money is needed that poorer families can ill afford. This is certainly an area where positive discrimination could well be applied to ensure that all children in schools can make the fullest use of the facilities available.

Investigation of cases of need is one of the tasks of the education welfare service. Education welfare officers visit schools and families checking on cases of truanting and non-attendance, assessing families for grants, and working with families where there are problems of child neglect or juvenile delinquency. Some workers are school based and do counselling work with children who have difficulties. Following the creation of unified social services departments in 1970 there has been considerable discussion about the future of education welfare officers. It was suggested that social services should provide social workers for the schools but this was resisted by many educationalists who feel that there was some advantage in an education based welfare service. In recent years local authorities have been allowed to experiment with different patterns of organization and the administrative issue is still unclear. But whichever department operates the services it is clear that the social needs of children can often be recognized at school and there is a great need for social workers to help make the link between home and school as effective as possible.

Higher education

The universities are not strictly a part of the statutory education system as they are independent, self-governing institutions. A large part of their income, however, now comes from the Exchequer. The University Grants Committee, which apportions this income, links the central government department with the separate universities and attempts to define a national policy for higher education. Moreover, LEAs play their part in providing grants for the payment of fees and for maintenance of students from their areas who enter on courses at colleges and universities. A committee was appointed in 1961 by the Prime Minister under the chairmanship of Lord Robbins 'to review the pattern of full-time higher education in Great Britain and in the light of national needs and resources to advise HM

Government on what principles its long term development should be based . . . .' The Robbins Report, published in 1963, contained a detailed analysis of patterns of higher education in universities, colleges of education and colleges of further education. It recommended dramatic expansion of the numbers of higher education from the figure of 8 per cent of the age group which obtained at the time of the report to one of 17 per cent of the age group by 1980–1. The increase in places was to be achieved by the foundation of some new universities and by the expansion of technological education through the creation of technological universities and special institutions for scientific and technological education and research. Some of Robbins' recommendations, for example for the setting up of a Council for National Academic Awards degrees for work in regional and area colleges and for the introduction of degree courses for suitable teacher-training candidates, have been implemented. Expansion has certainly taken place both in the older established universities and in some new foundations. The number of students admitted and taking degrees has more than doubled in the decade since Robbins. During the 1970s it is expected to level out at around 300,000 full time students*, of which just under half will be arts based and just over half science based. In addition to expansion of numbers of university students there has been dramatic growth in opportunities for higher education in the new polytechnics as was mentioned in the section on further education. It is envisaged that expansion of higher education within further education will continue until it takes up roughly half the demand. The opportunities for education offered by universities and polytechnics will continue to include degrees in a wide range of subjects, postgraduate work of a specialist nature, and a variety of vocationally oriented courses. It is intended that a new shorter two-year course be made available in both sectors of higher education leading to a Diploma in Higher Education. By the 1980s it is hoped that the percentage of the relevant age group able to take up higher education will be 22 per cent which is higher than Robbins suggested. This expansion is fairly dramatic but it has not taken place without considerable controversy. Higher education is a vastly expensive service and expansion has raised anxieties about costs. It has also raised some doubts about the relevance of degrees and academic work in general to the employment situation. Clearly some people regard expansion of higher

*For Great Britain.

educational opportunity as good in its own right while others are more concerned to see a return on the investment made in terms of a graduate contribution to industry and the professions.

An important part of higher education, and one that is in some ways a more readily acceptable investment because of its vocational purpose, is teacher training. Most teachers are trained at colleges of education, run either by local authorities or voluntary bodies, but some receive training at universities after graduation. The split between graduate and college trained teachers has always caused friction and the aim now is ultimately to have an all graduate teaching profession. Thus the college of education courses are becoming more of a general education with some training and practical experience added. An enquiry was held into the whole issue of teacher training and the *Report of the committee on Teacher Education and Training* (the James Report) was published in 1972. Not all its recommendations were taken up but those concerning expansion of in-service training have been accepted and its suggestion of a Diploma in Higher Education has been adopted for a wider purpose. The content and standards of teacher training courses are determined by a balance of the main interests involved, the Department of Education and Science, the LEAs, the universities and the voluntary colleges, with advice from the major professional bodies concerned. Notable among these are the National Union of Teachers, the National Association of Head Teachers, the Association of Teachers of Technical Institution and the Headmasters' Conference.

It can be seen from this brief survey that the present education system is highly complicated, and evaluations cannot easily be made. At a very simple level the need is for education and the service provides it, compulsorily and free of charge for all children between five and sixteen and more selectively for young people and adults thereafter. But one must ask if the education system does meet the needs of the state and of the individual fully, not just does it start to attack basic ignorance, but does it provide the right sort of education on the right levels to satisfy both the interests of the State and the individual? This sort of question, as the foregoing outline of the system will have shown, is not easily answered. It is easy to say that everyone should have the 'right' sort of education to the right level but how do we determine, for example, how many years of compulsory education we should have, or how specialized higher education should become? What demands ought society to make of its education system – should the content of courses be left to the teachers or should the state lay down what it wants? There is constant room for discussion on such topics.

Moreover, one must ask not only if the education system meets the needs of society, as far as we can determine them, but if it does so in the most just, efficient and economical manner possible. This raises questions about the meaning of equality and the definitions of efficiency in an educational context. Much emphasis has been laid in the past on the education system providing equality of opportunity for everyone to make the most of their lives. More recently it has been seen that even with educational priority approaches and comprehensives the school can only partly compensate for fundamental deprivations within the family and the community. We are now sharply aware that education alone cannot make amends for poverty but it still has a major part to play in shaping our society. Constant efforts must be made to understand and assess the education system, to see whether it is appropriate and relevant to the current social and economic structure, whether it does deal fairly with different sections of society, whether it is carried out in an efficient manner; and it is fair to say of the present British system that while it contains many features of which we may be proud it has many weaknesses that urgently require remedy. Some of these are relatively practical like the shortage of good teachers, outmoded premises, shortage of nursery school places, etc. Others are more concerned with the content of courses: whether these are too academic, whether they fail to encourage a lively, critical approach to society, whether they ignore much of what is most relevant in life in failing to teach their students enough about the implications of science, the meaning of aggression, problems of race, conflict and emotion, etc. Education ought to be a reasonably controversial field and most certainly a rapidly changing one, and it ought to be debated against the background of wider moral, philosophical and social issues. It is undoubtedly one of the most fascinating topics of study in the field of social administration.

Suggestions for further reading

Benn, C. & Simon, B., *Halfway There* (Penguin, 1972).
Blackstone, T., *A Fair Start* (Allen Lane, 1971).
Dent, H. C., *The Education System of England and Wales* (University of London, 1963).

Douglas, J. B. W., *The Home and the School* (MacGibbon & Kee, 1964).

Douglas, J. B. W., *All Our Future* (Peter Davies, 1968).

Jackson, B. & Marsden, D., *Education and the Working Class* (1962).

Pedley, R., *The Comprehensive School* (Penguin, 1963).

Robinson, E., *The New Polytechnics* (Penguin, 1968).

Rubinstein, D., *The Evolution of the Comprehensive School.* (RKP, 1969).

Reports of the Central Advisory Council for Education (England)

The Crowther Report, *15–18* (1959).

The Newsom Report, *Half Our Future* (1963).

The Plowden Report, *Children and their Primary Schools* (1967).

5   The housing problem

Housing need: The general problem

Housing is a very important and very complex issue. The basic need is for all people to have shelter, a roof over their heads. However, this is overlaid with more sophisticated needs for a suitable house, that is, one of the size, price, position, etc, to suit each household's particular requirements. Merely having enough dwellings for the number of households which claim to want one would not remove the housing problem: the question of standards, location, security of tenure and so on would remain. Further, the quality and price of available housing itself influences demand so the number of households requiring a separate dwelling cannot be calculated without reference to the prevailing standards. Housing need is hard to define and the social policy that is the response to the need is a complex one. There is no one clear social service to cope with such a universal need, and individual and commercial as well as public housing efforts must all be considered in looking at society's total response to the problem.

Apart from the simple need for shelter many factors contribute to the formation of housing need. Size of dwelling is clearly important: it must be related to the size of a family and its particular way of life; and the type of dwelling – flat or house for example – must be considered. Location is extremely important – the dwellings must be available in a part of the country that offers suitable employment opportunities and in the immediate locality of shops, schools, transport facilities and so on. The amenities of the house, standard amenities such as running water, bathrooms, indoor lavatories and more luxurious amenities such as garages, gardens, etc, are also important considerations. The condition of a house is vital, whether it is in good structural order, weather proof and not too damp. Personal tastes interfere in housing need – whether a house is in a socially acceptable area, whether it has charm, seclusion, architectural merit and so on. Finally two very important factors are those of price and security: housing must be available at prices, including hard to estimate or assess but very real, to the people who live in slums in their lack of opportunity to enjoy space and beauty and attractive surroundings and to take pride in their homes and gardens.

Slum clearance is clearly desirable but though it solves many problems it can also create them. The break-up of extended family and neighbourhood ties can put strain on welfare services, and re-housing on overspill estates can make difficulties. Long journeys to work can tire as well as prove expensive and new estates often lack a sense of friendliness and real community. Loneliness can become a real problem and over-competition in the decoration and embellishment of new homes can lead to severe financial strain. It takes longer to build new communities than it does simply to put up the houses and shops, schools and factories that form the physical structure of them.

The housing problem in Britain today

The list of damaging personal and social consequences of an unsatisfactory housing situation is a long one. Having looked at the problem in general terms let us now look at the actual situation in Britain today. There are currently approximately 17.5 million separate dwellings in England and Wales. This probably amounts to there being a slight overall shortage of dwellings to existing households, but there is very uneven distribution between the different regions, some having a surplus and others an acute shortage of accommodation. Of the total housing stock, around 54 per cent of separate dwellings are owner occupied, 28 per cent are local authority owned and 13 per cent are privately rented. The remainder are otherwise held as tied accommodation, or under housing associations. The total housing stock is increasing every year although, of course, new building is offset by losses through clearance and redevelopment. The proportions of owner occupied and council owned dwellings are increasing while the private rented sector is declining rapidly. About one third of the housing stock was built before the First World War. The 1971 House Condition Survey found 1.2 million houses in England and Wales unfit for human habitation. In addition nearly two million houses, though technically fit, lacked one or more basic amenities. Some experts dispute these figures as too low and it is certainly the case that in addition to 1.2 million unfit houses in 1971 there were many more that were below a reasonable standard. Since that survey, more houses have been cleared and improved but likewise, more have decayed and declined.

D

These basic facts of the current housing situation give some indication of the size and gravity of the problem. Far too many people are condemned to live their lives in grossly unsuitable accommodation. At the same time housing standards generally continue to rise and some people not only live in spacious, well heated, luxuriously appointed houses but have country cottages as holiday homes as well. Gross inequalities are apparent in the distribution of housing and the areas of greatest housing need are not being met. Undoubtedly the major problem area is the private rented sector of housing provision. On the whole, owner occupiers and council tenants get reasonable accommodation for the price. People who are forced to rely on private rented property tend to be worse off in terms of what they have to pay and what they get. This is partly because the major part of private rented property is old stock and, therefore, is most likely to fall below acceptable standards of fitness. But since this sector is declining, and demand outstrips provision in the other sectors, so demand, and hence prices, for privately owned, substandard rented accommodation remains high. Much of this older rented property is multi-occupied now, which tends to lower standards, and much is badly in need of repair. It is in the private rented sector that the evils of overcrowding, decay and disrepair, extortion and eviction mostly occur. Those who suffer most tend to be larger families, old people, fatherless families, immigrants – the most poor and vulnerable sections of the community. But perhaps the most extreme indictment of the present situation is the existence of actual homelessness. A substantial number of families, over 1000 in London alone, are literally without any home at all and have to seek temporary accommodation or submit to the break-up of the family unit. And many of these families, before they suffered the final indignity of homelessness, never knew more than the claustrophobic squalor of a one-roomed flat in a multi-occupied house with no bathroom, when, technically, they were housed.

The major housing problems today then, remain the familiar ones of overcrowding, slum dwelling and homelessness. But there are some problems which are relatively new; for example the difficulties of living in high flats and the problems of the new estates. In trying to tackle the slum problem and the long lists of people waiting to be housed, local authorities ran up against the fundamental difficulty of where to put all the new houses. In many cases building took place on city perimeters, far from work and old contacts and particularly when redeveloping clearance areas, it involved the use of high blocks of flats. Flats have been consistently unpopular and do in fact lead to some extreme difficulties, particularly for families with young children. Linked with this problem of where to put new homes is the whole vast topic of town and country planning. It has long been recognized that efforts must be made to preserve the countryside, and to limit the growth of cities – which, if unrestricted, tend to coalesce into bigger and bigger conurbations – so that city dwellers have some access to green fields and country air. Britain is predominantly an urban country, with over 80 per cent of the population living in cities or urban areas. And the problem of city life, traffic congestion for example, are very severe in their economic as well as social costs. But the growth of conurbations has continued, and in particular the growth of the Greater London area, despite general awareness of the damaging social consequences of this trend.

The administration of housing

Housing is a problem which to some extent affects everybody. All people need to find accommodation to suit their particular requirements and whether or not they succeed is determined by the total prevailing housing situation even if they are not actually caught up in the more dramatic and problematic aspects of it such as homelessness or slum dwelling. Similarly housing policy concerns all aspects of the housing situation and not simply those areas in which the state makes direct provision. The government is concerned with condition, price and distribution of housing generally, in addition to the actual provision of council housing. So although less than one in three households live in local authority homes, all households, including the majority looking for houses to buy or rent in the private market, will be affected by the national housing policy. For example, local government clearly determines the price of council housing when it fixes rents, arranges rebate schemes, etc. But the price of other, private accommodation is influenced by the availability of mortgage facilities, tax relief, rent regulation, the rent element of supplementary benefits and so on, which are determined or influenced by government action.

Inevitably housing policy and administration is confused because it concerns so many issues. There is a great deal of legislation relating to housing and town planning, rent control and so forth, some of it dealing broadly with the powers and duties of local housing authorities, some of it concerning particular and detailed aspects of the housing scene such as the prevention of eviction. The government's concern in the housing situation dates back to the nineteenth century. At the start it was a public health concern that led to the introduction of legislation empowering local authorities to clear slums and make bye-laws to improve building standards. This was because the unfettered jerry building of the early nineteenth century had led to major problems of sanitation and consequent ill-health. Housing was shoddily constructed and massed together in appalling densities and the rapidly increasing population of the new urban areas were forced into it under grossly overcrowded conditions. It was only really after the First World War that the government took a more positive role. Local authorities were urged not only to clear slums, but to build houses to meet general housing need and let them at rents the needy could afford. It was realized that only by such direct provision could there be any chance of a real improvement in the housing conditions of the bulk of the working class. Moreover the central government itself made subsidies available to help the local building effort. Henceforth the local authority concern for clearance and standards was matched by efforts to provide homes 'fit for heroes' to live in. Meanwhile restriction had been placed on private rent levels during the early war years and government concern for control in this sector continued to some extent. Gradually the area of state intervention widened and its policy grew more positive and comprehensive. Concern was shown for town planning, and the distribution of housing generally, and attempts made to relate housing need and provision to economic development, the growth of industry and transport facilities, etc.

Central government responsibilities   It might be helpful to summarize the current administrative position in this complex field. The three main sectors of housing are owner occupied, private rented and local authority rented. The central department, once the Ministry of Housing and Local Government and now the Department of the Environment, is responsible for the formulation of policy and the provision of some information and advisory services. But the principal providers of new homes to buy or rent are the local housing authorities, private builders and landlords. The department attempts to secure the co-operation of the local authorities in carrying out its policy with regard to slum clearance, for example. It also attempts to influence the amount of new buildings by its discussion with the building industry, building societies and so on. It also tries to control the quality, price, security and availability of accommodation in the private rented sector. But while its influence may be pervasive the department's power remains limited and many of the current trends and problems in housing are barely understood let alone directed and controlled as part of a clear housing policy.

The department has no overriding statutory responsibility for ensuring the execution of a national policy but it attempts to formulate one. It has powers of various kinds over the activities of the local authorities which in turn derive their powers direct from housing legislation. For example, the central department controls the subsidies which are a vital part of the local housing departments' revenues and it must confirm local clearance orders or compulsory purchase orders. It uses these powers to persuade local housing authorities to conform to a national policy though they not only play the major active role in housing but retain some scope from their statutory powers to determine their own lines of action.

From 1957 to 1975 the department was advised by a central Housing Advisory Committee which advised on policy, conducted investigations into specific problems and produced some useful reports. In recent years six regional offices situated at Manchester, Newcastle upon Tyne, Birmingham, Leeds, Bristol and Nottingham have been opened. Regional studies of housing need and planning policy have been prepared which attempt to consider housing in the context of industrial development, migration patterns, transport facilities and so on. Central government policy is formulated as a result of the information gathered from its advisory bodies and regional studies, together with the statistical material collected centrally and the results of research. It is announced largely by the publication, prior to legislation of White Papers which set out the main lines of policy, establish targets and priorities and tentatively attempt some forward planning. An example of these is the paper of 1965 entitled *The Housing Programme 1965–1970*. This purported to be 'the first stage in the formulation of a national housing plan'. It set out the objectives of housing policy and discussed methods of achieving them, setting, for example, a target of building half a million new homes a year. This was to meet the existing needs by clearing slums and eliminating overcrowding and to keep pace with rising needs from population growth, household formation and urban redevelopment. The paper discussed the question of who should build these houses, private enterprise or local authority, and considered the need for private building to let as well as for owner occupation. It discussed the building industry's capacity, the problem of land allocation and acquisition, standards, finance, building methods, tenancy and rent policy and improvement of existing housing stock.

This demonstrates the department's overall concern with the many aspects of housing policy, despite its lack of statutory powers of control. The main active public agents in the housing field are the local housing authorities and more will be said of their work later. The department does have various methods of controlling and influencing the local authorities and the building industry to persuade them to contribute to a national policy. Most contact between the central department and the local authorities now comes via the regional offices. These deal with matters relating to new house building, applications for loan consent and subsidy approval, matters of building techniques and questions of house improvement. The Housing Inspectorate conducts public inquiries into clearance and compulsory purchase orders. The Directorate-General of Research and Development, the responsibility of the Ministry of Public Building and Works is also run centrally. This attempts to co-ordinate the various building research groups throughout the government service, encourage the development of standardized and industrialized techniques for the construction industry and disseminate information on the best modern practices. This body was established in 1963 and at the same time the National Building Agency was set up as an independent, but grant-aided body, providing information and advice on all aspects of building, primarily in the housing field, and offering its services to private as well as public authorities. The central department is also responsible for the establishment of machinery for the setting of rents in the private sector. Finally the department has initiated the establishment of New Towns which are developed by specially appointed Development Corporations operating alongside the normal local government structure.

Local government responsibilities The role of local authorities in housing is an active and varied one. They have a general responsibility for meeting the housing need of their areas. There are a great many local housing authorities, as the Greater London Council, the London boroughs, the county districts of England and Wales and New Towns are all involved in this field. The administration of housing at local level varies considerably, not all authorities having a clear-cut housing committee, department and manager. Some authorities divide their housing responsibilities between different departments. This often reflects the varying priorities given to housing by the different local authorities. Clearly it is of extreme importance in a large city and less so in a sparsely populated rural area, and administrative arrangements reflect this. But the central department has recommended that housing management should be the responsibility of a major committee and the job of trained staff.

The first statutory concern for housing gave the local authorities' responsibilities first for the clearance of individual unfit premises and then of whole areas, and for the making of bye-laws to prevent further building of potential slums and to ensure some minimum standards. Most authorities acted slowly on their new powers since clearance and rehousing were such costly and difficult enterprises. But after the First World War, aided by government subsides, they embarked on a vigorous and positive housebuilding programme. Since then they have been prominent in the housing field not only for the enforcement of standards but also for their direct provision of accommodation. And today a major part of their task is the building, managing and letting of council houses and flats to meet the general housing need.

Since council building has been taking place for many years the present housing is quite varied. Some accommodation built early this century has become old and obsolete, while some is dramatically modern. Initially it was provided to rehouse people from the slums, then it became more widely available. Immediately following the Second World War there was an acute housing shortage and local authorities were encouraged to build as many houses as possible as quickly as possible, to meet the general need. Local authorities rather than private builders were relied on to ensure a rapid increase in the depleted housing stock. From the mid-fifties a change in policy led to an increased emphasis on private building and the public housing authorities were encouraged to concentrate their efforts on slum clearance and redevelopment rehousing. More recently they have been urged to make more provision of small dwellings, especially those suitable for older people. These changes in national policy are effected at local level partly by the operation of subsidies which can be paid to local authorities in respect of schemes which gain departmental approval.

The provision of local authority housing is always problematic. Because of subsidies from the central government and from the rates, and to some extent because of the relative economy of building on a large scale, council houses are available at comparatively low rents for the quality of accommodation they provide. They are therefore highly desirable for large numbers of people, especially those whose incomes and family commitments make the prospect of buying a house extremely remote. This results in long waiting-lists of people seeking council houses, and local authorities have to decide to whom they should give priority – those who have waited longest or those who live in the worst conditions. Moreover, the concentration on slum clearance often means that there is very little accommodation available for people on the waiting-lists as most new building is taken up by rehousing clearance families. This in itself is always a difficult operation. All too often rehousing is offered on local estates on the perimeters of cities and this means a loss of contact with familiar areas, long and expensive journeys to work, and adjustment to living in new, often rather characterless, areas that lack the neighbourliness of the old urban communities. Attempts to redevelop the cleared city centre areas usually involve the use of high blocks of flats in order to achieve high densities with some open space. 'Living high' itself imposes new problems and flats are disliked by many tenants. Then there are questions of who should pay for the housing, how far it should be subsidized, whether tenants should pay according to their income and so on. A continuing area of controversy concerns whether council housing should be offered for sale to its tenants. It is very difficult to keep everyone happy, and the role of local authorities in housing has never been clearly defined. Are they definitely operating a welfare service, providing housing for those who cannot provide it for themselves and, therefore, clearly giving priorities to those in greatest need, or are they managing, on a fair and reasonable basis, decent property at moderate rents for respectable tenants? If the latter is the case they can argue it is sensible to exclude the more difficult and unreliable families despite their genuine need. This is still very much an open question.

The local housing authority builds, manages and lets housing and this is one of its major functions. But it is also concerned with standards and conditions of privately owned and rented property. It makes bye-laws to ensure the maintenance of good standards in new property, and it has a variety of powers and responsibilities as regards existing property. The most obvious of these powers is that of the demolition and clearance of housing which is deemed unfit for human habitation. Local authorities have to ascertain the numbers of slums in their areas and plan to clear them and rehouse their occupants. They can then redevelop the cleared areas as they see fit. In recent years they have also shown increased concern for property that is not up to present day standards but is not yet included within a scheduled clearance programme. Some authorities have adopted a policy of 'deferred demolition'. They buy areas of old property that still has some future and put it into reasonable repair. It is then added to the stock of accommodation available to be rented. This ensures that the worst neglect is remedied and the tenants have a landlord, the council, who will keep the property in basic habitable condition. Local authorities have also had power since 1949 to make grants to the owners of old property for its improvement and repair. Recently some authorities have taken a more active role in promoting this policy of improvement. Following the publication of a White Paper in 1968, *Old Houses Into New Homes* (Cmnd 3602), local authorities have powers to deal with whole areas of unsatisfactory housing by systematic improvement. They also have wide powers and duties relating to rent regulation and rent allowance. Rent acts have brought more and more privately rented property under controls which effect both the rents asked and the security of tenure. Since the Housing Finance Act of 1972 they have some responsibility for the operation of rent allowance schemes which affect private tenants as well as those in council property. And finally, since 1974 they have had, as housing authorities, responsibility for housing the homeless on a temporary basis as well as a continuing and fundamental responsbility for providing for long term housing need.

Housing policy

In discussing central and local housing authorities and their organization and functions much has already been said about housing policy. The housing problem, with its present symptoms of homelessness, slums, land shortages and soaring costs, remains a major concern of governments and numerous statements are made about policies and priorities. The amount of legislation in the housing field is formidable but despite statements of intent and increasingly complex machinery for control the actual housing situation remains intractably difficult. This is due partly to the fact that housing policies are politically controversial and subject to sudden changes of direction when successive governments replace one another.

The broad and generally agreed goal of our housing policy is to provide a separate home at a decent standard for every household that needs one. The controversy begins when means of achieving this goal are considered. A major aspect of housing policy is basic supply of new dwellings. In this area there is less disagreement about how many homes are needed than about who should provide them. Targets for housebuilding have been put as high as 500000 dwellings a year but this level has never in fact been attained. The highest number of houses built was reached in 1968 when 425000 houses were completed in the United Kingdom. The level of completions has been dropping subsequently and the 1973 figure stood at just over 300000 dwellings. The job of building new homes is shared by local authorities and private enterprise and policies have differed over which should play the greater part. In the decade following the last war the local authorities built roughly three quarters of all new homes. During the next decade private building was encouraged and public building restricted mainly to clearance replacement. As a result the private sector overtook the public in building new homes. Private enterprise has maintained a substantial lead into the 1970s. In 1973, 102000 houses were completed by the local authorities while 190000 were completed by private builders. A further 11000 were provided by the public sector for police, prison and forces accommodation.

Local authority building has been open to much criticism in recent years on the grounds of its standards, amenities and location. Standards of building tended to decline for reasons of economy and the Central Housing Advisory Committee produced in 1961 the Parker Morris Report, *Homes for Today and Tomorrow*, to give authorities acceptable standards of space, heating and other amenities to conform to. A further report in 1967 entitled *The Needs of New Communities* suggested ways of improving the life on new estates and there has been some development of tenants' associations to encourage tenant involvement and improve social facilities in areas of new housing. Clearly the major priority is building homes but it is necessary to maintain standards both for individual dwellings and for whole areas of development. Some examples of imaginative and satisfying municipal housing schemes do exist but the general picture of local authority building is a depressing one with unimaginative layouts and poky dwellings being all too common. Private enterprise, it must be added, does not often do much better by way of developing attractive and viable communities and there is clearly much still to be learned about effective town planning and development. Part of the problem of new building has always been that of finding adequate sites. Brief mention must be made here of the New Towns policy, the most bold and imaginative solution adopted so far. New Towns are designed to provide homes for people alongside opportunities for work and leisure, education and welfare, shopping and transport, etc, altogether in accessible, community-conscious groupings. Following the New Towns Act of 1946 fourteen New Towns were designated by 1950, eight situated around London to cater, in part, for metropolitan overspill. After a gap during the fifties in which only one town was designated the sixties saw a steady addition so there are currently twenty-nine New Towns. Another solution to the problems of congestion and overspill is provided under the Town Development legislation. This facilitates the transfer of population from overcrowded urban areas to small towns wishing to expand. Both the exporting authority and the receiving authority can gain by this procedure which is less radical than that of founding actual New Towns. The success of these policies, however, hinges on whether industry and hence employment can be attracted to the new centres of population. Without work opportunities new houses are useless to the people who need them and in this area of housing policy the interdependence of industrial development and social policy is sharply drawn. Some interesting growth has resulted from New Towns policy but the experiment is still on a fairly small scale compared to the haphazard growth of new development in and around existing towns and cities.

A good many of the new homes built by local authorities are used to replace those lost by clearance and redevelopment. Slum clearance has been an important part of housing policy since government intervention in housing began. The work of clearing slums was halted during and after the Second World War but local authorities returned to it during the 1950s. In 1956 the general needs subsidy which encouraged building to house people from the waiting lists was abolished. Thereafter councils concentrated their housing efforts on clearance and redevelopment. After a decade of clearance, enthusiasm for wholesale redevelopment began to wane. There was mounting concern at the slowness of clearance programmes and the consequent blight on areas awaiting redevelopment. Following an enquiry into slums by the Central Housing Advisory Committee*

*The Report, published in 1966, was entitled *Our Older Homes: A Call for Action.*

the government adopted a policy favouring rehabilitation rather than clearance. This was set out in the 1968 White Paper, *Old Houses Into New Homes*, and endorsed by the 1969 Housing Act.

Improvement of existing homes has long been recognized as an important way of husbanding the housing stock. Since 1949 grants have been made available to owners of older property at the discretion of the local authority for the improvement of houses up to certain defined standards. The policy was hesitant at first and grants tended to be hedged around by conditions which put off a great many owners. Since 1959 authorities have been bound to pay grants to owners installing the basic amenities, baths and water supplies, etc, in their houses and have had wider discretion to pay towards general improvement. In 1964 the concept of the Improvement Area was introduced. This gave councils certain powers to compel improvements in designated areas. The 1969 Act built on existing improvement provisions but reduced the conditions around grants and extended its limits. It also made provision for the declaration of general improvement areas where improvements to the environment as well as to individual homes could be encouraged. After 1969 the level of grants, previously running at a very modest rate, rose sharply. In 1967 when the first National House Condition Survey was carried out nearly four million dwellings lacked basic amenities. A further survey in 1971 showed that this number was substantially reduced. The survey also showed, however, that the incidence of bad conditions was variable between different parts of the country and between different tenure groups. Only 4 per cent of owner occupied houses were found unfit as against 23 per cent of privately rented houses. As a result a higher grant rate for improvement was introduced in 1971 for Development and Intermediate Areas in which the largest concentrations of poor housing were found. In 1973 the White Paper *Better Homes: The Next Priorities* introduced the concept of Housing Action Areas to help local authorities give priority to the remaining areas of worst housing. The criteria for declaring an area a housing action area include numbers of households living in overcrowded conditions, numbers of furnished tenancies and shared accommodation, houses lacking standard amenities and the incidence of elderly people and large families in the neighbourhood. Housing Action Areas are fairly small, typically containing about 500 dwellings. The local authority is to work directly on improvement and to encourage existing landlords to cooperate. Housing associations are encouraged to acquire and manage accommodation so that it can be improved and rented. Preferential rates of grant are available for housing action areas.

As a result of these developments improvement has become a substantial element of housing policy. The change of emphasis from clearance to improvement has not, however, gone unchallenged. Many houses are now in better condition and many areas have been improved without wholesale destruction of older property and community life. But there have been criticisms over the effectiveness of improvement schemes partly on the grounds that they have not helped the worst housed, and partly because they encourage the postponement of necessary clearance and new building.

It is certainly true that the improvement grants have been abused both by property speculators and by second-home owners. More control of the use of grants has now been introduced and with the recent housing action area provisions, local authorities and housing associations should be able to make the benefits of improvements available to the tenants in the worst conditions. Much can be done both to ease the housing problem and to preserve the charm and neighbourliness of some older areas by energetic rehabilitation. Provided it does not replace clearance and redevelopment where this is justified – either because houses are structurally too unfit to merit improvement or because the environment is unhealthy – then improvement must remain a significant and permananet part of our housing policy.

In the outline of the present housing situation it was noted that the private, rented sector was shrinking. The greatest loss has been of cheap rented accommodation since there has been some development on the luxury apartment front. The loss is felt most seriously in urban areas and especially in London where it has been the biggest single factor in the rise in the numbers of homeless families in recent years. It is due primarily to slum clearance, which mostly affects cheap, rented property, and the fact that it has not been profitable to build or convert property to let. This last factor is influenced in part by the cost of land and building but also by the effect of rent control. Rents were controlled by government intervention during the First World War and since control implied not only fixed rents but also security of tenure it proved extremely hard to end without great hardship being caused. Undoubtedly frozen rents have at times been unfair on landlords who have received only nominal incomes from their property and consequently had little interest in maintaining it in good repair. The 1957 Rent Act brought a considerable measure of decontrol both directly by the immediate decontrol of property above certain rateable values and indirectly as a result of a clause which allowed decontrol on change of tenancy. The rate of this indirect 'creeping' decontrol proved to be much faster than anticipated and severe hardship resulted for many families as a consequence. Little if any new property came into the private rented sector as a result of the 1957 Act as rent control was not the only reason why investors were reluctant to build or buy property to let. A good deal promptly left the sector as decontrol enabled many landlords to sell their property for owner occupation.

As prices rose the rush to sell property led to an acceleration of unscrupulous practices on the part of landlords to gain vacant possession. The Prevention of Eviction Act was passed in 1964 followed by the Rent Acts of 1965 and 1968. These acts gave greater security of tenure and some protection of tenants from harassment or unfair eviction. The Rent Act of 1965 also introduced the concept of rent regulation to the unfurnished sector. Rents were to be set at a 'fair' level, having regard to current prices but discounting scarcity, by rent officers. Landlords and tenants both had a right of appeal to a Rent Assessment Committee if they disagreed with the rent officer.

The system of rent regulation was reviewed in 1971 by a Committee on the Rent Acts. The report of this committee, the Francis Report, claimed that by and large the system was working well and the principle of fair rents was later extended.

The protection to tenants afforded by the Rent Acts is that they can only be evicted for certain offences not merely because the landlord wants possession. This applied only to unfurnished tenancies at first but the Rent Act of 1974 extended protection to furnished tenancies where the landlord is non-resident. Where the landlord is resident the tenant can get up to six months' security from the rent tribunal. Security of tenure is vital to protect tenants from being forced out of their homes because landlords seek to sell or change the nature of the accommodation. Lack of security of tenure was a reason for many families becoming homeless. Unfortunately tightening up on security helps existing tenants but it does nothing to help those who seek homes to rent. The supply of accommodation to rent continues to drop and landlords become reluctant to let property when they feel the balance of advantage lies with the tenant.

Whatever the effect of the Rent Acts homelessness continues and in London especially has been increasing sharply in recent years. Clearly when the housing situation is bad in terms of availability of accommodation and security of tenure, some families will find it impossible to obtain a satisfactory home. The most vulnerable groups in society, the poor, large families, immigrants and single-parent families, tend to suffer most in the housing shortage and most often find themselves homeless. But when the shortage of rented accommodation is very acute, as it is in London, then even small, stable families in well-paid employment find it impossible to obtain homes.

Homelessness in London has twice been investigated and reported on and yet solutions appear impossible to find.* For most homeless families council accommodation seemed the only solution as the private rented sector shrank and was competed for by larger groups, especially of the young and single. But although councils have housed many families from temporary accommodation there seemed no end to the problem. The responsibility for providing temporary accommodation, originally a welfare or social services department function, was transferred to housing authorities in 1974. But many authorities cannot cope and the homeless are increasingly relegated to bed and breakfast hotels which provide accommodation but not a home. The long-term solution can only lie in making more accommodation available and in reducing the power of London to attract so many people. Powerful and coordinated policies are needed to achieve this which extend beyond the province of local authorities. In the short-term councils cope by increasing use of short-life properties and some have asked for more power to take over empty property for use in this way. Meanwhile illegal occupation of empty property has increased, especially among young people, as the homeless have taken to direct action. Squatting is not however usually much help as a solution to the ordinary family's needs as it can only be a short-term proposition in most cases. The work of housing associations is more helpful here in buying up old property for cooperative management and use. Housing associations have been actively encouraged since 1961 by government loans. In 1964 the Housing Corporation was set up to stimulate activity in this field. The help of housing associations is sought in improvement policies as well as in a solution to homelessness. The contribution of cooperative housing is a significant one but to date it has been on too small a scale to make a great impact on the problem of shortage of rented accommodation.

*See Greve, Page and Greve *Homelessness in London* 1971 for the most recent account.

Housing Finance A crucial aspect of housing policy is that concerned with finance. The cost of housing is affected by many factors including building costs, land prices and the cost of borrowing money. Local authority building is subsidized both from the rates and from central funds. The provision of private house buidling is encouraged by help to owner occupiers through tax concessions on mortgage payments and help to the building societies. Rent levels in the private sector have long been subject to control and regulation. Housing finance is both complex and controversial and government intervention at times appears contradictory and incompetent. House prices have risen sharply in recent years and so has the cost of borrowing money. Fortunes have been made out of property speculation while for most ordinary people housing of all kinds has proved more difficult and costly to obtain. Governments have been urged to make money available at low rates of interest for housing purposes to encourage building and help stabilize costs. The nearest we have approached such a policy in Britain was the Housing Subsidies Act of 1967 which made it possible for the government to subsidize local authorities by making up the difference between the cost of borrowing at 4 per cent and the actual cost. But there has been much dispute over the issue of equity between the different tenure groups and the whole subsidy system was changed by the controversial Housing Finance Act of 1972.

This important act set out to change the approach to housing finance and it was indeed a very radical departure from existing policies. In the White Paper *Fair Deal for Housing* (Cmnd 4728), which preceded it, it was asserted that subsidies to the public sector were inequitable because they were largely used to keep rents low rather than finance more building, while in the private sector rent control was acting unfairly to favour tenants at the expense of landlords. Help to owner occupiers was noted but the extent of it was not criticized. The solution to the problem of housing finance was therefore seen to reside in an extension of the fair rent's principle, coupled with rebate and allowance schemes to help the poorer tenants, and the concentration of Exchequer help on those local authorities with the worst housing problems.

The main provisions of the Housing Finance Act were three-fold: it extended the 'fair rent' formula, introduced by the Rent Act of 1965 for private rented unfurnished accommodation, to the public sector; it totally reformed the subsidy system for local authorities; it introduced a national, rent rebate scheme for all council tenants and rent allowances to the private tenants of unfurnished dwellings. Under the fair rent extension, rent officers were to fix the fair rents of all council property and rents would rise to these levels over a limited period. Rent scrutiny boards would consider the general levels set but not individual rents. On the subsidy side some subsidies were to remain for a transitional period but basically the new approach was to relate Exchequer and rate help to the state of the local authorities' housing revenue accounts. When these accounts were in deficit a subsidy of 75 per cent of the deficit would be met by the Exchequer and 25 per cent by the rates. But when accounts were in balance or surplus no subsidy would be paid. At 'fair rents' levels, which could be reset every three years, local authorities would easily achieve a surplus but with rent rebate schemes helping poorer tenants their accounts would show a deficit initially. As wages rose the rebate element would reduce over time and some authorities would move into surplus. The surplus made was to be paid to the Exchequer, first to offset the cost of rent allowances in the private sector and thereafter to be split between the Exchequer and the local authorities' general accounts. The scope of rebate and allowance schemes was so great that substantial numbers of average income earners were potential claimants of the new complicated means-tested benefits introduced by the Act as well as more vulnerable low income groups. The Housing Finance Act was implemented despite unprecedented opposition from some councils. It did allow some generous rebates to be paid but it was generally viewed as an attack on local authorities and their tenants. Local authorities lost their freedom to set rents and manage their accounts and council tenants were faced with steady increases in their housing costs with subsidies to poorer tenants both private and public being paid for by the better-off tenants.

In 1974, following a change of government, the Housing Rents and Subsidies Bill was introduced to replace the 1972 Act. This restored to the local authorities the power to set rents at 'reasonable' levels and created new and substantial subsidies to enable them to get on with the job of coping with the housing shortage. For the time being the procedures for allowances to private tenants were to continue but provisions for decontrol of rented property were removed. A searching inquiry into all the problems of housing finance was promised. A review of government policy in this area is clearly overdue and radical measures are needed. The 1972 Housing Finance Act was radical enough but its provisions reflected an accumulated prejudice against the public sector in housing rather than an unbiased assessment of the relative positions of different tenure groups in the total housing situation. There remains scope for strong measures and new departures in this field for problems of finance must be solved if the housing position of Britain is to be improved.

From this discussion it can be seen that to meet the housing need an informed, vigorous and comprehensive housing policy is required. In Britain we still have a major housing problem but we are pressing along the road towards finding effective solutions. Some people would argue our policy is too negative and hesitant, that we need to be bolder and more imaginative if we are to achieve success. Undoubtedly housing raises basic issues, of the role of government in society for example, which are not easily settled, as well as raising immediate concern because of its direct implications for all members of that society.

Suggestions for further reading

Berry, F., *Housing: the Great British Failure* (Charles Knight, 1974).
Cullingworth, B., *Housing Needs and Planning Policy* (RKP, 1960).
Cullingworth, B., *Housing and Local Government* (RKP, 1966).
Donnison, D. V., *The Government of Housing* (Penguin, 1967).
Greve, J., Page, D., and Greve, S., *Homelessness in London* (Scottish Academic Press, 1971).
Muchnick, D. M., *Urban Renewal in Liverpool* (Bell, 1970).
Ungerson, C., *Moving Home* (Bell, 1971).

Reports of the Housing Advisory Committee:
Cullingworth Report, *Council Housing: Purposes, Procedures and Priorities* (HMSO, 1969).
Dennington Report, *Our Older Homes: A Call for Action* (HMSO, 1966).
Parker Morris Report, *Homes for Today and Tomorrow* (HMSO, 1961).

6   The personal social services

The need for social care

The need for social care is a complex one and not easily defined or described. This is because there is no absolute need for care – it depends on what society acknowledges as reasonable at any point in time. The whole area of personal needs and social services is fraught with value judgements about the proper functions of the family or responsibilities of the individual and woolly ideas about communities. Nevertheless, put at a very simple level it is now accepted that some people need care because they cannot look after themselves and lack adequate family and neighbourhood support. The reasons why people need care are many and varied. Some people have extra handicaps to cope with: physical disability, the frailty of extreme old age, mental handicap and such like. Children will need care if their parents are unable to provide it or do not do so to the standards society currently considers necessary. Many people become casualties of over-rapid social change and inadequate social provisions. People cannot cope on poverty-line incomes with housing shortages and unemployment. Single-parent families and immigrants face added difficulties in finding and keeping a home together and many who have been ill or become redundant at work or been left socially isolated need help to rehabilitate themselves in society. The individual problems vary enormously but the need for some form of social care is common to them all.

Not only do some individuals and families need care: neighbourhoods and communities are often unable to function effectively. Industrial decline, slum clearance, changing patterns of transport and communication can destroy or debilitate communities leaving them vulnerable and disorganized, unable to adapt to change or to retain a fair share of resources.

The need for social care has long been recognized but only recently has it been perceived as a sufficiently discrete and coherent need to justify separate and distinct statutory provision. Traditionally statutory concern with the need for social care was interwoven with provision for destitution, treatment or control. Provision was usually of an institutional nature and the care element was subordinate to the primary objectives of the work house, asylum, infirmary, hostel or reformatory which offered it. Gradually provision of care became a separate function, distinct from the provision of income, medical attention, education or reform. But it was then limited to separate and distinguishable groups, such as orphaned children or the disabled to meet their needs. This fragmented provision focusses attention on the problems of specific groups and made possible the development of some caring services to a very high standard. For example local authority children's departments, responsible for children deprived of normal home life, provided a range of children's homes and supervised fostering and adoption with the help of specially trained care officers. But the cost of specialization was considerable. Specialization tended to isolate groups from the rest of society and even from their families. It led to some overlap in services, confusion of responsibility, gaps in provision and awkward career prospects for the social workers concerned. Concentration on need groups meant that services tended to operate on a casualty basis, only taking action when there had been a failure in family or community support and unable, therefore, to work to prevent failures. The specialist services remained tiny, with insignificant budgets and no say in vital planning issues which affected the total community. In each area of concern there was increasing anxiety over the need to provide more preventive work and support to the family and community and it became clear that the specific orientation of social care services hindered developments along such lines.

Disillusionment with institutional solutions to the need for care and a growing interest in community alternatives, together with increasing concern for prevention, have helped to form a more general view of the problem. It is now accepted that individuals, families and communities need care because they have problems they cannot deal with on their own. The reasons why people need help vary enormously and so do the motives of the state for intervening in their lives. But the general need for social care is now considered an appropriate focus for the organization of services to meet that need.

The type of care needed varies considerably. Some people actually need a home, a place to live, an accepting and caring environment. In some cases they may only need a temporary shelter, in others a fairly permanent home. A need for residential care has long been recognized for certain groups such as deprived children, old people and those with mental or physical disabilities. Other groups such as homeless single persons, wayward adolescents, ex-prisoners or battered wives, for example, have a need for care that is often less widely acknowledged.

Only small minorities need full residential care but many more people need a degree of help and support in the community. Many people have a home but need help in running it: practical help with maintenance or domestic work or adaptations to take account of disabilities, or general advice and support or help with meals or simply company. Many handicapped individuals have families who do devotedly care for them but need occasional relief or regular support. Care can be provided during the day for children, old people, the disabled and so forth, to enable them and their families to cope without the necessity for a full residential placement but without unnecessary stress or neglect.

Some individuals lack family support and need a substitute for the care a family could provide but many families need support in order to keep together. Families are particularly crucial for the care and socialization of children but many need help in these functions if they are to survive and provide adequate standards of care. Families may need practical help and all too often material aid; advice on the bringing up of children and support through day care services; help with a wide range of problems from housing to marital relations. Care of the family can be a valuable preventive measure reducing the need of children or the handicapped for residential care. In both family care and individual care there is a need for advice and help in using other statutory services, in obtaining maximum benefits, adequate medical care, better housing and such like.

The needs of communities vary though most share a need for better communication and involvement of people in the services and provisions which affect their lives. In some areas the need for greater self-determination is striking as people have opted out of conventional democratic processes and succumbed to feelings of helplessness in the face of technological change and bureaucratic bullying. Communities need encouragement to greater political participation in local affairs, they need confidence to express their interests and demands, they need a renewal of hope and determination to improve community life. In deprived areas community groups need active encouragement to become involved through better information, professional advice and support and practical services for aiding organization. In some communities there is a particular need to develop tolerance and improve race relations, in others the need is to reduce vandalism and violence, in others to develop a greater sense of neighbourly responsibility. At a time of increasing professionalism and bureaucracy the power and responsibility of ordinary people as individuals and neighbourhood groups need emphasizing and developing. The capacity of society to care for its more vulnerable members and to contain violence and disharmony depends as much if not more on ordinary families and communities as it does on statutory services and expertise but both families and communities may need professional support if they are to function effectively.

In the personal social services needs are often elusive and intangible and they are still very controversial. The need for residential care is well established, the need for community development much less accepted. But in fact the two are very strongly linked. It is easy to see a need for total social care when children are abandoned or old people isolated. But total care is not an adequate solution to such problems because institutions can generate and perpetuate difficulties themselves. If the need is seen as one of *preventing* family break-up or the isolation of the elderly, rather than one of coping with the consequences of such events, then the need for community development and family support becomes much clearer. In the pursuit of prevention a wide range of social needs for day care and domiciliary services have now become visible and serious problems of urban deprivation and social injustice are being revealed. The need for social care cannot easily be described or quantified partly because in this sensitive area the interrelated nature of social needs is so apparent. A need for care is often the result of a need for better housing or linked to the wider social problems of a whole area. Moreover our perception of need is limited by our ability to respond to it and it is easier to provide palliative care than to revitalize communities or achieve a better distribution of resources. But we have some idea of the dimensions of the problem and can see that it embraces an immediate need to provide social care and support to a variety of individuals and families; a longer term need to develop more effective family and community life; and an ultimate concern with social justice. In response to this curious mix of needs, for practical things like gadgets or mobile meals services to a vague ideal of social purpose and community welfare, we have evolved the personal social services whose structure will now be described.

The administration of personal social services

The provision of personal social services is the responsibility of local authorities. Under the Local Authority Social Services Act 1970, the counties and metropolitan districts of England and Wales and the London boroughs have to establish a social services committee. The committee appoints a director of social services, a local government chief officer, who runs a department of social services. The department is responsible for the provision of residential care services, a variety of day care facilities, domiciliary and advice services and social help to communities, schools and hospitals.

At central level responsibility lies with the Department of Health and Social Security which has a Personal Social Services division. Professional advice is provided by the Social Work Service which has a central establishment and twelve regional offices. The social work service is responsible for the general development of the personal social services and its role is basically constructive rather than regulative, although it does retain some inspectorial duties. Within the social work service is a development group responsible for generating new ideas and experimenting with best practice. The Secretary of State for Social Security, who has overall responsibility for this area of provision, is advised by a permanent Personal Social Services Council. The council has advisory, research and development functions. It can set up working parties to enquire into particular problems or needs and it has a special role in the dissemination of research findings and new ideas. It is financed by central and local government but remains independent of both.

The Seebohm Report   The effect of the Local Authority Social Services Act 1970 was basically to unify the previously fragmented and specialized social care services which had existed for the elderly, the disabled, deprived children and the mentally ill and handicapped. The act was passed following the recommendations of the Seebohm Committee which published its report *Local Authority and Allied Personal Social Services* (Cmnd 3703) in 1968. The Seebohm Committee was set up in 1965 to review the organization of personal social services and consider what changes were necessary to create a more effective family welfare service. The personal social services existed to promote the welfare of different groups of people with special needs. They were services which made use of social work skills to help people cope with special problems, and make full use of all available community resources from statutory services to neighbourly help and which provided such extra care through residential homes or day or domiciliary support, as was deemed necessary. Most of the social care provided was a response to the dependencies created by social, physical or mental handicaps but some was concerned with problems of social control, especially those arising from child neglect or delinquency. The main services were provided by local authority children's departments and welfare departments but some were the responsibility of local health departments which had particular concern for the care of the mentally ill and mentally handicapped and some families with difficulties. A good deal of specialized social care provision was also made by voluntary bodies sometimes aiding the statutory concern and sometimes pioneering with new services or new need groups.

As was noted in the previous section, policies of prevention and community care in all the services led to a renewed interest in family welfare. During the 1960s there was mounting concern at the lack of any clear statutory responsibility for the welfare of families and the consequent inadequacy, overlap and confusion of provision. Psychological and sociological studies were emphasizing the importance of the family and demonstrating its vulnerability in the face of social change. There was also a growing awareness of the need for coordination of policies and provision between services and of the need to strengthen the social care sector in local government. On the professional front social workers were increasingly conscious of the shortcomings of fragmented provision and were moving towards professional unity and generic training.

There was accordingly considerable interest in the Seebohm Committee's deliberations and evidence was obtained from a wide range of relevant organizations and professions. There was a fair degree of consensus on the need for administrative reorganization and the committee's call for a unified personal social services department was generally welcomed. The Seebohm Report went further 'than suggesting fundamental administrative reforms however: it put forward a radically different view of the role of personal social care services. To quote the opening phrase of the Report: 'We recommend a new local authority department providing a community based and family oriented service which will be available to all. This new department will we believe reach far beyond the discovery and rescue of social casualties: it will enable the greatest possible number of individuals to act reciprocally giving and receiving service for the well being of the whole community.' So the objectives of the local authority social services departments derive from the Seebohm Report. The 1970 act merely implemented the reorganization suggested by Seebohm and listed the legislative duties of the new departments but the report attempted to establish a new philosophy for social care. It emphasized not only the importance of the family but also of the community. It envisaged a department concerned with the welfare needs of all people not merely those minorities who had become casualties or had clearly definable handicaps. And it spelt out in some detail ways in which the social care services could be made more generally relevant and available so that they would become a genuinely universal and basic social service.

The legislative position Under the 1970 Act local authorities have established social services committees and departments and to these are referred a wide range of duties and responsibilities. Among the principal duties are the duty to receive children deprived of normal home life into care and duties to promote the welfare of children and to provide for children in trouble. Most of these duties are spelt out in the Children Acts and the Children and Young Persons Acts. Under the National Assistance Act of 1948 local authorities have duties to provide residential accommodation for the elderly and infirm and to promote the welfare of the blind, the deaf and the general classes of the handicapped including those suffering from mental disorders. Various functions which derive from the National Health Service Act of 1946 are now referred to social services. These include the provision of home helps, and certain responsibilities formerly belonging to maternity and child welfare including the provision of day nurseries. Social services also have responsibility for the registration of homes for old people and the regulation of nurseries and child minders. They have a responsibility to act as adoption agencies and a duty to provide and maintain reception centres for persons without a settled way of living. Under the Chronically Sick and Disabled Persons Act 1970 they have a duty to obtain information on the need for welfare services and a duty to make such provision.

These are the principal legislative concerns of the social services departments: the full schedule of related enactments is more detailed. It can be seen that the legislative position is very complex partly because of the background of social services in specialized and fragmented provision but largely because the needs they are responding to are so sensitive and variable. The list of statutory duties is long. It includes some very precise and inescapable responsibilities, such as those for providing homes and keeping registers, which still shape the output of social service department and determine much of their allocation of resources and development of work. But it also includes some decidedly vague duties to 'promote the welfare' of certain groups under which legislative sanction much preventive and community work is now being done and under which the Seebohm objective of a reciprocal community welfare service can be pursued.

Structure and organization of social services departments

Under the 1970 reorganization there was major structural change in the creation of new unified departments. There was also much concern to make those departments more efficient in the use of scarce resources and to create management systems within them which would assist in the development of a more universal service. Considerable interest in the application of management theory and technique to social service organization was manifest at this time. As a result the structure of many departments benefited from a conscious and informed intent to devise an organization which would match the objectives of the new service. There was concern to make the service more acceptable and accessible and to move away from the narrowness of specialist care. Accordingly attempts were made to ensure decentralization of provision, to allow flexibility and discretion at field level, to facilitate the flow of communication throughout the organization and to create a truly generic social work service. There was also concern to create the potential for effective planning and involvement in local corporate management.

Obviously local variations do exist but a typical social service department has some degree of decentralization through area teams and some division of responsibility along activity rather than need groups lines. Typically assistant directors head sections responsible for fieldwork, residential work, domiciliary and day care services and research and development. A small number of area teams are established each with an area office serving a given geographical area. The fieldwork services are usually decentralized, teams of social workers working with generic caseloads of families, children, old people, the handicapped or mentally ill as the need arises. The other main provisions vary, with residential provision largely run on an authority rather than area basis and some of the day and domiciliary services operating from area team level, others serving the whole authority.

The area teams of social workers mostly work generically but some specialization does exist. In some authorities specialist intake teams concentrate on diagnostic work and intensive short-term care. In most areas one or more community workers will be active in supporting community groups and stimulating local action. Liaison with voluntary bodies is an important aspect of the job and also the encouragement and use of volunteers. Area teams make contact with other social services, liaising with schools and community health services and working with the courts and hospitals.

The changes in social work consequent upon reorganization have been considerable. The move to generic work, the greater involvement in the community and the increased concern with prevention and social change had led to much anxiety about the role of social workers. A constant and often vigorous debate has been carried on around the relative merits of case work or community work or over the whole position of social workers in our society. It seems appropriate that at a time of reorganization, roles as well as structures should change and the debate is necessary. But it might be helpful nonetheless to offer a brief and necessarily limited description of the social worker's role.

All social workers have basically two functions. One is to put their clients in touch with all the services and resources statutory, voluntary, neighbourly and personal, which might be of help to them in coping with problems and to assist them if necessary in persisting with applications and appeals and understanding regulations. The other is to help clients to gain insight into the nature of their problems, to offer comfort and support in times of stress and to help clients either to adjust to their situation or move constructively to change it. These functions apply whether the client is an individual, a group or a family or a whole community. In all cases the social worker's aim should be to help with a mixture of practical assistance and the development of insight and understanding. Social workers therefore, need access to extensive resources and must develop skill in the diagnosis of problems and in the helping process. Their work must always be demanding because human problems are always and often deceptive and contradictory. Their work is often depressing because human problems involve suffering and solutions are not easy. There is often conflict between immediate help and long term prevention and the more social workers probe into the causes of distress the less possible it becomes to find easy answers and the more necessary it becomes to respond on individual, community and societal levels in the search for solutions. Inevitably at times social workers must feel frustrated and impotent and unsure of themselves but at other times they will feel they have helped and responded adequately to a need for social care.

Fieldwork is rightly regarded as the frontline service in social care because social workers should have the immediate and initial contact at the area office or in the client's home with the people they seek to help. But it is now well recognized that a range of practical services must be brought into play to help people. Day and domiciliary services are of growing importance in social service departments. Day care is provided for children whose mothers work or who are under stress. Day nursery provision is usually inadequate for the need and supervised child minding is also provided. Encouragement is given to local groups to provide playgroups for the benefit of mothers and children even where there is no absolute need for care because of a mother's absence. Day centres are provided for old people, offering a place to go, lunch, social and recreational activities and sometimes medical care. For the handicapped day centres usually aim to provide occupation and sometimes rehabilitation. Domiciliary services include the highly important home help service, especially useful for the elderly and disabled, mobile meals services, practical help with the problems of disability, laundry services, aids and adaptations for the blind, deaf and handicapped. Peripatetic foster mother schemes help children to stay in their own homes and when a substitute home has to be found for children boarding out with suitable families provides an alternative to the use of residential care.

The provision of residential care is still a major function of social services departments even though the community care services have received more attention recently. In fact residential provision still accounts for just over half the total cost of personal social services. Homes are provided for children in need of care and children in trouble. These are now known as community homes and local authorities are grouped in regional planning committees to provide a full range of homes from small family group homes to specialized assessment centres and schools. The largest group for whom residential care is provided is the elderly and physically handicapped. Again a variety of provision exists but the variation has much to do with the age and size of the buildings and less with different functions.

For the mentally ill and handicapped relatively little provision is made so far as economies have held back the building programme that should have increased provision for these groups. For other groups such as the homeless or young unmarried mothers provision is locally extremely variable. The provision of residential care is costly both in capital terms and current costs. It has suffered, in a time of interest in community care, from unpopularity and consequent neglect. But its contribution to social care must always remain an important one and efforts have to be made to avoid the isolation of this aspect of care from other services and developments.

One of the major points emphasized in the Seebohm Report was the poor quality of many social care services and the gaps in provisions. Far too many services were of a low standard, having poor facilities, untrained staff, long waiting lists and inadequate coverage. There was a considerable lack of information about the extent of needs for different services and consequently little attempt at rational ordering of priorities. Too many services were provided without any attempt to evaluate their effectiveness and shortfall in provision was largely guessed at. As a result Seebohm recommended that social services departments undertake research into needs and attempt to monitor the effects of different policies and compare the success of different provisions. Accordingly most, though not all, local departments have a research and development section. These sections collect data on their localities and assess needs so that the department is in a better position to plan its services and decide on priorities. They can evaluate provision, initiate and monitor change and examine the substitutability of different services. They are particularly important in the overall local government context to help give the social services department an effective say in the authorities' corporate planning. Research and development staff are also well placed to forge links with related services. Along with fieldworkers they can be involved on health care planning teams and contribute to such things as housing action areas and community development programmes.

The development of personal social services

The social services departments have only recently been established so it is not easy to comment on their progress. The Seebohm Report and the publicity over reorganization raised expectations of the new departments to unrealistic levels. Initially problems of structure and staffing were preoccupying and then departments had to take stock of their inheritance of buildings and services and attempt to even up standards and fill in gaps. The tasks of reorganization and improvement would themselves have been considerable but several other new responsibilities coincided with the changeover. The Children and Young Persons Act of 1969 was to be implemented and this placed heavy new responsibilities on the social services departments especially to provide court reports and supervision and also to develop new services of intermediate treatment. The Chronically Sick and Disabled Persons Act of 1970 gave the departments an entirely new responsibility to assess the needs of the disabled and to ensure provision was available to meet them and this resulted in enormous pressure of work. The White Paper, *Better Services for the Mentally Handicapped*, published in 1970, asked the local departments to take a much more vigorous part in providing community care for this neglected group. As a result of these measures and generally raised expectations, local social services have been under considerable pressure. Inevitably there have been some complaints of deterioration in standards, especially from the courts and the medical profession. But in fact the scope of their work has increased steadily: more people are receiving more services than ever before although much room for improvement remains. The social services departments have prepared plans for the DHSS showing current provision and projected development over a ten-year period. They are in a better position to assess needs and establish priorities and contribute to social planning. Their total output still accounts for less than 2 per cent of all public expenditure and under 15 per cent of expenditure on all health and welfare services and for that their impact is considerable.

Clearly staffing is a major issue in social development as the staff are the main resource of the departments. About half the staff are in residential care work and only about 10 per cent of the total involved, just over 150000 in 1973 in England, are actual field social workers. Much thought has recently been given to training. In 1971 the Central Council for Education and Training in Social Work was established. The council has a statutory responsibility to promote education and training in all fields of social work and to recognize the courses and award qualifications. It has members representative of employing bodies, educational establishments and professional associations.

The central council recognizes courses which lead to the Certificate of Qualification in Social Work. This qualification is obtained after successful completion of either a two-year training in social work or a one-year training for graduates with social science qualifications. In addition there is some special provision for mature entrants to social work and those who have entered the services unqualified but have much practical experience. The CQSW is now the standard social work qualification but in the field of residential work several courses and qualifications remained in existence while a working party examined the whole issue of education for residential work. The main recommendations of the working party have now been accepted by the Council and they have far reaching implications. There is now to be a common pattern of training for residential and fieldwork. Since large numbers of residential staff are untrained it has also been decided that there will be another level of training, less academically demanding than that required for the social work qualification. This level will lead to a qualification in social service and the training for it will be largely on an in-service basis.

These radical proposals have yet to be implemented but they constitute a determined effort to bring residential care into a clearer partnership with community care and to improve the overall quality of service to clients. If they are implemented a wide range of staff in social service departments could become eligible for some form of training. Given the importance of staff such as home helps and day care workers this could prove an important shift of emphasis from social work to service delivery within the social services.

A major training problem in personal social services concerns the administrative staff. Senior staff at director and assistant director level include many with professional social work backgrounds. While this has proved important to the development of the services it does mean that many lack specific management skills. Some attempts are now being made to offer courses to senior and middle management grades from social services to provide some training in management and social planning. This cannot be covered in professional social work training and anyway benefits from older post-experienced personnel.

The personal social services are still in a very formative period. There are many problems to sort out, especially on staff training and roles, and much basic provision still needs to be made, especially in the residential and day care fields. New social problems, such as the high level of child abuse coming to public attention or the rising incidence of drug abuse, put new demands on the services while old problems, of dependency among the old and handicapped or juvenile delinquency, do not get any less. When departments are under stress due to lack of resources and high levels of demand for services they tend to fall back on the provision of their statutory duties because these alone are difficult enough to fulfil. But some of the wider objectives of a preventive, community-based service are being pursued despite these constraints. Above all the links between services and the general levels of employment and resources in society are clearer and new ways of strengthening individuals and developing communities are emerging. The personal social services and social workers operate where change shows and often where it hurts so they need to be flexible, variable, even uncertain of their role if they are to move with it. Although in monetary terms this service is tiny compared to income maintenance or education it is a challenging and fascinating area to watch and merits further study.

Suggestions for further reading

Foren, R., & Brown, M. J., *Planning for Service* (Knight, 1971)

Jones, H. (Ed.), *Towards a New Social Work* (RKP, 1975).

Jones, K. (Ed.), *The Year Book of Social Policy in Britain 1971* (RKP, 1972).

Rodgers, B., & Stevenson, J., *A New Portrait of Social Work* (Heinemann, 1974).

Rowbothom, R. *et al.*, *Social Services Departments Developing Patterns of Work and Organization* (Heinemann, 1974).

Townsend, P. *et al.*, *The Fifth Social Service* (Fabian, 1970).

The Seebohm Report: *Report of the Committee on Local Authority and Allied Personal Social Services*, Cmnd 3703 (1968).

Part Two
Special need groups

7 Child deprivation and family welfare

The problem of child deprivation

The need for children to have a stable home life and happy upbringing has long been recognized. Children are dependent on others for their very survival, and the quality of the care they receive, physically and emotionally, will go far to determine the sort of adults they will grow up into. So it is vital that they are given the right sort of care, so they can grow up to be well developed and strong physically, mentally alert, contented and emotionally stable. Only then can they grow up able to enjoy full lives, to become responsible and useful citizens and to make good parents in their turn.

Most children are reared by their natural parents and most are cared for well. As recognition of the importance of the early formative years has deepened, the state, however, has taken an increasing part in concern for child care. It has demonstrated its concern in three main ways: by aiding parents in their job of child rearing through the provision of services such as maternity and child welfare, schooling etc; by taking care directly of children who have no parents and by taking over the care of children whose parents are not providing properly for their physical and emotional well-being.

Aid to parents is provided mostly through the basic social services. Family allowances indicate the state's recognition of the financial implications of parenthood. As we saw in the chapter on social security these do not, however, keep the very low paid workers over the officially defined poverty line. But the aim is to help parents financially even though the actuality falls short of the intention of preventing family poverty. The maternity and child welfare services have been developed to help parents do their best for their children. Mothers are given ante- and post-natal care and children are medically inspected, vaccinated, etc, periodically. The health visitors at the clinics and on domiciliary visits offer advice and help on many aspects of child rearing and can refer children for further specialized attention where necessary. Education services, of course, are a vitally important aid to parents in providing schooling and ancillary services. Welfare foods such as subsidized milk and orange juice again acknowledge the need to cater for the welfare of children and aid parents in their job.

The state, then, offers a fair amount of help to all parents in their task of rearing children. It also has to assume responsibility for those children who lack parents or are not receiving proper care. In the case of orphan children the position is relatively clear: a child without parents needs someone to care for it. But children, with parents, who are not receiving proper care are a more complicated category to define. The state has, in a sense, to define what proper care is, or at least, what falls short of it. It has to take powers to intervene in family life and take into care children who are being neglected or badly treated. So the reasons why many children are in care depend on what the statutory powers and duties of the child care service are. These have tended to widen as our understanding of the needs of children has developed. Initially only orphaned or abandoned or destitute children were cared for by the state; then those who were cruelly treated or delinquent, and today any child who is deprived of normal home life on a temporary or permanent basis. Before looking more closely at the reasons why children come into care, and at the numbers involved, it is necessary to look briefly at the main legislation in this field and the powers and duties of the child care service.

Child care

The main legislation relating to child care is the Children Acts of 1948 and 1958 and the Children and Young Persons Acts of 1933 and 1963 and 1969. Central responsibility for the administration of these acts, which relate both to children deprived of normal home life and to juvenile offenders, was with the Home Office for many years. The Home Secretary was advised and aided in this task by the Central Advisory Council of Child Care, the Inspectorate in Child Care and the Central Training Council in Child Care. Following the 1970 social services legislation, responsibility for most matters relating to the care of the deprived child is now transferred to the Department of Health and Social Security in order that the child care services can be better coordinated with the other personal social services. The responsibility for development and inspection is taken over by the Social Work Service there, while the work of the Councils has been merged with that of the new Personal Social Services Council and the Council for Education and Training in Social Work.

At local level, counties and county boroughs became responsible for child care under the 1948 Children Act. This gave them a statutory duty to appoint a committee and a chief officer specifically for the care of children. Local children's departments were staffed by social workers, known as child care officers, together with administrative and residential staff. The Children Act followed the 1946 Curtis Report on the care of children deprived of a normal home life which had recommended the creation of a specialist children's service to replace the existing provision fragmented among various departments including public assistance. Following the 1968 Seebohm Report legislation has now brought the work of children's departments into the new social services departments, as indicated in the previous chapter.

Local authorities have a duty under the Children Act 'to receive into care where it appears to the local authority that their intervention is necessary in the interests of the welfare of the child, any child in their area under the age of seventeen years who has no parent or guardians or has been abandoned or lost, or whose parents or guardians are prevented, for the time being or permanently, by incapacity or any other circumstances from providing for his proper accommodation, maintenance and upbringing'. This is section 1 of the act and under it a very wide variety of cases are received into care. Furthermore the social services departments have to receive into care children committed by the courts under the Children and Young Persons Acts of 1933, 1963 and 1969. The major reasons why children are committed into care are that they have themselves committed an offence, they are in need of care, protection and control or they, or another child of the same family, have been victims of an offence, or are in the same household as a person convicted of a serious offence such as manslaughter, cruelty and so on.

Most of the children who come into care under section 1 of the 1948 act do so at the request of their parents and their parents can take them home whenever they wish. Indeed under the 1948 act the local authorities have a clear duty to restore the child to his natural parents as soon as this is consistent with the child's welfare. In the minority of cases in which the child does not return home he will remain in care up to the age of eighteen if necessary. In some cases, where the parents are dead or permanently unable to care for the child the local authority assumes parental rights over the child. Children who are committed by the courts to the care of the local authority cannot, of course, be taken home by their parents whenever they wish. The authority is given parental rights over the child by the court order and unless this is revoked these remain in force until he reaches eighteen. However, children over whom the local authority exercises parental rights may be allowed to return home on trial if this seems to be in their best interests.

Social services departments thus receive children into care for a variety of reasons. The bulk of receptions are under section 1 of the Children Act. Some of these are children who have no parents or who have been abandoned and these will be long-term cases. But the majority are children who have come into care because their parents are unable to look after them. A very large number of cases, about half the total receptions into care, are received because of the short-term illness or confinement of the mother. Other reasons include long-term illness, particularly mental illness, the imprisonment of the parent, the desertion of the mother, unmarried mothers unable to support their child, and homelessness of the family through eviction or other reasons.

Not all requests for admissions into care are complied with, of course. Parents are encouraged to make their own arrangements where possible and are helped by such means as the admission of younger children to day nurseries. Concern for the prevention of break-up of families has greatly increased since the Children Act of 1948 and local authorities now have statutory duty to develop preventive work as the next section will show. Where children do come into care close contact is maintained with the parents and they have to pay towards the cost of their children's upkeep according to their means. Children who come into care through the courts are committed to the care of the local authority, either because they are themselves offenders, or because they are the victims of offences or because they are found in need of care. A child is found in need of care, protection and control if the court establishes that he is not receiving the sort of care a good parent may reasonably be expected to give and he is falling into bad associations, is exposed to moral danger, or the lack of care is likely to cause him suffering or seriously affect his health or proper development, or if it establishes that he is beyond control of his parents. Obviously children who have been neglected to the point that they are the subject of care proceedings are likely to be difficult and sometimes very disturbed. They are likely to need very careful handling if their substitute parents are to establish a happy relationship with them. Older children who are beyond control and difficult or delinquent will not take easily to substitute homes and will often cause a good deal of trouble there. They might need a non-emotionally demanding environment in which they can recuperate and relax before they are able to tackle relationships again.

While the children sent by the courts are likely to be, on average, more disturbed than those received under section 1, the differences are not too noticeable. All children will tend to suffer from the loss of their home and separation from their parents, siblings and familiar surroundings. Short-term cases are often small children to whom the separation is so alarming that its temporary nature is irrelevant to them. Often children come into care after upsetting events at home, such as a mother's illness or following the trauma of eviction and homelessness. And often they come from homes where there have been difficulties, rent arrears, marital troubles, sickness and so on, for many years, before a further crisis causes the children to be taken into care. Many of the children will have experienced poverty and insecurity if not actual neglect and they will often have been known to the health or education authorities as children at special risk before they come into the care of the social services department.

In short, some children will come from relatively stable homes for temporary care, others have had very damaging and painful experiences and come from permanently broken homes and are likely to require long-term care. All will be disturbed and unhappy to some extent at the loss of familiar surroundings and some will be deeply hurt in their capacity to trust and respond to the people who endeavour to provide substitute homes.

There are currently over 95000 children in the care of the local authorities in England and Wales. The total has grown steadily since the present service was set up in 1948, but in fact the proportion of children in care per thousand of the total population under eighteen has not altered much. At present it is about 6.5 per thousand. But the turnover is very great so that 52680 children were received into care in the year ending 31 March 1974, the vast majority being short-term cases.

The type of care offered to children must vary according to their needs. But in every case the aim of the social services departments is to find the child, until such time as he can return to his own home, a substitute home as near to a good, normal home as possible. While good standards of physical care, hygiene, nutrition and so forth, are clearly vital, it is now realized that the most important need is for the child to receive personal attention and genuine affection. Only in a secure and loving atmosphere can he cope with the shocks that have preceded and accompanied his coming into care, and develop to his full potential. This realization has led to the abandonment of the large institutional type of children's home and a policy favouring the boarding out of children in ordinary homes where possible. Boarding out, or fostering, has been practised for many years and the Curtis Committee on the care of children strongly urged that this should be the first choice in finding substitute homes. Under the Children Act of 1948 the local authorities now have a duty to place a child in foster care unless this is not practicable or desirable in the child's best interests. Where it is not possible children's homes are kept as small as possible and are not isolated from the community around them.

The range of substitute homes offered by the local authorities varies considerably and it is of course essential to try to match the different children coming into care to the most appropriate home. Accordingly, all authorities must provide facilities for the initial and temporary reception of children with the necessary skilled staff for observing and assessing their physical, mental and emotional condition. These reception centres are also used for the temporary care of children where it is necessary to change the foster or other home. In some cases where it proves very difficult to place a child the reception centre might end by providing relatively long-term care but this is not usual or desirable.

After assessment by the child care officer or reception centre the child is placed in a suitable substitute home. This is, as already indicated, a foster home where practicable. About half the total number of children in care are in foster homes, but the proportions of children boarded out vary between different areas. Foster parents are paid a weekly allowance that covers the basic costs of maintaining a child but care is taken to see that fostering does not become a materially profitable exercise. In selecting foster homes social workers interview and assess would-be foster parents for their general suitability, then great care is taken in placing a particular child in a particular foster home. Where the arrangement works well the child obtains a secure substitute home. He is able to form a good relationship with his foster parents and he has the advantages of remaining in a normal setting, going to school, making friends and generally participating in the life of the neighbourhood. But fostering does not always work out so well. The reasons for success or failure of fostering are not well understood. Clearly in some cases the parents expect to lavish care upon a poor, neglected child who will respond with gratitude and affection. They receive a child that has been badly let down in the past, who has to learn, painfully, how to care and trust again. Far from experiencing simple gratitude, such a child will most likely feel terribly torn and anxious when faced with his foster parents' offer of affection. If he comes out from his defensive withdrawal and hesitantly accepts the affection he is likely to need to test it out, to see whether it can withstand some heavy strain or whether, like past ties, it can be broken. So a hurt child will be moody and often intensely provocative, testing out the validity of the proffered affection and expressing some of the pent-up anger and agony from the past. Not surprisingly, some foster parents are bewildered by the bad behaviour.

It is the skilled job of the social workers to help the foster parents cope by understanding their anxiety, explaining the child's difficulties and helping them to get along together. It is hard for foster parents to cope with a very demanding and disturbed child and no less hard to part with him once they have learnt to love him. Foster care is not permanent and many children will return to their natural parents, and here again foster parents will need support and help in easing a parting.

It is not easy to find enough foster parents to care for very difficult children, and all too often fostering breaks down and the child has to be returned again to the reception centre. Repeated failures in fostering are obviously very damaging to a child to whom it means repeated rejection. So for some children it is deemed better to place them in small homes where it is easier to maintain continuity of care. Most local authorities now run small family group homes instead of the larger children's homes common before the 1948 Act. These typically cater for up to a dozen children, boys and girls of various ages, and they are run by a housemother with some assistance by day. Often the housemother is a married woman whose husband goes out to work but acts as a father to the children in the evenings and at weekends. The home will usually be a converted older house or even a large council house on an estate, and the children will go to the schools and churches and clubs in the neighbourhood. At some small homes children from the same family can be kept together where fostering would entail splitting them up. Also, various children deemed unsuitable for fostering, because of behaviour problems, or physical handicaps for example, or because there are strong ties with the natural parents, can be accommodated, together with those who have had a foster placement breakdown.

Following the 1948 Act efforts were made to foster a deprived child where possible and homes were regarded on the whole as second best. But in recent years the wisdom of fostering in all cases has been questioned and the merits of a less emotionally demanding atmosphere which a home can provide have been increasingly accepted. Some authorities now favour homes taking fifteen to twenty children particularly for the difficult medium-term cases where the child is away from his natural home for more than a few months. Practice varies quite widely in different areas, of course. In addition to the provision already described some authorities still retain some of the older type large homes and several run residential nurseries. But broadly speaking, the aim is to provide, whether by fostering or small family group homes, as much individual attention and as near normal an environment as possible for the child who has to come into care. Alongside this aim is that of returning the child to his natural home wherever possible. This is a duty in respect of section 1 cases, and even with children committed by the courts, efforts are made to ensure their eventual return to their own homes. This involves allowing the children home on trial, a practice which has increased sharply since 1948, and taking whatever steps are necessary to rehabilitate the family so that full parental responsibility can be resumed.

Apart from their major task of receiving children into care and providing substitute homes for them, local authority social services departments have various other responsibilities in the child care field. One of these concerns the supervision and arrangement of adoptions. For children permanently deprived of their natural home adoption provides a secure alternative home. Under the 1958 Adoption Act local authorities have a duty to secure the well-being of children awaiting adoption. Persons who wish to adopt a child may contact their local social services department who may either place children for adoption itself or contact a registered adoption agency or make direct arrangements with the child's parents. The social services departments supervise the child during the statutory three-month period which elapses between the notification of adoption proceedings and the making of an adoption order by the court and a social worker is usually appointed as a guardian *ad litem*, i.e. for the duration of the case, to interview the prospective adopters, investigate the relevant circumstances and report to the court.

Attempts are made to consider the best interests of the natural parents and the would-be adoptive parents, but the interests of the child are, of course, of paramount importance.

There has been mounting concern about some of the problems of adoption and fostering recently and a department committee was set up to investigate. Its report on the *Adoption of Children* was published in 1972. This recommended a change in procedures so that adoptive parents would be assured that no changes of mind by the mother at a late stage could result in the removal of a child. Moreover it suggested that foster parents who had had the care of a child for five years or more should be able to apply for an adoption order without risk of removal by parents before a hearing. Despite considerable controversy a Children Act was passed in 1975 based on these recommendations. It seems to improve adoption procedure and provides for more say from the child, as well as from the adults in a disputed case. But however much care is taken there are situations where it proves extremely difficult to be fair to both natural parents and prospective adoptive parents and this will always be a sensitive and emotional aspect of child care work.

Another function of the departments is that of child protection. Under the 1958 Children Act local authorities have a duty to ensure the well-being of children who are fostered privately. The social work staff visit and inspect and offer advice and guidance where necessary in the interests of the child. Social services departments also provide care and after care for older children, by running hostels for working boys and girls and help with the costs of further education and training, or simply by offering friendship and advice.

Social services departments co-operate closely with voluntary organizations concerned with the welfare of deprived children. They can place children in homes run by voluntary organizations and make contributions to their costs and they have certain powers to inspect voluntary homes. Voluntary effort has been prominent in the development of services for deprived children. Organizations such as Dr Barnardo's, the National Children's Homes, the Catholic Rescue Society, pioneered methods of child care during the nineteenth century and still play a very active part in the child care service. Approximately 12000 children are currently being cared for by voluntary organizations.

Prevention: from child care to family welfare

As the preceding paragraphs have shown child care is based on the 1948 Children Act under which one major duty of the local authorities is to receive children into care and provide them with adequate substitute homes unless or until they can be returned to their natural parents. The majority of children come into care at the request of their parents, because they are temporarily unable to look after them and they will return to their own homes in due course. But a substantial proportion of the long term cases are children who have been taken into care against the wishes of their parents because they have not been receiving adequate care or control.

The 1948 Act initiated many changes in child care. The terms under which children could be received into care were considerably widened, the methods of care were made more sensitive to the needs of children and the unified administrative structure ensured more uniform standards of care over the country. Moreover major advances were made in training child care staff both for the fieldwork of finding substitute homes, supervising fostering and keeping contact with parents and for residential work. Nevertheless the twenty years following the Act were ones of such rapid development in policy in the child care field that by 1968 the Seebohm Report recommended the absorption of the child care service by unified social services departments and the merging of specialist child work into generic social work. The emphasis had shifted radically from the child centred approach of 1948 to the Seebohm concern for family and community. This change was essentially the outcome of concern for prevention in the child care field.

Interest in prevention of the break-up of families was discernible from the inception of the child care service. There are several reasons why it received greater emphasis as the years went by. More knowledge of the emotional needs of children demonstrated the importance of maintaining a warm and continuous relationship between a child and its mother or mother substitute. The study of sociology began to show the importance of the family and class and cultural factors in child development. The increased use of trained child care officers who had studied the growth and development of personality meant that more people were aware of the difficulty, if not the impossibility, of compensating a child for the break-up of his natural home. Practical considerations, such as the difficulty of finding enough foster placements and adequate staff for children's homes, also lent weight to arguments in favour of preventing children from coming into care. Moreover there was some evidence of a feeling in the country that the state must not too readily take on the care of children lest it undermine the responsibilities of parents.

So efforts were made to prevent children from coming into care. Essentially this meant working with families at risk of break-up. In some cases it meant helping families, who had applied for their children to be taken into care, find an alternative solution. But it also meant trying to contact families and individuals – doctors, schools, health visitors, housing departments, etc, when they felt a family had too many problems. This resulted in the children's department undertaking general family casework and finding they lacked the power to provide much constructive help in many cases. Their powers were accordingly widened by the 1963 Children and Young Persons Act which gave local authorities a duty to prevent and forestall the suffering of children through neglect in their own homes. Under this act they were given responsibility 'to make available such advice, guidance and assistance as may promote the welfare of children by diminishing the need to receive children into or keep them in care'. Assistance could include assistance 'in kind or, in exceptional circumstances, in cash'. Preventive work now had full legislative sanction.

Children's departments were not the only agencies involved in family welfare however. Within the local authorities, health departments were increasingly concerned, especially through the work of the health visitors, who were often closely involved with families in difficulties, and also welfare departments through their responsibility for homeless families, and education authorities through the education welfare services. Voluntary bodies also played, and still do play, a prominent part in family welfare, especially in the larger towns and cities. A description of some of the more prominent of these will indicate the scope and style of their contributions.

In many centres of populations there exists a Family Welfare Association. These associations can often trace their origins back to the nineteenth century when they were, under different names, primarily concerned with giving relief in cash and kind to families in distress. In London the Charity Organization Society did pioneer work in developing a casework approach to the families who came to it for aid, helping them to solve their problems and help themselves rather than become dependent on charitable funds. The COS became the Family Welfare Association shortly after the Second World War and its functions have widened in scope as the need for basic relief has been reduced by the growth of statutory income maintenance services. The story is similar in other areas, with an older organization or group of charities coming together as a local Family Welfare Association. Today the organization and staffing of the local FWAs varies but they have roughly the same aim: to promote family welfare by helping families overcome their problems. They still have funds to dispense and many clients initially come in financial distress, but they also have social workers available to give advice and support as well as the occasional cash assistance.

Another very important, but very different, family service is provided by a national organization, the Family Service Units. The FSU operates through local units many of which are generously grant aided by local authorities. All the major conurbations have units which provide an intensive casework service to families referred by other statutory and voluntary social agencies. The FSU was founded in 1947, and was based on the experience of the Pacifist Service Units which had helped families who were overwhelmed by the destruction, separation, chaos and strain of the war years to cope and re-establish themselves. This experience showed that the problems of many families had little to do with the actual wartime conditions which were only an additional stress for families already overwhelmed by financial, housing and emotional problems of their own. The need for help did not, therefore, end with the war, and FSU continued the work subsequently. The essence of the FSU approach consists of the family caseworkers having very small caseloads so that they can visit families frequently, several times a week if necessary, and help directly with the practical as well as emotional problems the families face.

The National Society for the Prevention of Cruelty to Children is increasingly concerned with helping families to cope better with the demands of rearing children. There are also various bodies concerned with the particular problems of the unmarried mother or with single-parent families who increasingly see their role as contributing to family welfare. At national level the National Council for One Parent Families acts as the central organization which draws together the various statutory and voluntary bodies concerned and generally offers advice and information in this field. At local level voluntary welfare organizations, usually run on a diocesan basis, often act as agents for the local authority in providing facilities for the reception of unmarried mothers and some provide long-term ccommodation for mothers and their growing children or general ocial work help as long as it is necessary. Increasingly evident in this field are self help organizations such as Gingerbread or Mothers in Action. Marriage Guidance is a voluntary organization with a national council, coordinating the activities of local councils, which aims to promote successful marriage and parenthood and thereby helps to maintain family welfare by improving marital relationships. The list of all the voluntary agencies concerned directly or indirectly with family welfare would be too long to provide here. Facilities vary considerably from area to area. For example, in some areas in addition to statutory departments and the main voluntary agencies there are family rehabilitation units or holiday and recuperative homes for mothers and children. So it is impossible to generalize about the extent of the provision. Suffice it to say that in this field voluntary effort has long played a considerable part.

From the experience of voluntary bodies and of the different local authority departments concerned much was learnt about the difficulties of families and of the ways in which they could be helped. Initially it was felt that some families failed to take advantage of the services offered by the welfare state and despite the basic social services they fell into poverty and sickness, remained ignorant of the skills and attitudes needed to cope with life and failed to find accommodation for themselves. Subsequently, especially during the late 1960s after the mounting evidence of shortcomings in the basic provision, there was a contrasting tendency to blame the services and society for forcing people into intolerable positions. It is undoubtedly the case that poverty and bad housing conditions are still very much in evidence, that the poor have alarmingly inadequate provision of health care and educational opportunity and that homelessness is a very real threat. It is also the case that people who live with financial anxieties, poor health, insecurity of employment income and accommodation are rarely happy and usually suffer not only from the actual privations of poverty or homelessness but also from a demoralizing sense of failure as well. Society makes certain demands and assumptions and when families cannot live up to them, they can be made to feel outcast and inadequate and this does not help their ability to cope. It is humiliating to be living in debt and squalor in the midst of affluence and bewildering to feel helpless in the face of laws and regulations and procedures which one cannot understand. The strain and tension created by constant difficulties can lead to other problems and it can be hard to sort out which came first and all too easy to blame the surface symptoms of child neglect or indebtedness or irresponsible parenthood rather than on an unjust social system.

In fact, as more is known and understood about problem families it becomes apparent that there are many reasons why families fail to stay together or to bring up their children adequately and the reasons differ widely from family to family. In most cases there is a mixture of individual and social and economic reasons behind a family break-up. Factors commonly found among the complex causation of family stress include ill-health, low intelligence, mental instability and immature personality, low wages and/or reliance on social security payments, irregular employment, single parenthood, large families and bad housing conditions. It does at times become impossible to sort out causes and effect and to distinguish the environmental factors from the personal ones, to separate, for example, poverty wages from work shy attitudes or homelessness from marriage breakdown. One essential paradox which lies at the core of the problem is that the poorer a person's own resources are in terms of intelligence, energy, emotional stability and maturity, the more he is likely to have to cope with. A less educated and intelligent man is usually low paid and will frequently have a larger family so he will have to make less money go further and have fewer skills with which to organize his affairs. Similarly it is often women in poor health left on their own, with immature personalities, who have to cope with several very young children in cramped conditions without a circle of supportive friends and without expensive labour saving aids. Many families who get into difficulties have been struggling to cope with problems which would daunt the most energetic and resourceful people. So it is not surprising that the worse the environmental stresses are the more people fail to cope and those who fail are the most vulnerable. If wages plus allowances fall below subsistence level families will become poverty-stricken however hard they work or carefully they budget, and large families will suffer first. The worse the housing situation becomes in terms of shortages and high rents and insecurity of tenure the more people will become homeless – people, who could cope perfectly well with their housing needs if reasonably priced and secure accommodation was available – and the first to become homeless will be the large families, the single-parent families, and those moving in search of work and so forth.

Some families in difficulties appear to have had long histories of problems. Perhaps the parents themselves are from broken and unhappy homes, have married hastily in search of much needed security, had several children quickly and are struggling on a low income for unskilled work, dependent on privately rented furnished rooms. It is hardly difficult to see why problems multiply and may get out of hand for such families. More disturbing in some ways are the families who have coped adequately for years but are plunged by sudden misfortune into a downward spiral of difficulty and demoralization. Much suffering is involved in family failure. The 'social' problems of debt or child neglect or abuse are the ones which attract attention but the misery of the parents is easily ignored. Whatever the initial cause of failure families are not helped by condemnation and rejection as those who feel guilty and inadequate can become depressed or in turn rejecting and aggressive.

What can be done to help families and prevent, not only their break-up and the admission of children to care, but also the problems of child neglect and abuse and the general unhappiness of those who feel overwhelmed by problems? Just as the causes of family failure are many and varied so too the approach to family welfare must be on a wide front. Insofar as the causes lie in faulty social provision there must be action to change such things as the social security provision and to improve housing. Insofar as the causes lie in individual problems help must be made available to families, help which is not only relevant but is made accessible and acceptable even to those who are very angry or demoralized or despairing.

In terms of official policy the movement from child care to family welfare resulted in demands for the creation of a more effective family service. There was a desire to create a single referral point and a truly accessible and localized service that everyone would know about and use. The growing concern for a unified approach meant that when the Seebohm Committee concluded its review of personal social services it recommended the creation of a single local authority welfare department. This has already been described in the previous chapter. One of the major tasks of the social services departments is that of helping families in difficulties.

Help starts with social work and this is now more readily obtained locally through the area team structure. Social workers must first diagnose the problems and then help with such practical aids as they have at their immediate disposal. They can now offer some material aid, including at times of emergency some cash assistance. They have a major part to play in helping clients get their rights from other social services. As services have become more selective the importance of the welfare rights movement has increased. There are now a whole range of benefits – family income supplement, free school meals, rent and rate rebates and allowances etc, which can help families in financial need and the processes of application and appeal for these are complex enough to warrant the assistance of social workers in many instances. A vital part of family welfare involves help with housing by social workers taking a client's part in helping them get an application for council housing considered or by encouraging the formation of community housing associations. The day and domiciliary services of the local authority can be brought to bear if relevant – day care of small children can help enormously in many family problems where the welfare of children is at risk. Liaison with other agencies and people concerned with families and children remains important. Where, for example, children are considered at risk of physical harm it is important that medical authorities pass on relevant information about non-accidental injuries and teachers report cases of obvious neglect or comprehensive risk registers are compiled.

Despite many years' experience of child care and family casework there is still a lively debate about the causes and extent of family failure and about what further measures should be taken to reduce it. The DHSS is currently cooperating on special research projects to investigate patterns of transmitted deprivation where families appear to hand down problems from generation to generation. In contrast to this approach, which seems to look for causes and solutions within families, the Urban Deprivation Unit at the Home Office, is concentrating on the problems of inner city areas. Stressing the significance of an environment dominated by industrial decline and urban decay, the unit is seeking ways of helping the vulnerable people who accumulate in certain areas by revitalizing neighbourhoods rather than assisting individuals. Meanwhile the social services departments and the voluntary bodies concerned continue to help as best they can utilizing a wide range of approaches and practical aids.

It is clearly important for social services departments to strike the correct balance between policies of prevention which involve family and community support and policies of intervention where the immediate interests of the children are given priority. Social services departments have been strongly criticized recently for not taking more effective action to protect children at risk. Considerable public anxiety has been roused by the apparent increase in the number of children subjected to severe neglect and physical assault. It has been suggested that in some cases concern for the family has been allowed to outweigh concern for the children who had suffered at the hands of their natural parents even while the social services departments and voluntary agencies attempted to help. A particularly distressing case was that of the manslaughter of Maria Colwell in 1973 while the child was under local authority supervision. The publication of the fairly critical *Report of an Inquiry into the Care and Supervision Provided in Relation to Maria Colwell* in 1974 led to much heart-searching by social services departments, social workers and other concerned groups. Doubts was expressed about the wisdom of supporting the natural family in certain circumstances. Other tragedies have been publicized which underline the extreme vulnerability of children and urgent attention is now being paid to ensuring the prevention of child abuse. Particular concern is focussed on problems of communication between the individuals and agencies involved with the welfare of families. It does seem that at times the ability to take prompt and effective action to prevent severe child abuse is frustrated by bureaucratic confusion, professional rigidity and shortages of appropriate resources. The Colwell inquiry and others like it sadly demonstrated how vital it is for the social services concerned with children to be alert and flexible: any rigidity of attitude or procedure can be fatal in this extremely sensitive area of social service.

Children in trouble

It became increasingly clear that the family must be supported and assisted if child deprivation was to be avoided and the development away from specialist child care to unified social services was the result. The importance of the family for the prevention of delinquent behaviour has also been recognized and it is now widely accepted that the delinquent child and his family are in need of the same kind of attention as the deprived child and his family demand. There have accordingly been several moves in recent years to bring services for the young offender closer to those for the deprived child. These culminated in the 1969 Children and Young Persons Act which brought about some radical changes in the treatment of young offenders.

The arguments for treating disturbed, delinquent and deprived children alike are based on the assumption that the child is the product of his home and not a totally separate responsible individual. Deprivation at home can lead to various forms of maladjustment, including delinquent behaviour, and court procedures and punishment are seen as an inappropriate response to this situation. It is considered better to work, over a period of time, with the family as well as the child, providing whatever support, training or care appears to be appropriate at different stages of development. In this approach a court order following an isolated offence is regarded as too rigid a way of tackling a complex problem and one that fails to involve the family adequately.

In the mid 1960s, when these arguments were much canvassed, there was some pressure to abolish the whole system of juvenile courts and to rely instead on family councils and family courts. Radical proposals were put forward in the 1965 White Paper, *The Child, the Family and the Young Offender*. These proved too controversial and modified proposals appeared in the 1968 paper *Children in Trouble* which formed the basis of the 1969 act.

Juveniles who break the law have been dealt with by separate courts since 1908 and since 1933 the courts have been specifically charged to have regard to the child's welfare in all their dealings. The courts have had a variety of treatment orders available in respect of the children brought before them, including placing children on probation, sending them to attendance or detention centres or to approved schools. The juvenile courts have also had powers to place children in care and the old children's departments had to receive children in need of care and protection and find them substitute homes. Child care authorities were also involved in running remand homes and approved schools.

The 1969 Children and Young Persons Act retained the juvenile court system but reduced the effective powers of the juvenile magistrates. Action to deal with offenders is now to be taken on a voluntary rather than court basis where possible. Prosecution of children aged ten and under fourteen has ceased. If a child has committed an offence *and* his parents are not providing adequate care, protection and guidance, or the offence indicates he is beyond parental control, then he can be brought before the court as in need of care, protection and control. For the age range fourteen and under seventeen, prosecution is only possible for a limited number of offences on the authority of a magistrate and the extended care, protection and control procedure is used in most cases. The courts must now make care orders, committing children to the care of the local authority. The local authority, now the social services departments, must decide on the most appropriate form of care. For all children in care a comprehensive system of community homes is now being developed, organized on a regional basis and managed by local authorities or by voluntary organizations in collaboration with local authorities. Community homes include former remand homes and approved schools and former children's homes. So children sent from the courts whether they were offenders or offended against can now be placed in whatever type of residential care is deemed most appropriate to their needs at the discretion of the social workers of the local authority. This part of the act has been strongly criticized and to some extent misused for a minority of very difficult cases. Since magistrates are no longer able to make approved school orders it appears that some are sending children to the higher courts for possible borstal sentences. Another problem is remand for very difficult children. At present too many young offenders are being remanded in prisons because local authorities lack enough secure accommodation for them. Steps are being taken to provide more secure places for the unruly and disturbed children who would otherwise disrupt community homes and reappear before the courts.

The local authority also undertakes supervision of children, and this replaces the previous probation order. Supervision is by a social worker who can make certain requirements such as that the supervised person resides in a specified place, or participates in specified activities. Under these provisions local authorities are expected to provide Intermediate Treatment designed to replace attendance and detention centres. Intermediate Treatment was meant to help not only children in trouble but those at risk of getting into trouble. The idea was that a wide range of activities would be developed for groups of young people which would allow them to gain a sense of personal involvement and achievement. Children under supervision could be directed to such projects as appeared appropriate to their needs although the projects would not be exclusively for young offenders. Projects would be run by youth groups and voluntary organizations as well as local authorities. Many social services departments have appointed special Intermediate Treatment organizers to develop suitable projects but progress has been slow. Intermediate Treatment needs enormous enthusiasm, imagination and energy in the design and carrying out of projects and the necessary resources of staff and funds have not been forthcoming. This has seriously weakened the therapeutic and remedial potential of supervision orders and it is to be hoped that greater priority will be given to this area in the next few years.

Essentially the 1969 Children and Young Persons Act involved a transfer of responsibility from the courts to the local authorities. This means in practice that magistrates have less say in determining what happens to children in trouble while social workers have more say. This is in accordance with the expressed intention of the Act to merge the previously separate concepts of delinquent and deprived into the one category of children in trouble. The changeover has not proved easy. Local authorities had to implement the Act, which involved a considerable increase in responsibility for them, at the time when the creation of the new social services departments was preoccupying the child care and social work staff. As a result the magistrates, never entirely happy with the act, have been quick to criticize the way it has been carried out. They have claimed that the courts have been inadequately served by the new social services departments. More fundamentally they criticize the reduction of their power to make residential orders and the merging of treatment for delinquent and non-delinquent children. So severe was the criticism that a special inquiry is currently being held into the working of the Act, prompted in part by the apparent increase in juvenile delinquency and in part by anxiety over its effects. Many people fear the 1969 act was too radical and makes life too easy for young delinquents. Others feel that its implicit emphasis on home and family as formative influences on young people deny the importance of sociological explanations of delinquency. They would seek an even more radical approach that would tackle not the individual offender but the wider deprivation and social injustice they consider him a product of. Nevertheless, although there is still much controversy over the 1969 Act it was a notable step forward and one consistent with a renewed general concern for the importance of the family. Basically it extends society's consideration for deprived children towards those groups who have previously excited anger rather than compassion and as such it is a progressive and humanitarian measure. It is to be hoped that the controversy which surrounded its inception and the shortage of resources, especially of trained staff, which have weakened its early implementation, will not prevent it from being a durable one.

Suggestions for further reading

Bowlby, J., *Child Care and the Growth of Love* (Penguin, 1953).
Donnison, D. V., *The Neglected Child and the Social Services* (Manchester University Press, 1954).
Heywood, J., *Children in Care* (RKP, 1959).
Holman, R. (Ed.)., *Socially Deprived Families in Britain* (Bedford Square Press, 1970).
Kellmer Pringle, M., *The Needs of Children* (Hutchinson, 1974).
Packman, J., *Child Care Needs and Number* (RKP, 1968).
Philp, A. F., *Family Failure* (Faber, 1963).
Stevenson, O., *An Approach to Family Social Work* (1969).
Timms, N., *Social Casework* (RKP, 1969).
Wynn, M., *Fatherless Families* (Michael Joseph, 1964).
Younghusband, E., *Social Work with Families* (Allen & Unwin, 1965).
The Curtis Report, *Report of the Interdepartmental Committee on the Care of Children*, Cmnd 6922 (1946).
The Ingleby Report, *Report of the Committee on Children and Young Persons*, Cmnd 1191 (1960).
Children in Trouble, Cmnd 3601 (1968).
The Finer Report, *Report of the Committee on One-Parent Families*, Cmnd 5629 (1974).

8   Services for old people

The problem of old age

Simply to grow old is not in itself a problem. The urge to survive is fundamental to our nature and inherent in our fight against disease and poverty and in our attempts to control the environment. In a sense, then, survival into old age is a triumph, but a triumph that brings with it many problems, problems that tend to increase the longer one survives, the greater age one attains. The problems arise because old age is a period of increasing dependency, materially, physically, socially and emotionally. If the special needs which arise from these states of dependency are met fully and promptly then the problems will be kept to a minimum and on balance old age will be experienced as a time of contentment. If they are not met, old age may become a problem both to the individual and to society.

Material dependency arises because the old cannot earn their living and financial arrangements must be made to see that they have an income which is adequate to their needs. Physical dependence arises because for most people the process of ageing involves a general physical and sometimes mental weakening. The old are more frequently ill than the rest of the population and more frequently suffer from physical disabilities such as partial loss of hearing or arthritic joints. Gradually their capacity to care for themselves fully is reduced so that they require help with heavier cleaning jobs or gardening, then help with routine tasks such as shopping and cooking and finally, in some cases, help even with feeding and washing and dressing themselves. Many of the aged, therefore, need help in the home, or perhaps residential care, and a considerable number will require intensive medical and nursing care at some stage.

These material and physical states of dependency are fairly widely recognized since, for example, increasing frailty is a fairly easily discernible consequence of growing old. Less readily acknowledged are the social and emotional problems which ageing can bring. Old people cannot get out so much, for physical or financial reasons, or both. They have less opportunity to make new friendships and tend to depend for companionship on the continuity of longstanding relationships. As spouses and relatives and friends of their age move away, or die, old people look more and more to their few surviving relatives and neighbours for affection, friendship and reassurance and can easily become very dependent on a small number of people for social contact. Moreover, growing old often involves very considerable adjustments for the individual who has to accept increasing physical dependency and consequent loss of autonomy and status. Many find it hard to accept a dependent role and fight to assert an independence which they lack the means to substantiate, often, in the process, alienating and exasperating the very people they depend on. The old have to accept changes in patterns of living and cultural standards which they cannot understand, and cope with rejection by the younger generations, and a good deal of sentimentality and shallow stereotyping in private and public references to themselves. Adjustment to their changing role and position in society can be so painful that some old people fail to achieve it satisfactorily and live at odds with society in bewildered but proud withdrawal.

If these social and emotional needs are to be met the old must have every facility for preserving the contacts they have with relatives and friends and possibilities for some compensatory relationships when deeper ties are ultimately broken. They deserve a more sensitive environment that does not so harshly relegate them *en masse* to the category of 'old people' and does not emphasize, in attitudes and actions, their increasing dependency; and many need help in coming to terms with the process of ageing and the major adjustments it entails – to retirement, to relinquishing their home, etc.

It is a fundamental point about the aged, and one which is applicable to any group of people who need special help, that they will differ very widely in their capacities and in their needs. Old age begins officially on retirement but the majority of people in their sixties and many in their seventies remain reasonably fit, independent, active and content and in many cases they will remain so until the end of their lives. For some, though, some of the problems are evident from the point of retirement, or even before, and for very old people, in their eighties and nineties, the chances of considerable dependency are clearly rather high. Not all of these dependent old people can rely on consistent family care. So although many old people cope smoothly with the problems of ageing, others fail in varying degrees to obtain the special help they need. As a result they suffer from poverty, physical hardship, neglect, sickness and disability, loneliness, humiliation and fear. Old age becomes something to be dreaded and endured rather than enjoyed by the individual.

In Britain today we tend to consider old age as a social problem. We know from research and investigations and general observation that many old people are desperately poor and neglected, appallingly isolated and lonely. At the same time we are worried about the mounting costs of the social services intended to meet the needs of the aged. There are several reasons why the problem appears to be particularly acute at the moment and some of the more important ones need stating. First, the proportion of old people in the population is rising fast. In 1900 the proportion was 4·7 per cent, in 1950 it was 10·8 per cent and today it is between 16 and 17 per cent. This means that there are more old people needing special help and proportionately fewer people of working age to provide for them. Old people also live much longer nowadays. This is one reason why the proportion of over sixty-fives has risen, but it also means that many more old people will grow very old, with much higher chances of becoming very dependent and physically feeble. Average life expectancy was only forty-three years in 1880; it had risen to sixty-two years in 1939, and by the 1960s it was over seventy.

At the same time as the number of old people in the population is rising several factors are operating which have tended to reduce the ability of the family to cater for the needs of old people, especially their needs for care and companionship. Prominent among these factors are increased social and geographical mobility consequent upon greatly increased educational opportunity and a rapidly changing economy; the marked trends over recent decades towards smaller families, higher marriage rates and earlier marriage; and the growing numbers of women continuing in or re-entering full-time work. The greatly increased life expectancy of both men and women today means that the children of many of them may themselves be entering old age when they, the parents, are really in need of care.

A further problem of ageing which in part follows from a greater life expectancy is the problem of retirement. This is most relevant to men, some of whom, if they are still fit on retirement, will have another fifteen years of life ahead of them. Apart from the possible financial hardship of retirement many find it hard to adjust to having little to do. They are bored at home and yet feel ill at ease in their former places of enjoyment, pubs and sports grounds and so on, and with their former friends if these are still working. They feel useless being no longer productive workers and yet having little to do at home. This problem is much worse for those who are forced into premature retirement through redundancy. The sense of uselessness and the boredom of empty days, the abrupt, often humiliating change of status from worker to 'old age pensioner' can lead to severe depression and consequent physical and mental deterioration. There is a real need here both for a more flexible employment situation, which could absorb older men in less arduous or part-time work, if they required it, and for more efforts to prepare people for retirement, helping them to develop time consuming, absorbing and possible profitable hobbies in advance of finishing work.

The problem then, which old age presents, is partly inherent in the process of ageing, and partly the consequence of certain current demographic and social trends. In 1973 there were 9·3 million people in the United Kingdom over retirement age. The vast majority need pensions to meet their financial needs, almost all will be registered with a doctor and will make use of the health services, many require special housing or residential accommodation and some degree of help in coping with the problems arising from increasing frailty, social isolation and their dependence role. Clearly the social policy required to tackle the problem must be comprehensive in scope and its instruments flexible and imaginative in application.

Services for old people

There is no one social service designed to meet all the needs of old people. Society has accepted responsibility for seeing that their needs are met in a piecemeal fashion; tackling the most obvious needs first, those for financial provision, medical care and residential accommodation. A considerable part of the total range of need is met through the basic social services of income maintenance, health and housing and personal social services. In special welfare services for the aged voluntary organizations play a prominent part. This fragmentation of concern for the aged is sometimes criticized, but clearly when we are considering a particular *group of people*, like the aged, rather than a particular *problem*, like sickness, it would not be possible, or desirable, to provide all that is needed through one statutory service. The aged, like any other group, have special needs which arise because they are aged, but they share the basic needs of all human beings. It is quite appropriate that they utilize the health services and income maintenance services which are provided generally, and also utilize the special services provided particularly for them.

Financial provision　A fundamental need of the aged is for adequate financial provision since the vast majority are unable to earn their living. In endeavouring to meet this need numerous problems are encountered, notably how to find enough money to provide adequately for the increasingly large proportion of the population who are in retirement, and therefore by and large non-productive, and how to define 'adequate' in this context. In a previous chapter the present social security system was described and it was noted that the bulk of the work of social security is concerned with pensions and benefits for old people. In principle we accept that people should be helped to provide for their own needs in old age by contributing throughout their working life to a pension scheme. This method of financing old age is widely practised through the media of private insurance and occupational superannuation as well as that of statutory national insurance. Because of this it is particularly important, in devising an effective social policy, to meet the financial problems of old age, to consider both the long-term and the short-term aspects. We must try to meet the needs of those people who are in retirement now, and try to create an effective scheme whereby those who are working now will be able to retire with financial security in the future. The effectiveness of retirement pension schemes is greatly threatened by increasing longevity, the problem of keeping pace with the cost of living in an inflationary economic situation, and the problem of rising standards of living which bring new affluence and expectations.

At the present time, then, the majority of old people claim retirement pensions under the national insurance scheme. The basic rate at the time of writing is £13.30 per week for a single person and £21.20 for a couple, but some pensioners are entitled to somewhat higher rates because of graduated contributions or deferred retirement. Some old people who were not included in the scheme as contributors receive a lower rate of pension. Many old people receive occupational or private pensions in addition to their basic retirement pension and a large number have personal savings or private incomes of widely varying amounts. Those old people who are virtually dependent on the retirement pension and who find it does not meet their needs can claim a supplementary pension from the Supplementary Benefits Commission. This means that all people over pension age who are not in full-time work have a statutory right to have their income brought up to a guaranteed weekly level. This consists for a single person of the long-term scale rate of £13.70 per week, or for a couple of £21.55 per week, plus the actual cost of rent and rates. Supplementary benefits are, of course, only paid on test of need, but in assessing a person's means certain forms of income such as disability pensions and a reasonable level of capital are to some extent disregarded.

When the present national insurance scheme was introduced in 1946 it was hoped that the benefits paid under it would be adequate for subsistence. This has proved impossible partly because of the wide variations in need imposed by disparate rents, and partly because of the steady rise in the cost of living. Accordingly, a substantial number of today's retirement pensioners need to claim assistance and submit to some form of test of need. Through pride or ignorance many people failed to do this. A deliberate attempt was made in 1966 to make assistance known and acceptable, when it became known as supplementary benefits. Now, it is hoped that all who need supplement to their basic pension obtain it, but there is still evidence that many do not. In addition to supplementary benefits many old people make use of the range of selective benefits such as rent and rate rebates which have been introduced to tackle poverty. But there is always anxiety that some of the most needy old people will fail to take advantage of their rights. Recent increases in basic pension rates, made possible partly by the introduction of earnings related contributions in 1975, and promises of effective annual uprating to keep pace with rising costs of living should help to improve the position of current pensioners. But, as a group, today's old people are still relatively deprived in our society and this must be seen as a major failure in social security policies.

To avoid the perpetuation of this failure recent policy changes have moved the insurance system towards a wholly wage-related scheme to provide a form of national superannuation. Various proposals have been made with different emphasis on the relationship between state and occupational pension schemes. It has been a feature of post-war Britain that occupational pension schemes have proliferated and they must be brought into some form of partnership with state provision. It has been seen that a wage-related scheme that gives people a proportion of earnings on retirement is both desirable and acceptable but it has not proved easy to overhaul the existing state system to provide this. After various suggestions for change the proposals outlined in the 1974 paper *Better Pensions* are currently being debated and should be implemented by 1977 to 1978. These aim to provide within twenty years, to everyone who retires, a wage-related pension fully guaranteed against inflation. 'Everyone' means women insured in their own right as well as men. Traditionally women have depended on men for their livelihood in marriage and child rearing and subsequently in retirement although single women who work have always earned separate pension rights. But nowadays most women both work and marry. Many work full- or part-time for much of their married life and are now able to claim equal pay and equal chances of career and promotion with men. In this changed situation it would clearly be inappropriate to consider the long-term needs of the elderly without making provision for women as workers rather than as dependants. *Better Pensions* aims to make such provision and this will be a radical but overdue change in social insurance. The proposed scheme should also help the lower paid because pensions will be built upon a base level which will be a relatively higher platform for those with lower earnings. By basing pension rights on contributions paid in the best twenty years of working life those in manual work should have equal chances with professional and clerical groups of obtaining a decent pension. The scheme will operate in partnership with existing occupational structures and people in suitable schemes will be able to opt out of part of the cover and pay lower contributions. If it works – and it is difficult to project so far ahead – it should eventually end our present reliance on supplementary benefits for a substantial number of retired people and give women a more equal place in social security. It should end the threatening aspect of old age for many people by affording a genuine financial security rather than, as now, guaranteeing a precarious subsistence.

Health services　Old people make considerable use of the full range of services provided under the National Health Service Act. Even if those who are living in institutions are excluded, it is estimated that one half old people under seventy-five and about two-thirds of those over seventy-five are suffering from a long-standing illness in addition to normal minor ailments. Large numbers of the elderly suffer from some degree of disability or impairment of physical or mental function. It is not surprising, therefore, that old people make fairly heavy demands on medical care.

General practitioners spend a good proportion of their time with elderly patients and this is acknowledged in the rates of payment for different categories of patients on the GP lists. Some have adopted a system of routine visiting of all the old people on their lists in order to check that health is maintained and to ensure that diseases and disabilities are tackled at the onset. Many GPs cooperate closely with the community health services which are particularly valuable for the old. Health visitors call to give advice and help on the problems of increasing infirmity and the management of disability, and encourage the maintenance of adequate standards of hygiene and nutrition. District nurses can attend to give injections, change dressings, etc, under the supervision of the old person's doctor. Chiropody and laundry services can be provided and a wide range of aids and appliances.

Despite the general practitioner and domiciliary medical services many old people have to enter hospital for treatment or care. As old age advances this can become a very disturbing experience and even where the medical problem is not grave the hospitalization itself can accelerate confusion and frailty among old people. In recent years this has been more widely recognized and both doctors and nurses have increasingly made a speciality of the care of the aged. Geriatric units are being established and consultant geriatricians appointed. Efforts are made to rehabilitate patients after treatment to ensure that where possible their hospital stay is temporary. Nevertheless a large number of elderly patients do come into hospital with terminal illnesses or chronic diseases, including mental disorders and they require long-term care. They do make heavy demands on the resources of the hospital service so steady efforts are being made to improve the preventive aspects of geriatric care.

Social care Under part III of the National Assistance Act of 1948 local authorities have a duty to provide residential accommodation for old people who need care and attention. This is now the responsibility of the social services department but until 1970 it was the job of welfare departments. Residential care is provided by local authorities for about 100000 old people in England and Wales. A further 15000 are cared for in homes run by voluntary organizations. In 1948 local authorities had a variety of old premises used for accommodating the elderly, mostly old public assistance institutions. The aim of the new welfare authorities was to provide homes rather than institutions and so private houses were acquired and converted and then modern purpose-built homes were constructed. These accommodated about thirty old people, which was originally considered the optimum size, but over the years purpose-built homes grew larger and up to seventy places became quite common. The bulk of local authority homes are now purpose-built and accommodate thirty to seventy old people. There are still some larger homes in existence and a small number of old premises used jointly with the health authorities but it is planned to close these eventually. The 'ideal' old people's home has about fifty beds, mostly in single rooms, and accommodates both men and women. There is usually a large dining room, several lounges and a sheltered garden area. Accommodation for residents is on the ground floor or well-serviced by lifts. Staff have separate self-contained accommodation if resident. The home is situated within easy access of shops and other facilities and in the heart of the residential area from which the old people come. The furnishings will be modern and colourful and residents will be encouraged to bring small items of their own furniture with them to give individuality and interest to their rooms. All meals and full care, including night attendance, will be provided and visiting strongly encouraged. The aim of the staff will be to make people feel as much at home as possible. Residents pay for their care according to their means and all will have at least a minimum amount of money for personal use.

Naturally homes differ. Ideal standards are not always achieved. Many homes are too large to be homely. Some still have dormitories, lack space for pleasant sitting rooms and have poor staff accommodation. Some of the converted premises are isolated and inconvenient to run. Some of the modern homes are too clinical, impersonal and routinized for comfort. The quality of the staff, from matrons to cooks, is probably the biggest single factor which determines whether a home has a happy atmosphere and good staff are hard to get for the demanding, albeit rewarding, job of residential care. Residential staff have tended to become isolated from field staff and their training and pay have lagged behind that of field social workers. Current proposals by the Central Council for Education and Training in Social Work should improve this situation. After lengthy consideration of the problem of residential work and training the council has put forward a clear statement that residential work should be seen as part of social work and share a common pattern of training. It remains to be seen how this suggestion can be worked out but at least it indicates that residential care is seen as being of fundamental importance to the social care services. The provision of homes for old people by local authorities is still for only about twenty places per thousand old people in an area, and many of these will be for very old and frail and disabled people. For this minority residential care is a vital service. For others it could be a pleasant existence if places were available and there was room for flexibility and experiment in provision.

When welfare departments were created in 1948 their major concern, as regards old people, was with residential accommodation but gradually this concern was widened to include the provision of a broad range of services for old people who remain and wish to remain, independent in their own homes. This wider concern was of course shared with health authorities, voluntary organizations and housing departments and it is now explicit policy in the unified local authority social services departments. From 1963 with the publication of the command paper *Health and Welfare: the Development of Community Care* local authorities have been encouraged to see as their principal responsibility the provision of services to enable the aged to live independently in the community. From the 1968 Health Services and Public Health Act they have had the powers to promote the welfare of old people.

Social services departments now have a variety of services available to promote the community care of old people. Social workers in the area teams visit the elderly and assess their needs and provide such services as seem appropriate and are available. One of the principal domiciliary services is that of home helps. Home helps, often recruited within an area by a home help organizer at area office level, call regularly on old people and provide domestic services such as cleaning. They also provide a friendly contact which is extremely valuable for detecting and referring any other needs. Mobile meals services can be provided or luncheon clubs for the more active old person, where company and entertainment can be obtained as well as a meal. Telephones can be installed, emergency call-card systems operated and local neighbourly help recruited to reduce the isolation of many old people. Most authorities now run day centres where old people can obtain care and recreation and most use their residential homes for temporary admissions where necessary. Transport is sometimes made available and clubs, holiday schemes, outings and social evenings encouraged. Many of these services help old people living alone but some also help old people living with their families and reduce undue burdens on relatives.

The scope of day and domiciliary care has grown sharply in recent

F

years. But the majority of old people do not make use of social services and the coverage is still uneven between authorities. The most widely used service is that of home helps and this essentially practical provision could be extended. Local authorities have difficulty in knowing which old people need help and of getting help to them in time. Area teams can be very busy with the full range of social need and lack time for regular visiting of the elderly. So it cannot really be said with confidence that community care of the elderly is fully operative although local authorities do have the intention, if not the means, of providing it.

Housing and the elderly   Clearly if old people are to continue to live alone they need not only the support of domiciliary health and social care services but also suitable premises. Size, location and quality of housing are important to all people, but clearly the old, with their reduced mobility and increasing frailty, have a special need of decent accommodation. The sad fact is, however, that in Britain the old have the worst housing of any group. Higher percentages of the elderly than of the general adult population live in accommodation built before 1919 which is often poorly maintained. Higher percentages of the old lack fixed baths, indoor WCs and adequate heating arrangements. There is, therefore, a real and urgent need to improve the housing conditions of the elderly.

Recognition of the importance of housing, especially for community care policies, has led to the building of an increasing number of small dwellings by local authorities including one-bedroomed flats and bungalows. Attempts have also been made to provide sheltered housing, that is groups of small dwellings with some communal facilities and a warden in attendance. Sometimes small bungalows have been built in the grounds of residential homes, in other developments they have been linked to a warden's bungalow by means of alarm bells. Groups of bed-sitters with communal lounge facilities have been tried, and in some places the shared lounge has been available for social facilities for the old people of the neighbourhood. Housing associations as well as local authorities are involved in the provision of sheltered accommodation.

The essence of good housing for old people is that it should be easy to run, easy to heat, clean and move around in, conveniently situated, afford independence and privacy to the occupant, with opportunity for sociability and the security of regular contact. Most sheltered housing schemes are extremely successful and together with the domiciliary services allow some old people to retain their independence and their interest in life. The trouble is there are just not enough places available at the moment. In the owner-occupied and privately-rented housing sectors old people do not often have the means or the energy to make use of improvement grants. They remain very vulnerable in privately rented accommodation as they can often be ignorant of their rights. Efforts are now being made to ensure that more old people are using rent allowances and rate rebates where these apply but there is a need for constant vigilance to protect the most vulnerable groups of old people from the worst aspects of bad housing.

The voluntary contribution Voluntary organizations are particularly active in the care of old people. They play a large part in the provision of welfare services, especially in running clubs and recreational activities and helping with the provision of meals, and they make a substantial contribution to the demand for residential care. Too many organizations are involved to list them all, but nationally organized groups such as Red Cross and WRVS are prominent, and were frequently pioneers in the provision of meals services. The National Old People's Welfare Council, now known as Age Concern, coordinates and encourages the activities of a vast number of local groups concerned with old people's welfare. These local committees offer, either directly or by coordination and encouragement of local effort, a wide range of services such as visiting, holidays, social clubs and even sheltered workshops for the elderly. Age Concern acts also as a pressure group on behalf of the elderly, publishing information on their needs and on services available. The National Corporation for the Care of Old People is primarily a research organization funding enquiries into the needs of old people.

In recent years there has been much imaginative development of the use of young volunteers for work with the elderly. Organizations such as Task Force and Young Volunteer Force have recruited young people from schools and clubs and involved them in regular friendly visiting of old people and work on gardening and home decorating. Many schemes for housing old people have been developed on a voluntary basis. They include schemes like that of the Abbeyfield Society which aims, by converting large older-type houses, to provide old people with the personal security and independence of their own room and furnishings, combined with the advantages of the degree of companionship and care which a communal dining room, the provision of main meals and the friendly attention of a resident house-keeper afford. One of the latest areas of voluntary activity is the provision of classes on preparation for retirement. These can help many people to adjust more happily to the changes retirement brings about in their lives.

Not only are voluntary organizations active among the aged, the aged are also active in voluntary work. The relatively young old person is free to contribute a good deal of time, energy and experience to voluntary action and large numbers take advantage of retirement or reduced family responsibilities to increase their participation. Many younger old people run clubs for the elderly and help organize meals services. A very large number help, informally, their neighbours and relatives older than themselves. This activity is doubly advantageous in that it helps to meet the needs of the more elderly for a variety of services and also helps to give the younger elderly person a sense of usefulness, a strong interest and in some cases a degree of insight and preparation for the inevitable transition to a greater ageing which must be faced.

We have pursued an official policy of community care for the elderly for more than a decade. Services have been developed, co-ordination improved and concern stimulated. There is still, however, room for doubt on the effectiveness of our social policies for old people. The failure of the insurance scheme to provide adequate social security has been noted. The elderly are amongst those most adversely affected by the current housing problems. There are acute shortages of staff, some depressingly poor conditions in many geriatric hospital wards and shortages of many community social services. Perhaps more depressing than actual shortages of provision is the tendency to alienate the old in contemporary society. This occurs when too much provision becomes labelled as especially for old age pensioners. Administrators of services do need to be careful not to isolate recipients too much. The old need help but they do not necessarily need a massive range of old people's services. Clearly some of the needs now met by social services departments would be better met by the old people themselves if they had the financial means to preserve their own independence. It is worth remembering that most people cope quite adequately with the practical problems of old age if they have financial security and decent housing and it is on the provision of these we should concentrate. Moreover, despite the importance of professional social care, it is the family which still plays the major part in meeting the social, emotional and general physical needs of the dependent old. The role of the state in services for old people should be to create conditions which maximize the ability of the individual, the family and the community, to cope independently. There are, after all, many aspects of the problem of old age which no formal statutory provision can deal with. Only the family, the community and above all the old people themselves can solve the need to belong, to have a place, meaning and dignity in life. The role of the social services here is the vital but subordinate one of enabling them to meet this need effectively.

Suggestions for further reading

Goldberg, E. M., *Helping the Aged* (Allen & Unwin, 1970).
Meacher, M., *Taken for a Ride* (Longmans, 1972).
Roberts, N., *Not in my Perfect Mind* (1961).
Shanas, Townsend, Wedderburn *et al.*, *Old People in Three Industrial Societies* (RKP, 1968).
Shaw, J., *On Our Conscience* (Penguin, 1971).
Townsend, P., *The Family Life of Old People* (RKP, 1957).
Townsend, P., *The Last Refuge* (RKP, 1962).
Tunstall, J., *Old and Alone* (RKP, 1966).

9   The physically disabled

The problem

The terms physically disabled and physically handicapped cover
people with a wide range of disabilities: the blind and partially
sighted, the deaf and hard of hearing, people with congenital de-
formities, those who have suffered serious injury, those who suffer
from crippling diseases such as arthritis, tuberculosis, 'organic
nervous disorders', and so on. Clearly the needs of each person, and
the problems they present, will differ, according to the nature and
severity of the disability and according to the individual's personality
and social and economic situation. But all the physically handicapped have one need in common – the need to be helped to overcome their disabilities and live as near normal a life as possible, being
a part of, and contributing to, the life of the community.

It is perhaps useful, in considering the problem, to differentiate
between a disability and a handicap. It is possible, within limits, to
assess a physical disability. Blindness can be ascertained, the degree
to which a person suffers from loss of hearing can be measured, and
the extent to which an injury or disease is physically disabling can
be assessed in a fairly precise manner. But the extent to which a
given disability will *handicap* a person in education, work, social
relationships, enjoyment of leisure, etc, will depend on his social as
well as his clinical state, and on the timing of the disability. If a
person is born severely disabled he will need a great deal of help in
overcoming the effects of the disability, but he will possibly be able
to adjust to it better than the person who has enjoyed perfect health
and led a full, normal life and is suddenly injured or crippled by
disease. If someone has acquired skills in early life for a job involving
considerable strength and mobility he will be more handicapped in
finding work if he becomes wheelchair-bound than someone similarly
afflicted who has qualifications and experience in a field which allows
him to do a sedentary job demanding intellectual skills. Similarly,
the person who has a great love of music might find blindness less of
a handicap in obtaining pleasure than would the person who had a

passion for football. Various factors will strongly affect the extent to which disability leads to handicap, primarily the ability of the disabled person and his family to cope with disablement. The family may encourage independence, or they may stifle it, the individual may rise to the challenge but may equally be overcome with bitterness and despair.

It is still difficult to indicate the size of the problem of physical disability in this country, as there are no exact records. At present we have to rely on several sources of information, which sometimes overlap, and which definitely leave great gaps. We have registers for certain groups of disabled people, those registered with local authorities, those who are listed as disabled with the Department of Employment, records of certain groups receiving treatment or pensions, and so on. The total picture is incomplete, partly because not everyone who is disabled is necessarily in receipt of a pension or special welfare service and many of the lists of those on the disabled persons employment register, for example, include those with mental handicap as well as those with physical disabilities.

Since 1971 we have had the results of a major survey on the prevalence of physical disability which was undertaken to provide reliable estimates of the numbers of handicapped people. This commented, in the report *Handicapped and Impaired in Great Britain*, that the term disabled tended to be used for the more obviously and severely disabled and the report used the term impaired to identify the numbers with measurable disability. The report concluded that there were just over three million people of age sixteen and over in Britain with some physical, mental or sensory impairment, 1·25 million men and 1·75 million women, the majority being over retirement age. It is obvious that this figure blurs the borderline between what is often generally considered as disability and what is considered the increasing frailty of old age. It proves impossible to keep to rigid categories when examining this issue.

Although it is not possible to give any exact statistics of the physically disabled, it is possible to give some indication of the extent of the problems they face. We have already noted that these will differ according to the actual disability and according to the individual's circumstances. This simple fact cannot be overstressed and it accounts, in part, for the continuing lack of precise data on the numbers of physically handicapped in the country: we do not know exactly how many people are physically disabled because they are not a clear homogeneous group that can be counted. Nevertheless, we need to consider what problems might arise and make provision accordingly, accepting that such provision should be very flexible if it is to cope with the range of need presented by the disabled. Some problems are fairly obvious: whether the disability is congenital, or the result of an accident or disease, whether the maximum amount of medical care available is required, in order to minimize the effects of the disability, or arrest the causative condition. Advances in medical science have made possible extensive treatment, by medical, surgical and rehabilitative techniques, which can remedy some defects and compensate for others. Some of the disabled will need, despite medical treatment, intensive care and regular nursing all their lives, others will need steady attention from their doctors even if they are relatively mobile and independent.

For many of those who are disabled from birth or during childhood special education is obviously necessary. Clearly the blind, the deaf and the crippled cannot be expected to make do with ordinary educational provision but require specially adapted teaching methods, and in some cases peripatetic teachers if they are confined to their beds at home. On leaving school most of the disabled will need help in finding suitable employment; some will need a permanently sheltered working environment; many will need financial assistance as they are unable to earn a living. The majority of severely handicapped persons need some help in the routine of ordinary living, as travel, shopping, housework, catering and so on are bound to be difficult and sometimes impossible. Many will need, because of their restricted mobility and their sense of difference, assistance in establishing social contacts and suitable leisure activities.

Finally, all the physically disabled, however seriously or slightly they are handicapped in obtaining education, work, financial security and so on, do have one need in common: the need for understanding and acceptance. For many of the disabled the greatest hardship they suffer is not the frustration and practical problems of lives that are limited by disability but the sense of being in some way segregated from the rest of society. They feel, and in many cases they are, stigmatized, rejected, objects of disgust or pity in other, normal, people's eyes. They feel, in a world which tends to cultivate an oversimplified and idealized image of normality, members of an abnormal, deviant group. This is a very great hardship indeed, and only a very determined effort by society will ensure that the disabled achieve real acceptance and integration. The disabled may sometimes need help themselves in overcoming feelings of bitterness, despair or resentment towards the rest of society, and help in adjusting to and accepting the consequences of disablement without succumbing to a withdrawn resignation or unnecessary isolation.

Provision for the handicapped

The special needs of different categories of the physically handicapped were recognized first by individual philanthropists and this led to the establishment of numerous national and local voluntary organizations aiming to promote the welfare of the disabled. Many of these pioneer voluntary bodies still exist, and they have been joined by large numbers of organizations which have arisen in recent years to tackle the needs of particular groups among the disabled, so that voluntary effort continues to play a major part in meeting the needs of the handicapped. It is only during this century that statutory services have been developed and they came in a very piecemeal fashion. For example, some educational provision was made for the handicapped child once the universal state education system showed the need. Rehabilitation services were boosted by the world wars which greatly increased the numbers of severely disabled persons needing help in adjusting to their handicaps and finding suitable employment. After the Second World War the coverage of the needs of the disabled became fairly comprehensive in scope, although there was no attempt to set up a single department or authority to be responsible for their needs. Instead the various statutory authorities concerned improved their provision, and the voluntary effort was further encouraged. There was not, however, much discussion on the overall needs of the disabled and research into how the needs could best be met was minimal.

Only very recently has there been a development of more comprehensive concern for the disabled. This was precipitated by the Chronically Sick and Disabled Persons Act of 1970. This act generally strengthened and added to the welfare powers of the local authorities. But it had a particularly important clause in section 1 which laid a duty upon the authorities to inform themselves of the numbers of disabled persons in their areas and to make arrangements to meet their needs. In carrying out this duty local authorities have found themselves attempting to assess the numbers and needs of the disabled on a scale never before attempted. The Act occasioned a considerable debate about the needs of the disabled and as a result much publicity was given to their cause and many of their problems received greater critical attention. Particular reforming efforts have been made in the areas of welfare services and of financial provision. The general position remains one of fragmented concern and years of relative neglect of this group cannot, of course, be easily compensated for by debate and good intentions. But at least the issue is now more lively and from 1974 the disabled have had a special Secretary of State, at Health and Social Security, to champion their cause and coordinate provision for their needs.

Medical provision   All aspects of the National Health Service are involved here. The maternity and child welfare service contributes by ensuring early diagnosis of problems, such as deafness, through its system of regular medical examinations and the observation of health visitors. It also plays a prominent part in preventive work through the vaccination and immunization programme designed to give children protection against crippling diseases such as poliomyelitis and the damaging effects which can follow relatively mild diseases such as measles. General practitioners are available to identify problems and refer them for further investigation, and to cooperate with the hospitals for long-term treatment. The hospitals play a major part in treating diseases, in dealing with the victims of accidents, and their rehabilitation. The largest group of persons registered as suffering from general handicap are those who suffer from organic nervous diseases which include polio, multiple sclerosis, epilepsy and so on. Arthritis and rheumatism are prominent crippling diseases. Hospitals provide not only active treatment, by surgery and medicine, but also long-term care of the very severely afflicted, research into the causes and treatment of disabling disease and the rehabilitation of patients, both those recovering from diseases and those disabled by accident. Through such techniques as occupational and physiotherapy, and by the inspired use of artificial limbs, walking aids, powered wheelchairs and so on, many severely disabled persons can be helped to adjust physically to their situation, develop compensatory skills and achieve considerable mobility. Medical rehabilitation units attached to some hospitals specialize in helping the disabled patient maximize his potential and overcome his disabilities and rehabilitation is increasingly seen as an integral part of a full treatment programme. Under the NHS patients can obtain artificial limbs, wheelchairs, special vehicles and various other aids and appliances, while hearing aids and spectacles are available where necessary. The community health service provides home nursing, which can be very useful to handicapped persons, and in some areas physiotherapy classes and transport are available.

Educational provision As was noted in Chapter 4 local education authorities have a duty to provide special schools for numerous categories of children covering both the mentally and physically handicapped. These are the blind, partially sighted, deaf, partially hearing, physically handicapped, delicate, maladjusted, epileptic, educationally subnormal, children with speech defects and the mentally handicapped. In 1973 there were 1421 special schools, including some voluntary ones to which LEAs sent children, and a total of 119098 pupils receiving special education. About half of these children are educationally sub-normal but nearly one-third are physically disabled in varying degrees. Special education is part of a general duty to provide educational opportunities according to age, aptitude and ability for all children in their area. The children are given special education only if they need it, not simply because they are disabled. If they can manage at ordinary schools they do so and are not segregated unless their handicap necessitates this.

The special education provision is currently adequate in terms of numbers of places for the physically handicapped, but it is subject to some confusion as to aim. On the one hand, it is felt that segregation of handicapped pupils is wrong and that they ought to be taught in ordinary schools, albeit with special lessons and equipment, in order that they do not lose touch with ordinary children. On the other hand, it is argued that to maximize the benefits of special education it should become even more specialized with schools focussing on a particular problem and designed and equipped exclusively with this in mind. So in some areas there are experiments in teaching blind or other handicapped children at ordinary day schools, while at the same time separate provision is being made, by voluntary effort, for spastic and for spina bifida cases. In other areas some compromise is reached by a move to build more purpose-built schools in urban areas and to provide transport to them so that more children can receive special education and yet remain at home. Previously many schools were in converted country houses and were of a residential nature.

Meanwhile more thought is being given to providing a varied education within the special schools to meet the needs of pupils who might have a common handicap but whose aptitude and intelligence vary widely. There remains a shortage of real secondary education with opportunities for further and higher education where appropriate, and a shortage of teachers specially trained to work with the handicapped child. There is also a lack of facilities for the multiply-handicapped child. In short, although the provision is there, it needs to be improved in many instances, and in particular made more flexible and sensitive to the needs it is attempting to meet.

A further problem facing the physically handicapped is that of finding employment when finishing education. The Youth Employment Services are responsible for handicapped school-leavers as well as children leaving ordinary schools but clearly the problems faced by the handicapped child are very great and in 1964 a report on the subject* urged that more youth employment officers have special training in the work. The handicapped school-leaver is usually behind his peers in educational attainment owing to loss of education through time spent either under treatment, or overcoming disabilities affecting learning, and he also has special difficulties in finding a suitable job. Even if a suitable job is found he might well have difficulties in getting to and from work. More facilities are needed for further education or prolonged education, possibly at regional centres, to enable young people to reach the general educational standard required for admission to vocational training courses. Many of the younger disabled could make good use of further training if they had a chance to get to it and there is a lack of flexibility in many of the existing special schools which condemn them to operate at a lower level than their abilities warrant. There is also a grave lack of suitable adaptations in many institutions of further and higher education which could enable handicapped young people to benefit from courses for which they were intellectually capable. For example, few colleges are equipped to cope with chair-bound students and only the exceptionally courageous young disabled person can surmount the sheer practical difficulties involved in attending a course.

Employment needs and special provision There are a wide range of facilities available to help the disabled overcome the difficulties they face in finding and keeping suitable work. These are mainly provided under the Disabled Persons (Employment) Acts of 1944 and 1958 and are run by the Department of Employment, formerly the

---

The Handicapped School-leaver, report of a working party commissioned by the British Council for Rehabilitation of the Disabled.

Ministry of Labour. A disabled persons employment register is kept at local offices of the department and the disabled can register themselves and obtain the special attention of the disablement resettlement officer. It is the DRO's job to find suitable employment for the disabled and this entails building up a knowledge of suitable work available in the locality and of sympathetic employers, as well as discussing the individual disabled person's particular problems and inclinations. The DRO can follow up a placement to discuss any problems which may arise between the disabled worker and his employer. The acts also provide for a quota scheme which makes it compulsory for every employer of more than twenty men to take on a quota of at least 3 per cent registered disabled. Further, certain occupations can be designated as reserved for registered disabled. At present only two jobs, car park attendants and lift operators, have been so designated.

The DRO may recommend that a disabled person attend a course at an Industrial Rehabilitation Unit. He will liaise with the medical rehabilitation teams and with the IRUs to know something of the overall picture of the person's employment problem. The IRUs provide short courses for men and women who need help in regaining their confidence and fitness for work. They offer no specific training, but they assess a person's capacity and carry out vocational aptitude tests as well as offering a working routine to re-accustom the disabled person to the normal demands of a working day. The IRUs can, if necessary, be followed by periods of vocational training at training centres and colleges which teach the disabled new skills so that they can obtain work again. If they cannot immediately find open employment the Department of Employment might find them a place in the government-run sheltered employment scheme which is known as Remploy. There are currently over ninety Remploy factories up and down the country which employ disabled people in productive work which earns them a reasonable wage. Remploy factories produce a wide range of goods from kitchen furniture to overalls and they also do contract work for other manufacturers. They are, however, subsidized to some extent, and although the Remploy workers do a full day's work they do not have quite such demands made on them as they would encounter in open employment. A considerable number of Remploy workers do move on to work in open conditions but many remain semi-permanently in the sheltered environment.

The disabled person's employment services are reasonably comprehensive, and the Piercy Report on *The Rehabilitation Training and Resettlement of Disabled Persons* (1956) expressed general satisfaction with the scheme. Nevertheless there is room for improvement and change. It has been argued that the scheme is geared too closely to the needs of the industrial worker who is disabled by accident or disease in middle life and who, following full medical care and rehabilitation, needs help in returning to the routine of work, in adjusting to his disability and in finding new skills within his capacity. The scheme is less helpful for the person who is handicapped from his youth and has no experience of work, and it is not always suitable for those who are unused to and ill-suited for industrial work, for example, those from clerical work or service trades. In particular, the IRUs fail in some cases to rehabilitate the men who pass through them largely because it is not the men's physical disablement but their attitude which is handicapping them in returning to normal working life, and the IRUs are not really equipped to change these attitudes. Their routine is quite demanding and in some ways it expects a level of determination on the part of the rehabilitee which would probably be high enough to get him back to work without a course of formal rehabilitation.

Criticism of the retraining schemes is often that they train men for jobs which are not always available to them and they expect too much mobility from people who have further reasons, in their disability, for being reluctant to move from their familiar surroundings. There has been discussion over whether the DROs should not be better trained, possibly in other social work, in order that they can help the disabled adjust psychologically to their change of status as well as help them in practical ways. There is, too, a need for a greater awareness of the changing demands on the scheme. For example, there are today many fewer tuberculosis cases and far more mentally handicapped persons using the services than there were in the 1950s and this means new demands are placed on the staff which they are not always able to meet.

Financial provision   Obviously most severely disabled persons are likely to have financial problems as they have either a limited earning capacity or even none at all. Moreover disability can itself make extra demands on financial resources because the disabled need extra care and special services. State financial provision for the disabled is very complex and patchy. It has operated on the rather inequitable basis of paying different amounts of money or none at all according to the source of disability rather than its extent. Persons disabled by war or in the armed forces and those disabled at work as a result of injury or prescribed industrial disease have for many years enjoyed reasonable financial provision. Those normally at work but disabled by non-industrial illness have had a limited cover under national insurance and those who have never been in the work force have no special provision but must rely for subsistence on supplementary benefit if they lack resources. The result of this anomalous position has been that the majority of the disabled have had to suffer great financial hardship. Only in the last few years have real efforts been made to equalize provision for different groups of the disabled and there is still a long way to go before we can claim to have adequate social security in this area.

Provision for the industrially disabled comes under the 1946 National Insurance (Industrial Injuries) Act and it is operated alongside the main insurance scheme. Injury benefit is payable to anyone injured or disabled at work regardless of contributions. It is payable for up to twenty-six weeks if a person is incapacitated for work at the rate of £13.85 a week plus earnings-related supplement if appropriate. If incapacity for work continues thereafter a person can obtain invalidity benefit. In addition to benefit to replace earnings there is a disability benefit which is in a sense a compensation for the disability itself. This is paid according to the degree of disability and is £21.80 a week for 100 per cent disablement. Disability benefit continues whether or not the person returns to work and it can be added to for various reasons. Special hardship allowance is payable if a claimant cannot return to his regular job or obtain work of a similiar standard. Unemployability supplement at invalidity pension rates is payable, with increases for dependants, for those who cannot work, together with extra allowances varying according to the age of onset of disability. There is also a Constant Attendance Allowance, Exceptionally Severe Disablement Allowance and a Hospital Treatment Allowance, each payable where appropriate.

The industrial injuries scheme is reasonably fair and sensible. It recognizes the basic need of the severely disabled for maintenance and the special needs for nursing care and attendance and it takes into account the actual disability and, whether or not it handicaps a person in working, it provides some financial compensation for it. Similarly the war pension scheme pays out relatively flexible and generous pensions for disability arising from service with the armed forces or wartime civilian casualties. These schemes are regarded as a model which should be extended to those whose disability is congenital or arises out of non-industrial disease or accident. In contrast to them, cover for other groups, though recently improved, is still only partial.

Insured workers who are off sick are entitled to draw sickness benefits. If they remain chronically incapacitated for work they can now claim invalidity benefit which is at a higher rate as explained in Chapter 2. If the 1975 pensions reform, also described earlier, becomes law, invalidity pensioners will eventually have inflation-proofed, earnings-related pensions. At present, invalidity benefit is now payable at the single person rate of £13.30 per week, with dependants benefits. Invalidity allowances are now added on according to the age of onset of chronic invalidity. These vary from £2.80 to £0.85 and are payable in retirement also.

Those who are not in the work force have had to rely on supplementary benefits for maintenance. In 1974 proposals were made to provide a new non-contributory invalidity benefit and these became law in 1975. They will be implemented by the end of 1975 and will afford an invalidity pension, at 60 per cent of the rate of the national insurance pension, to those people of working age who do not qualify, for lack of contributions, for the present invalidity pension. The majority of those likely to qualify for this new benefit will be currently reliant on supplementary benefit but a small number will not have been previously receiving any benefit. The financial situation of many will not improve, therefore, as most will still need to be supplemented to the usual level, but the new benefit will not be means tested so it is an important extension of rights. A further new benefit introduced is a small invalidity pension for in-patients of working age in mental hospitals. Left out of the 1975 provision were disabled housewives. They are still totally ineligible for help since they cannot even claim supplementary benefits. This is a very considerable hardship because the disablement of a wife and mother is likely to mean, quite apart from any suffering involved, severe financial stress and/or the neglect of home and children. Strong protest was made at this omission and a promise has been made to include disabled housewives in the invalidity pension scheme but probably not until 1977. This promise is welcome but it is still inadequate as the extension is only likely to be towards the very severely disabled housewife who is totally incapacitated and herself in need of care.

Most of the above benefits are towards the maintenance of disabled persons unable to earn. There is now some provision to meet the costs of the disability itself.

In 1970 an Attendance Allowance was introduced which is payable where a person is in need of substantial care and attention. Claims are submitted to an Attendance Allowance Board: The constant attendance allowance is currently £10.60 for those requiring day and night attention, while an attendance allowance of £7.10 is payable for those requiring less attention. This allowance is only available in practice to the more severely disabled. There has been considerable controversy over who should be eligible for the allowance and the qualifying conditions are quite stringent.

Those who are unable to go out to work because they are caring for a severely disabled relative in receipt of an attendance allowance can claim, when the 1975 legislation is implemented, an invalidity care allowance. This will not be payable to married women. Promised from 1975/76 is a new mobility allowance of £4 a week to help people whose walking ability is severely restricted. This allowance replaces the provision of invalid vehicles, which will continue to be available as an alternative, but it will cover those who cannot drive as well.

Children who are disabled cause an extra financial burden to their parents and there have been some moves to acknowledge this. Following discussion of the settlement of private claims for compensation for thalidomide children a special fund was set up to help other congenitally handicapped children. The fund is administered by the Joseph Rowntree Memorial Trust. Set up in 1972 it was established with £3 million to help parents with the costs of some special provisions. It is, however, more in the nature of a charitable gesture than a true extension of state responsibility for this area of need.

The financial hardship of the disabled has recently aroused considerable protest, particularly from among the more articulate of the disabled themselves. A pressure group known as the Disablement Income Group or DIG was formed to campaign for better provision. Disappointment with the 1974 proposals led to the formation of the Disability Alliance, a consortium of groups concerned with the disabled, to continue to fight for a better deal. The ultimate goal of the pressure groups is a universal disability allowance, paid on assessment of disability and not related to age, income, working position or marital status. This would involve some acceptance by society of compensation to the chronic sick and disabled, not just of a responsibility to maintain them. It seems unlikely that this will occur in the near future. Although there are now many benefits available they all have fairly stringent qualifying conditions. Vast numbers of people, especially among the elderly, receive no financial recognition of their moderate disability. Difficulties in defining disability, together with powerful limits on society's generosity towards handicapped groups, seems likely to continue to restrict the scope of financial provision for the disabled for many years to come.

Welfare and personal social services

Local authorities were made responsible for the welfare of the handicapped under the National Assistance Act of 1948. Initially they only had a duty to promote the welfare of the blind but from 1951 they had power to promote the welfare of the deaf and of the general classes of the physically handicapped. From 1960 this power became a duty. The services which the authorities developed for the handicapped followed the model already established for the blind. They included keeping registers; providing help to the handicapped in overcoming the effects of their disabilities and obtaining any available general, preventive or remedial medical treatment necessary; advice and guidance to handicapped persons on personal problems and also on any relevant statutory or voluntary social services; encouragement of handicapped people to take part in social activities and arrangements for voluntary visitors. The services also included practical help by way of aids and adaptations to the homes of the disabled, provision of recreational facilities and travel and holiday schemes. For the blind the services offered included the teaching of Braille and the home teacher of the blind was a specialist social worker who provided this service. For the deaf welfare officers had to provide a communication and translation service where necessary. The pattern of provision was based on a partnership between the local welfare authorities and a wide range of voluntary organizations, many of which acted originally as agents of the local authorities in discharging their responsibilities. Provision for the blind and the deaf was reasonably comprehensive as a result, but often rather isolated, but provision for the heterogeneous general classes of disability was very slight and uneven between authorities.

From the start of welfare provision for the disabled it was recognized that social workers would have a key role to play in putting the handicapped in touch with the provision available. Since 1959, when the Younghusband Report on *Social Workers in the Local*

Authority Health and Welfare Services appeared, there have been systematic training courses for social workers designed to include the welfare of the disabled in their scope. Gradually the idea of welfare work for the physically handicapped has become more professional. Social workers were trained to perceive the psychological as well as the practical problems facing the disabled. Disablement arouses severe anxieties and strong resentment in people. Not surprisingly, a disabled person, suddenly threatened by a role change from head of the family to dependent invalid, can become frustrated and bitter. Social workers should be able to help handicapped individuals express their feelings, adjust to new roles, find new sources of strength and generally cope with the psychological impact of disability.

But the most striking development in welfare services have been on the service delivery side rather than the personal counselling aspect. As with the elderly the aim of welfare became the provision of community care. For the disabled, who by and large do not live in institutions, this meant services to help them become a more effective and integrated part of the community. Community care services included provision of places in occupation centres, development of transport services, encouragment of self-help groups and voluntary action, the provision of aids, adaptations and holiday schemes, and liaison with other bodies such as health authorities, housing departments and social security offices. Local authorities gradually developed such services but the extent of their coverage and the quality of their provision was remarkably uneven. Some authorities maintained up-to-date registers and a full range of services, even if not enough of each, while others barely acknowledged the need at all.

In 1970 there were two major developments. Welfare services for the disabled became part of the new local authority social services departments and the Chronically Sick and Disabled Persons Act was passed. The first meant that the handicapped can now hope to enjoy more generic provision of social work, day care and residential care; a generally extended and localized service; the greater use of home helps and meals services; and the more effective encouragement of community work. The second meant that local authorities became heavily involved in researching into the numbers of disabled and attempting to assess their needs and the public became much more aware of the whole problem of disability.

Research findings in this field have often proved depressing reading. Most local surveys on the prevalence of handicap indicated that existing registers were badly understating it. Surveys of provision have indicated that this still falls short of a desirable level. In most areas there were simply not the resources to meet the expectations which the 1970 act raised. The gap between provision and need was too great to be bridged rapidly and many shortcomings have con-tinued to be revealed by the considerable glare of publicity directed at the local authority services for the handicapped. More seriously there was, and still is, great confusion about need and demand for service. The 1970 act, for example, gave local authorities power to install telephones and television sets in the homes of the disabled but the social services departments have been bewildered by how to decide on priorities between services and as between individuals needing services. In the absence of explicit rationing devices various un-desirable practices which obscure or delay demand have developed. As a result there has been bitter criticism of the local authorities and much disappointment among the disabled and their families. With a more sober view of what is possible local social services departments are now beginning to plan for the provision of more comprehensive and effective welfare services for the disabled. It will take time for the resources and expertise to build up, but hopefully the will and intention to provide a first-class service now exists.

Accommodation

The need for accommodation is a real one, as many of the disabled are clearly handicapped in the ordinary housing situation. At present the local authorities have a duty to provide residential accommodation if this is required for any one who needs it by reason of age or in-firmity. But many authorities lack separate provision for the younger disabled who have to join the old people in residential homes. More separate provision is being provided and many authorities make good use of the facilities made available by voluntary organizations.

As part of the growing concept of community care, spelt out in the 1963 *Health and Welfare: the Development of Community Care* plans, many authorities have recognized that the physically disabled, like the elderly, usually want to retain their independence and avoid entering homes as long as possible. Also, when families are providing care for a disabled relative they usually want to continue to do so if this is at all possible. Local authorities have, therefore, begun to help the disabled in their own homes by providing meals services, domestic help and so on, and in some cases they make arrangements to take the disabled person on holiday to give the other members of the household a break. A further logical step is to consider the provision of specially adapted housing. As mentioned earlier, social services departments can and do make adaptations to premises to make life easier for the disabled person. They can put in ramps instead of stairs, widen doorways, fix rails in bathrooms, lower working surfaces in kitchens, extend tap handles, place electric points within reach, etc. All these things can make life much easier and increase the independence of a disabled person, though clearly it would be simpler in many cases to provide bungalows or flats designed especially for the disabled, in particular those confined to wheelchairs. Some authorities are now doing this, in others ground floor accommodation in blocks of flats are reserved by the housing departments for disabled people. Some areas have made some provision for sheltered housing, that is specially built flats with some services provided by a warden. This is an area of provision which needs urgent expansion, since proper living accommodation is essential for those who are restricted in their mobility. The Department of the Environment issued a circular in 1974, *Housing for People who are Physically Handicapped*, which gives guidance to local authorities on how to assess the need for special housing and advice on provision over such things as design and siting. This should serve as an encouragement to the authorities to develop this important aspect of community care.

The voluntary contribution

Voluntary effort has already been mentioned, but a further comment is required to underline the very large contribution of voluntary agencies in this field. They cannot all be named, but examples of different types of organizations will indicate the scope of the effort. In many aspects of work for the disabled the voluntary agencies were pioneers. Major organizations such as the Royal National Institute for the Blind and that for the deaf provide services on a national basis, aiming to promote better understanding of and provision for the needs of the people they represent. The RNIB produces Braille literature, the talking book library, and educational aids. It runs specialized homes and schools for the blind, such as a social rehabilitation home for the newly blind, and several training establishments, workshops, and a placement service. The RNID runs similar services for the deaf, and in both fields there are large numbers of local and several regional welfare organizations which cater more immediately for the welfare of the blind and deaf of their localities. The Central Council for the Disabled is a coordinating national body which encourages the development of voluntary effort for the disabled, and the British Council for Rehabilitation of the Disabled conducts research into their needs and problems and acts as an information body. There are a large number of societies and associations promoting the welfare of different groups of disabled people, large societies such as the Spastics Society and small spontaneously formed groups of, for example, muscular dystrophy sufferers. Some provide extensive facilities and pioneer new methods of treatment, education and care, others are small social clubs meeting in members' houses for companionship and leisure activities. The range of effort is very great and its contribution extremely important, not least in quickly meeting new needs as they arise, for example, the special needs of thalidomide children.

It was noted at the start of the chapter that not least amongst the needs of the physically disabled was the need for understanding and true acceptance in society. The provision of the services already described is important but this must take place in a society which fully accepts the implications of disability, otherwise the disabled feel they are rejected and discriminated against. Rejection of the physically disabled is not uncommon, for disfigurement and malformation have been associated with evil in earlier, superstitious times. Today few people would openly express any repugnance for the disabled, but many probably feel it, and it is implied, for example, in over-solicitous or embarrassed responses to people in wheelchairs. Many deaf people complain, with some justification, of being treated as stupid simply because they cannot hear, and many crippled people complain of being avoided, or pitied, and rarely accepted for themselves.

There is, therefore, a real need, since this rejection, obvious, implied or felt by the disabled themselves, is a great handicap in their struggle to feel part of the community and to lead normal lives. To overcome this discrimination, public education is needed, and less segregation of handicapped people, so that acceptance is increased by widening the concept of normality. If attitudes are hard to change, it is at least possible to create an environment less hostile to the disabled, for example, by a vigorous campaign to improve access to public buildings. The extent to which society is prepared to divert resources of money and skilled manpower to the treatment, education and care of the physically handicapped is always a telling indication of the extent to which society accepts them and truly cares about their welfare.

Suggestions for further reading

Boswell, D. M. & Wingrove, J. (Ed), *The Handicapped Person in the Community* (Tavistock, 1974)

Hunt, P. (Ed), *Stigma: the Experience of Disability* (Geoffrey Chapman, 1966).

Lees, D. and Shaw, S., *Impairment, Disability and Handicap* (Heinemann, 1974).

Parker, J., *Local Health and Welfare Services* (Allen & Unwin, 1965).

Sainsbury, S., *Registered as Disabled* (Bell, 1970).

Sainsbury, S., *Measuring Disability* (Bell, 1973).

Topliss, E., *Provision for the Disabled* (Basil Blackwell & Martin Robinson, 1975).

10   The mentally disordered

The problem of mental disorder

Mental illness and mental subnormality are grave social problems. Any form of mental disorder is a serious handicap to the *individual* since it can involve great suffering and prevent him or her from living a full and satisfying life. But the *social* problem posed by mental disorder is a particularly awkward one: on the one hand, facilities for care and treatment are necessary and on the other, some form of control may be required, because the more serious states of mental illness and subnormality involve some failure to live a responsible and well ordered life which conforms to the demands of society. For the protection of society some form of control of the mentally disordered is needed and great care has to be taken, since control means some infringement of individual liberty, to ensure that the control is not abused, and also that it does not clash with the other needs for care and treatment.

It would not be appropriate in a book of this kind to go into details over the clinical manifestations and classifications of mental disorder, although the book list at the end of the chapter contains some introductory reading on the subject. But some brief description of the nature of mental handicap is necessary before the social implications, with which we are largely concerned, can be fully grasped.

Mental subnormality is the formal term used for a condition of arrested or incomplete development of the mind, previously referred to as mental deficiency. The term mental handicap is now currently used in general literature and discussion. It covers a very wide range of cases in which some degree of subnormal intelligence is the only common factor. In certain cases, often of severe subnormality, there are recognizable clinical abnormalities as well as low intelligence. These include cases of mongolism, which is a condition caused by a chromosome abnormality and those affected show distinctive 'mongoloid' features from birth; cases where the condition results from disturbances in metabolic or hormonal functioning, for example cretinism; and cases of brain damage at birth. In most of these conditions low intelligence is accompanied by physical handicap, sometimes of extreme severity. In other cases there are no apparent pathological attributes and no clear clinical causes, so the subnormality cannot be deduced from appearance or symptoms and is diagnosed gradually from performance and development in early childhood. In many of these cases, usually referred to as 'subnormals', as opposed to 'severe subnormals', the diagnosis is made on starting school on the basis of educational tests. Because it is hard to distinguish whether poor educational performance arises from low intelligence rather than, for example, severe emotional disturbance, diagnosis and assessment of subnormality cannot always be accurate, and even where it is, doubt remains as to its causes. Parents of low intelligence tend to produce children of low intelligence but it is not clear to what extent this is a result of hereditary factors or the influence of a poor environment lacking in intellectual stimulation. Poverty, deprivation and low intelligence do tend to go together, but it is hard to disentangle cause and effect.

The causation of much mental subnormality is, therefore, obscure, and diagnosis of many cases must rest on social and educational grounds rather than on clinical criteria. Cases range from the severely handicapped person who is physically helpless and incapable of coherent speech to an acceptable, responsible person, earning a living, looking after himself, obtaining considerable enjoyment from life but generally regarded as not very bright. The needs of the subnormal vary accordingly. At one time it was supposed that subnormality was a condition which could not be treated or improved upon. But today some cases are susceptible to medical treatment, and all respond to some degree of training and education. In many cases even of quite low intelligence considerable learning and development can take place although the pace may be extremely slow. Despite this it is fair to say that the subnormality will be a permanent disorder, although the degree to which it handicaps a person will vary over a lifetime.

Mental illness, unlike subnormality but like physical illness, may occur at any stage of life, and may be chronic or acute, mild in form or severe. Some forms of mental illness are linked to organic disturbances, such as brain tumours, others to physical deterioration such as the senile psychoses. But most mental illness lacks any clear physical symptoms and it is recognizable only from the patient's abnormal behaviour. This is why some forms of mental illness are confused with criminality, for example, because they are manifest largely by anti-social behaviour. Some definitions of mental illness beg the question of what constitutes normal behaviour.

It has gradually come to be accepted that there are no clear lines dividing normal and abnormal behaviour only several continua on which people might be placed which shade very gradually from the recognizably normal to the clearly disturbed. Mental illness is a very complicated subject, and pyschiatry, the study and treatment of it, is not yet well enough developed to permit of an easy, agreed classification. To oversimplify, the more obvious (not necessarily more serious) illnesses, generally regarded as 'madness', are often referred to as psychotic disorders. These illnesses are manifest by a wide variety of symptoms from paranoid delusions or auditory hallucinations to total withdrawal from normal communication into silence or bizarre, apparently meaningless jargon, and they have in common some degree of loss of contact with reality. Neuroses, in contrast, are often extreme forms of normal behavioural or emotional patterns, such as depression or anxiety, and the patient usually retains some insight into his condition. Personality disorders are conditions where the individual's whole personality appears to be permanently warped rather than that he is suffering from some actual illness at any given time. But these distinctions are necessarily very loose and easily blurred when actual diagnosis is attempted. They do, however, give some indication of the very broad spectrum of behaviour grouped under mental illness, which tends to confuse public reaction and policy in regard to this problem. Where the mentally ill person is potentially violent the social problem is quickly perceived, where he is withdrawn and depressed the individual agony may be overlooked.

It is not easy to assess the size of the problem that mental disorder poses. Not only does the extent of mental disability vary so widely that it ultimately defies definition, but the extent to which a given mental disability, insofar as it can be measured in clinical terms, handicaps a person, will depend not only upon the disability itself but on the patient's social circumstances as well. This is true of all the special need problems discussed in this book, but particularly so in the case of the mentally ill and subnormal when a breakdown in normal social relationships is often part of the actual disorder. Some examples might help to clarify this. If a child is born with some degree of subnormality of intelligence, and he has parents able to handle the situation calmly, without undue guilt or anxiety, creating a relaxed home atmosphere, encouraging the child's full development however slow it is, making use of the best educational facilities available and providing a stable, reassuring, affectionate home, then such a child might well not be severely *handicapped* by his disability, but grow up relatively independent, sociable and self confident. If on the other hand a child with a roughly similar basic disability is a cause for acute anxiety to his parents, who either make excessive demands on him or over-protect him, and fail to make use of the available care and educational facilities, rapidly rejecting him altogether as unrewarding and unmanageable, such a child might find his subnormal intelligence a severe handicap. The same is true of mental illness. If a person is suffering from a fairly severe mental disorder and has close friends or relatives who sympathize, encourage early treatment and make full rehabilitation possible by providing a tolerant but secure home after hospitalization, then the person has a fair chance of ultimately coping with his illness without it handicapping his general performance in life too severely. But if a person with a roughly similar disability is socially isolated, or his home environment has actually precipitated or exacerbated the illness, then he will be gravely handicapped in attempting to return to normal life after a period in hospital.

Clearly it is not easy to be precise about the numbers of mentally disordered persons who need help, but some figures of those actually receiving care or treatment are a rough guide to the size of the problem. In 1973 there were about 60000 beds in subnormality hospitals and 120000 beds for psychiatric patients in separate hospitals or wards of general hospitals. Approximately 45 per cent of the total number of occupied hospital beds in Great Britain were occupied by the mentally disordered. At the same time roughly 104000 subnormals and 92000 mentally ill persons were receiving some attention from the community services. But a great many people with some degree of mental disability will not be receiving any formal care or treatment.

The needs of the mentally disordered vary as much as their disabilities. Treatment is necessary as far as the advance of medical and psychological knowledge permits. In some cases this will involve hospitalization. If the disorder is severe the patient may also require full care and, very occasionally, physical control. In many cases mental disability will prevent a person benefiting from normal education or from earning a living and therefore special education and financial help will be needed, even if care in an institution or home is not actually needed. For those who are able to work special help might be needed in finding suitable employment or creating a sheltered working environment. But the needs of the mentally handicapped are perceived differently at different times according to prevailing attitudes towards mental disorder and the extent to which it is understood. At the start of this century it was generally accepted that the care and control of the mentally ill and subnormal should be a public responsibility. But little was known of the nature and causation of mental disorder and so provision for treatment was minimal. Informed opinion considered that care was best provided in hospitals for the mentally ill, the old lunatic asylum, and institutions or colonies for the subnormal. Total care within a segregated institutional setting was seen as the best answer to the social and individual problems arising from mental disorder. Today, however, we tend to emphasize the value of care within the normal community wherever possible. This change of policy, which reflects a growing understanding of the nature of mental disorder, and the development of the social services generally, means that we perceive the needs of the mentally handicapped in a different light.

We are now attempting to provide care on a community rather than an institutional basis, on the assumption that it is good to retain the mentally handicapped within the community as far as possible and help to rehabilitate and re-integrate those who have had to go into hospitals for treatment. So today we see the needs of the mentally handicapped as demanding a wide range of facilities: homes, centres, clinics and so forth, linked by a body of trained social workers and placed within a tolerant, accepting and truly caring community.

The mental health service

The main provision of mental health care comes under the National Health Service, which is responsible both for the psychiatric and subnormality hospitals and the community health services, and the local authority social services departments. The local education departments and the Department of Employment also have parts to play, as well as many voluntary organizations concerned with the needs of the mentally ill and handicapped. Up to the creation of the National Health Service in 1946 responsibility for the mentally ill and subnormal was carried largely by the local authorities, which ran hospitals and institutions for the mentally ill, and organized some care and supervision in the community for the mentally subnormal. Their powers were laid down by the old Lunacy and Mental Deficiency Acts, which were concerned with the definition, ascertainment and committal of mentally disordered persons as well as with the administration of the services. In 1948 the National Health Service took over all the hospitals and institutions as psychiatric and subnormality hospitals under the regional hospital boards while local health authorities continued the provision of community services. Meanwhile, in addition to these administrative changes, important developments were taking place within the hospitals as knowledge of mental disorder increased. More patients received voluntary and out-patient treatment and the social aspects of mental welfare were acknowledged. It was increasingly apparent that the old laws, which were particularly concerned with the legal procedures for certification of patients, were obsolete in a period when the medical and social concern for mental disorder was of much greater importance. In 1954 a royal commission was set up to investigate and its *Report on the Law Relating to Mental Illness and Mental Deficiency*, published in 1957, was followed by the 1959 Mental Health Act. This act is the statutory basis for our present mental health service, and it is concerned with definitions of mental disorder, the administration of hospital and community services and the procedures for admission and discharge to and from hospital. It is a lengthy and comprehensive act, and its provision must be looked at in some detail.

The 1959 Mental Health Act   Mental disorder is defined as mental illness, arrested or incomplete development of mind, further defined as subnormality and severe subnormality, and psychopathic disorder. This last category of mental disorder is a controversial one which aims to include those persons who do not appear to have a specific illness but whose behaviour is pathologically anti-social. It is further defined in the act as 'a persistent disorder or disability of mind . . . which results in abnormally aggressive or seriously irresponsible conduct . . . and requires or is susceptible to medical treatment'. Responsibility for the administration of services had been laid down by the National Health Service Act of 1946 but the 1959 Act further defines the powers and duties outlined there. At central government level the Minister of Health was ultimately responsible for the service. This responsibility is now held by the Secretary of State for Social Services who is head of the combined Department of Health and Social Security. This department, which has a Minister of

State responsible for the field previously covered by the Minister of Health, is concerned with the overall direction of the service, and is particularly responsible for the provision of hospital accommodation for psychiatric and subnormal patients. This is now provided by the Area Health Authorities. The responsibility had existed since the NHS Act but the Mental Health Act went further and dissolved the old Board of Control, which had at one stage been responsible for administration of services but had subsequently been reduced in scope to become a quasi-judicial body. The board was dissolved, its functions taken over by the Department of Health and Social Security, and Mental Health Review Tribunals were established for each Health Region to deal with any applications or complaints arising from compulsory admission procedures.

At local level the county and county borough councils had had power under section 28 of the National Health Service Act to provide for the prevention of illness and the care and after care of patients. The Mental Health Act spelt out the functions in respect of the mentally disordered which should be included under that section. These were the provision of residential accommodation, centres for training and occupation, mental welfare officers, the exercise of guardianship and the provision of any other services which might benefit the mentally disordered. The provision of these services was made a duty upon local authorities very shortly after the Act was passed. Following the Local Authority Social Services Act of 1970 responsibility for these services was transferred to the new social services departments.

Regarding admission and discharge to and from hospital the object of the 1959 act was to make admission to a psychiatric hospital as informal as possible. Patients can now be admitted for care and treatment without any formalities and without liability to detention. In some cases, however, compulsory admission is necessary in the interests of the patient and society and the act provides for three types of compulsory admission orders. An observation order lasts for twenty-eight days and a treatment order is for longer periods – one year, then two years at a time – if it is deemed necessary. These orders are made only on the written recommendation of two medical practitioners, usually with special experience and qualifications in psychiatric work. An emergency order which lasts for only three days can be made on the initiative of a relative of the patient or a mental welfare officer with the backing of one medical recommendation. These orders can only be made if certain conditions are satisfied. These relate to the degree of disorder suffered by the patient and extent to which his behaviour warrants detention in hospital in the interests of his own health and safety and the protection of society.

The 1959 Mental Health Act, in essence, laid the emphasis in the care of the mentally disordered upon informality of treatment and admission to hospital and care within the community where possible. It did not actually initiate any great changes in the mental health field, but rather endorsed the developments which had taken place within the hospitals and in the concept of community care and in public attitudes after the Second World War. But it did give considerable encouragement to the growth of services, particularly community services, and to the improvement of public understanding of the complex problems arising from mental disorder, and it was, accordingly, widely welcomed.

Hospital provision

Looking now in more detail at the actual provision of services, hospitals are still, for both psychiatric and subnormal patients, of the utmost importance. It is clearly necessary to have centres for the active treatment of the mentally disordered and for the long-term care of the chronic cases. The actual form that hospital provision should take is still very much a controversial issue. Our present psychiatric services have to work with many large old hospitals which were built during the nineteenth century as lunatic asylums. These are generally considered unsuitable for modern treatment of the mentally ill, but so long as demand for beds continues to rise it is difficult to do more than try to upgrade and improve them. However, during the 1950s the introduction of new drugs, popularly known as tranquillizers, brought about a 'therapeutic revolution' within the hospitals. It became possible to control, if not cure, the symptoms of many psychiatric disorders by the use of drugs, and therefore it was possible to discharge patients after fairly short stays in hospital, continuing their drug therapy, in many cases, as out-patients. This made possible an open door policy in the hospitals both in the sense that patients were out quickly and that within the hospital a more relaxed atmosphere could be achieved as drugs controlled excessive behaviour of severely disturbed patients. The coming of new and dramatic types of treatment, however, only heightened rather than diminished the controversy over the old hospitals. Some people argued that it should be possible to run down the existing hospitals almost entirely, replacing them by short-stay psychiatric units at general hospitals and long-term care within the community. It was certainly true that many of the older hospitals needed running down. They were often structurally unsound and costly to maintain, hard to staff because of their physical isolation and far too big. Above all, the hospitals greatly impeded the patients' treatment and rehabilitation because they were the objects of contempt and fear in the eyes of many people in society – the high walls and isolation symbolizing that the hospitals held society's rejects. The patients felt stigmatized and ashamed upon entering them. Moreover, their vast size, around 2000 patients in many instances, together with their past custodial traditions, tended to produce a form of organization that was rigid and hierarchical and threatening to the patient. It was argued that a lengthy period within a mental hospital could itself produce symptoms of social disorientation, apathy, loss of initiative and so on, which amounted to institutional neurosis, an illness which could persist long after the original illness had cleared up. In short there were considerable grounds for arguing that the old hospitals should go.

There was, however, no agreement over what should replace the mental hospital. Against those who advocated the end of any separate provision for the mentally ill were those who argued that some patients could best be helped by care within specialized institutions provided these were not huge, obsolete in design and rigidly organized. Some patients truly did require an asylum from the strains of the world. For their best treatment a place with grounds for walking in, and space to develop occupational therapy, away from the atmosphere prevailing in a well run general hospital, was probably necessary. Indeed, some psychiatrists had developed a whole approach to treatment in which the hospital itself, the total environment, was organized therapeutically. Various names are used, such as administrative therapy, but the technique is most generally referred to as the therapeutic community approach. It aims to involve all the members of the hospital, doctors, nurses, ancillary staff and the patients themselves, in the healing process. These ideas, pioneered in this country by Maxwell Jones, amongst others, were in part the outcome of studying the mental hospital as a social organization. It was seen that the traditional system, in which the patients were at the bottom of a communication and status hierarchy and were denied autonomy or participation in the running of the institution, exacerbated the problems many patients had, or produced the characteristic 'institutionalization' which was to be deplored. Further, it was seen that the same institution which was so damaging could be therapeutic if it was organized deliberately to foster social confidence and responsibility in the patients. In other words, many mentally ill people were defined as ill because of a breakdown in their social relationships; drugs might relieve some of the symptomatic tension but help was needed to remedy the causes by encouraging patients to participate in a community which improved the capacity of all its members, patients and therapists, to relate in a meaningful way to one another.

It is obvious that those doctors who practised the therapeutic community approach had doubts about the complete integration of psychiatric patients into general hospitals, which must perforce be organized and run in a radically different manner. The more telling critics of those who advocated the end of the mental hospital argued on a more immediately practical basis. They pointed out that large numbers of patients, especially amongst the old, were unlikely ever to be really fit to enter normal community life, and that for many others the community care services were still woefully inadequate. However much one wanted to run down the existing hospitals, demand for beds would keep them open unless patients were quite unscrupulously discharged while still needing considerable care.

It can be seen that the role of the present-day psychiatric hospital is a very controversial issue, one in which official policy is very much involved. The 1962 Hospital Plan aimed at a reduction in hospital beds for the mentally ill of roughly one half the total, together with a move towards more provision within general hospitals. Since the publication of the plan, numbers have been reduced, though not at the anticipated rate and only in the face of strong criticism from some quarters.

Despite the controversy it is becoming increasingly clear that there is no real ground for argument between hospital and community care and that they should complement rather than rival one another. A blurring of the distinction between hospital and community medical care is one of the aims of the 1974 reorganization of the health service. There is a place for psychiatric units at general hospitals and for separate, perhaps isolated specialized hospitals where a therapeutic community approach can be implemented, and for effective community mental health services. A flexible array of service is called for that can meet the very varied needs of different

G

groups of the mentally ill. Meanwhile the present position is that we have a few small modern psychiatric hospitals, able to make good use of a wide range of therapeutic techniques, some psychiatric units at general hospitals, many doing excellent work with the short-term cases, rather too many old, large institutions and the beginnings of day hospital care and community psychiatry.

Many of the large old psychiatric hospitals have succeeded in making good use of their facilities, in breaking down the whole organization into smaller, semi-autonomous units, and in ensuring generally that the emphasis is placed on the treatment and rehabilitation of the patients rather than simply on their care and custody. But some hospitals and some wards of other hospitals have failed to cope with the demands of too many chronic patients, and lack adequate staff, money and enthusiasm to prevent them becoming mere dumping grounds, especially of the psycho-geriatric cases. Shortages of professional staff are very severe in some places and over-reliance on foreign staff is not always in the patients' best interests in this area where personal communication is so important. So despite much that is progressive and encouraging in psychiatric hospital provision there is still much room for improvement.

There has been some of the same controversy over the role of the subnormality hospitals but on the whole the issue is clearer: subnormality hospitals ought to be replaced by smaller units, ranging from hostels and homes to specialist hospital units able to provide intensive nursing for the severely handicapped minority. The whole idea of large hospitals for the handicapped is indefensible: there is evidence that many patients do not need, and do not receive, treatment, and a hospital routine is wholly damaging to them. There has been an undercurrent of anxiety about the subnormality hospitals for many years and lip service has been paid to the idea of replacing them with community hostels. But in recent years criticism has become intense. In 1967, following allegations of ill-treatment of patients, an official inquiry was instituted into the conduct of certain members of the staff at Ely Hospital, Cardiff. The report of this inquiry found that some ill-treatment of patients had indeed taken place but also it found much to criticize in general: lax standards of nursing, inadequate medical care, poor conditions and bad management. Other highly critical reports were subsequently published following inquiries into conditions at subnormality hospitals. In all these inquiries the main conclusions were that abuse of patients where it existed was the consequence of acute shortages of staff, overcrowding and lack of facilities for patients and that general neglect pervaded in subnormality hospitals. As a result of the first inquiry the Hospital Advisory Service was set up in 1969 to visit, assess and criticize hospitals constructively and to help bring about improvements in their general standards. A further outcome of the scandals was renewed pressure to replace outmoded hospital care by care in the community. This culminated in the publication of a White Paper in 1971, *Better Services for the Mentally Handicapped*, and a renewed commitment to community rather than hospital provision. Meanwhile, however, since subnormality hospitals cannot be closed down overnight, there is a need for constant vigilance to avoid abuse and for much greater resources to be channelled to them. For many mentally handicapped people the hospital will be their sole environment for many years to come and it would be tragic if hopes for alternative provision were allowed to stifle any change or improvement within existing hospitals.

Community care

It is currently the accepted policy in the mental health field to provide more services in the community for the mentally ill and mentally handicapped. Provision of community mental health is divided between the health authorities and the local social services departments so there is no one, coherent, community mental health programme to describe. Community care is partly a reaction against a policy which overemphasized hospitalization and saw the institution as the answer to most social problems. It is also a practical answer to the difficulties of continuing to maintain and staff isolated institutions in an age when few people are prepared to make a career in residential work. More positively, it is the recognition that all people should have the right to live within the community, contribute to it and benefit from it, and simply be a part of it, except in very rare circumstances. The hospitals themselves make a very important contribution to the care of patients in the community. Most have out-patient clinics which enable many patients to be treated while remaining in their own homes. In some areas day hospitals are run for patients who need considerable care but who can still return home at night. In others, there are facilities for helping patients to bridge the gap between total hospital care and complete independence in the community. Hostels or discharge units within the hospital grounds enable some patients to go out to work daily and have a relatively autonomous and responsible life, while retaining some of the security of the hospital environment. Rehabilitation is fostered by developing workshops at hospitals which aim to give patients confidence in their working ability and experience in social relationships and responsibility. Psychiatric social workers work with doctors obtaining reports on the patients' home situation and helping patients retain contact with the outside world. They can provide a vital link between hospital and community although many hospital based social workers have traditionally concentrated on team work within the hospital setting.

The bulk of community care work is now the responsibility of the local authority social services departments. They took over the statutory duties and provisions of the old mental health departments. This has to some extent retarded the development of a community mental health approach because social services operate on an area team basis with a broadly generic approach to social work and the more specialist mental welfare work has inevitably suffered from this. New links need to be forged to develop a combined approach to community mental health in which both health and local authorities play a part. The new health care planning teams should facilitate this but meanwhile the NHS side remains hospital dominated and the local authority is struggling with more social care responsibility for both mentally ill and handicapped than it can at present cope with. What follows is a picture of optimum local authority provision. The actual situation is one of wide variation from authority to authority.

Social services provision for the mentally disordered is through the full range of social work, day care and residential services. Social work help is vital in all community care services and can be part of the total treatment programme for the mentally disordered. Social workers are needed to help the families of mentally handicapped persons as well as the mentally ill or subnormal themselves. A family with a severely subnormal child will have many problems and the social worker can help to overcome these. The parents may be tied to the house, they will usually be financially disadvantaged, the mother is likely to be overworked, trying to cope with the duties of a normal housewife and mother and the special needs of a helpless child. Moreover, the family may feel very guilty at having produced a handicapped child, over-anxious about the child's future, worried about their feelings towards him or the effect on other children in the family. In both these areas a social worker can help. She can ensure that the family receives all the practical help available from statutory and voluntary bodies, perhaps the use of a day nursery, better housing and so on, and she can help to reduce the parents' guilt and anxiety and encourage them to be accepting and relaxed towards their handicapped child, and neither reject him nor over-protect him. Of particular importance is the social worker's con-tribution in helping parents make full use of the facilities offered by the mental health services. Parents may feel suspicious of these, or resentful, and will need help in using them to best advantage. Similiarly, the families of the mentally ill need help in sudden emergencies when they cannot cope with a very disturbed relative, general help in understanding and accepting the nature of the dis-order and support if they have to make difficult decisions such as agreeing to the compulsory admission of a severely disturbed relative to hospital. The strain of caring for a disturbed relative can be considerable and the need for an understanding and reliable friend to talk to and share the anxieties with, is often very great.

Social workers can also help the mentally disordered themselves. For example, they can help a subnormal in the difficult school-leaving period, encourage him to find work, keep an eye on his activities if he is trying to take on too much, or is getting into bad company, help him to cope with family relationships and to become as independent and content as possible. They can help the mentally ill, encouraging them to seek treatment when necessary, supporting them in the trying period after hospitalization, encouraging their efforts to find work, lodgings and companionship despite their disabilities.

Day care facilities for the mentally handicapped include what used to be known as adult training centres. These vary considerably in the facilities provided for the handicapped adults. Some are pur-pose built and others are in makeshift premises. Some are glorified minding places while others attempt to develop social skills, en-couraging handicapped people to learn about such things as public transport and the handling of money. Some concentrate on occupa-tion and are run as industrial units. In some cases the day centres genuinely act as training centres preparing those who attend for eventual independence while in others the aim is simply to offer a daily change of environment and relief to their families for those too handicapped ever to lead independent lives. Day centres for the mentally ill are a more recent innovation. They exhibit similar variations in aims and activities. Despite variations, however, the day care facilities are enormously important and can make a tremendous difference to the lives of the mentally disordered. Provision is still far from adequate in this field.

Domiciliary services can help the handicapped and their families, especially when the mental disability is accompanied by physical handicap. In the area of social help and rehabilitation a variety of clubs can also help both subnormals and the mentally ill to make social contacts and gain the confidence to reintegrate themselves into society.

Residential provision is extremely important and at present totally inadequate in quantity for the extent of the need. Local authorities have been providing hostels since 1959 but only in very small numbers. They were envisaged as an alternative to full institutional care but tended to be used by those within the community who had hitherto remained dependent on family or friends. For the subnormals especially many hostels were welcomed by relatives who, often at great cost to their freedom and independence, had struggled to keep a close relative out of a stigmatized hospital, but were prepared to see them safely cared for in a local purpose built home. So new provision uncovered new need and the numbers actually in hospital did not get any less particularly among the mentally handicapped. The 1971 white paper promised expansion here but the building programme needed is huge and economy cuts repeatedly reduce it.

Hostels for the mentally ill are needed no less desperately than those for the handicapped. They have an important part to play in providing care to those discharged after long stays in hospital and also in providing temporary homes and rehabilitation to those trying to re-establish themselves in the community. There has been much confusion over their exact role for many years but clearly there is room for a variety of provisions: some rehabilitative, some permanent, some intense therapeutic communities, some experimental homes for disturbed adolescents. It is good that the demanding job of running hostels for the mentally ill and the mentally handicapped, together with other provision of residential care, should now be recognized as an important aspect of social work, for much needs to be done in this field and many able people need to be recruited for the work.

In addition to casework, day care and homes there is still the elusive community in community care. Ultimately the family and neighbours care and cope and so need understanding and support from those without such burdens. We have still a long way to go before the public really accepts the mentally ill and handicapped without fear or resentment and with genuine respect and trust.

Other services for the mentally ill and handicapped

Education also has an important role in the mental health field. It provides special education, as noted in Chapter 4, for educationally subnormal children and for those previously described as ineducable. In some instances it provides child guidance clinics, which offer psychiatric and social work help to children who have behaviour problems or manifest symptoms of mental disorder, and to their parents. It offers special education facilities for children who are maladjusted, usually those referred by the child guidance clinics. The Department of Employment is responsible for the provision of services under the Disabled Persons (Employment) Acts. These include keeping registers of the employable disabled, the provision of disablement resettlement offices and running of industrial rehabilitation units and government training centres. These services are available to the mentally handicapped where this seems suitable and both subnormals and mentally ill persons can be helped in finding and keeping suitable employment in open industry, and given courses of rehabilitation. Most of these services were designed primarily to help the physically disabled, especially those who had been in work but who were unable to continue as a result of a crippling accident or disease. Since the 1959 Mental Health Act the services have increasingly extended their help to the mentally disabled. Finally the DHSS takes responsibility for meeting the financial needs of the mentally handicapped mainly through the national insurance and supplementary benefits schemes, although there is virtually no help available at the moment to the *families* of the mentally handicapped despite the costs to them of caring for severely subnormal or disturbed relatives.

The voluntary contribution

Mention must be made, albeit briefly, of the voluntary effort in the field of mental welfare. The National Association for Mental Health, founded in 1946 as a result of the amalgamation of several older bodies concerned with the welfare of the mentally handicapped, is an important coordinating body for research and propaganda now known as MIND. It aims to spread information on the principles of mental health, promote research and aid experimental projects in the field. It also promotes local associations, runs training courses, and various homes, schools and publications. The NAMH has been of enormous importance in widening understanding of the social aspects of the problem of mental handicap and stimulating progressive work in this field. The National Society for Mentally Handicapped Children likewise aims to publicize the needs of the handicapped and encourage better provision for them. Where statutory provision is inadequate, the society aims to supply aid directly through its local branches.

There are many other bodies concerned with the mentally ill and handicapped. The Richmond Fellowship, for example, provides hostels, run as small communities, which offer a secure environment, an opportunity to regain confidence in social relationships and an enthusiasm for living, to a limited number of mentally disturbed adults and young people. The Rudolf Steiner schools are renowned for their fine educational work with the mentally handicapped. Various colonies exist under voluntary foundation where the mentally handicapped can live useful and happy lives, to some extent sheltered from the outside world, but permitted a considerable degree of independence and self-determination.

Voluntary effort is prominent in work with special problem groups, alcoholics and drug addicts, for example, where it both innovates and complements statutory provision. Disillusionment with traditional psychiatry has led to much interesting experimentation with small communities using new forms of therapy and espousing new philosophies and explanations of mental illness. Many new and fascinating approaches to care and treatment can be worked out in the voluntary setting and provide a base for constructive criticism of statutory provision and a fund of enthusiasm for change. In this as in so many fields of social service the voluntary contribution can be great both in a pioneering sense and in the steady provision of research, public education and good facilities.

The problem of mental disorder is a considerable one, both numerically and in the range of needs which it gives rise to. Partly because the public has been forced into awareness of the grave social problem the mentally disordered can present, the services are relatively well developed. But much still needs to be done to recruit staff at every level, consultant psychiatrists, mental nurses, social workers, teachers, etc, to up-grade the hospital and residential facilities particularly for the chronic cases, and to make available a more flexible range of services to those individuals or families who are coping with mental handicap without resort to hospital care. Last, but by no means least, much still needs to be done to improve public attitude and understanding, both to aid prevention of mental disorder, and to help the mentally handicapped overcome their disabilities and find a tolerable place in society. Only then could we hope to have both a community mental health programme and meaningful community care.

Suggestions for further reading

Barton, Russell, *Institutional Neurosis* (John Wright, 1960).

Bayley, Michael, *Mental Handicap and Community Care* (RKP, 1973).

Bone, M., Spain, B., & Martin, F. M., *Plans and Provisions for the Mentally Handicapped* (Allen & Unwin, 1972).

Clarke, A. M. & Clarke, A. D. B., *Mental Deficiency: The Changing Outlook* (Methuen, 1974).

Hays, Peter, *New Horizons in Psychiatry* (Penguin, 1964).

Jones, Kathleen, *A History of the Mental Health Services* (RKP, 1972).

Jones, K. & Sidebotham, R., *Mental Hospitals at Work* (RKP, 1962).

Jones, K. *et al.*, *Opening the Door* (RKP, 1975).

Jones, Maxwell, *Social Psychiatry* (RKP, 1952).

Jones, Maxwell, *Social Psychiatry in Practice* (Penguin, 1968).

Martin, Dennis, *Adventure in Psychiatry* (Cassirer, 1962).

Morris, Pauline, *Put Away* (RKP, 1969).

Rehin, G. F. & Martin, F. M., *Patterns of Performance in Community Care* (Oxford, 1968).

Roberts, Nesta, *Mental Health and Mental Illness* (RKP, 1967).

Stafford-Clark, D., *Psychiatry Today* (Penguin, 1952).

Tizard, J., *Community Services for the Mentally Handicapped* (Oxford University Press, 1964).

Todd, J., *Social Work with the Mentally Subnormal* (RKP, 1967).

Part Three
Some general issues

11 Financial and administrative issues

Clearly the social services which exist to cope with social problems of various kinds are large organizations. It follows that they absorb a large part of the national resources in terms of money and man- and womanpower, and that the financing, staffing and administration of them is very complex. This chapter will draw attention to some of the more obvious financial and administrative implications of the social services.

Public expenditure on the social services is considerable: the money spent in recent years has approached an amount equal to one-quarter of the Gross National Product. Social service costs account for over half the total amount spent in the public sector. In 1973/4 total public expenditure amounted to £33 825 million and expenditure on social services including housing amounted to £17 866 million. Collectively, the social services are by far the largest item on the analysis of public spending, and single services such as social security and education head the list. Expenditure on education in 1973/4 was £4571 million while that on military defence was £3420 million and the whole of law and order, including the police, cost £971 million. As the breakdown shows social security now dominates the list and the personal social services use up a relatively modest amount.

Table 1: *Public expenditure on social services in 1973/4 (United Kingdom)*

	Millions of pounds
Social Security	5559
National Health Service	2926
Education	4571
School Milk & Meals etc.	78
Personal Social Services	547
Housing	2360
Environmental services	1828
Total	**17869**

Source: *National Income and Expenditure 1963–1973*, HMSO, 1974.

Public expenditure generally, and expenditure on social services in particular, have been growing rapidly in this century. At the turn of the century an amount equal to only approximately 2·5 per cent of the GNP was spent on social services, by the outbreak of the Second World War the percentage had risen to between 11 and 12 per cent and since the war it has risen to nearly 25 per cent. This is a trend which is sometimes viewed with alarm, but then at the turn of the century social services were virtually non-existent and the social problems of poverty, sickness, squalor, ignorance, child neglect and so on were barely recognized, let alone tackled in any effective manner. Once the problems are recognized and society accepts some degree of commitment in the battle against social evils then, naturally, public expenditure is bound to rise and there is nothing inherently wrong in this situation. If we want to build a better society we have to be prepared, collectively, to pay for it.

Nevertheless a high level of public spending does raise problems especially when the general economic situation is bad. The money has to be raised by the government and this means high taxation levels which are always unpopular. Moreover, it means a greater proportion of national income is in the hands of public officials, and care has to be taken to ensure that it is used well. A demand for a reduction in public expenditure can mean that the weaker services suffer because they lack powerful support groups.

It is sometimes argued that the country 'cannot afford' such a high level of social service expenditure. But social services are not a luxury: any complex industrial society must expect to spend a lot on social services. Although their output cannot be easily measured like the productivity of a factory, nevertheless they are vital to the nation's economy as well as to its stability and happiness. Education, which is a major item of social service expenditure, is clearly a necessary investment if the nation is to have the trained people who are as necessary to production as raw materials. Where the services cannot be seen as making an economic contribution they are clearly improving the quality of life for members of our community, which is presumably the ultimate goal of raising productivity and standards of living anyway.

Where does the money for our social services come from? Excluding the voluntary contribution element, the public money is raised by taxation and by contributions for specific services, by local rates and by charges for some services. The bulk of the money is raised by taxation, and is part of general revenue.* Total taxation in the United Kingdom amounted to nearly £25 000 million in 1973/4. Income tax raised nearly £7300 million of this, while profit and corporation tax amounted to £1870 million; taxes on expenditure, including VAT and customs and excise, produced roughly £6500 million and motor vehicle licences £500 million while revenue raised from national insurance contributions amounted to nearly £4000 million. In addition local government raised £2600 million on rates for financing local services. So the government raised some 33 per cent of current revenue from taxes on income and 29 per cent from taxes on expenditure. Payment of contributions to national insurance and towards the cost of the NHS and to the redundancy fund amounted to nearly 18 per cent of revenue and taxes on profits and corporation tax raised roughly 8 per cent of the total. As we have seen just over half of public spending goes on the provision of the social services discussed in this book, the rest on defence, roads, employment, law and order and so on. So the level and type of taxation and the direction of social policy are clearly interconnected. If the policy is to develop statutory services that are organized and paid for collecttively, then public expenditure is likely to rise. If services are reduced in scope and operate on a more selective basis, that is only to serve certain categories and income groups within the population, then public expenditure could be reduced and if it rises or falls this will naturally affect taxation.

Some social economists argue that while social services such as health and education are clearly necessary, and a sound investment, they need not be financed entirely or even largely by public expenditure. If more were financed privately then taxation could be reduced and incentives increased accordingly. Some of the arguments and assumptions used to support this line of thinking are misleading. It is, for example, often assumed that one sector of the community finances social services while other sectors benefit from it; that, in effect, social policies contribute to a massive redistribution from rich to poor. Apart from the arguments for or against such a redistribution it is clear from the breakdown of taxation given above that this is greatly oversimplified. Taxes are not raised only or largely from any particular section of the community: everyone is subject to the expenditure taxes, on consumer goods, entertainment and so on, and all the working population pay the national insurance

*The disparity between income from taxation and public expenditure is accounted for by rents, interests and dividends and changes in financial assets.

contributions. Indeed, studies of who pays what and who benefits from the overall redistribution of income involved in the social services have revealed remarkably little difference between the percentages of income left to family units of different income levels after they have paid taxes and received benefits in cash and kind. Where there is some clear redistribution of income, as a result of social policy, it is between families with children and the single and childless. Families of virtually all income levels do definitely get more out of the social services than they pay towards them and towards other public expenditure. A further misleading assumption is that taxation levels are dangerously high in this country. Comparisons with other countries of roughly similar social and economic development do not bear this out. There is little evidence that the economy 'cannot stand' the present level of taxation or public expenditure just as there is little evidence that some people are forced to pay for services from which they do not benefit.

Nevertheless, it should be clear from these few facts that the financing of the social services is likely to cause political controversy. The social services are a large item of expenditure, and the financing of them affects everybody. They are, accordingly, the object of much heated discussion by economists and politicians as well as by social scientists. Decisions about them, their expansion, scope and so on, have such important economic implications that they cannot be, and are not, taken simply in the light of our knowledge of social needs. Social services set out to meet needs, and to solve problems, but they can also be used to bring about changes in the social and economic structure of society. For example, the social security system exists primarily to prevent poverty. But it could be used as an instrument to achieve greater equality in the distribution of the nation's resources. If it becomes a major instrument for redistribution of income then it is involved in the political arguments over equality and social justice as well as in meeting basic need. So the economic implications of social services can go far beyond the immediate practical ones of financing the current provision. Social policy is ultimately economic policy and cannot be viewed satisfactorily in isolation.

The few points mentioned here are, however, very rudimentary and the full study of the economic implications of social policy is a field on its own. While students of social administration need not all become social economists they must, at least, be aware of the broad economic background to all social action.

Administrative issues and the making of social policy

Like finance, the administration of the social services is a vast topic which can only be touched on here. Something of the administrative framework of the social services will have been gleaned from the preceding chapters on particular social problems and the services created in response to them. Both central and local government are involved in the provision of services. Central government administers some services directly, such as social security, while others are a local responsibility, exercised under varying degrees of central government control.

We have looked at social problems and services mainly as they exist at the present. But most studies of social services tend to look at them from the historical or development view. This is certainly extremely illuminating. Apart from being a fascinating story, a study of the development of social policy explains much of the present confusion of services, particularly of their administration. Few things are consistent in the social services: each service tends to be financed differently; the statutory basis, the context of the central/ local government relationship and distribution of control, and the underlying social principles all tend to vary from service to service. The history of social action accounts for this to a considerable extent and all students of social administration must turn to some reading of the development of social policy.

The historical view is noted here because it is particularly relevant to the current administration. Central administration has been continually adapting itself to the new demands made upon it by the creation of services. Local administration, as we know it today, was itself the product of social action to a considerable extent. Local government had to be devised in order to operate local health, welfare and housing policies, and local government today is still very strongly involved in the social service area.

Central government is primarily concerned in the working out of policies, and only partially in the direct administration of services. The formal expression of a social policy is the legislation that creates services to tackle social problems. So the National Health Service Act, the Children Act, the National Assistance Act, etc, are statements of policy. They are passed by Parliament and are subject to debate and discussion, and reflect party political views on the nature of social problems. They are drafted by permanent government officials who are concerned to seek out expert opinion on the issues

H

in question. Moreover, in many instances major acts follow the recommendations of the reports of royal commissions or inter-departmental working parties and so forth, which try to discover the facts about a particular problem and seek advice and opinion from all the people concerned. For example, the 1959 Mental Health Act, which consolidated the present policy of informality of treatment and community care for the mentally disordered, followed the report of the royal commission on mental illness and mental deficiency in 1957. The commission, which itself included a wide range of eminent people involved with the existing mental health services, took evidence from local authority associations, hospital authorities, government departments, professional bodies, the major voluntary organizations in the field and 250 individual persons concerned with mental health work.

The passing of an act, though, is not the end of policy making. The actual administration of services authorized by acts is a process which itself contributes to the making of social policy. On the whole acts, despite their legal precision, are fairly loose guides when it comes actually to setting up the services they authorize, and the decisions made by the administrators of services at central or local level are of great importance in shaping the provision.

It is not always clear who actually makes important decisions. At both central and local level of government there are elected repre-sentatives and professional administrators and other staff. The balance of power between the Houses of Parliament and the Civil Service and between the local council and the town hall officials is never clearly defined, and can vary enormously in different areas and functions. Similarly, it is not easy to generalize about the balance between central and local government when services are administered locally, and that between administrators and professionals within a particular service is equally obscure and variable.

The context of central/local government relationships is of particular interest to the student of social administration as many of the social services are a local responsibility. The statutes of Parliament legally determine the shape of local government and the scope of its action. They impose certain duties, to provide education or residen-tial accommodation, for example, and give local authorities certain powers, to provide other services, such as day nurseries or family planning. In many areas of social policy, local authorities have been given permission to provide a service, then, when the need for the service has been clearly demonstrated and resources for it are more widely available, the provision has become mandatory. For example, local authorities had power to provide a service promoting the welfare of the general classes of the physically handicapped from 1951, and in 1960 the provision of this service became a duty. Through the statutes central government can ensure some uniformity and minimum provision in certain areas of social need and encourage flexibility of provision, within certain limits, in others. In some areas acts lay down clear central powers of control, the 1944 Education Act, for example, but in others the main statutes merely indicate by a variable form of words that the Minister or Secretary of State of the central department is in the position of ultimate authority and will provide a general overall guidance. Some acts require the local authorities to submit schemes and plans for approval by the central department in order to carry out their powers and duties. Subsequently the central department can influence events by issuing circulars, guiding, instructing or exhorting the local authorities, and it can carry out inspections, exercise confirmatory and adjudicatory powers and so forth. But the major instrument of central control is probably finance. The central government raises the bulk of the money used by local authorities for education, welfare, housing, etc. Clearly the departments intend to keep a check on how it is spent, and they can even check the local authorities' own financial manoeuvres by the powerful instrument of loan sanction.

Central government, then, exercises considerable power, not only over the services it administers directly, such as social security, but also over those which are the local authorities' own concern such as education or personal social services. There has been much anxiety about the role of local government in the last decade. Some critics have considered it to be too weak and idiosyncratic to carry responsibility for major public and social services. Local responsibility has meant variations in standards which some regard as scandalous, especially since the bulk of local authority finance comes from central revenue. Other critics have felt that local government was a crucial democratic check on central bureaucratic control, that needed to be strengthened and given more autonomy and independence and greater say in determining local affairs. Ironically public interest in local government in terms of voting levels at local elections and knowledge of local provisions does not indicate a very healthy democratic base. Nevertheless local government does have a powerful democratic role as well as an important executive one and much thought and effort has recently been given to improving and updating the system to improve its performance.

Major criticisms of local government were directed towards its financial weakness; the relatively poor calibre of staff for the demanding professional work of modern services; public apathy and lack of interest; the inexcusable variations in local standards of basic provision; and the anomalous division of the country into authorities based on old historical boundaries rather than demographic and economic realities which resulted in a population range of from less than 50 000 to over a million. Response to this criticism has been a spate of reports and committees culminating in radical reform and reorganization of the system. The Maud Report on the *Management of Local Government* published in 1967, and the Mallaby Report on *The Staffing of Local Government* published in the same year, were both concerned with internal organization. The Maud Report considered there was urgent need for reform and change within local government. It recommended, in brief, that council members confine themselves to debating broad issues of social policy leaving the professionals responsible for the detailed execution; that there should be fewer committees and a management board of about seven council members supported by a corresponding group of chief officers to make most policy decisions on a corporate basis. Officials should be clearly headed by a chief executive, the chief officer to the management board and head of the small team of officers who should work closely together. Regarding central/local relations the report urged that local authorities should have greater powers to determine their own structure, organization and policy and should be put in a stronger financial position. Finally the Maud Report made some interesting suggestions for improving the image of local government and its relations with the public. The Mallaby Report commented in detail on staffing problems and examined ways of improving the quality of staff in local government.

The more fundamental issue of the size and nature of local government was investigated by a Royal Commission which issued its report in 1969. The Royal Commission proposed radical changes to create a reduced number of unitary authorities, responsible for the provision of all services, to replace the existing pattern of 172 first tier counties and county boroughs and over 1200 second tier district authorities. These recommendations were not accepted in total, and alternative proposals were put forward in a series of White Papers which involved a more complex change. These proposals became law in

1972 and new councils were elected in 1973 becoming fully operative in England and Wales from April 1974.* The position in England is now that in all areas there are two levels of administration, the county and the district authority. There are thirty-nine counties, usually the product of a merger between the previously independent county and county borough. These are responsible for the provision of education, personal social services, roads and planning. The smaller district authorities have responsibility for housing and environmental services, and some developmental control. In addition there are six metropolitan counties divided into a number of districts which are each responsible for all the main services. The metropolitan counties are based on the major conurbations and were modelled on the pattern already existing in London. London government was reformed in 1965 to create 32 London boroughs with, roughly speaking, responsibility for most main services.† In Wales there are now eight counties each with a number of district councils.

Local government reorganization coincided with NHS reorganization, coming into effect from April 1974. It has resulted in a smaller number of major authorities, a total of 116 for England and Wales, and a surge of interest in local democracy. Inevitably the actual process of reorganization has proved expensive and time consuming and extremely unsettling for many staff. It is hoped that in time the benefits of the new look will begin to show in improved performance and service provision.

Some critics of the inequitable distribution of services and resources and of the poor quality of much local provision have argued that the fault lies not only with local government but with antiquated central government organization. Some argue for much greater administrative decentralization, to remove the 'Whitehall bottleneck' and urge that central government gives more thought to the formulation of clearly defined policies so that local authorities can be safely left to get on with the job within a clear policy framework. Some changes are, of course, taking place, such as the move towards regional housing offices that are able to deal with many of the problems of local housing authorities and maintain a uniform national policy without recourse to Whitehall for every small detail. But very much more could be done. At present, as indicated, central policy is often very vague and control over detail too meticulous. So

*Similar proposals were made for Scotland, and implemented at a later stage.
†The Inner London Education Authority complicates the picture and the Greater London Council has some overall responsibility.

local authorities make their own policies which sometimes leads to conflict with central government and always to diversity of provision. Up to a point diversity is good; local government would be useless if it did not permit some variety and flexibility in provision. Needs vary locally and what suits one area might not be right for another. The advantages of diversity, however, cannot ever outweigh the need for a uniform minimum standard, which is not the same as rigid uniformity. At present diversity all too often means that some areas are simply deficient in provision, particularly for minority groups such as the disabled. So it is not easy to strike the right balance between over-control by central government and the consequent stifling of local initiative, and too little check on local action resulting in serious neglect of some social needs.

Concern for the preservation of local democracy is linked to the revival of strong interest in regionalism and the nationalist movements. A royal commission accordingly examined the working of the constitution and its report, the Kilbrandon Report, was published in 1973. The Kilbrandon Commission rejected suggestions for complete regional self government but recommended considerable devolution of power. It proposed a transfer of legislative power to new assemblies in Wales and Scotland along with wide executive responsibilities. For England a series of regional councils was proposed mainly for advisory and coordinating purposes. These proposals are still under consideration but if they were implemented they would have a considerable impact on the administration of social services and on the development of social policy.

Local government finance is currently being studied by the Layfield Committee which hopes to find ways of strengthening the financial position of local authorities. Their reliance on rates is problematic and the central government's contribution, through rate support grant, is controversial.

The protection of the rights of the citizen in the face of ever-widening government powers must also be considered. Two points only are noted here very briefly. First the existence of administrative tribunals, operating in the areas of national insurance, family allowances, supplementary benefits, rent assessment and mental health. These listen to appeals against official decisions by people who dispute the official interpretation of their rights. Tribunals are an essential check on the powers of officialdom but at the moment they do not work as well as they should to ensure justice in welfare provision. Too often their proceedings are confusing to the ordinary person and the quality of judgement at such tribunals is reportedly inconsistent. Their procedures should be made more intelligible and appellants need more support and help in putting their cases.

The other important check on bureaucratic dominance is the provision of a high level complaints procedure through ombudsmen. In 1967 a parliamentary commissioner was established to investigate complaints passed on by members of Parliament about maladministration in government departments. This was extended later to cover the national health service and as part of local government reform a commission for local administration was established in 1974. Local commissioners can now accept any complaint from members of the public about maladministration in local government. These measures are an important extension of consumers' rights and some safeguard in individual liberty.

It can be seen that there are many issues on the administrative side which affect the social services. Relatively clear ones arise from the structure of central and local government, their internal problems and their relations with one another. The issues which stem from the nature of administration itself are more complex. It is becoming increasingly clear that this whole process, defined in one recent study as 'a set of procedures for uniting those who control the resources necessary for certain tasks (the members of a municipal council or the shareholders in a company, for example) with those who use the goods or services produced from these resources (pupils, patients, tenants, customers, etc)',* is itself part of policy making. More attention is therefore being given to it. In short, it is not enough to discover needs and legislate to meet them: the actual means by which our legislative intentions are put into practice are of equal importance. In previous centuries needs were recognized reluctantly, if at all, when social problems were of such proportions they could no longer be ignored. Measures to deal with problems did not always meet the underlying needs: sometimes they ignored them, sometimes they reflected total ignorance of them. The classic example of this is the Victorian Poor Law which tried to deal with the very obvious social problems of poverty which led to high costs and corruption in the administration of relief and social unrest. But it did not deal with the reasons why people were poor, it did not get down to the underlying needs of the sick and disabled and fatherless and so on. Today, however, we make a conscious attempt to identify and

*D. V. Donnison, V. Chapman *et al.* in *Social Policy and Administration Revisited* (Allen & Unwin 1975).

measure social needs and to evaluate our services which try to meet them. The attempt is conscious, but it is still imprecise and unsure. Social administration itself is, as Chapter 1 explained, the academic study of social needs and problems and social policies and services. But it is a comparatively new, still fairly rudimentary, study.

Some formal, institutionalized ways of identifying need have been already indicated. The government can initiate enquiries by means of royal commissions, interdepartmental committees and so on. It can also carry out research, through the Central Statistical Office and the Government Social Survey, into a variety of topics. The government also finances research bodies and institutions, such as the Medical Research Council and the Social Science Research Council, which themselves initiate, approve and finance research topics into particular problems.

In addition to this research and inquiry, the government collects, through the various central departments, statistics and information relevant to the social services and attempts some forward planning on this basis. Collection of statistics, such as the housing returns, has always been part of the central department's work, but the more specific information currently requested which can form part of long-term planning is a relatively recent development.

Outside the governmental research activities major work is carried out by the universities, through departments of social administration, sociology, applied social science, social medicine and so on. Research bodies such as the Institute of Community Studies, the Centre for Environmental Studies and the Centre for Studies in Social Policy, also conduct inquiries into both social needs and the working of social policies. Large numbers of voluntary agencies also have a research function, sponsoring or undertaking research into needs. The big research foundations such as the Rowntree or Carnegie Trusts are of vital importance in financing much of the work carried out by universities or other organizations.

Finally a good deal of inquiry is made at a local level by local authorities or local voluntary bodies, attempting to assess a particular problem in the immediate area. Much of this small scale enquiry is the result of the curiosity and the anxiety of the people currently working in the social services, whether statutory or voluntary. Part of the agitation for reform of local government concerned ways of improving this research function. Most local authorities now have a research and intelligence unit to collect and analyse information on their areas. Social services departments have a particular concern to research into needs on a more systematic basis. Following the establishment of statutory links between the reorganized Area Health Authorities and local authorities, through the joint consultative committees, there have been some experimental attempts to establish joint social information units so that health and local government can share data collection and analysis.

Research is increasingly concerned with evaluation of services as well as assessment of need. Elementary evaluation involves collecting data on service provision but examining the effectiveness and efficiency of services is a more demanding task. Evaluation is still rudimentary but it is increasingly accepted that with services as massive and costly as those described we must develop techniques for measuring their impact and comparing the success and failure of different approaches.

Staffing

The growth of the social services to cope with existing social problems has necessitated the development of whole new professions to cope with the work. The more sophisticated and specialized health care is, the more people, and the more different kinds of people, we need to provide it. So the medical profession has developed, not only in numbers, but into increasingly numerous specializations. It is backed by research chemists, biologists, etc, and teams of professional and general ancillary staff such as radiotherapists, as well as by nursing staff. This growth and specialization means that more and more people must be found to staff the hospitals and clinics and rehabilitation units, and that they have to be trained. Training schemes, recognized qualifications, professional institutes, salary negotiating machinery and so on have to be developed. This is so in every field of social service: we need teachers, social workers, housing managers and town planners, etc, to fill all the posts, and training establishments and programmes to produce the trained people. At the same time we need increasing numbers of civil servants and local government officials to administer the services and social science research workers to continually investigate needs and assess the provision.

Staffing becomes ever more complex. Any change of policy has enormous repercussions on the staffing situation. For example, the Mental Health Act indicated the need for much greater expansion of the community care services for the mentally ill and subnormal. But

H*

workers for these services cannot just be recruited from the general population, because they should be trained to do the specialized work with which they are faced. So, ideally, we need to forecast changes in demand for personnel, particularly highly trained professional personnel, in order to have time to develop and staff more training institutions – medical schools, professional social work departments and so on – and then to recruit suitable trainees and give them the necessary education and training before we try to implement a major change in policy. In the social work field this was strikingly acknowledged by the Curtis Committee on the care of children, which recommended the setting up of a Central Training Council on Child Care before it published its final report recommending radical changes in the organization of the care of deprived children. Courses for training both residential and casework staff were organized rapidly so that when the 1948 Children Act came into force some influx of trained staff was anticipated to man the new children's departments. But such instances are, unfortunately, rare: usually the need for staff is allowed to reach alarming proportions before steps are taken to boost the recruitment and training programmes. The need to plan for staffing as well as financing of the social services does not apply only to the professionals: we cannot decide to double our output of houses in order to deal with housing shortages and obsolescence without regard to the manpower resources of the building industry as well as to the availability of suitable architects.

Many factors affect the supply of workers to various aspects of the social services. The numbers involved are large – nearly a million people are employed by the National Health Service alone – and the social services have to compete with industry, trade, other public services and, significant especially with doctors at the moment, the attractions of work abroad. It is impossible to give a meaningful figure of the total personnel employed in social services as definitions vary too much, but the social services are now an important sector of employment, and many of the personnel involved require training. Developments within the social services often mean that more training is needed at the same time as more staff and it is difficult to decide on priorities. If one wants to increase the output of trained social workers or teachers one can reduce the length of their training and dilute its standard but this will conflict with the need for more specialized staff, for the more specialized needs and problems which better services reveal.

Broad demographic factors can affect particular services sharply.

For example, the change in the sex ratio of recent years has resulted in fewer women remaining single, but single women were heavily relied on in certain social service fields, as teachers, social workers, nurses and residential staff; a shortage could have a marked effect on the staffing position in these fields. Clearly the need to recruit more men or take account of the problems facing the married woman who wants to return to work is vital. But while salaries are low in many social services as compared to work in industry, many men are put off, and the employment of married women creates problems which society is not yet willing to face – the need for day nursery accommodation, for example, (which itself creates a further demand for staff), and for a more relaxed public attitude towards the working mothers.

The overall employment situation is, of course, a key factor. Many social service jobs tend to be filled when unemployment increases the attractiveness of the more secure job which local government, for example, affords. But the motives which attract people to work within a social service are as variable as the jobs themselves and generalization is not very useful. Instead, particular professions try to improve their individual staffing position. The Mallaby Report on the staffing of local government has already been mentioned. Other committees have considered the staffing of different services, and the recruitment and training of, for example, social workers, health visitors, residential care workers, nurses and teachers. These reports assess the situation for a particular service or type of trained staff and usually make recommendations for improving quality and supply.

The overall position on staffing tends, therefore, to defy much generalization beyond that the social services need a very large number of trained people, and that by and large they fail to get them. Shortages vary somewhat over the country. London and the South East tend to have more psychiatrists, teachers, medical social workers, etc, than other regions. Some areas, particularly in the North, are very short of staff, and make do with less well-trained people. Throughout the social services there is a need for more and better training and better distribution and deployment of staff. The rate at which people can be absorbed into the public social service sector, or are willing and able to enter it, does not depend on the social planners alone, and there is much scope for improvement in our whole approach to manpower and womanpower problems.

Suggestions for further reading

Bell, Kathleen, *Tribunals in the Social Services* (RKP, 1969).

Brown, C. U. & Dawson, D. A., *Personal Taxation, Incentives and Reform* (PEP, 1969).

Brown, R. G. S., *The Administrative Process in Britain* (Methuen, 1970).

Buxton. R., *Local Government* (Penguin, 1973).

Culyer, A. J., *The Economics of Social Policy* (Martin Robertson, 1973).

Donnison, D. V. & Chapman, V., *Social Policy and Administration Revisited* (Allen & Unwin, 1975).

Forder, A., *Social Casework and Administration* (Faber, 1966).

Forder, A., *Concepts in Social Administration* (RKP, 1974).

Glennerster, H., *Social Service Budgets and Social Policy* (Allen & Unwin, 1975).

Griffiths, J. A. G., *Central Departments and Local Authorities* (Allen & Unwin, 1966).

Prest, A. R. (Ed), *Public Finance in Theory and Practice* (Weidenfeld & Nicolson, 1974).

Warham, J., *Social Policy in Context* (Batsford, 1970).

Webb, A. L. & Sieve, J. E. B., *Income Redistribution and the Welfare State* (Bell, 1971).

Social Trends (HMSO, 1970–4).

The Maud Report, *Management of Local Government* (HMSO, 1967).

The Redcliffe-Maud Report, *Report of the Royal Commission on Local Government in England*, Cmnd 4040 (1969).

The Williams Report, *Caring for People, on staffing residential homes* (1967).

The Younghusband Report, report of a working party on *Social Workers in the Local Authority Health and Welfare Services* (HMSO, 1959).

The Aves Report, *The Voluntary Worker in the Social Services* (1969).

Community Work and Social Change, report of a study group on training, set up by the Calouste Gulbenkian Foundation (Longmans, 1968).

12 Problems of policy in the social services

In the first chapter we looked at some definitions of social administration and saw how the subject had gone beyond a straightforward description of the social services. Social administration is now the study both of social problems and of the social action which arises in response to the problems. Next, we examined some of the main problem areas and some of the major social services which are the outcome of society's response to these problems. We have not however looked closely at some of the main areas of conflict in social policy. We have, in fact, tended to assume that the recognition of social needs and problems means that some positive action will be taken to deal with them, and that the main area of action with which we are concerned is the action of the state, the collective response of society, expressed through the growth of statutory social services. Mention has been made of the voluntary contribution, which has been and still is of enormous importance in meeting need, and is likewise a collective response to social problems albeit on a much smaller scale than the major statutory provision. Little mention, however, has been made of the private enterprise activities which are also concerned with social needs – the private schools, the insurance companies and so on – or of the growing sector of occupational welfare, that is health schemes, pension funds and the like provided by firms and employers for those who work for them. The balance, however, between public, statutory provision and private and occupational provision for the income maintenance, health, education and housing needs of individuals, is a highly controversial one. There are those who argue that having recognized needs the state should provide for them universally, and those who argue that the state should only provide for people who, for various reasons, are unable to provide for themselves. This argument affects several major areas of social policy, and is currently of some importance.

The debate about universal or selective provision of services mainly affects the basic social services. There is general agreement, on the whole, that groups with special needs should receive attention and welfare services provided collectively by society, although there is still some argument even in this sphere. The main argument concerns social security, health and education, but the debate is one which concerns all the aims of social policy and the assumptions behind the concept of a 'welfare state' – the unofficial title which was given to the collection of social services described in this book. The term 'welfare state' implies that the state has assumed responsibility for the welfare of its individual members and for the removal of, or at least the tackling of, the major problems of society. The state does indeed concern itself with most of the major aspects of life and of human need. It does try to see that people can work, be educated, live in pleasant houses and environments, have medical attention when they require it and receive care and help if they have special handicaps. To that extent it is a welfare state. But at no one time did society adopt a blueprint for a welfare state or suddenly decide to deal with social problems. The historical development of social policy shows that we concerned ourselves about different problems at different times and acted upon them in different ways, and only gradually did the scope of state concern for welfare become reasonably comprehensive, and almost consistent in its approach.

The origins of our present social services go back well into the nineteenth century. They are inextricably bound up with the social and economic effects of the industrial revolution. But the phrase 'the welfare state' has only been used since the Second World War; a result of the remarkable spate of post-war social legislation, creating some new social services and involving the wholesale reorganization of others. One of the more significant features of this reorganization was that, in some of the major areas of social policy, the principle of universal provision was firmly adopted. That is, that services should be available to all, provided by the community as a whole for the benefit not just of certain needy sections of society but for all its members.

The principle of universality was not, of course, applied in every sphere of social action. It was never, for example, assumed that the state should actually provide houses directly for everyone, although the public housing sector has grown considerably since the war. The principle was adopted, however, on a wide enough scale for it to mark a new era in social policy, and to occasion the widespread use of the term 'welfare state'. It is seen most clearly in the National Insurance Scheme of 1946 which brought basic income maintenance services to all members of the community irrespective of income levels or occupation; in the National Health Service Act which in 1948 made free comprehensive health care available to everyone; and in the 1944 Education Act. None of these acts initiated new social services, but they were all a significant point in the development of social policy because of the universal scope of their coverage.

Since the war the universal principle has been attacked, and a strong body of opinion has argued for a reduction in the role of statutory provision and financing of social services. This is not to say that people argue that the social problems of poverty, sickness, education and so on should not be tackled. Simply, that there are different ways of tackling them from those we have adopted. We have a considerable consensus of opinion that problems should be eradicated, but considerable diversity of opinion regarding the best way to do this. It is always easier to agree on negative goals than on positive ones. This is primarily because, as the previous chapter indicated, social services are sufficiently important in financial and administrative terms and in the ways in which they affect the social and economic structure of society that they can themselves bring about radical change in social organization. It is hardly surprising that there is considerable argument over what form this change should take, and how far it should be allowed to go.

To take an example, already raised in this book, of social security provision: we can agree that poverty should be eradicated from a civilized, relatively affluent society – but some people feel that the state should go further and use social policy as a means of effecting greater equality, while others accept the existing unequal distribution of resources as natural and necessary for a thriving society.

Those who currently attack the present provision of relatively universal social services do so on several grounds. One is that it is too costly. To find the money for universal services means very high taxation levels which reduce incentives and slow down economic expansion and productivity generally. Furthermore, universal provision means that some people receive benefits, in cash or kind, which they do not need, which is wasteful, while others cannot receive adequate services because the provision is too thinly spread. Too much state provision, it is claimed, undermines the stability of the family: a man does not have to feel so responsible for his family if he knows that the state will help him with the costs of their keep and education and medical care, etc. Moreover, it undermines an individual's independence and freedom if he is not able to choose how he spends his money or what kind of service he gets. If the state takes his money by taxes and provides free medical care, he has no choice over how much of his income he wants to spend on medical care, rather than on holidays, for example, and he has no say in the type of care he is offered. On the other hand if he buys the services he requires, in a free market, he exercises choice and can influence the provision by taking his custom to the most satisfactory service. How much more important, it is argued, that an individual should exercise choice in welfare, which is so fundamentally important to the quality of life, than merely in consumer goods.

The arguments range from practical ones of cost to ideological ones about freedom. One outcome of such arguments is a demand for more selective provision. That is, state services should be available only to those who cannot afford to buy their own security, health care, education and so forth. The opponents of these views, who defend universal state provision, argue that selectivity would mean a double standard of service in areas which they agree are of fundamental importance. The wealthy would buy a better standard of, say, medical care, than the poor could obtain from the statutory service. This is partly because the relatively wealthy would be financing the state provision as well as their own private provision and they would not want to see it on an equal standard, otherwise there would be no incentive to people to improve their position and buy better care. Better quality resources would tend to accumulate in the private sector: private education, for example, would command better facilities and attract better teachers than a state system that was merely provided for a minority. Furthermore, two services, public and private, would tend to exacerbate the divisions of society and perpetuate inequalities. There are enormous practical difficulties in distinguishing the recipients of state care from those who look after themselves. For example, it is necessary to have some kind of means test to determine eligibility for free, state provision, and it has not yet been proved that a means test can operate without stigma and humiliation for those who have to admit their relative poverty. Means tests are clearly a disincentive to some people who find that if they earn more they lose their entitlement to free provision and so are hardly better off. Arguments about the effect of state welfare on family responsibility are dismissed on the grounds both of historical evidence and current sociological investigations.

The essence of the argument of those who oppose selectivity of provision according to income is that it implies some basic justice in the initial distribution of resources. Within a free enterprise, capitalist society resources are very unevenly distributed. If social services accept this by providing only for the poor, this implies that the poor in some way are poor because they are of less value in society. They earn less because they contribute less. But many people feel passionately that the inequalities do not reflect worth in any way, but are the consequence of a complicated economic system that tends towards social injustice, and that social policy should attempt to cancel out this injustice and provide greater equality for all members of society.

So the basic ideological conflict tends to be between 'freedom' and 'equality'. Universalists argue that freedom is illusory for it is only the freedom of the better off – the poor cannot choose. Selectivists argue that inequality is natural and desirable, and the state should only intervene to the extent of preventing gross exploitation and suffering but must not interfere with man's natural inclination to better himself.

In practice, of course, there are different arguments appropriate to particular services. For example, it is pointed out that education should be a state service because it is provided largely for children who cannot themselves exercise choice. Health care is regarded by many as a commodity which cannot be equated with consumer goods and left to the market, as demand is too unpredictable. There are many variations of the basic universality/selectivity conflict: in some cases one can argue for state provision but private finance, or state finance but private provision: services provided and financed by the state versus services provided and financed by the private sector is only one possible model.

These arguments are currently prominent for several reasons. The main one is probably the economic situation which has caused grave anxiety and led to measures ranging from devaluation of our currency to the monotonous regularity of credit squeezes. In times of financial stringency it is clear that public expenditure has to be closely scrutinized, and as social service expenditure accounts for over half of total public expenditure, there is a ready demand for a cutback on spending on the social services. At the same time those working in the services, or doing research into social problems, have revealed startling deficiencies in the existing provision: poverty exists despite the social security system; the conditions in some primary schools and hospitals are appalling; community services are inadequate and wildly understaffed. We are therefore plainly in a dilemma: more money should be spent to improve the provision yet we feel we must cut back on public spending. It is hardly surprising that many people have seen the answer to this dilemma in greater selectivity; provide more for the minorities in greatest need, and let the rest take care of themselves. This line certainly has an appealing simplicity. But, as we have seen, it ignores the practical and ideological problems that selectivity gives rise to. On the other hand, it could be argued that if more needs to be spent in total on, let us say, health care, it would not make much difference if less came from the public sector and more from private spending. So one could argue for greater public expenditure on essentials such as medical care and reductions in the private sector generally, in the interests of national economy. But this is always a politically awkward solution and therefore rarely canvassed.

Different political parties quite rightly reflect different views of social organization and social justice. The Conservatives are traditionally concerned with upholding individual rights in a free market system while Labour advocates a socialist conception of collective action for the common good. So trends towards greater selectivity or universality in social policy are primarily determined at a political level. Selective measures proliferated after the change of government in 1971 – family income supplement and rent allowances are two examples of selective measures introduced thereafter – and much official emphasis was placed on finding ways of maximizing the take-up of means tested benefits. Since the government changed again in 1974 the trend towards selectivity has slowed down but not really reversed. There is still a lack of commitment to a truly universalist approach and a tendency to cloud the ideological argument with economic distractions.

Frustration at the lack of conviction among political leaders has been partly responsible for a growing disillusionment with a social reforming approach to social policy generally whether it be on universal or selective principles. For many people the last decade has been one of repeated and mounting evidence of the failure of the welfare state. Few people could dispute the fact that poverty and inequality continue to exist, that the education system operates most inequitably, that the health service and the personal social services are woefully short of resources and that housing continues to be dominated by shortages and squalid conditions. Much of the evidence for this depressing picture is the consequence of the more systematic study of the scope and effect of social provision which has occurred as social science has developed. Descriptions of unmet need and inequitable provision are not always placed in an historical perspective and might be less depressing if they were. Nevertheless the shortcomings of the social services are now so well documented that there is no room for easy complacency. The assumption that once society has identified need it will exert itself to meet it, cannot any longer be made. Moreover we have good reason to doubt that a piecemeal reform of the most glaring faults of our social conditions will ultimately lead us to a more just and egalitarian society: in many ways basic inequality has increased rather than decreased alongside the growth of social services.

The result of contemporary evidence of failure in our welfare system has been great disillusionment with social service provision. Many critics would reject the whole pragmatic, reforming approach which has dominated the growth of British social services and seek more radical solutions. One group of critics argue the case for an extreme selectivist approach, a return to much greater reliance on the market and on self help. Another group argue that socialist welfare cannot co-exist with capitalist economy: so long as our society is based on economic competition there must always be failure and it is useless to seek to eradicate failure without changing the basic system. These critics see social welfare programmes as largely irrelevant or palliative, taking the edge off despair for the most deprived but effecting no radical redistribution of resources or of power. Their solution would be a drastic change in the social and economic structure of society without which, they claim, all social policies are bound to prove ineffective. There are also those who argue that the development of social services has resulted in an over-professionalization and bureaucratization of life which has disastrously reduced people's capacity for self reliance and meaningful community activity. Unhappy at the whole development of a technological age they seek solutions in self-supporting communities and small mutual aid groups avoiding large organizations and formal institutions for social welfare.

Such extreme responses can be appealing but neither *laissez faire* nor revolution nor the drop-outs' nostalgia for a more peaceful age are very realistic solutions. We have developed social services which have achieved some valid improvement in the quality of life for many people. Insofar as they fail to achieve better standards and greater social justice how can we realistically set about improving them? Despite the prevailing climate of gloomy criticism and cautionary notes some important and hopeful trends are now discernible. It cannot be too often stressed that social services must be flexible and new approaches must be tried to maintain the dynamic of social policy.

To look first at the ideological base. Some of the arguments for universal or selective social provision have been discussed. It should be clear that these issues are not just practical ones but also concern values. It is tempting to reduce the debate to over-simplified economic terms or to insist that it is merely a question of social engineering and not of social ideology. But fundamentally social services concern people both as individuals with needs and as a group, a society with common problems. If we wish to preserve real humanity and afford the maximum dignity to all people then the collective provision of universal social services is not only meaningful but essential. Put in other words, social policy and administration is the study of our struggle to eradicate not only poverty and ignorance but also humiliation and discrimination from our society. Our social services have evolved for many different reasons but they are based on certain values, or value assumptions, about collective action and social equality. If these values are eroded too far, in the name of economy or expediency or some illusive freedom, then we will no longer have social services as we currently understand them but only relief measures and safety nets. So it is important to hang onto the principle of universality. Nevertheless its failure, in an unequal society, to work well for everyone is a grave problem that must be tackled. It is at this point of dilemma that we have moved on to argue for positive discrimination, the direction of additional resources to areas or categories of special need on a basis of universal provision. The late Richard Titmuss put the case for positive discrimination most clearly and forcefully in *Commitment to Welfare* in which he said: 'The challenge that faces us is not the choice between universalist and selective social services. The real challenge resides in the question: what particular infrastructure of universalist services is needed in order to provide a framework of values and opportunity bases within and around which can be developed socially acceptable selective services aiming to discriminate positively, with the minimum risk of stigma, in favour of those whose needs are greatest.' He goes on to argue: 'In all the main spheres of need, some structure of universalism is an essential pre-requisite to selective positive discrimination; it provides a general system of values and a sense of community; socially approved agencies for clients, patients and consumers, and also for the recruitment, training and deployment of staff at all levels; it sees welfare not as a burden but as complementary and as an instrument of change and, finally, it allows positive discriminatory services to be provided as rights for categories of people and for classes of need in terms of priority social areas and other impersonal classifications.'*

Moving on from ideology to practice some efforts have been made to shift social policies in this direction. The establishment of educational priority areas as advocated by the Plowden Report was a pioneering example. Extra resources were channelled to areas or institutions with special needs. EPA schools receive higher equipment grants and teacher quotas, priority capital allocations and staff salaries. In 1969 the Local Government Grants (Social Need) Act was passed which created the Urban Programme. Urban aid is administered by central government and it is designed to direct additional resources to urban areas of special social need. Resources are directed towards local projects with a wide range of objectives run by local statutory or voluntary bodies with particular emphasis on multiple projects. Initially aid went to the improvement of nursery facilities, children's homes and community centres. Priority in selecting projects is now given to those which cater for newly perceived community needs or utilize new methods of meeting needs rather than those which add to existing facilities. Urban aid is not a large programme in financial terms but it has encouraged an imaginative and flexible approach in dealing with old problems and directed more resources to areas of extreme urban deprivation. The Community Development Programme, of which more will be said later, was also launched in 1969 and in 1972 the 'Six Cities' studies were inaugurated. These latter projects were experimental action and advisory programmes for the improvement of the environment taking a total approach to problems of declining towns and inner city areas. The legislation for Housing Action Areas is a further example of positive discrimination, an attempt to concentrate help on particular areas with special housing problems.

Positive discrimination has not been operated on a large scale to date but it remains an important ideological step forward out of the universal/selective dilemma and a practical tool of great potential for evening-up standards of provision and directing extra resources to the most deprived without undue stigma. Moreover from the

*From 'Welfare State and Welfare Society', Chapter XI of *Commitment to Welfare*.

tentative practical measures taken so far much can be learnt for future policy on a larger scale.

Another essentially practical response to the problems of the social services has been to seek solutions in organizational change. The argument here is that services would work well if they were better managed, if they were planned ahead, if priorities were allocated on an informed and rational basis, if different services coordinated their activities better. To improve service delivery we have recently seen the total reorganization of personal social services, the National Health Service and local government. There has also been considerable interest in many services in better management and in social planning. While administrative reform alone cannot make amends for inadequate resources or inequitable provision it should help to provide more efficient organizations for the operation and delivery of social services. In particular the greater emphasis now placed on research into need and the monitoring and evaluation of provision should provide at least the information base on which to act more decisively in future. Moreover although reorganization has moved us towards even larger public bodies, with their inherent problems of impersonal, bureaucratic control, we are increasingly seeking to understand the operation of such organizations. The hope is that if we understand the behaviour of organizations and people in them we will eventually find the ability to control them to our own advantage and direct them more effectively, to fulfil our social aims.

Improved administration and social planning can, of course, only lead to improved services insofar as there is knowledge and agreement about the aims and objectives of social provision. There are real conflicts here, between objectives of social control and social change, for example, but at least these are becoming more explicit. And the final, most encouraging response to the generally accepted failures in service aims has been a renewed concern to ask the recipients of services what *they* want and will accept. Greater participation of people in running their lives is now seen as a desirable end in itself. It is also recognized that only by involving people more in plans and provisions can there be any hope of real success in social policy. Participation was encouraged formally by the Skeffington Report *People and Planning* issued in 1969. This suggested that people should be better informed about policies and plans and services and be allowed to express views on them and have their views taken into account. People must feel that they can take an active part in social welfare, contributing as well as benefiting and having some say in the decision making process. During the 1970s interest in participation has grown sharply. Involvement is now seen as the key to more effective social change. It is certainly a crucial factor in avoiding the growing alienation between people and authorities that militates against success.

Participation has already been felt in the housing and planning areas. The new social services department's interest in reciprocal services and accessibility show their concern for participation. The Community Health Councils are a gesture to public involvement in the delivery of medical care. In many other areas participation is still little more than a word. This is partly because involvement needs time and confidence as well as opportunity. It is necessary to create new openings for participation within the social services and to develop people's capacity and confidence for involvement. In this last area community work has a major part to play. As evidence has accumulated on bad housing conditions, poverty and urban deprivation there has been a growing suspicion of explanations of social pathology that locate the blame with the inadequacy of the individual rather than with an unjust or ill-organized society. And there has been a logical growth of interest in forms of social work which attempt to generate positive community action to secure better social conditions and greater participation of local people in decisions which affect them.

The burgeoning concept and practice of community work has borrowed its ideas and methods from the ex-colonial community development movement and the American civil rights and war on poverty experiences as well as from the more traditional community organization approaches that indigenous councils of social service or university settlements have practised. The methods employed by community workers vary as much as their locations and are still in rather an experimental stage. Where a lack of a facility or service is regarded as the major issue then the worker will tend to be engaged in getting the existing services to function better and might work largely with officials or council members. Where the people's sense of apathy and impotence in the face of authority and bureaucracy is regarded as most crucial, then the worker will want to maximize the involvement of the people and even encourage direct action, such as rent strikes, demonstrations or the forcible occupation of vacant premises or waste land, as much for the effect such action has on community morale as for its more tangible gains.

In 1969 the government gave official sanction to the community work approach by establishing the Community Development Programme initially in only a few selected areas of high social need. The project aimed to 'find ways of meeting more effectively the needs of individuals, families and communities, whether native or immigrant, suffering from many forms of social deprivation'. It is also hoped to do this by methods which helped people to achieve greater involvement and self-determination. The projects are largely financed by central government but are run in cooperation with the local authorities who actually employ the community workers. After starting in four pilot areas the CDP is now widening out in scope, but it is still experimental in method.

The CDP has been criticized by some observers as too hesitant in approach, particularly because it places the workers within the local authority setting and emphasizes their role in encouraging cooperation between the social service departments and achieving change by working for the consensus of the authorities and organizations involved. Nevertheless the projects have begun to clarify some very important issues and point the way for future developments.

The basic assumptions underlying the CDP were that social problems were concentrated in certain areas and could be solved by a combination of better coordination of services and the mobilization of self help and mutual aid. The project teams are now abundantly clear that the symptoms of disadvantage they are dealing with are not caused by concentrations of problem families but by structural constraints. Industrial decline has created a general depression of the areas and vulnerable groups are left behind as the skilled and mobile move out in search of better opportunities. They have noted that the key issues of the deprived areas are unemployment, housing and income rather than poor social service facilities or low take-up of benefits. Much can and should be done to improve the personal social services and educational facilities of deprived areas, to stimulate involvement and encourage neighbourhood projects. But the key issues are beyond the present scope of the project teams. There is an urgent need, if the deprived are to be helped, to create work opportunities and to find better ways of guaranteeing income than the present multitude of means tested benefits. The main message from CDP so far is that if we are to tackle acute deprivation we need a radical reallocation of resources rather than marginal rearrangement of services. This must include a genuine rather than a token involvement of the deprived in pressure for change. But it must also include a massive shift of resources in the direction of decaying and declining areas to revitalize their industry and refurbish their environment. What is needed is positive discrimination in the distribution of basic resources as well as social services.

New projects called Comprehensive Community Programmes were announced in 1974 based to some extent on the CDP findings but these are on a tiny scale. It would be tragic if they were to become mere window dressing while the real injustices in the distribution of resources were neglected. We are now at a stage when social policy must move radically into the economic field. Too many failures of social provision are blamed on existing social services, which cannot hope to combat the deficiencies of the basic socio-economic structure of society. What is needed is an extension of the methods and ideologies developed in social administration to new problem areas. Social services are a response to problems and these, as the first chapter indicated, are not fixed. As we redefine and reformulate our problems so we must redirect our social policies.

In the preface it was claimed that my intention was to keep this introduction to the subject of social administration simple. If readers who have persevered thus far have found that it has become progressively more difficult to follow, this is partly the consequence of the shortcomings of the book, but also, alas, very largely the consequence of the inherent difficulties of the subject. I hope some degree of confusion will not deter anyone from following the suggestions for further study of social administration for it is an increasingly rewarding, although constantly challenging, activity.

In the preface to *Commitment to Welfare*, Richard Titmuss says: 'The more I try to understand the role of welfare and the human condition the more untidy it all becomes.' If such an eminent scholar and original thinker in the field of social administration can be so honest about his confusion no reader of this introduction should feel ashamed to admit a similar bewilderment – and carry on the study regardless!

Suggestions for further reading

Donnison, D. V. (Ed), *A Pattern of Disadvantage* (1972).
Goetschius, G., *Working with Community Groups* (RKP, 1969).
Hall, P., Land, H., Parker, R. A. & Webb, A., *Change, Choice and Conflict in Social Policy* (Heinemann, 1975).
Halsey, A. H., *Educational Priority* (HMSO, 1972).

Jones D. & Mayo M. (Eds), *Community Work One and Two* (RKP, 1974 & 1975).

Lapping, A. (Ed), *Community Action* (Fabian, 1970).

Marris, P. & Rein, M., *Dilemmas of Social Reform* (RKP, 1967).

Marshall, T. H., *Social Policy* (Hutchinson, 1975 edition).

Mayo, M., *Community Development and Urban Deprivation* (Bedford Square Press, 1974).

Morris, M., *Voluntary Work in the Welfare State* (RKP, 1970).

Pinker, R., *Social Theory and Social Policy* (Heinemann, 1971).

Pinker, R., *The Idea of Welfare* (Heinemann, 1975).

Robson, W. A. & Crick, B. (Ed), *The Future of the Social Services* (Penguin, 1970).

Robson, W. A., *Man and the Social Sciences* (Allen & Unwin, 1972).

Tawney, R. H., *Equality* (1931).

Titmuss, R. M., *Essays on the Welfare State* (Allen & Unwin, 1958).

Titmuss, R. M., *Commitment to Welfare* (Allen & Unwin, 1968).

Titmuss, R. M., *The Gift Relationship* (Allen & Unwin, 1971).

Titmuss, R. M., *Social Policy: An Introduction* (Allen & Unwin, 1974).

Wedge, P. & Prosser, H., *Born to Fail* (Arrow Books, 1973).

The National Community Development Project:
Inter Project Report (1974); *Forward Plan* (1975).

Publications of the Fabian Society: eg *Socialism and Affluence* (1967); *Social Services for All* (1968); *Labour and Inequality: A Review of Social Policy 1964–70* (1971); *Positive Discrimination and Inequality* (1974); *Towards Participation in Local Services* (1973).

Publications of the Institute of Economic Affairs: eg *Towards a Welfare Society* (1967); *Universal or Selective Social Services?* (1970).

Index

To Nicolas James Prisco
Welcome to this world

CHAPTER ONE

Sleeping on the deck between a pair of cannon had drawbacks; the planking was hard and the ship rolled enough on the swell to require John Pearce to jam himself against the bulwarks. For all the discomfort it had two distinct advantages: the tiny cabin of HMS *Larcher* was not comfortable for two people seeking to avoid any kind of tactile contact, which he must do with Amélie Labordière, his passenger and one-time mistress. In addition, even if he was the captain, he was, on such a small vessel as an armed cutter, required to share the watch, which meant no more than four hours sleep and often not that if anything untoward happened.

The only other option, and one to which he had condemned *le Comte de Puisaye*, his other passenger, was to sling a hammock 'tween decks, which, in terms of space on such a cramped vessel made the cabin seem palatial, and that said nothing about an atmosphere replete with snoring and the all-pervading odour of endemic and malodorous flatulence – all the French aristocrat had to protect himself from that was a canvas screen, and John Pearce, needing to be quick on deck in an emergency, would not have been granted even that; besides, fresh air was so much more to his liking.

· The night being cloudy, the heat of the day had been trapped and, unusually in the northern quadrant of the Bay of Biscay, if there was a decent swell coming in from the Atlantic the wind was no more than a zephyr. That meant, with a slight breeze on her quarter and few sails aloft, the ship was making little headway in what was a Stygian darkness. Pearce had added to the lack of light by shading the lantern that illuminated the binnacle. A candle could be seen at sea for miles in clear weather and they were in hostile waters, close in an arc of shoreline in possession of the enemy, and obliged to cross, on the way back to England, several well-worn routes to the major French ports, both commercial and naval, and that took no account of French cruising warships or privateers in search of prizes.

'Wake up, Captain.' The voice was soft yet insistent enough to penetrate a rather lubricious dream full of scantily dressed women and bring him to full wakefulness. 'There's something odd.'

Disturbed slumbers at sea went with the position of commander; while men could be left to con a ship set on an unchanging course, if anything untoward occurred, and very much so if danger threatened, only he could make the necessary decisions. The sleeper rolled up the cant of the deck and out of his boat cloak to look up into the ghostly face now inches from his nose, hoping that whatever was odd did not include the danger of a lee shore. As a man who knew his navigational limitations, Lieutenant John Pearce lived in dread of an error that would see his ship wrecked. Then he remembered that he had discussed the course they were sailing with his master, Matthew Dorling, who might be young but knew his stuff.

'What is odd?'

'Listen.'

All Pearce could hear was the groaning of the ship's timbers and it took a firm hand to get him upright so that he could allow such aural examination to extend further. The first slapping sound was unmistakable – the well-known thud of an object hitting a heavy body of water, and wherever it was coming from it was not the bows of the armed cutter. This reprised the fear of going aground, the second rhythmic slap doing nothing to bring about reassurance. Yet as it continued it carried with it none of the other sounds associated with waves cascading on a shore, no hissing of trapped water escaping over rocks. Then some timbers moved so seriously as to send a crack of strained wood out into the night and it was not off his own vessel.

'A ship?' Pearce hissed.

'Reckon,' came the soft reply.

Peering outwards Pearce looked for any glint of light, only to conclude there was none.

'Holy Christ, it could be a ghost ship.'

That whisper had an air of panic about it, reminding Pearce of just how superstitious was the average Jack tar, even if in this case it was no tyro but a leading hand. The temptation to scoff was high – the man in command of HMS *Larcher* did not believe in spectral spirits – yet it seemed inappropriate in the circumstances so instead a firm hand was applied to a barely visible shoulder to induce calm.

'Steady now, man. I will take the wheel. Go below and rouse out the crew, but quietly. No bells, no drums and make sure they are silent as they ascend to the deck.'

'Aye, aye, sir.'

No sooner had Pearce got his hand on the spokes, having released the leather strap by which it had been secured, than the rocket went up, seeming to rise from nowhere, a red streak of flame shooting skywards to form a starburst as it exploded, that accompanied by the flash of a signal gun, he thought somewhere to windward. What followed was both astounding and alarming as all around the armed cutter great stern lanterns began to be lit over a vast expanse of sea, not in single figures, not even by the dozen, but to Pearce's vivid imagination by the hundreds, each one illuminating a small patch of deck on those he was close to, showing a sliver of white and phosphorescent

10

wake, as well as the lower sails of what constituted an armada.

'Mother of Christ, if we're not in the middle of a fleet.'

Given the darkness of a moonless and starless night, it was like being placed in a candlelit galaxy, and if they were moving at a snail's pace, Pearce quickly realised the ships all around them were very obviously on an opposite course to his own. Even in the dark he knew the voice of the man who had uttered that curse to be his friend Michael O'Hagan; there was no mistaking that deep Irish brogue and the religious nature of his blasphemy. He also sensed that the required warrants had taken up their places beside him, which proved to be so when each one named their task so he would know they were present.

That was followed by silence as Pearce contemplated the dilemma in which they were trapped; given their location there was no way this fleet of vessels was friendly, but against that, from what he could see – and granted that was limited – they were not warships. They looked to be, certainly by the shape of their transoms and bluff bows, too squat for fighting, more in the line of merchant vessels, which in turn led to the deduction that this was a French commercial convoy, with the qualification that one of such dimensions must have an armed escort and very likely a potent one.

'Mr Dorling, we need find a reasonable patch of sea in which to come about, but very quietly. Can the hands do what is necessary without any calling out or shouted orders?'

'I would say yes to that, sir.'

The tone of voice in that reply was worthy of examination; much as he had come to like the crew of HMS *Larcher* and as much as he had seen their competence when sent about any particular duty, he still had areas of ignorance. It was as well to take into consideration that he was not their titular captain, but merely in temporary command from the mission upon which they had been so recently engaged. Dorling had sounded very assured and really there was no choice but to go with his judgement.

'Please relay the necessary orders, then come back to inform me when all is in place. Also tell our passenger below on no account is he to come on deck. Gunner?'

'Capt'n.'

'Mr Kempshall, as soon as we are come about and have settled on a new course I want the flintlocks in place, the guns run out and loaded on both sides, bow chasers too, then hauled back in and left behind closed gun ports, but slowly and with minimal noise.'

There was a silence then, as the gunner contemplated the ramifications of that, for a trundling gun could be noisy and then there was the damage they could do. Fired at closed ports, which they could be in a panic, would cause serious damage to the woodwork and, in the dark, who knew where the splinters from such an act would go; they could easy kill or maim the crew and anyone else. Pearce misunderstood that long pause and remarked on what he thought was troubling the man.

'Difficult as it is, Mr Kempshall, I would rather have to worm them later than seek to load in an emergency.'

'Weren't that, your honour; I was thinkin' of the work I'd give my carpenter brother. I'll set my mates and the gun captains to work and get below and start preparing charges, sir.'

'Make it so. Michael, get the muskets out and loaded and every weapon we have available by the guns.'

'Jesus, we can't fight this lot.'

'They are merchantmen, Michael, and they will not fight, but if any of their escorts come snooping, then I must seek to use what little gunnery we have to get away. The best way to achieve that is to give them something else to think about, so when you have seen to the swords and tomahawks I want you working on some strong combustibles that we can sling at another ship.'

'A vessel ablaze will keep them busy, happen?'

That made Pearce smile in the dark; he had not been sure Michael would smoke his aim. He was about to say so when he realised the Irishman was gone. All around him men were doing likewise, going about their duties, and it was a testament to the efficiency of the Royal Navy and the massive amount of sea time the fleet enjoyed that they could do so without being able to see anything, albeit such actions were usually carried out with a great deal of noise. Not now; they were appreciative of the danger they were in, could see just as he could the myriad number of lights all around the ship, so the shrouds were climbed by touch; likewise, the way the men eased their bare feet into the foot-ropes and made their way along the yards was done in silence, and if they did call to each other it was in voices so low as to not even carry to the deck.

Somewhere forward and amidships Dorling was peering skywards, trying to see by the odd white flash of a bare foot that the hands were in the required places, sure that, on deck, those allotted to pull on the falls were standing by to release them from their cleats, prepared to haul hard and swing round the yards before sheeting them home once the cutter, aided by the hard-over rudder, was on a reverse course. On the wheel, Pearce would also take his cue from the master, a man so much more competent in the art of sailing than he.

The actual turn was far from noiseless, for with so many men employed in physical tasks such a thing was impossible. All Pearce could hope for was that the odd call or curse, the sound of ropes whirring through blocks or the creak of a swinging yard would not carry to the other vessels around them, and if it did, they would have few men alert at this time of night aboard a merchant vessel to hear them. Even if they were attuned to the danger of an enemy, they must surely feel safe in the cocoon of their armada. Added to that was the constant sound of their own timbers, which would be creaking and groaning as all wooden and rope-rigged vessels do.

Pearce sensed a presence. 'You with me, Michael?'

'I am.'

'Sneak into the cabin and find the flag locker – there's a tricolour in there. Don't unshade the lantern until the door is shut.'

'And if I wake the lady, who might need some comfort?'

'Tell her to stay off the deck,' Pearce snapped, for he could discern the trace of humour in his friend's tone.

There was no setting of a course; Pearce steered to keep an equal distance between two of the nearest vessels, only troubled by a series of flaring rockets and booming signal guns that were clearly imparting some message of which he had no knowledge, these briefly and partially illuminating the seascape, luckily not close by. That did tell him the escorts, who would seek to control the convoy movements, were way off to windward, a position from which they could protect their charges from interdiction, the added advantage being that should a threat emerge from another quarter, they had the wind with which to deal with it.

Time lost all meaning, which gave him a period to think, and once he recalled his previous course and where he had set out from the day before it seemed to suggest this fleet was heading for the mouth of the Loire, which would take them up to the main French commercial port of Nantes. The other thought which occurred was that such an event was of some importance. Given the overwhelming superiority in numbers that the Royal

Navy could deploy across the oceans, this sort of convoy should, in theory, be impossible to assemble and even harder to escort to home soil. Given the size, it must have some bearing on the ability of Revolutionary France to continue the war, especially since he had been informed by one of the male passengers that the nation was in the grip of famine, not that he had entirely believed a man with an agenda of his own to pursue.

'The escorts will form an outer screen,' Pearce said, really thinking aloud as he included Michael O'Hagan in his ruminations. 'Something this size, I should think they are numerous, mostly with the weather gage to give them control, but I should not be surprised if there are warships bringing up the rear to scare off our cruisers.'

'Seems to me they might be the ones to give us worry, right enough.'

Pearce nodded, unsure if it could be observed. He asked Michael to fetch Dorling and, after a talk about their previous course and their likely location now, was obliged to conclude that the merchant convoy expected to make landfall early in the morning, possibly at first light. If their navigation was good then it would be the Loire estuary, but even slightly off it would be simple to correct and begin the next stage of the operation, which was to send the ships, one by one, upriver to the port of Nantes as and when the tide permitted.

'Which means we must not be in the same position then as we relatively are now.'

'Soon as it's light, sir, we will be spotted, and for my money that — a strange ship right in the middle of this lot — would bring someone to have a look-see.'

'Can't fault that.'

Looking out into the darkness as he contemplated Dorling's opinion, Pearce was suddenly aware that even in the pitch dark one of the nearby merchantmen had fallen off its course and was being brought closer to them by the leeway forced upon it by the current. Those lower sails, which had been ghostly, now had a more defined shape, there was no sign of a wake, while the stern lantern was no more than a glow hidden by the bulk of the vessel. Unsure if it was imagination or vision, he thought there was a bowsprit too close for comfort and possibly heading for his shrouds. Spinning the wheel he let the head of HMS *Larcher* fall away and spoke as soon as that had an effect.

'Take the wheel,' he hissed to Dorling, making for the side as soon as the exchange was complete, hands cupped to his mouth and about to yell. For a split second he held his tongue, as it came to him that to call out in English was unwise, so he did so in French, demanding to know what the *sal cochon* was playing at. That his words had an effect was obvious; someone on the merchantman's wheel was hauling hard on the rudder, this evidenced by the way the light from that lantern altered that which it was illuminating. Pearce, leaning over the side, was certain that if he reached out he could touch the bowsprit rigging of the other ship; he could certainly hear the noise of the bow itself breasting into the swell, the slapping sound loud in his ears. Then a voice called back.

'What in the name of Jesus does that mean?'

English, and with it an accent of some kind? Pearce decided to stick to French and informed the man on the other deck that he had nearly run them down.

The response was querulous. 'Have you got anyone aboard who speaks a proper language, you Gallic booby? And might I enquire, if you do, what in the name of creation you are doing sailing in the middle of this damn convoy with no light showing?'

'I speek a leetle English,' Pearce replied.

'Then get some lights aloft if you don't want to be run down, monsure.'

It was the last word that nailed the speaker as a Jonathan. What was an American doing in a ship off the coast of France?

'I pilot,' Pearce replied, wondering if that would make sense; no ship in this convoy would risk the Loire sandbanks without one.

'Well, monsure, you're not much of one, I'd say, but if you want all this goddamn grain and barley we have fetched over three thousand miles of ocean, you better have a care where you lay a course.'

'Grain and barley?' called Pearce, too surprised to think.

'Thousands of tons of it, friend, enough to feed the whole of France for a year and some left over.'

While they had been talking the voice had been fading slightly, evidence that the merchant vessel was resuming a proper course, this while Pearce was trying and failing to calculate the kind of total cargo being borne by what ships he knew to be around him. Without another thought he raised himself up on to the bulwarks, then half climbed the lower shrouds and began to try and count the lanterns he could see, lit because the convoy was close to shore and clearly in no danger in the opinion of the man in charge of the escorts.

'Michael,' Pearce said, when he had jumped down and made his way back to the wheel. 'Have you got out that tricolour?'

'I have.'

'Then get it bent on and our ensign down and out of sight. Mr Dorling, we need to change course once more and get back on to the original heading. I do not want to be enclosed by this lot when the sky gets light.' That was followed by a sigh. 'And if you are a praying man, beg for a bit of a decent wind and from the right quarter.'

That manoeuvre was carried out with more noise than previously; clearly his crew had heard the exchange and thought they had little to fear from an armada of Jonathans, indeed there were one or two willing to suggest that they press a few into the King's Navy, given the high chance that many of them were deserters over the years and from that same body. Once on a new course and cursing the lack of that wind, Pearce steered by the light of those lanterns, sailing in line ahead, keeping HMS *Larcher*'s head equidistant between them. Being summertime the dawn came too early and they had not got clear by the time he could apply the standard naval test and see a grey goose at a quarter-mile. What he could see, off the stern of the last convoy vessels, was a pair of frigates beating to and fro, while to windward there were visible the higher topmasts of a pair of ships of the line.

That he was not immediately spotted was, no doubt, due to their concentration being to seawards, the area from where danger could threaten. It would take time, perhaps more than a day, to feed those merchant ships even into such a wide estuary. The rest, stationary and waiting their turn, would be exceedingly vulnerable to anything coming in from the wide Atlantic like a squadron of British warships, which would certainly save him and *Larcher*. Such a thing was too much to hope for: all he had was that tricolour and the hope that being a small warship sailing along with closed gun ports, he would be seen as no threat.

It was a risk to sail close to one of those frigates, to seek to convey an expression of unconcern, which he added to by raising his hat, too far off to be seen to be British, wise that such an action was not taken too far; he did not want to get within anything like hailing range. Sam Kempshall, as ordered, had loaded the signal gun and in time-honoured fashion Pearce ordered that the distant flagship should be saluted, an act that received a reply in what was, on both ships, a total waste of powder.

'Time to worm those cannon, Mr Kempshall, but I

would beg you leave one of the chasers loaded.'

That took time – worming guns to get out the ball and the charges was a slow process, a period in which, even in light airs, the gap opened up substantially until any visible French warship was no more than hull upon the horizon. When all was ready John Pearce called for the ship to heave to and presented to his enemies a broadside view.

'Michael, put back out the ensign, if you please.'

The proper flag was bent onto the halyards and as it raced aloft and the tricolour came down, the temporary captain of HMS *Larcher* hauled on the lanyard that fired the flints of the three-pounder cannon. That he wasted a ball – it landed harmlessly in the sea – was of little consequence. The purpose was to alert those Frenchmen to what was happening, to let them see, as they trained their telescopes on what had taken their attention – the noise of a cannon fired and the billowing smoke that produced – that the vessel which had sailed so serenely past was one they would have done well to intercept. The nature of that convoy and what it might contain would soon be known in London.

'Your guests are desirous of being allowed the deck, Captain.'

'Make it so, Mr Dorling, and set us on a course for home.'

'Aye, aye, sir.'

CHAPTER TWO

Jahleel Tolland had not endeared himself to the hard-working folk at Buckler's Hard, but then, being a fellow of rough manner and impatient with it, he was not much given to being pleasant to any living soul; to his way of thinking these New Forest folk were too close-mouthed for their own good and a whip would not go amiss to get them to mind their manners and have them respond to his enquiries. Franklin Tolland had been found to be easier to deal with; indeed it was he who had elicited the replies to the questions the pair had come to ask.

Even if they had been previously supplied with information and from an unimpeachable source, such was the endemic mistrust of the Tolland brothers they needed to be certain of the facts. Yes, the armed cutter,

HMS *Larcher*, had set out from Buckler's Hard a week past and was expected to return to the River Beaulieu in short order, though only providence knew when. And yes, the man in command was a lieutenant who went by the name Pearce, though they could not swear to his given name being John, for he had bedded down elsewhere and had not spent, if you added it all up, much more than an hour or two ashore in the vicinity.

To that was added a physical description, confirmation that the Tollands were in the proper place to lay by the heels the man they sought, and that had allowed them to mount their horses and return up the road to the town of Lyndhurst, where they had left the rest of their gang, each of whom, it was decided, would take it in daily turns to ride down to a point that overlooked the estuary of the River Beaulieu to catch the return of the ship.

To stay in Buckler's Hard itself was difficult given the lack of accommodation in what was no more than a maritime shipyard inhabited by those involved in construction, impossible without they arouse suspicion as to their motives for being in a place few visited. The Tolland name would likely not be known to anyone locally but that could never be certain, and when you lived outside the law, as these smugglers did, it was best to never take a chance on it being recognised.

'This Pearce bugger could be gone half a year,' opined one of the band, a near-toothless and bent-nosed ruffian called Cole, this after four days of waiting, during one of which the rain had come down in buckets to depress any high spirits with which they had come to the place.

'Never,' Franklin Tolland replied. 'We have it on good authority that he would be gone two weeks at best an' it could be less.'

'Weeks in which,' Cole hissed through his gums, 'we would see not a coin turned.'

'Stow it,' Jahleel growled. 'When did you ever earn a crust that me and my brother did not provide?'

'All I is saying, Jahleel, is that we are men of the sea wereselves.'

'So?'

'So we knows she is fickle, mate, an' if what you say is true, this Pearce feller is set to go ashore over the water and that be hostile, so he might get himself killed. Besides that, goin' there an' comin' back won't be easy on a sea crawlin' wi' French ships of war. We could be here till doomsday.'

Jahleel Tolland looked round the tavern table and assembled faces to see if there was general agreement with Cole, hard to discern with few of the others present prepared to catch his eye; to a man they were in fear of him which was just the way he liked it.

'Has you lost all recollect of what that bastard did? He stole our ship and our cargo from under our noses and damn near put us in the workhouse.' A gnarled hand slammed down on the bare wood of the tabletop. 'An' that's an act for which he has to pay and pay high. I want to see his bleached bones after he's told us what we need to know.'

'You mean to slit his gizzard?' asked one of the gang quietly.

'After he's told us where to find the rest of his gang and I've made him scream for death in place of what I will do to his carcass.' Jahleel Tolland produced a large knife and began to carve out marks on the tabletop. 'Happen I'll leave my name on him, afore I get to his throat.'

• 'It might be a bad idea to do him in, brother.'

Jahleel looked at Franklin, making a point of aiming his gaze at the red and far from fully healed scar on his younger brother's cheek, the result of a sword swipe given to him by the very same John Pearce. If the older brother was scarlet of face and, with his pockmarked cheeks, both intemperate and unprepossessing, Franklin was the opposite. He had always been a ladies' man, a comely-looking cove and proud of it, to which he added the manners of speech and behaviour of what he considered himself to be, a gentleman. Now, none would look at him, male nor female, without first seeing the scar, which would class him as villainous.

'And you with that face?'

'We don't want the law on our tail.'

'Christ, we live outside the law.'

'Smuggling is one thing, Jahleel, murder another.'

'You goin' soft, Franklin, for I don't recall you bein' shy of killing afore?'

Grunts of agreement greeted that comment; in a game where trust was unknown and acts of thieving and

25

disloyalty common, Franklin Tolland had been as swift as the rest of the crew to take the life of anyone light-fingered, twice as much so when it was a sneak or a turncoat willing to dob them in to the excise for a cash reward.

'Never, but if we do in one of our own kind in the act of shipping contraband, who's to give a care? This Pearce might be as much of a scoundrel as any in our game but he is King's Navy too and that might get us a whole heap of trouble. They look after their own and the last thing we want is Jack tar seeking vengeance when we get back to our proper trade. We want them to pay us no heed so we can come and go without fuss.'

'Then it has to be out of sight,' Cole wheezed. 'Happen we let him land, an' take him when no soul is about. Plenty ground and soft round here to bury him in once you'se got what you want, then it be a mystery.'

'Never,' Jahleel spat. 'That sod has slipped me four times now, so he's getting taken up as soon as his feet touch soil.'

The door swung open and the eighth member of the gang bustled in. He had been doing his duty on the seashore by the hamlet of Lepe, which overlooked the deep-water approach to the winding River Beaulieu.

'I think I sighted that cutter bearing up for the river.'

'You sure?' Franklin demanded.

'Christ no, couldn't see her transom even if she does bear a name, but she has a naval pennant, the right lines and has two bow chasers and four six-gun ports a side, which fits what I was told to watch for.'

'Tide?'

'On the rise, and she was getting her sweeps out, given the wind don't favour her.'

Jahleel was already on his feet, his face even redder than normal with rising passion. 'Get the horses saddled up, all of you. I want us to be well hidden afore he makes the final bend.'

That accomplished, they gathered outside and mounted up, being just about to set off and take the road south when a shay came hurtling down the street, drawn by a single sweating horse. Sat under the canopy and being free with his long whip was an elderly fellow in the heavily braided uniform of a rear admiral, and if Jahleel Tolland had a high colour on his face he was well outdone by the sailor, who seemed able to match him in passion too.

'Stand aside there, damn you to hell!' the admiral cried, his protruding eyes raking the assembled horsemen who threatened to impede his progress. 'I am on the King's business.'

'You'll be on a funeral slab, you old bugger,' Jahleel shouted after him, having been obliged to haul hard on his reins to get his mount out of the way, while the shay had gone through a deep puddle left over from the heavy day's rain, an act which threw up a spray of mud-filled water.

'Quiet,' Franklin called, waving a hand to cool his brother's passion, a sideways glance showing that the good citizens of Lyndhurst had stopped to stare. What followed was a quiet hiss. 'We don't want our faces remarked upon.'

'Too late for you, Franklin, so let's get going and sort out that bastard who marked you for life.'

Pearce, standing on the tiny quarterdeck of the armed cutter, realised that the positive mood in which he had allowed himself to wallow since clearing that grain convoy was fast evaporating and that had nothing to do with matters nautical. Perhaps it was to do with the weather, for after a day of heavy rain in which he had required his oilskins it had turned sunny, which in itself seemed to mock his previous sanguine mood. Reality came home to roost as HMS *Larcher* sailed past the mouth of the Lymington, a river that took its name from the port to which it led. More tellingly, for his happiness as well as his future, Emily Barclay was there, waiting for him to return and this had forced him to revisit an unpalatable truth – to wonder how the person he loved would react to him arriving back from this short voyage bearing, as a passenger, a woman who had previously been his mistress?

Emily was somewhat prudish in an English county way. This had everything to do with her stable, parochial and provincial upbringing, which so contrasted with his own life of endless wandering in the company of his combative father, none more so than the formative years he had spent in Paris in the immediate aftermath of the French Revolution. The city, eighteen months after the fall of the monarchy, had been exciting and vibrant then, full of optimism, an air of adventure, gossip, the discussion of radical ideas and of course, beautiful women.

Coming of age there, tall and slim, with a handsome, unblemished countenance, John Pearce had caught a come-hither look in more than one female eye. With the exuberance of youth and eager for experience he had taken full advantage of what was very obviously on offer, finally settling into a more serious liaison with Amélie Labordière, this with the full cognisance of her understanding husband; a rich man and no hypocrite, he had his own pleasures to pursue.

Emily had experienced nothing of that nature: from her parental home she had gone on to be trapped in a loveless marriage to the odious Captain Ralph Barclay, a husband seventeen years her senior and a man Pearce saw as his mortal enemy. This was an encumbrance from which he was in the process of rescuing her, a task that had been fraught with many complications, not least Emily's own disinclination to acknowledge their mutual attraction or to succumb to his advances.

Circumstances had favoured his suit, though she had only become his lover in the few days before his departure and he knew such a position left her, even if she sought to hide it, with a residue of deep Anglican guilt. He suspected she would not readily take to the unexpected presence of the aristocratic and Catholic Amélie, while he also assumed that any attempt by him to explain it away as pure coincidence stood a very strong chance of being treated as so much stuff.

Yet it was nothing more than happenstance; he had been charged by the Government to undertake a mission to the Vendée to assess the state of the revolt there – was it worth supporting or should it be left to wither? He had come across Amélie in the company of those who were fighting the Revolution on behalf of their region, their religion and their monarchy, the latter two concepts ones to which John Pearce could only take exception. Nor could his undertaking be said to be a success, this exemplified by the other person he was fetching back to England.

In the few days the *Comte* de Puisaye had been aboard, and for some days prior to that, the man had become a sore trial to John Pearce and he was now wondering if keeping him below when they were in some danger – in the same way he had confined Amélie to his cabin – had as much to do with the man's insufferable nature as a need to ensure that any interference he might produce could have a negative effect. He had been raised by an extremely radical father to see the world as an inequitable place in need of change, where the fortunate few had an excess of money and land while many lived in poverty, where the twin pillars of the Church and the Crown ensured nothing was allowed to disturb the status quo. Good manners had obliged Pearce, many times, to bite his tongue.

Puisaye was an unreconstructed aristocrat whose sole wish was that life should return to that which it had been before the fall of King Louis. The *comte* could neither see nor accept that the world had changed, nor could he or his ilk seem to accept that they bore a great deal of the responsibility for what had befallen their class. If the guillotine was barbaric in the frequency with which it was now being employed, if the terror sweeping France was indiscriminate in whom it killed, the men who had occupied positions of power under the monarchy, by their indifference to the plight of the mass of their fellow countrymen, only had themselves to blame.

The count was likewise convinced that he and his fellow rebels in the Vendée held the key to the defeat of both the Jacobin Terror and the Revolution. All they required was that Albion support them with a massive injection of naval assets – warships of every size, regiments of infantry and batteries of artillery – plus several tons of gold to pay for their return to power. Given such aid they were convinced they could advance from their coastal swamps to overcome the forces sent from Paris to defeat them. From what John Pearce had observed they were living in cloud cuckoo land.

Puisaye was less of a pressing personal concern than Amélie Labordière; the fellow could be passed on to William Pitt and Henry Dundas to be dealt with, and those two politicos as well as the government they led were welcome to him. Less cheering was that Amélie, in the few conversations he had allowed himself with her – any hint of intimacy had to be avoided – had made it plain that she too held the same opinions as Puisaye, which left him to wonder how his discomfort at her stated views had never surfaced during the months they had been lovers. The answer was, of course, obvious: ardent youthful lust and carnal engagement took precedence over any concern for politics of any hue. John Pearce was too busy enjoying himself, added to that the fact that he had been far from wholly convinced of his father's opinions then and he still questioned some of the more outré notions now, not least the innate goodness of the human race.

Such thoughts recalled his last visit to Paris, a city much changed from that which he had enjoyed in the company of Amélie, and that dragged up, in turn, the memory of the last contact he had enjoyed with a parent known throughout England and Scotland as the Edinburgh Ranter. This soubriquet had been given him for his years of radical stump speeches and pamphleteering, all denouncing the privileges enjoyed by the monarchy, the Church, the aristocracy and the greedy mercantile class.

Adam Pearce had been hated by these pillars of the British Government for the way he stirred up discontent and sometimes even riot; a marginal nuisance for most of his life, all that had changed with the fall of the Bastille and the revolution that swept France. Suddenly his activities and growing fame – he called for a similar overthrow in his homeland and the notion was welcomed by many – presaged a potent threat, so much so that Adam and his son had been imprisoned for a short spell in the Fleet. Set free Adam had not kept silent; he had taken up his cause again only to be forced to flee to France from a King's Bench warrant for sedition, a crime which could be punished by hanging.

Initially welcomed in Paris as a famed supporter of republicanism, as well as a victim of reactionary justice, Adam Pearce had been feted and admired by the men then in power. But both that power and his welcome had begun to pall over each month; never one to hold back on what he saw as morally right, John's father found that the people who had taken over the revolutionary government had no more love of his honesty than the ministers of King George; in a city increasingly febrile, that was dangerous; there were no warrants in France, just arbitrary and revolutionary justice.

John Pearce had returned to England to plead for that King's Bench warrant to be set aside only to find himself being pursued by men intent on serving it and clapping him in gaol. On a cold winter night he had taken refuge in a crowded tavern hard by the River Thames, in a part of the city called the Liberties of the Savoy, much used by men avoiding the long arm of the law. Called The Pelican, it proved to be a poor choice in terms of safety; he had been illegally press-ganged into the King's Navy by none other than Emily's husband, Captain Ralph Barclay of the frigate HMS *Brilliant*.

As much good fortune as bad had attended his service since that night: he had been cast ashore and nearly drowned in a cutting-out expedition, got he and his companions back to safety and obliged Ralph Barclay to release him and them from the navy only to be pressed for a second time on the way home. The commander of his new vessel had promoted him as a way to stifle a troublemaker; he had then found himself obliged to take command of the vessel in the first successful naval action of the war and was hailed for that as a hero, which resulted in Pearce being given his present rank by order of King George.

In the interim, in Paris, matters had gone from bad to worse for his father. The party of the Girondins, who took control of the Government, cooled towards him and sought to still his criticisms by disapproval. The Jacobins, who overthrew the Girondins and sent their political enemies to the guillotine, imprisoned Adam Pearce to silence him completely. Appraised of this his son hastened to rescue him, finding him too ill to give any attempt a chance of success. Knowing he was near to death, Adam substituted himself in place of another prisoner, a fact his son discovered too late; he was already in the tumbrel and on his way to the place of execution by then. John Pearce failed in the race to seek to save him, instead witnessing a decapitation by that same infernal device which had lopped off the heads of so many before him, accompanied by the screams of a bloodthirsty revolutionary mob.

Duty came along to chase away such gloomy recollections, for over the prow lay the sandbanks that protected the entrance to the River Beaulieu and those he examined carefully. He must take cognisance of the state of the tide, for he would need it to be rising or at flood to take him, on a north-westerly breeze, up to his anchorage at Buckler's Hard on what was a tidal waterway. Once there he would quit the ship and his temporary appointment. That brought its own feelings of regret; if he did not have much love for the navy, he had enjoyed being in command of the young men who manned this vessel.

As he looked along the deck at the hands that had been called up to their duty, he hoped they too had appreciated his being there, at least the majority, for the man he had replaced and who would return was a tyrant. There amongst them, chatting easily and causing the occasional ripple of laughter, was his good friend Michael who, if he came across as the jolly Irish giant, was a proper handful sober and could be fierce when inebriated.

On their first ever encounter, the same night when both had been taken up in the Pelican Tavern, Michael had been near blind drunk. Pearce had been obliged to duck a haymaker that, from such massive fists as the Irishman possessed, would have removed his head. Much water had flowed since that day when they and many others had been the victims of the press gang. For a small group, stuck together as messmates, the name of that tavern had given them their own soubriquet: they called themselves the Pelicans. Even if he was not truly a friend then, nor the cause of their subsequent troubles, John Pearce could not avoid feeling responsible for what had become of them since that night: old Abel Scrivens had perished in his place; Ben Walker was now a slave to the Musselmen, if he was not expired too.

For them he could do nothing, but his primary task once ashore, Emily Barclay and potential complications notwithstanding, was to get out from under the thumb of Ralph Barclay the two remaining Pelicans, Charlie Taverner and Rufus Dommet, with whom he and Michael had been press-ganged. First he must bear up for the river entrance and, given he still held himself to be short on experience, being a naval lieutenant by good fortune rather than long experience, Pearce thought carefully before issuing the necessary orders.

'Mister Dorling,' he called, 'prepare to shorten sail and, I think, given the wind is not favourable, we will need to employ sweeps to progress upriver.'

'We could warp her up with boats, sir.'

'No,' Pearce replied with a smile, before taking off his blue coat. 'That would burden a few men. With sweeps we will all share the task, myself included.'

'Monsieur!' the *Comte* de Puisaye exclaimed when, minutes later, he saw John Pearce grab the end of a sweep. 'This is undignified for an officer.'

'Dignity be damned,' came the reply, in English, which made the crew chuckle.

CHAPTER THREE

Emily Barclay was sat on a stool, by a stream and under a wide-brimmed straw hat, at a place the Lymington locals called Batchley Copse. She had a brush in her hand, pigments on a trestle by her side, while behind her sat an elderly fellow, there to instruct her on the finer points of watercolour painting as she tried to capture the midsummer sunlight dappling on the water. Apart from walks and a nightly visit to Lymington harbour – there was some hope that John Pearce would come to anchor there rather than Buckler's Hard – this was part of her daily routine, clement weather permitting, which it had been most days, though the ground was still damp from when it had poured.

Concentrating, the image she was trying to get on canvas took her mind off a sea of troubles that seemed to grow in difficulty the more she gnawed on them, not least what kind of future she could expect with the man who had so recently become her lover. It was true that when her thoughts did turn to John Pearce and what they had enjoyed together, worries gave way to fond recall as well as a trace of a blush, for he had shown her what pleasure two people could enjoy when happily coupled.

But that did not last; such memories inevitably took her back to the previous experience of the same acts with her husband and they had been anything but pleasurable, having ranged from painful, through mind-numbing to, on one occasion, an act of downright brutality bordering on rape. This had shown her clearly that far from marrying a man of some stature and refinement she had become attached to a beast rather than a gentleman, and Ralph Barclay had become someone from whom she was determined to permanently separate.

As an act it had proved easy, she simply found somewhere to reside apart – but as a condition of living it was far from that. Emily knew only too well the world in which she lived and the mores of the society in which she had been raised: marriage was for life, a sacred trust, not something to be taken up and discarded on a whim. John Pearce might say and truly believe that society could go to damnation but it was not his reputation that would be shredded. Men were expected to be weak in the article of sexual temptation but no woman was allowed the same licence; to stray off the conjugal path was to be tarred as not much better than a whore.

It was impossible not to dwell on what their joint

future might be and in truth that had barely been discussed, though they had the means to impose silence and acceptance on her husband. In their possession was a copy of the details of a court martial in which not only had Ralph Barclay committed perjury, it provided evidence that he had induced or coerced others to lie as well, a document that could see him hanged. Now in command of a 74-gun ship of the line, he was presently at sea as part of the Channel Fleet and that was a position, his naval rank and responsibilities and his life notwithstanding, he would never let be put at risk; Ralph Barclay saw himself as defined by his rank as a senior post captain.

How foolish she had been at seventeen years of age, how easily she had allowed herself to be persuaded that a match to a man of such status was not to be missed. Only later had it occurred to Emily that the parental pressure, seemingly gentle but now perceived as persistent, had more to do with their comfort and happiness than her own. By marrying she had secured the continued possession of the home in which her mother and father lived and in which she had been raised, a dwelling entailed by inheritance to her soon-to-be husband. Had she refused him he might have taken his revenge on them by repossession, which would have seen the whole family on the streets.

'Might I suggest, Mrs Raynesford,' said her elderly instructor, 'that a deeper green be applied to show the more heavily shaded leaves.'

The use of that name made her jerk and move

the brush too rapidly, smearing part of the work, for if Raynesford was her maiden name, it was not her wedded one. She turned her head away so he could not see any trace of her deep blush, for it was inclined to induce both shame and guilt; in a moment of indecision and under pressure that was the name by which John Pearce had booked them into the King's Head in Lymington as man and wife.

There was a sigh from behind her back. 'Perhaps another tree branch, even if you cannot observe one, will rescue the work, which has a degree of promise.'

'Yes,' Emily said, biting her lower lip as she sought to concentrate on what was before her eyes rather than behind them.

Ralph Barclay was sitting on the sunlit quarterdeck of the Third Rate, HMS *Semele*, the round-backed captain's chair lashed to ensure it stayed in place, watching as the crew worked hard to repair the battle damage she had so recently suffered. Underneath his uniform coat, left sleeve pinned to his chest because of his lack of an arm, he had been obliged to wear ducks instead of his normal breeches, making him feel improperly dressed. This was due to the wound in his thigh, sliced open by a musket ball in the encounter with the main French battle fleet, which had bled so copiously he had passed out. As a precaution against repetition, the leg was heavily bandaged.

Thus placed on his chair he was unable to see much of the rest of the Lord Howe's command as it sailed up the Channel towards Plymouth in the company of those French warships that had been taken as prizes. If the fleet was abuzz with talk of the victory, and it would be if it were anything like HMS *Semele*, then a large part of the conversation would be about prize money, that much favoured wardroom and 'tween-decks topic. Even the great cabin was not immune to speculation and Ralph Barclay could happily contemplate his own booty, for a great fleet victory brought reward not just in terms of glory but also in terms of wealth to the whole ship's company, the captain most of all.

That would dominate every waking thought now the dead had been committed to the deep, the wounded were under the care of the surgeon and the last vestige of loss, the auctioning of the possessions of the deceased, had been completed. Ralph Barclay had engaged in endless calculations of the various forms of payment in which he would be entitled to have a share, the hulls of the prizes of course being the most valuable. But there was the value of the stores they carried, as well as the rigging, the canvas, head money for the captured sailors, gun money for the weapons, both cannon and muskets – his only worry that those who decided such things would not properly take into account the sinking of the *Vengeur du Peuple*, the vessel with which he had been heavily engaged and the enemy that had inflicted the damage now being repaired.

A seventy-four like *Semele*, she could not have been crewed by much less than six hundred men, yet from what he could tally only just over half that number had been taken off alive. Beresford, third lieutenant at the start of the encounter, now, due to the expiry of the pair above him, the first, had recounted to a recumbent commanding officer what had happened after he passed out. It was plain that attempts at rescue had been hampered by the fact that many of the crew of the dismasted French warship had perished because, having broken into the spirit room, they had been drunk. That did not alter their worth; representations must be made in writing to ensure such men or their money value was not ignored just because they had drowned.

'Sir,' said Lieutenant Beresford, approaching his captain. 'The surgeon was wondering if you would be up to visiting the wounded. He is sure such a thing would lift their spirits.'

Spirits, Ralph Barclay thought, his face taking on a savage look; the only spirits those sods care about are the same ones that killed the Frogs aboard *Vengeur*. His next thought was that they were hardly likely to get any emotional lift from the sight of him either, for he was no soft-soul commander but a strict disciplinarian, a man who ran a taut ship and was as likely to flog a fellow as praise him. Yet it had to be, it was his duty.

Looking up at Beresford he saw how different the youngster appeared from the fellow he had been in his company prior to the contest, more sure of himself, and he could guess why. There would be promotions, especially for first lieutenants, even if they came to it by the death of their superiors. They would be entitled to become commanders and be given unrated ships, sloops and armed cutters of their own if they were lucky enough to have the influence to be granted a commission; even languishing on the beach that would mean prize money to spend, an increase in pay and a ready audience if they were called upon to regale their neighbours, not least the young daughters of the local gentry, with the story of the battle; many an advantageous match had been founded on less.

'I will require aid, Mr Beresford,' Barclay said, lifting his empty sleeve, 'for I am a one-winged bird.'

'Sir,' the lieutenant replied, embarrassed, for he had not contemplated the need.

'Add to which my wound—'

'Of course.'

'As you know, Devenow, the fellow I usually rely on, is one of those under the care of the surgeon.'

Beresford tried but failed to hide his distaste at the mention of that name; Devenow had acted as the captain's servant, a task to which he was wholly unsuited, which had raised questions of probity in the wardroom. He was a nasty bully and a man inclined to drink himself insensible, having threatened many of the crew to acquire their grog; what his captain was doing relying on such a creature escaped almost the entire crew.

'Perhaps we could ask Gherson?'

Ralph Barclay nearly spat out 'That dammed coward!' but he contained the temptation to abuse his clerk, for it would only diminish the man who chose to employ him, even if the accusation was palpably true. Gherson had tried to hide in the cable tier during the battle, needing to be hauled out by a midshipman and forced to stay in the place of danger; it was doubly galling that he had survived unscathed.

'I shall fetch a pair of hands to help you, sir.'

It was unfortunate that the two closest and barely occupied were Charlie Taverner and Rufus Dommet. Poor Beresford could not know that, if they were now volunteers, these men had once been press-ganged by his captain from a tavern set in a place where such acts were illegal. It took some time for Ralph Barclay to both look at and acknowledge them but when he did so his thoughts of prize money and what he could buy with it evaporated.

'Not that pair, damn you,' Ralph Barclay cried, for even if he was looking at them he was thinking of that scoundrel John Pearce, with whom they were associated under that stupid Pelican soubriquet of theirs. 'They would as like cast me down a companionway as help me.'

If Ralph Barclay had the right to fix the two men with a basilisk stare they did not have the freedom to respond in kind, for Charlie and Rufus were nought but common seamen, who lived at the mercy of such men as the ship's captain. Dismissed, without once ever matching his stare, they knuckled their foreheads and turned away as Beresford called forward two other souls to help the invalid.

'Chance gone begging there, Charlie,' hissed Rufus, his freckled face alight.

'Not half, mate,' came the whispered reply from Taverner. 'Nought would give me greater joy than to see that bastard take a tumble.'

'As long as it did for him it would be sweet.'

'Trouble is, Rufus, he knows who we are, an' that can't be to the good.'

'You sayin' he did not know we was aboard before?'

'Can't have done, Rufus, or I reckon we'd have stripes on our back by now.'

'Happen when we make port, Charlie, John Pearce will be waiting there to take us off.'

'Pray for it mate, for with Devenow and that bastard Gherson aboard as well, we've got three devil's on our tails, not just the one.'

In the great cabin, Cornelius Gherson was working on the endless logs required by the Admiralty and Navy Board that gave evidence of the proper running of one of His Majesty's ships of war; every item of food, drink and stores consumed had to be listed and accounted for, while after a battle the repairs that required the use of canvas and rigging, ropes, pulleys and chains, as well as timber, nails, paint and even turpentine seemed to never end. This was a task for which he was well suited, though there was some sorrow that the various peculations he had carried out so far since HMS *Semele* had been commissioned would be required to be set aside.

The clerks who examined these logs had a fearsome and completely unjustified reputation for diligence; in truth they were as lax in the pursuance of their duties as any man who acted without too much supervision and was overpaid for their task, more interested in their privileges and the quality of their claret than their responsibilities. Most submitted logs got no more than a cursory examination, meaning that a certain amount could go missing without being spotted. A fleet action changed that and eagle eyes would scour the books for signs of sloppiness brought on by the euphoria of victory; those Admiralty clerks hated the notion that another might prosper.

Yet even as he added, subtracted and listed, Gherson's thoughts were on other problems, not least his relationship with Ralph Barclay; never entirely sound, it was now much diminished by his recent behaviour. Worse, over the horizon lay not just the coast of England but also the lies he had told to get him out of a tight spot. Tasked to get the copy of the court martial papers that would damn his employer, he had not only failed to even find them, he had assured Barclay that his mission had been successful and they had been destroyed by burning.

If he did not know where they were precisely, Gherson assumed they had to be in the possession of Emily Barclay and that presaged great trouble. That they could see his employer hanged if ever produced in a court of law was less of a consideration; Cornelius Gherson was only troubled by that thought in the sense that it would impede his own progress to where he wanted to be, clerk to an admiral either on a profitable station or in command of a fleet, a position from which could be extracted, by fair means or foul, a great deal of money. It might be time to seek another employer.

He had done well so far, going from press-ganged sailor at the outbreak of war to his present position, which he could hope to hold, given Barclay needed his skills to ensure he made the most of what could be procured by a little light peculation and the care of his investments. It was even better considering he had ended up at sea after an attempt at murder by chucking him off London Bridge, brought about by previous thefts as well as the seduction of the young wife of his then employer, the city nabob called Alderman Denby Carruthers.

He had survived the raging River Thames by dint of a strong hand on his shirt and ended up in the navy, obliged to mess alongside all those unfortunates taken from the Pelican Tavern. Still, for Gherson, in a life of continual ups and downs, its twin, good luck, had always followed misfortune, so he put aside matters of which time itself could only take care. He concentrated instead on ideas of how he could best extract personal profit from Ralph Barclay's sudden acquisition of increased wealth.

Alderman Denby Carruthers knew nothing about the construction of ships and was well aware that a devious seller would know how to use paint and putty to make look better some tub likely to leak through its timbers. No fool, he had engaged the services of an experienced old salt who was long past the age at which he desired to go to sea, a one-time ship's master who had sailed merchant vessels on the triangular passage all of his seaborne life. Not that he was in search of a true blue-water boat; the vessel he had been tasked to buy, specifications given to him by the Tolland brothers, required a shallow draught added to decently copious holds and it also needed to be dry and weatherly. No point in loading it with valuable contraband only to have it ruined by the seepage of seawater.

Even if he had never engaged in the illicit trade, Carruthers knew only too well that smuggling had ever been a profitable enterprise. That had only increased with a war going badly and that was doubly the case recently: the Duke of York had taken an army to Flanders, marched it to and fro only to begin to bring it home again, so he was now the butt of a wonderful ditty that had been composed on his return, a song that everyone was singing, much to the chagrin of his father, King George. Nor did it go down well at the Horse Guards building, the place from which the army was run.

Indeed he was humming 'The Grand Old Duke of York' as he paced the deck, waiting for his old sailor to come up from the bilges where he had claimed the smell alone would tell him half of what he needed to know. The Tollands had said they did their trade out of Gravelines on the Flanders coast, now in the hands of the armies of Revolutionary France. His worry that such a force would impede the trade had been set

48

aside; even Jacobins needed to trade for gold and the smugglers brought in that commodity while taking away the fruits of the luxury French trades. That they had lost their previous vessel he knew, if he was not aware of how; it mattered little – they were in need of financing and he had the funds to support them and that was all he would do. They would take the risks and between them they could share the rewards.

A very successful man of business he did not live a life without concerns, though none of that related to his business or his substantial wealth. His gremlins lay in the domestic sphere, for he now realised that it had been folly for a man of his age to marry a much younger bride, who had not only cuckolded him with the clerk he had once employed, but was now, he was certain, trying to make contact with the fellow again. That had him glaring at the River Thames, hard by which the vessel being examined was berthed, and it was as though that waterway had failed him. He had seen Cornelius Gherson, short of the fine clothing bought for him by Catherine Carruthers, his besotted paramour, chucked by two brawny helpers into the river at a point where the water flowed fast and deadly through the arches of London Bridge. How had the swine survived to come back and haunt him?

Then the second plan he had hatched to take care of Gherson had failed and he could only console himself with the fact not every venture in which he had engaged returned a profit; that was the way of business. If anything, his scheme had added to his troubles by placing him in obligation to a low-life villain called Jonathan Codge, the man he had engaged to rid his world of Gherson; in fact he had sought to get shot of both of them in one fell swoop by dobbing them to the Bow Street Runners but somehow Codge had got out of that too, which left him having to buy the man off with a monthly stipend.

Still, matters were in hand to solve all his problems and if not fully formed they soon would be; if he was short on the kind of hard bargains who would see to his needs, he was fortunate to be related by marriage to a man who did know where to find them. Edward Druce, as a successful prize agent, knew the kind of men who made up the London press gangs and they fitted the bill when it came to muscle. Not only would he rid himself of Codge but also something had to be done about his wife Catherine.

He had forgiven her once, yet it would be folly to do so again – and then there was his new clerk: Gherson's replacement, Isaac Lavery, seemed to have taken her side. Dismissal would serve for him, plus the word put around that he was light-fingered; such an accusation would see him in the workhouse, for no one would employ him after a city alderman, a man destined one day to be mayor, had trashed his probity. Such thoughts evaporated, for his white-haired sailor was coming up from below and it was time for business; time to work out, if all was well, a price. That was where Alderman Denby Carruthers was at his happiest; the thought of driving a hard bargain, given the other meaning of the expression on which he had just been cogitating, made him laugh for the first time in days.

In the tangled web that had been created by an illegal act of pressing seamen from the Pelican Tavern there was one other person of consequence in the mix – even if he had not actually been present – and that was Emily Barclay's nephew, Midshipman Toby Burns. He, a weak character, had been coerced by his uncle into lying at a court martial set up to examine the accusation made by John Pearce and his fellow Pelicans, all four of them sent off on a mission to the Bay of Biscay along with anyone else privy to the truth of the matter, leaving depositions detailing the facts of the case of illegal impressment.

Toby Burns claimed in court to have been a member of the party who attacked the Pelicans when in fact he had been all the time aboard HMS *Brilliant*, berthed off Sheerness. His contribution to saving the skin of his uncle by marriage had been to take responsibility for getting the press gang ashore at the wrong part of the Thames riverside, which had provided enough leeway for a deliberately appointed and benign court to acquit.

If the act of committing perjury had been uncomfortable, then the price paid could hardly have been said to be better. Toby Burns now saw himself in the clutches of people determined to do him harm, not least the man who had chosen the officers to sit in judgement at that court martial off Toulon, the same man who made sure that the Pelican depositions went unrecorded. He was the senior officer who had issued orders that sent away the hostile witnesses, those very same Pelicans, as well as any member of *Brilliant*'s crew who could vouchsafe the truth.

Sir William Hotham was a well-connected and very political admiral; he was also the second in command of the Mediterranean Fleet and he had protected Ralph Barclay because he was a client officer, a man who could be trusted to offer support in Hotham's ongoing battle with his superior, Lord Hood. Toby's reward for his lies had been a posting to HMS *Britannia*, Hotham's flagship, where those who shared his rank saw him as much cosseted and granted opportunities to distinguish himself. The midshipman saw matters very differently: to his mind Hotham kept putting him in situations in which he stood a very high risk of being killed or maimed.

These last weeks had been even more uncomfortable as each day he reached into his sea chest to reread the letter that had arrived from London with the fleet's despatches. There, in plain ink, was the upshot of the whole affair, the intimation from a Grey's Inn lawyer, a fellow called Lucknor, that the truth of the whole court-martial charade, as well as his part in it, was known. If the missive did not actually say that – indeed it was couched in a spirit of cool enquiry and requested a response – even a brain as slow as Toby's own could, from the words used, extrapolate the true meaning.

It was nothing more than a threat to dish him, which, if it had merely meant dismissal from the navy he would welcome. But a few seemingly disinterested enquiries of his own as to the penalty for perjury had elicited the probable outcome – it was a hanging offence – information which made him run a hand round his throat and did nothing for his ability to sleep at night; his dreams were nightmares and awake in the dark it was even worse, the whole compounded by the fact that he had no one to confide in, not being gifted with anyone he could really call a friend.

Toby Burns could guess that the man at the centre of his troubles had to be John Pearce; the only other person who knew of his offence, apart from Hotham and Ralph Barclay, was his Aunt Emily and he could not believe that she would sacrifice him and disgrace the family in the process. Yet curse Pearce as he did and frequently, to do so provided no solution to his dilemma – what to say in reply to this Lucknor fellow.

The sight of HMS *Agamemnon*, refitted at Gibraltar and rejoining the fleet after weeks of absence, provided a possible solution. Dick Farmiloe, a fellow mid aboard HMS *Brilliant*, who had truly been at the Pelican Tavern and had been part of that illegal press gang, was serving with Captain Nelson as an acting lieutenant. Could he be asked for advice, given he was a culprit in the original offence and therefore at some risk himself?

The stiffening of those around him was a clear indication that Admiral Hotham had come on deck and Toby Burns likewise became erect while ensuring his hat was straight. Passed a telescope, Hotham raised it languidly to his eye and fixed the approaching sixty-four. If he admired her lines, and many did for she was the fastest ship of the line in the fleet, it was not that which brought forth the subsequent comment but the nature of the man who commanded her, a fellow whom the admiral despised.

'Prepare, gentlemen,' Hotham intoned to no one in particular, 'to be treated to yet another boring account of Captain Nelson's glittering destiny.' The pitch of his voice changed perceptibly, became abrasive. 'One day I look forward to putting the popinjay in his proper place, which for me would be a bumboat. Let him find a burial spot in Westminster Abbey from there, eh?'

Everyone laughed, even if few agreed; the younger men admired Horatio Nelson, as much if not more than the ship he was lucky enough to command. Yet it was the nature of the service that when an admiral made a remark of that kind, then it was politic to seem to be seen to concur. Toby Burns did laugh with true heart, for he approved of the sentiment.

CHAPTER FOUR

On arrival back at the King's Head, Emily Barclay was perplexed to see what appeared to be her trunk and valise outside the front entrance. The latter, a small case being near new and part of her trousseau, it was quite distinctive enough for there to be no mistake. So it was with a degree of deep curiosity that she thanked and dismissed her elderly limner-cum-instructor and watched him as he took off in his rickety single-horse hack, the easel she had used poking up from the rear.

Carrying the work she had done that day, a single canvas, Emily came out of the dipping sunshine into the cool and dark interior, her eyes slowly adjusting to the change of light making it difficult to discern the nature of the two men standing there. That soon eased, allowing her to see the owner of the inn, as well as his concerned face, but her gaze was quickly transferred to the furious and florid countenance of the other fellow. He was a short and rather fat naval officer, bewigged under his tricorn hat and an admiral by the gold frogging that heavily adorned his coat. Added to that, he had a horsewhip coiled in his hand and that was twitching in such a way as to be a matter of some concern.

'Madam!' he cried, lifting the whip and pointing it at her, his eyes sinking to take in the hem of a dress made muddy by traversing the still wet fields. 'Though I doubt the appellation to be the correct one, I demand to know who you are and under what pretext you dare to call yourself the wife of a naval officer, one, I might add, that does not exist.'

The shock of the accusation seemed to pass through her body like that she received when two rubbed pieces of cloth produced an unpleasant effect and even on some occasions a spark. With a tremulous voice she made the only demand she could think of.

'And who, sir, are you?'

'He is Admiral Sir Berkley Sumner,' the owner of the inn responded, wringing his hands and clearly worried. 'A person of consequence in the county.'

'That I am, just as I am here to expose you for what you are, as well as the lying scoundrel whom, I suspect, seeks to dun this poor innkeeper fellow out of his due. I will not use this horsewhip on a woman, God forbid I should stoop so low, but I have it in my hand to chastise the false Lieutenant Raynesford when he dares to appear, and I can tell you he will feel its weight up and down the entire High Street of the town. The reputation of the King's Navy demands it!'

Shocked as she was, Emily had been given those several seconds to think by the length of that tirade. The use of the Raynesford name and the accusation that it was false nailed at least part of the problem. If she knew her situation to be one of deep concern, she also knew that she had no choice but to go on the offensive, mixing truth with some very necessary lies.

'How dare you, sir!'

'What?' the admiral responded, his already ruddy face going puce as he seemed to fill his rotund body with air, in the production of a reply he was given no time to make.

'I am the wife of a serving naval officer, sir, and I expect to be treated with the courtesy that position carries.'

'There is no Lieutenant Raynesford,' the innkeeper said, 'and between you and the man who uses that name you have brought my humble tavern into disgrace. Your names were mentioned in the *Hampshire Chronicle* as being a respectable couple. Now the word is out you ain't and the town's abuzz with it.'

'I do believe my husband paid you a deal of money before he left, enough to cover his absence – enough, indeed, for over a month-long stay.'

'He did, but—'

'Then how can this old fool say he has set out to dun you when I have not been here that long?'

The horsewhip was loosened then, the leather tip falling to the floor. 'Old fool!'

'I cannot think you anything else, sir, since you did not enquire if my husband had put my staying behind here on a bill to be later settled or paid well in advance.'

'Bill be damned.'

'Mind your tongue, sir! I will have you know I am not accustomed, nor will I tolerate even from my husband, such foul language in my presence.'

That again was true; she had checked Ralph Barclay any number of times when he transgressed and John Pearce had not escaped censure either, though he had laughed off her sense of decorum as if it was nonsense.

'Do not seek to divert me, madam. I contacted the Admiralty seeking to find out who this Raynesford was and the reply came back from the secretary himself that there was no one known to them of that name in the service. It therefore follows the man you call your husband is an impostor, which can have only one reason and if there is no criminality in his dealing with this fellow at my side, I am sure there is some somewhere, either now or in the future.'

'I must ask you to leave, Mrs . . .'

The confusion of the innkeeper's face, added to the continued wringing of his hands, infuriated Emily. The man had been happy enough to take their money without enquiry as to their true status and now he was bleating about his loss of face. No doubt, with the fat little red-faced admiral shouting his mouth off, the whole town was abuzz with the fact that the King's Head was home to a pair of adulterers, as if such a thing was uncommon, when such liaisons sustained half the inns in England. Yet that was a minor consideration: underlying everything was the precariousness of her position, for she had willingly given credence to that impression, willingly engaged in criminal conversation with John Pearce under a false name, and what would be the consequences of such an act? Somehow, in this place she must save face, or at least do enough to ensure her reputation until she could get away.

She had no idea when Pearce would return, so to stay in Lymington, possibly for days if not weeks, as the butt of gossip and finger pointing from the prurient locals, was anathema. However, Emily was not prepared to be tossed out into the street like some common trollop. She and Pearce had lied when they came to this place and for now it was imperative that falsehood be not only maintained but also reinforced, so she manufactured a most imperious tone.

'Nothing, my man, would convince me to stay in your hovel a day longer than I require, but since you have been paid for my accommodation and food you will oblige me by fetching back inside my valise as well as my trunk and, as there is no coach out of Lymington until morning, you will have to put up with my presence for one more night.'

Throughout these irate exchanges her mind had been working on another level, seeking a way to deflect her accuser and she dredged up one card to play that might see this Admiral Sumner off. She knew the nature of the mission that Pearce was carrying out on behalf of the Government, just as she knew it was one shrouded in secrecy, for if he had told her what he was setting out to discover he had also sworn her to keep the information to herself, as well as why.

William Pitt ran a government permanently on the cusp of being outvoted, indeed he depended on the support of his political opponents to stay in office and pursue the war. These were men who would not take kindly to anything smacking of a diversion from what they saw as the main effort and that was an expedition to the Caribbean to take the French sugar islands, this while many of the thinking classes in England harboured a deep suspicion of what was happening in the Vendée due to its openly Papist bent. Thus Pearce's mission had to be kept from scrutiny, the very reason it had been financed by funds hidden from parliamentary examination.

Fixing her countenance in a stern and reproving expression, she turned to Sumner and went on the attack. 'As to you, sir, I think it best you crawl back into whichever hole from which you have emerged, for you are in danger of being exposed as not only a fool but a danger to the nation.'

'What?'

'It did not occur to you to enquire where my husband is or what he is about?'

'Why would it?' Sumner sneered.

'It should have. Do not be surprised, sir, to receive from the Admiralty an admonishment for poking your flabby nose in to matters which do not concern you, for endangering the safety of the nation and for risking the life and reputation of a gallant officer held in high regard by those whose task it is to run the country and prosecute the war with France.'

'What stuff and nonsense is this?'

'I admit my married name is not Raynesford and nor is it that of my husband.'

'Ah-hah, the truth at last.'

It is, Emily thought, but not as you see it, though that allowed her to speak part of what she was saying with utter conviction.

'But you would have been better wondering why a naval officer would choose to employ subterfuge by using a false name rather than jumping to a conclusion that it indicated illegality. My husband is, as of this moment, at sea in command of a King's ship, sir, and I do not know that they are such fools at the Admiralty as to entrust a vessel to an impostor.'

'What ship, by damn?'

'I am not at liberty to tell you that and nor, if my husband were here, could he. Nor would he be able to enlighten you to the nature of the mission in which he is presently engaged, for that, sir, is a secret.'

For the first time Emily could see a crack in the admiral's certainty; if he did not yet look troubled, he looked perplexed.

'Secret?'

'Just that! It is also vital to the security of Britannia, so I suggest it would serve you to depart and put from your mind what it is you have been about, for not to do so could see you in the Tower. The least I can offer you is not to inform the Admiralty of your foolish actions, though I cannot guarantee that my husband, once he has been appraised of your interference in matters which are none of your concern, will not pass on to the powers that be the fact that you have threatened to destroy what it is they are trying to achieve. What the consequences of that will be I cannot tell you, but possible disgrace looms and it will certainly find no favour at the Admiralty.'

Emily could not know how those last few words played on the mind of Sir Berkley Sumner. He was, to those who had known him throughout his naval career, a prize dolt and, in terms of naval competence, a proper danger to those with whom he served. Having got to his captaincy through family connections rather than ability, from there he had, with age and seniority, though without a scintilla of sea time, risen to his admiral's rank. Never likely to be entrusted with a command, Sumner was destined to be and remain a 'yellow admiral', the soubriquet for an officer who might carry the rank but would never raise his flag at sea.

These were opinions of which he was unaware and did not share: Sumner reckoned himself as a genius both in the art of command at sea and the tactics required to achieve a great victory over his nation's enemies, sure that those now leading the fleets were inferior to him in all regards. Thus he bombarded the Admiralty with pleas for a position suited to the talents he held were his and lived in constant fury at the rebuffs he received, however politely they were couched. His face, now showing doubt, told Emily that she had struck home, that Sumner was wondering if he had inadvertently overreached himself.

'The Tower,' he said weakly.

'Perhaps not that, sir, but certainly censure. I decline to mention the fate of Admiral Byng.'

No word could have hit home harder to a vainglorious fool; Byng had been shot by firing squad on his own quarterdeck for his failures off Minorca. But there was the matter of dignity, not to say the need to cover what might prove to have been a mistake.

'Madam, I will not receive censure for doing my duty.'

'I was rather referring to your exceeding it, sir.'

Sumner pulled himself up to his full, if insubstantial height and again used the horsewhip to point at Emily, jabbing it to make his purpose plain. 'I judge by your manner and facility of tongue that you are a lady of some intelligence. It may be you speak the truth. Have no doubt I will make enquiries regarding that—'

'Do so, Admiral Sumner,' Emily responded, cutting right across him again and forcing onto her face a knowing smile that did not lack a trace of pity; she did not feel as relaxed as she hoped she looked, for in her chest her heart was pounding, as it had been since she had come through the door. 'I see you as a man who cares not one jot for the peril to which he may expose himself and perhaps it will be seen as such. Then again, perhaps it will not. What a sad end it will be to a long and no doubt distinguished career, in the service of His Majesty.'

That got a meaningless grunt, but it also got him brushing past her and out into the street. Emily did not turn to see him go, she looked hard at the innkeeper.

'Be so good as to fetch my luggage and then, when you have done that, make sure that a place is booked for me on the morning coach. I shall, of course, eat in my rooms tonight, and as to payments made and reimbursement, I will leave my husband to deal with that on his return to England. Added to that you will observe the mud on the hem of my dress. I require that to be cleaned.'

The entirely made-up posture held until Emily was safe in her little parlour. Only then did the facade crack and tears begin to wet her pupils as she realised what a close call it had been. She had lied so convincingly and, looking around the rooms in which she and John Pearce had made love against all the laws of the land and holy matrimony, it made her wonder just how much

64

the standards by which she had been raised had been eroded, which was not a comfortable state of mind.

The use of the long oars, even with the tide to help, ensured that progress was slow, so it was late afternoon before Buckler's Hard came into sight. HMS *Larcher* swept round the last bend in the river, a turn of ninety degrees that allowed the wind to play on what little sail Pearce had kept aloft and they assisted the forward movement. This relieved a weary crew to go about the duties required to get the armed cutter to a berth and obliged Pearce to put back on his heavy blue coat, for a boat had set off immediately they were sighted to lead them to the mid-river buoy to which they were to tie up.

There was little to see other than that for which the hamlet had been created by a long-dead Lord Montague; it was a site for shipbuilding set at the base of the New Forest, with enough water to float out empty hulls at high tide and an ample supply of suitable timber, long-matured oaks, near at hand from the forests planted eight hundred years before by William the Conqueror to facilitate his love of hunting. Boats had originally been built on the single hard that stood between two rows of red-brick cottages, these sitting at right angles to the River Beaulieu, literally rising from frame to hull outside the front doors of the resident workers, a practice that lapsed as vessels grew too large in size.

Now twin slipways rose out of the still waters, they

containing the vessels presently under construction, one a sleek frigate, the other hull a much more bulky seventy-four. The cottages remained, the homes of the workers and their families, creating a charming aspect given the open ground between them. There were more than a dozen trades accommodated in those cottages and many more workers came in from the surrounding countryside; shipwrights, ironworkers, caulkers, the sawyers with their ten-foot serrated blades used to cut the great planks from solid oak trunks. There were coopers and smiths, plumbers and riggers, all the way down to labourers and oakum boys. Over the intervening distance came the sound of hammers on wood and metal, while smoke rose lazily into the warm evening air from the pitch heaters and forges.

'I got your dunnage ready, sir,' said Michael O'Hagan, very quietly. 'As well as that of the French lady and gent.'

That 'sir' made Pearce smile; if ever there was man not naturally a servant it was his friend and, in truth, it had been no more than a convenience; Michael was to be admired for his loyalty, his strength and his good sense but not his gentility. Pearce's reply, made without turning round, was equally soft, though it was hardly necessary as the commands began to be issued as shouts by the various warrants that would see the armed cutter at anchor.

'You'll be able to go back to calling me John-boy as soon as we're ashore, Michael.'

'Sure, and won't I be grateful for it, for I'm weary of the sound of my grovelling. Mind, I might have occasion to curse you an' all, given you've become too fond of that blue coat of yours, as well as ordering folk about.'

There was no need to turn to note that the remark was intended to be humorous, it was in the deliberately mordant tone. 'Somehow, Michael, I don't think any curses heading my way will be coming from you.'

'There's a rate of trouble awaiting, that's for certain.'

'I'm sure Emily will see sense once matters are explained,' Pearce replied, more from hope than conviction; he was not about to be open on the subject of his doubts even with a close friend.

'Weren't her I was thinkin' of. Your Frenchie might not go quiet.'

'I've already told her that she's . . .'

'Not your squeeze,' Michael said, filling in the gap Pearce had left by not quickly finishing the sentence. 'She might have said that to you, but I see the look in her eye when your attention be elsewhere and you allow her the deck. It is not short of hope.'

'You're mistaken.'

Michael laughed softly. 'Holy Mary, if I were you I'd be looking for an easier life, like puttin' about and seeking out to tackle those French escorts we slipped by a few days past.'

That conversation and the aid of the wind had got them near abreast of the village so that the twin lines of cottages were in full view; so was the lack of anything beyond them, for behind the twin rows of red brick lay a flat landscape bereft of any distinguishing features barring a few fields and endless forest. Both Pearce's passengers were on deck to observe the arrival.

'Monsieur,' called the Count de Puisaye in his own tongue, his face bearing a look of distaste as he gazed at the barren and open countryside now exposed. 'Surely we are not to land here?'

'We will do so,' Pearce replied, speaking in the same language and including an equally distressed Amélie in the statement. 'This is from where we set out and I am obliged to bring the vessel back to this anchorage.'

Obliged, Pearce thought sadly, because of the temporary nature of the command. For all I know, Rackham, the fellow who holds the post permanently, is fully recovered from whatever ailed him and, at this very moment, is gathering his own dunnage to come back aboard, where he can ply his flogging cat and keep going his various peculations, all spotted in the logs Pearce had studied when coming aboard.

'But there is nothing here,' Puisaye cried, employing a sweeping gesture accompanied by the kind of hurt tone, evidence of his personal vanity, which had already irritated his host since their first meeting. It was as if he was expecting a guard of honour as well as a delegation from St James' Palace to be waiting in all their finery, so the reply was short of understanding; in fact it was downright brusque.

'There is a road, monsieur, and one that will take you to where you need to go, just as soon as I can arrange transport.' Then he turned to Michael. 'We will need to take that strongbox ashore as well and find a way to get what's left safe to London.'

'Some of those hard-looking sods that delivered it would be handy. It would make a good day's work for any thief who could get their hands on it.'

'I fear, Michael, the task will fall to you and I.'

'Then happen we'll be travelling with loaded pistols.'

The item referred to had come to them in a sealed coach with a strong escort, having originally held a sum of some thousand guineas, albeit the coins were from various countries such as doubloons and louis d'or, Dutch guilders, and even the not long minted American dollar. They had been provided in ten evenly filled bags by the Government, or more precisely by the prime minister's right-hand man, Henry Dundas, the purpose to facilitate the rebellion in the Vendée if it was seen fit to disburse it. The strongbox now contained in value near four hundred pounds in gold coins.

Between them Pearce and Michael O'Hagan had carried six of the pouches into the marshes where the rebels resided and they had left the money there for the intended purpose, even if Pearce had serious doubts it would do any good. Given Dundas had said it had come from something called the contingency fund, Pearce reckoned it to be money that had to be kept from public view – such a fund had to have a secret purpose. He could not just hand it over to anyone, which meant the safe option of boating it to Portsmouth and putting it in the care of the Port Admiral was not available. Besides, since it was his personal responsibility, he had signed for it, so there was no choice but to keep the residue under his own care until it could be formally handed back and accounted for.

'Come to think of it, I will have to raid one of the remaining bags to pay for a coach to London for our count as well as the strongbox itself. I'm damned if I'm going to facilitate the journey for either out of my own purse.'

'And who, sir,' Michael asked with a twinkle in his bright blue eyes, 'is going to pay out for the lady?'

'Dundas can pay for her as well,' Pearce snapped, as he turned and entered his tiny cabin, Michael on his heels. 'Now I need to go ashore and bespeak some kind of conveyance big enough to get our charges to Lymington.'

'Are you sure that's were you should take them?'

'I have no choice, Michael,' Pearce responded, as he unlocked the strongbox. 'The coach that will get Puisaye to London goes from there.'

'Sure, John-boy,' Michael hissed, too softly to be overheard, 'you've not thought it through. The coach passes and picks up at a few places on the way, an' if my memory is right some of them ain't much further off than Lymington.'

The response came when Pearce was standing up, a thick canvas bag in his hand, which he was unlacing to open: the prospect of getting Amélie away without Emily ever knowing he had brought her back. 'Now why did I not think of that?'

'Don't you know, sir,' Michael said in a louder voice, as well as one not short on irony, 'that the donning of a blue coat, from what I have been able to see with my own eyes, does little for clear thinking or common sense?'

CHAPTER FIVE

Heading back up the main New Forest road towards his home in Winchester, at a much more leisurely pace than that with which he had made the original journey, Admiral Sir Berkley Sumner was busy composing in his head the letter he would send to the Secretary to the Board of Admiralty. Sir Phillip Stephens was the person to whom he had despatched an enquiry regarding Lieutenant Raynesford, prompted by the appearance of the name in the social column of the *Hampshire Chronicle* as having recently arrived at the King's Head in Lymington.

First he would acknowledge that his curiosity about serving naval officers was an indication of his deep interest in his profession (to others he was a nosy old soak). Then he would show appreciation for the man's acuity, as well as the quite proper discretion he exercised in failing to include him in what was a covert undertaking. He would then tell Sir Phillip of how he had, by pure accident, come across and aided the secret scheme being undertaken by the aforesaid Lieutenant Raynesford, indeed he would make the point that, thanks to his timely input he could modestly suggest that matters were on course for an improved conclusion.

This would back up what would inevitably follow, for he was much given to pestering Sir Phillip and the Board, a repeated request that, given he had proved his worth as a gallant and intelligent officer he be given his due in terms of employment at sea, or if that was not available, a shore command that went with his rank and abilities.

If the *Comte* de Puisaye had been troubled by the sheer lack of anything of prominence in the appearance of Buckler's Hard, the same notion occurred to Jahleel Tolland when he actually got round to examining how he was going to accost John Pearce. He and his brother, when making enquiries, had not attracted more than the slight level of interest accorded to strangers, albeit Franklin's scar being so obviously recent had aroused comment; the same could not be said for a group of eight armed and mounted men riding in to the place at a pace to send up clods of the greensward, and that was not aided by their appearance. They looked like what they were, a band of right hard cases, and in a spot full of toiling labourers they stuck out like a sore thumb.

Seeing they were being eyed by and pointed to by the locals and not with kind expressions, Jahleel ordered a swift about turn before they were a third of the way to the jetty, seeking by his expression to imply that somehow they had taken a wrong route and ended up not where they intended to be. They made their way back to the point at which the road divided and took the turning back towards Lyndhurst, Jahleel calling a halt when they came to a wooded copse about half a mile distant, there to get out of sight and to formulate a new plan of action.

The Tolland gang thus missed an unescorted John Pearce coming ashore to seek a way of transporting his 'guests' out of the area and on to meet the northbound coach at Lyndhurst, not that he was given much more in the way of satisfaction. Buckler's Hard was a place truly at the end of the line – there was no bridge across the river and little beyond it to attract outsiders not connected to the work being carried on or shooting the local wildfowl in the marshlands and forest that extended to the seashore.

The only visitors to the place tended to be naval surveyors or people in some way connected with the acquisition of the ships being built and they made straight for the home of the master builder, which stood some way outside the village on a higher elevation. Anyone else would be a carter delivering those things needed to build the hulls that were not available from the surrounding countryside, and there was a ramshackle inn in which they could stay, a place that also served as an alehouse for the workers who lived and worked on the hard.

Though amply provided with horseflesh and carts, these needed to move the heavier objects such as shaped timbers and forged metalwork from the workshops to the slipways, there was nothing of a more comfortable nature to be had, certainly no covered coaches, and not even a shay for hire. The only conveyance Pearce was offered was an open-topped cart normally used to carry bales of oakum and looking as if it had seen much better days; two of the wheels appeared set to come adrift as soon as they hit a deep mud patch or, when it was dry, the kind of ruts he had been obliged to negotiate on first coming here.

That he declined for the very simple reason that such a humble conveyance would further serve to upset the *Comte* de Puisaye – and probably Amélie Labordière as well – so it came down to a quartet of the local New Forest ponies, which, if they were animals of no great height, would suffice. He also bespoke a carthorse and panniers to carry the luggage of the ongoing travellers, the whole, including harness and saddles, rented at what Pearce reckoned to be an exorbitant price and that took no account of the deposit the fellow required to ensure his property was returned in prime condition.

Having made his bargain, the stablekeeper, perhaps because he observed how piqued was this client at the cost, became much more sociable, extolling the virtues of his ponies, they being sturdy beasts and very suited to the area in which they lived regardless of season. Bred wild they were captured to either be trained or culled in order that the numbers remained sustainable, the best breeding stock kept and the rest sold on for work in tunnelling and mining where their size and strength was valuable.

'I was a'telling the very same thing to that friend of yours.'

'Friend?'

'Aye, the fellow who came by a few days back asking for you.'

Pearce had never subscribed to the theory that humans had hackles that could rise at a sign of danger, but the way the hair at the base of his neck behaved felt remarkably like that of a dog.

'Looking for me?'

'You is Lieutenant Pearce?' That acknowledged the man continued. 'He was asking when you would be making your berth in the river agin, not that I or any other could say fer certain.'

'Did he give a name?'

That had the stablekeeper sucking his teeth and looking perplexed. 'Don't recall he did, sir.'

Working hard to control his voice, Pearce said, 'Then you'd best tell me what he looked like.'

'A lone, fresh scar on his left cheek, Michael, and when I asked about on the hard he was not alone, and from the description of the two together . . .'

'Mother of God, how did they know where to find you?'

'A question I have been gnawing on since the man mentioned that scar.'

'Not much chance of the two of them being alone?'

Pearce did not respond immediately, he was wondering if discovery of him included knowledge of the whereabouts of Emily; if it did there was not much he could do about it, the only positive thought being that at least she had not booked into the King's Head under the Barclay name, which should protect her.

'None. Eight of them we faced in London and we would have to reckon the same here.'

'Any notion of where they are now?'

Pearce shook his head then sat upright and slowly looked around the anchorage, a place surrounded by ample woodland – there was a dense oak forest to the west on a slightly higher elevation – and his brow cleared somewhat. He was thinking that there had been no sign of any danger while he was renting those ponies, which led to an obvious conclusion: the Tollands were not in the village. If they had been, and with him alone, what he was doing now would be idle speculation for he would already be in their hands – all it needed was a pistol in the ribs and a demand he do as he was told.

How, then, did they intend to proceed in taking him for he had no doubt that was their aim? If not in the village it could only be on the road that led to both Lyndhurst and, by a detour, the quickest route to Lymington. But to do that they would need a clear sight of his departure, a point he made to the man sitting with him.

'And if they have the ship under observation they will know when we depart.'

'But not how many?'

'The addition of Puisaye and Amélie will not aid us, Michael, quite the reverse.'

'I was thinking the presence of others might give them pause.'

'And what if it does not? Do you recall the words of the older brother when we overheard them talking, that he would have his money or my skin in place of it? That same fate could stretch to anyone who is with me if I'm caught, you included, and I would remind you, we on this ship are the only folk who know of our French pair. Think what it's like out there – miles of deep forest, most of which never feels the feet of man, and ask yourself what our combined fate could be?'

Both men fell silent for a moment as that thought struck home: they could just disappear.

'What about seeking a parley, John-boy and telling them the truth of the matter, that you was robbed as much as were they?'

'They would scarce believe that, given I still cannot credit what I fell for myself.'

No one likes to be reminded that they have been a fool, as had he, and it was near as uncomfortable now as it had been when he first realised just how easily he had fallen for the deception. A sharp fellow who called himself Arthur Winston – not his real name – had dangled before him what looked like a chance to make a great deal of money from the recovery of a contraband cargo, made up of items becoming more expensive by the day as the war failed to progress: bolts of silk and lace, barrels of brandy, fine French wines, perfumes, all the commodities so beloved by those with money to buy.

How much had his own stupidity contributed to his being drawn in to the scheme, how much had it been the prospect of being able to offer comfort to Emily Barclay without the need of anything from her husband rich with prize money? It mattered not; he had recruited his Pelicans then sailed to the Flanders port of Gravelines, seeking to recover 'Winston's' ship and cargo, one for which he claimed to have already put up the money, to free it from a local who had refused to release it without a second massive payment. And he had succeeded, the only trouble being that it had never been 'Winston's' ship or his cargo; it had been the property of the Tollands, professional smugglers who very likely now sat athwart his route out of Buckler's Hard, and if he had scant real acquaintance with them it had been enough to show they were murderous. They were also serious and clearly had connections – had they not pursued him first to Dover, then to London and now, amazingly, to here?

Still convinced that he had carried off a legitimate coup regarding the contraband, Pearce had sailed their ship into St Margaret's Bay just north of Dover and beached it, so that too had been forfeit to the excise. It might be their legal property, but only a fool would reclaim a vessel just taken in the act of smuggling. The cargo? That had disappeared with John Pearce watching and helpless, immobilised by an injured foot, this as the bay filled with men come to make the arrests for which they had been tipped; at least he had been able to get Michael, Rufus and Charlie Taverner away along the tidal shore that led to Deal before they arrived to arrest him.

It was in the nature of things that the two friends reprised the whole affair in detail, being in search of a solution, an exchange that took place at the very prow of the ship and it was one designed not to be overheard because Pearce had made it plain to the rest of the crew that he wanted some private space to talk to his friend-cum-servant. He should have known better; if you could not keep a secret on a ship of the line – it was held as an absolute truth that Jack tar could hear a whisper through six inches of planking – the chances of doing so in a cramped armed cutter were zero. A ship's crew were always agog to know what was being planned; captains made decisions regarding their future, including matters of life and death, without so much as a by your leave and since they cared for it more than any officer it was as well to know what fate awaited them over the metaphorical horizon.

Not that all were privy to what was being discussed;

the bosun, known to all as Birdy, slight of frame if well muscled, had slipped into the space below the prow under the bow chaser gun port, open on a warm day to let in to the 'tween deck air enough to dry out the timbers. Birdy learnt enough to make out that if nothing had been said that the crew should be concerned about, what he had overheard meant a threat to their temporary commander and soon, once he had extracted himself from his eavesdropping, that was disseminated.

It would be stretching things to say that the crew of HMS *Larcher* loved John Pearce – few of the lower deck loved any officer and the armed cutter had as well a small number of endemic malcontents who hated him just for his coat. But in the main they had come to esteem him, given the contrast with the real ship's captain, a well-named tyrant. Unlike Rackham, Pearce was honest and fair-minded, given to smiling instead of scowling, polite when called upon to be so instead of in a state of constant ire at slights and failures real or imagined.

He had also shown real flair in a fight, as well as trust in the crew to perform to their best and had said how pleased he was when they did. Sailing through that armada of merchant ships without alerting them or their escorts had been skilful and much appreciated; if he had failed, the best his crew could have hoped for was a French dungeon, with a watery grave a real possibility. Given that their opinion of him stood as it did, one of their number was elected to speak for them all.

'A word, if you please, Captain?'

Half sat on the prow bulkhead and deep in conversation with Michael, Pearce had not noticed the approach, which had been made by a master who in such a small vessel, like the rest of the crew, worked barefoot.

'Mr Dorling.'

Looking up into the man's face, round and clean-skinned, he sensed that Dorling was worried, for his normally smooth forehead was slightly furrowed, while the eyes, small for the size of his head, were narrowed. A fellow who always appeared to Pearce as serious – hardly surprising given his responsibilities at such a young age – his temporary commander felt that underneath lay a personality much more inclined to humour than misery; in another life and at another time Dorling would have been a companion of sharp wit and scant respect.

Given the master did not speak immediately, this allowed Pearce to look beyond him and see that, if they were trying not to look in his direction, the whole crew were somehow attached to this approach, the only disinterested person the Count de Puisaye, who was sitting in a quarterdeck chair plying a makeshift fishing rod; Amélie was in the cabin avoiding the sun, which she was sure would damage her delicate skin.

'It has come to our attention, sir, that you seem in some way troubled. If I were to refer to smugglers I think that would nail the concern.'

Having looked at Dorling as he spoke these opening words, a sharp shifting of the eyes caught the fact that everyone else on deck, who should have been engaged in the raising of sails for drying, was immobile, which only lasted till they realised he was looking in their direction; the sudden burst of movement was obvious as ropes squealed and canvas flapped.

'Sure you been at the keyhole, have you not?' growled Michael.

Pearce leant backwards and glanced at the open gun port, a clear indication that he too had guessed what had occurred. 'I'm not much given to flogging, but sometimes—'

If he had hoped to cow Dorling he failed; the voice was firm and quick to interrupt, which was ill disciplined in the extreme and very out of character. 'I speak out of respect for you, sir.'

It was O'Hagan who replied, underlining what everyone had believed: whoever the giant Irishman was, and they knew as little of him as their temporary captain, he was no servant. 'And what is it you have to say?'

'Only this, your honour, that if you has a problem then the men aboard would not feel it beyond their duty to help out. From what we know, numbers seem to be the problem an', well, we has that to more'n match, I reckon.'

Pearce had dropped his head before Dorling finished, deeply touched by the sentiment, even if there was still a residue of irritation at the eavesdropping, and the response, when he spoke, went mostly into his chest. 'I'm not sure that would do, Mr Dorling, using men of the King's Navy to settle a private dispute.'

Dorling finally smiled, which wholly improved the look of his features and hinted at the good companion he might be. 'Don't see how you can stop us, sir. All you has to do is allow enough of us ashore, which, I would remind you, can only be done on your say so.'

'And how many do you speak for?'

'To a man, your honour, to a man,' Dorling replied, with real force. He was gilding it, for there were some who maintained it was none of their concern that an officer was in trouble; they could be ignored, there were more than enough willing. 'Christ, even the ship's boys are up for it.'

'Even when they have no idea what they face?'

'Can't be worse than a fleet of Frenchies.'

'It is,' Pearce replied, with much in the way of passion, 'or at least close enough to give pause.'

In the ensuing silence Michael O'Hagan knew that his friend was thinking the thing through, for it was not as simple as either the master or the crew supposed. This was no shore-going barney like you had in a port-side alehouse or gin den, where the worst you would face was a well-aimed fist and maybe being crowned by a chair leg. The Tollands were proper hard bargains and smugglers who carried the weapons they needed to protect themselves and their smuggled goods. They would be armed with swords, at least, and very likely pistols as well and such men were inured to the need to kill when called upon to do so; they could not have survived in their game without it.

'Would you let us talk of this, Mr Dorling?' Michael asked.

'As you wish, Paddy.'

That got a frown. 'I thought it was known that being called Paddy I did not much take to.'

'Sorry.'

Michael grinned. 'Sure, it is the first time you have erred, Mr Dorling. It's the second time that ends in a fuss.'

That had the master looking at O'Hagan's ham-like fists; he knew what a fuss meant. As he made to leave Pearce added, 'I would like this conversation to be completely private.'

'I will make sure it is, sir.'

As he turned and walked away there was a cry from the bulkhead near the wheel, in French, which told them that Puisaye had caught something. His makeshift rod was bent and a couple of hands had, unbidden, gone to help him, given they saw him as an old crock of a fellow, near to being infirm. One grabbed the line and whipped it up and over the side, to show on the end a wriggling trout.

It was a mordant Pearce who said, 'I think I know just how that poor creature feels.'

'We have a good offer, John-boy.'

'Do we, Michael? How can I accept when I have no

idea what kind of danger these lads might be exposed to? The Tollands will be well armed and they know how to use their weapons.'

'There are guns aboard the ship.'

'Which could turn Buckler's Hard into a battlefield.'

'They are not in the village, remember.'

'I wonder if we might be able to bluff them by a mere show of strength.'

'I would be more minded to a real one, for bluff only buys time.'

'Which could possibly be achieved without someone being either seriously wounded or killed. If you want to set hares running with magistrates and the like, that would be a good way to do it without any notion of where it might end. I have been had up for too many things in my time, Michael, I have no notion to be arraigned for murder.'

'There is another way, John-boy: we take to a boat and head for another place to land.'

Pearce shook his head slowly. 'Think on how they found us.'

'I can think but I cannot find answer, yet it tells me what has been done once can be done again and since I am by your side I am as much at risk as you. My face is known to them and for all I can tell my name as well. We can run from them now but will that mean running for ever? That is a question to which we have no answer. We have been so very lucky, you and I – even Mrs Barclay – and that must run out sometime.'

'So,' Pearce sighed, which indicated his level of optimism, 'you are saying that it must be faced here and we must find some way of gaining resolution.'

'I am saying you must let the crew aid us. At least with numbers we have a chance.'

That led to a long silence, but Pearce responded finally. 'It might up to a point, Michael, but only up to a point.'

'Frenchie coming,' Michael said quietly.

'Monsieur,' the count demanded. 'When will we depart for London?'

The thud of a boat coming alongside and with no shortage of noise distracted both Pearce and the count. Bellam, the ship's cook, began slinging onto the deck a case of wine, various sacks of fresh victuals, one of which, by its shape and being wrapped in muslin, looked to be a substantial rib of beef that Pearce had asked him to seek out for his last meal aboard, which he intended should be something of a celebration and, to please his guests, one held at a more shore-common hour. The three o'clock naval dining hour they had found as hard to accept as the quality of what they were given to eat.

'We cannot leave today, monsieur, it is too late in the day. Perhaps on the morrow.' The disappointment, if not downright disapproval, was obvious. 'But, for tonight, I promise you a capital dinner, and since you have caught one fish and that will not feed three, I would admonish you to ply your rod again and get us another for it would make a fine opening course.'

'What was all that about?' Bellam asked as he hauled himself aboard.

'Christ knows, mate,' came the reply from Brad Kempshall, the ship's carpenter, dark-haired twin to the blond gunner Sam. 'Lessen you know the lingo you can't tell. But that apart, I would take it as a kindness if, when you was bringing a boat alongside, you showed a bit more care.'

The reply was loud and on such a small deck was taken in by all. 'An' there's me seeking to straighten out the wood you left warped and you plying the trade of Christ's old father hisself. Some folks never give thanks.'

Pearce found himself looking along a deck of laughing tars; he was not laughing, he was trying to work out how to play his hand, which, despite the promise of support, did not seem an exceptionally good one, yet in being barracked by Michael a germ of a solution began to present itself.

CHAPTER SIX

'Light's fading,' wheezed Cole, the man first set to watch HMS *Larcher* and newly returned. 'Added, there's no sign of a boat castin' off. Looks to me as if they was setting out a table on the deck and there's smoke coming from the galley chimney.'

'Damn the sod.'

'We ain't got now't to keep us goin', either, and I'm sharp set.'

'For the love of Christ,' Jahleel spat, 'stop thinkin' on your belly.'

'If'n you can stop it a'rumblin', Jahleel, I'll stop moanin' for sure.' He jerked a thumb to where the hobbled mounts were grazing. 'The only things getting fed are the horses an' that's what we will be on, plain grass.'

'Never mind the rumbling,' Franklin interjected,

'somebody has to go back and make sure Pearce stays aboard.'

'Ain't goin' to come off in the dark, brother,' Jahleel said, for once without any trace of rancour, looking skyward at what was rapidly turning from light blue to a deeper hue. 'Even if it is a starry night, it is not a road to be travelling by moonlight.'

'A tankard of ale might ease things,' Cole said.

'Now there's a good notion,' Franklin responded with a sneer. 'The only place to get that is in the hard tavern and that is full of the locals. Jahleel's planning to do Pearce in and you want to sit blathering to them and let them see our faces close up.'

'All I is sayin' is I don't fancy sitting out all night with not a drink to pass my lips nor a bite of food to eat.'

Jahleel Tolland laughed, a low chuckle really. 'Should get you in the mood to take it out on Pearce of a mornin', I'd say.'

'Will do an' all,' Cole snarled, 'that is, if you stand back long enough to give a body a chance.'

'Cephas,' Jahleel said to another of the gang, as he pulled out and peered at his Hunter. 'Go keep watch for a bit; I'll send someone to take over after a while.'

'Can we light a fire, at least, Jahleel?'

'It's a warm night and we are sound here, unless you reckon this here forest be full of demons.'

'Why'd you say that?' Cole wailed.

'I know you're a'feard of them, that's why,' Jahleel roared, 'an' if they's ever comin' for you Cole, this night is as good as any. Bless me, did I see yonder tree move a bit closer?'

A chorus of ghoulish wails from all of the gang followed that, which had Cole covering his ears; he was man who believed very strongly in evil spirits. But Cole got his way; enough dry kindling was found to get a blaze going, bits of broken-off and seasoned branches, of which the forest was well supplied, only dampened on the bark by the recent rain, turning that into a warming fire that each man was reluctant to leave when it came to their turn to take over the watch on the armed cutter.

A small table had been set up on the tiny quarterdeck, with lanterns rigged above to provide light when the last of the sun disappeared, a more comfortable way to dine than they had enjoyed at sea, sitting on the casement lockers in the ship's cramped cabin, yet it was far from a relaxed occasion despite the improved quality of the food. Pearce gnawed on what he had planned while the Count de Puisaye was once more in the kind of expansive and confident mood regarding the future of his country, claims that grated on his host's nerves, given it was so divorced from reality.

The citizen armies that had defeated the likes of the Duke of Brunswick and forced the coalition raised against the revolution to retreat, and had, from what he knew, made life a misery for the British Army's action in Flanders, would be swept aside by the ragtag peasants of the Vendée, for they had their faith as well as God on their side. A great host would be gathered on the march to Paris as people rose up in their thousands to sweep aside the apostates who had so ruined proud France. For John Pearce the only way to avoid his direct gaze, demanding agreement to these preposterous claims, was to hide behind the rim of his tankard and pretend to drink deeply.

Amélie was silent throughout and Pearce wondered if it was because of her fellow countryman's hyperbole of if she had an inkling of what was going to happen on the morrow, which seemed to add a deepness and unhappiness to the looks she threw in his direction, not dissimilar to those mention by Michael O'Hagan. If he had seen them, Pearce had worked hard to avoid them, yet he knew they were present. He had been deliberately indifferent to her over the preceding days for the very good reason that any show of sympathy could have untoward consequences, not that his attempts to get to sleep were unsullied by temptation; he could hear her movements, and worse for slumber he could remember the pleasure of their previous couplings.

At least the food was good: fresh trout – for Puisaye, with much assistance, had been successful twice more; the beef was pink and the vegetables were fresh from a cook who, at anchor on a calm river and with no discernible wind, reckoned there was scant reason to boil the meat and instead oversaw it being properly roasted; likewise the carrots and greens were crisp rather than soft, the potatoes allowed to roast in the juices alongside the beef. Proud of his efforts, the fellow hovered until he was complimented for his efforts.

'It is so good, Mr Bellam, it could match any meal I had in Paris.'

As soon as the words were out of his mouth, Pearce was aware that if he had drunk little, it was enough to loosen his guard; a mention of the French capital was not a good idea in the present company, the truth of that immediately apparent when the count asked for a translation. Much as he tried to weave a tale round it, the name of the city still hung in the air, causing Amélie to respond.

'Do we not have many fond memories, Jean, of our time together in Paris?'

This being almost the first time she had spoken without she was responding to a question from Puisaye, Pearce found he needed his tankard again, this time to avoid her eyes, which had about them a pleading look. That could not stay at his lips for ever and when it was downed he had to reply.

'That is in the past, Amélie.'

'And what is to be my future?'

Pearce was not only cursing the question but the fact that it had been posed in the presence of Puisaye – the few exchanges he had allowed outside normal conversation had been done out of earshot of the only other French speaker aboard; not now, and it was as plain by his expression that the count was just as curious as Amélie, which was damned annoying.

'You are a charge upon my conscience.'

'What a strange expression, Jean.'

It is, he thought, but I am not going to say I will take care of you, for that is an expression too loaded to employ.

'I cannot give you what you lost, but . . .' The tankard came up again to be drained, for he did not know how to conclude the sentence.

It was telling the way her hand went to her cheek, as if she was underlining that her beauty, with which he had been so struck on first meeting her, was no longer as it had once been; Amélie had suffered in her flight from a life of luxury to a Vendée swamp, but it was more than that, for she had also aged. So had he, but time had been unkind to a woman who was already many years older when they had first met, her worldly knowledge being, to an inexperienced youth, a great part of her attraction.

'No one can give me back what is gone.'

'Your husband—'

The interjection was sharp. 'I was not referring to Armand.'

'He died in a noble cause,' said the count in his customary sententious way.

'Odd,' Amélie replied, a sour note in her voice, 'that all causes are termed noble, monsieur. I have heard Jacobins use the same expression and I am sure it is one used by that ogre Robespierre and his Committee of Public Safety.'

'You cannot doubt that the cause we represent is anything other than just!'

Amélie dropped her head and spoke the single word, '*Non.*' It implied the exact opposite, inferred that such sentiments were for fools, and if Puisaye had possessed half a brain – a department in which he was seriously lacking – he would have spotted it. His next words underlined that.

'In the future you will recover that which was both yours and that which belonged to your late husband. France will once again have a king and will once again have our prelates and priests, as well as a docile and contented peasantry. I have no doubt of my ability to convince the Government of England—'

'Great Britain,' Pearce interjected, losing patience with this posturing. 'England is only part of the country of which you speak.'

Puisaye waved that away as if it was no account, which annoyed Pearce even more; if he was far from even slightly rabid in the cause of Caledonia, he still came from Scottish stock. Failing to mention that country or Wales was a habit hard enough to bear in the English and not to be borne at all in a foreigner.

'As I was saying, when I have outlined to them what can be achieved with support, I am sure that they will despatch powerful forces to the Vendée. Then it is we who will employ the guillotine to rid our beautiful land of the scum who have despoiled it.'

'You have yet to answer my question, Jean.'

'I . . .'

'You are committed elsewhere.'

'I am not sure the lady of whom you speak would understand.'

'What is to understand? We were lovers – that has cooled but we can still be friends.'

How could he say that such a thing could not be, that this was stuffy England not lax Paris, to even attempt it might destroy the thing he sought most at this moment in his life? He was sure that even to mention Amélie to Emily – God they share a name, which he had not realised previously – would cause complications over which he would have no control. The chance to speak the truth was there for him to take advantage of; prevarication won hands down.

'Let us leave that aside for now,' Pearce finally responded, picking up the full bottle that had replaced the one just emptied. 'More wine?'

HMS *Queen Charlotte* had raised Penlee Point and with much banging of signal guns from the flagship the Channel Fleet entered Plymouth Sound. Those vessels most in need of repair were sent upriver to the dockyard, the rest anchoring as commanded by the flagship. As soon as they were secured and the necessary reports and logs were delivered to *Queen Charlotte* the ship visiting began and along with that invitations to dine.

Ralph Barclay was forced to decline that he should be called upon to move – he pleaded his wound – and so missed the first round of dinners, instead receiving aboard HMS *Semele* the following day a pair of officer acquaintances who esteemed him as a colleague and had been made aware of his infirmity. Whistles blew and marines saluted as they came aboard; Albemarle Bertie from HMS *Thunderer* and Anthony Molloy of HMS *Caesar*, accompanied by their premiers, the table made up to full with the addition of Ralph Barclay's own remaining lieutenants and a spotty midshipman.

He was in possession of ample stores, having been a recipient already in this war of a decent amount of prize money, and he had been granted ample time to send ashore for the very best local produce. Thus Ralph Barclay was able to set a good table and ply his guests with wine of a high quality. Throughout the meal the battle in which they had so recently been engaged was re-fought in a manner that allowed it to move from the experience of each of the commanders individually to a collective appreciation of the whole.

With the guests as cheered by victory as their host it did not take long, and this was the nature of the service, for Lord Howe's actions in the battle to come under a less than flattering scrutiny. Had he pressed home the attack with sufficient vigour? Could more have been done to confound the enemy? Why had the fleet not pursued the fleeing French to seek to take more prizes, given the damage to many of their ships was greater than that of the British Fleet? On the whole it was agreed any captain present – indeed most of the lieutenants, they were informed – could have done better.

'He's far too old for the task,' opined Bertie, his round, childlike face being shaken to underline the folly of giving command to a man of such advanced years. 'Word is he left the deck before the action was over. Past his three score years and ten, and as for Curtis, well he's an old woman, to my mind.'

There was a moment of silence as that thought was ruminated upon; as Captain of Fleet, in essence the executive officer and advisor to the commanding admiral, Sir Roger Curtis would have had a great say in what actions had been undertaken and he would have taken over direction of the battle when Howe retired to his cabin. His abilities were equally traduced.

'Then there is the grain convoy,' Ralph Barclay said, this to fellow officers who looked mystified at the reference, causing their host to add, with a degree of caution, 'You surely recall that the purpose of the fleet being at sea was to intercept that convoy, which we signally failed to do.'

'Never saw the damned thing,' Molloy responded.

This was said in a tone more forthright than he had employed in discussing the battle, an action from which HMS *Caesar* had emerged unscathed, having not been in a position to close with the enemy. His peers had nodded sagely as he explained why that should be, accepting that regardless of Howe's orders to do so, the state of his ship and the nature of the wind had made such a thing impossible.

'Precisely,' Ralph Barclay said, slapping the tabletop

and fixing his guests with a knowing look. He reminded them of the first sighted frigate and what had followed as they, indeed the whole Channel Fleet, had pursued it. 'I have an inkling that we might have been deliberately drawn off by that fellow. Led us straight to his main fleet, did he not, and quite possibly away from the grain convoy.'

Nods were all his fellow captains would allow themselves as they recalled what their host was saying was true and what it might portend; France was rumoured to be on the verge of starvation after yet another poor harvest and if that came to pass the revolutionary government was bound to fall. The convoy in question, up to, it was said, a couple of hundred deep-hulled merchantmen, had set sail from the United States weeks before with enough grain aboard to alleviate the problem of famine, which, in essence meant the continuation of the war.

Ralph Barclay carried on talking, the note in his voice emboldened by a decent amount of claret. 'Might have been better to have ignored that frigate and gone in search of the convoy. Happen Black Dick Howe will get a rap on the knuckles instead of the praise and the dukedom he expects.'

'You might have the right of it, Barclay,' Albemarle Bertie insisted, 'but you'll have the devil of a job persuading anyone now of such a view. Hindsight rarely does the trick in such matters.'

'Not so, Bertie, given I took the precaution of noting

that possibility in my log at the time. We are talking of foresight not hindsight.'

'How much do you reckon on the prize money, Barclay?' Molloy asked, looking bored with what was being discussed.

That changed the subject swiftly and it was generally agreed that the sum to be distributed for what had been taken, this calculated by men who knew their stuff, could not be much less than a quarter of a million pounds sterling, which had the junior officers trying to silently calculate what it meant for them on fiddling fingers hidden under the table.

Bertie raised his glass at the sum mentioned. 'Then I say, damn the grain convoy, let's drink to that.'

'Hear him,' chorused the assembled lieutenants and the solitary mid, as hands appeared to lift and empty their wine.

The meal on the deck had a dual purpose; if HMS *Larcher* was being watched – in truth, John Pearce – then he being in plain sight was highly desirable, ten times more so as the light began to fade and the rigged lanterns made it easy to concentrate on the trio sitting at the table. What would not cause comment was a couple of boats going from ship to shore picking up stores – fresh bread and newly baked biscuit, as well as vegetables that even as temporary captain Pearce had an obligation to purchase by a warrant drawn on the Navy Office. It would have taken a sharp eye to discern that each time one returned laden it had two fewer men aboard than had set out. That allowed for the gathering of a small party to go out and ensure, first, that the Tollands were not as Pearce suspected in the village, but encamped somewhere off the road he must take out.

Dorling and another hand had taken the jolly boat downriver, rods out and seemingly fishing, to seek out the second part of Pearce's plan and that had not happened until the master had assured his captain that he was prepared to be on the wrong side of the law in carrying out what was proposed, the crew likewise, though, in truth, the risks for the future and any censure all lay with Pearce. He and Puisaye were consuming some of Rackham's supplies of port, Amélie having retired, when Dorling returned to say he had found what was required.

'Then, once the lanterns are doused I will make a show of bedding down for the night. Let us hope that whoever is watching has no trouble keeping their eyes open.'

'As long as they see you at first light, sir, they will be confident.'

The last word produced a frown; he might have thought the whole matter through but John Pearce was very far from sanguine about everything going to plan, even when Dorling knelt to tell him all was in place on the shore.

CHAPTER SEVEN

Sleeping through noise at sea was necessary: the wind whistling through the rigging, the creak of moving timbers. On a ship sat in a quiet tidal waterway it should have been different, with only an anchor watch set and no requirement change every four hours or to be up at first light. Yet the ship's hour bell still tolled and that by habit caused a single eye to open. Then came the dawn birdsong, the odd cawing seagull included, but these were not the only things to disturb a fitful night's sleep as, once more huddled on deck in his boat cloak, John Pearce gnawed on all the problems that beset his life and not just his fears for the coming day, the whole compounded by the buzzing in his ears of insects made more numerous by the recent rain, which provided many shallow puddles in which to breed.

Intent on feeding off his blood they had been inside his boat cloak leaving behind itches that demanded to be scratched, but really it was the early dawn that made sleep impossible. Forced to be up with the lark and uncaring about being observed from the shore, Pearce stripped off and dived naked into the chill water of the river. Michael O'Hagan, through habit, was also awake and by the ship's side to haul him out, a towel at the ready added to an expression that told the swimmer he was mad to so expose himself. Dressed before the hands were piped to breakfast Pearce was, in all respects, ready for whatever the day might bring.

'Mr Dorling, is all prepared?'

'As much as it can be, sir; all we need now are your passengers.'

Pearce was eager to depart, but he was required to wait while Amélie used his cabin to carry out a lengthy and elaborate toilette, which had her one-time lover pacing the deck with impatience and asking Michael more than once if they might ever get ashore this day or any other. Not that matters would have been hastened by more alacrity on her part – *le Comte* de Puisaye likewise devoted much attention to both dressing and applying fresh powder to the wig he had not worn since coming aboard. He then produced from his travelling chest a fine crimson velvet jacket as well as a pristine white stock, breeches and stockings, to set off his silver-buckled and freshly blackened shoes, that before he began to festoon himself with various orders studded with jewels.

'Monsieur, that coat is inappropriate,' Pearce barked, then forced to produce an excuse that had nothing to do with facing armed and dangerous smugglers he added, 'we are travelling on horseback over dusty tracks, indeed there may still be mud.'

'Nevertheless, Captain, who knows what we will encounter on the way?' There was a terrible temptation then to tell him. 'I would not have your countryman think me anything other than that which I am.'

Pearce had to bite his tongue a second time then, to stop himself from saying, 'A pompous old dolt.'

Like the count Amélie Labordière had dressed as if she was going to a levee, in a gown of silk set with patterns of sequins, albeit she had covered her garments with a cloak. She had also taken much trouble with both powder and rouge, which went a long way to restoring her to an image of the beauty he remembered. That she knew it to be so was in the cast of her eye and the slight smile as she nodded to John Pearce, which had him turn away to meet the amused gaze of Michael O'Hagan.

He was carrying short pieces of rope, at the ends of which he had expertly fashioned a sort of cradle, this to carry the remainder of the Dundas gold, that not being something he could leave behind. The strongbox was too big and would have required a carthorse of its own so Michael had suggested a repeat of what they had done to transport it in the Vendée, only this time it would be carried in individual sacks which could be slung over the carthorse's flanks and not their shoulders, he having sworn he still bore the marks of the weight.

Pearce fished for the key to the great padlock, which had never left his coat pocket, and made his way into the cabin, there to extract from the strongbox the four weighty bags, these secured in Michael's contraption once his friend had extracted from one what he thought he would require to facilitate the journey, a sum in fact in excess of the suspected requirements, given there was no knowing how the day would turn out.

'Don't go back in the water with that in your purse,' Michael joked, seeing how much he had taken, 'or you'll sink to the bottom.'

'Might be a blessing for all concerned.'

'I have not packed your pistols and they are loaded and primed.'

There was a moment then when the two locked eyes, for in planning his scheme, Pearce had been insistent that no risks be taken that might see anyone killed. But Michael held his gaze and Pearce knew he would not budge, so he shrugged and threw the padlock and key into the open box, wondering what the man he had temporarily replaced would make of its presence when he came aboard.

'Keep them out of sight.'

'Place smells a mite better than normal,' Michael said, a twinkle in his eye, as he sought to kill off the crabbed mood. 'A lady's perfume is better than vinegar any day.'

Pearce was not in the mood to be ribbed. 'If you are going to keep this joshing up I can see where those pistols you loaded might come in handy.'

He grabbed his logs and returned to the deck. The boat was over the side waiting for them and Pearce was touched to see that the oarsmen had taken as much care in preparation for his departure as their French passengers had for their own; whether it was play-acting or genuine he did not know, but they were wearing their best shore-going rig, the long pigtails were greased and ribbon-festooned, each oarsman sitting stony-faced and looking forward as if they were crewing an admiral's barge.

Nor did they deviate from that as Pearce made a short speech of thanks to those lined up on deck, shaking hands with the warrants before going over the side, boat cloak over his arm, to the high-pitched whistle of the bosun's pipe. With chests occupying space and the sheer bulk of O'Hagan there was scant room to sit and misfortune had him pressed against Amélie on the same narrow thwart; with the sun now well up on a warm morning he could smell both the familiar perfume, the same as had infused his cabin, as well as the musk of her body, both of which played upon his memory. Added to that was the heat of her skin as their flesh inadvertently made contact, at which point he was made aware by his own bodily changes just how far he was from being immune to her charms; in short, his folded cloak, over which he had laid his sword, was a blessing.

The occasion of the party coming ashore was unusual enough to have a few idlers gather to watch their landing, which took all of two minutes from ship's side to the jetty, the sight of a finely dressed pair of French aristocrats certainly being far from normal in such a backwater. Curiosity turned to amusement as the mounts were brought forward, animals that so contrasted with the sartorial elegance on show – one, the carthorse, with a set of leather harness with which to strap on luggage.

Puisaye had about him an expression of aristocratic sangfroid even when faced with a fourteen-hand pony; he was not going to demean himself by showing the local peasants that this was anything other than normal and he got aboard his animal and sat on it as if it was the finest steed in creation, his nose high and eyes fixed forward as if he was about to lead an armed host into battle. Amélie, even on such a short-legged mount, had to be aided by Pearce, which produced more unwelcome intimacy.

Michael, once mounted, a satchel containing the encased brace of pistols over his shoulder, looked as if he could walk and ride the animal simultaneously; Pearce, albeit his legs were shorter, was not far off the same and thinking the sword he was wearing a damned nuisance. Loading complete they trotted out of Buckler's Hard, pursued by the local urchins making ribald comments about which arses were the fattest, equine or human.

'Shall I dismount and clip a couple of these cullies, John-boy?'

'Leave them be, friend, for if you don't look like a fool, I'm damn sure I do.'

'They're coming, Jahleel. I watched them land then mount and now they just left the cottages behind, our blue coat up front.'

'"They", Cephas?'

'Aye, four in all,' the smuggler replied. 'You recall that big bugger we traded blows with in London? Well he's along bringing up the rear an' towing a packhorse, but there's two right strange coves in't middle, a woman in a cloak and a man dressed like a nob on the way to a ball, powdered wig an' all. Whole party's aboard ponies too small for proper ridin', so we can take 'em as easy as kiss my hand.'

'Four makes matters altered,' Franklin said, as he primed and loaded his pistol, left till late because of the dampness of the forest. 'I was set for two to deal with.'

'Not to me, brother, if others are along where they've no right to be, that will be their misfortune. Now, let's get mounted and be at 'em.'

'Jahleel, think on it, for the love of Christ! Four folk and as described by Cephas won't have departed Buckler's Hard unseen. They might have made a right show and if that be the case they will be talked about all over the county in time. They go missing and there will be a hue and cry for certain.'

The lack of a response showed that Franklin had struck home and not just with his sibling.

'Go too far and you'll risk the rope for us all.'

Jahleel aimed his pistol at one of the trees and squinted down the barrel, which had the virtue of allowing him to avoid his brother's eye. 'He's not goin' to slip me again, Franklin; I said it an' I meant it, and if worst comes to worst, by the time their loss is noticed we will be long gone.'

Now it was the younger brother's turn to point up his scar, this done with his fingertips. 'I has even more cause to want revenge than you, Jahleel, but what is it we really want?'

'Blood – Pearce's blood.'

'No, we want that for sure, but just as much to know what happened to our cargo and the money it raised, sold on. Happen he was only a small part of it and if his blood would be a bonus, which I grant you, we'd be better served finding out the names of those who had the means to get our stuff ashore and profit by it.'

'We ain't got time for this,' Jahleel insisted, as two of the gang, sent to fetch the already saddled horses began to make their way back.

'They's movin', but dead slow,' Cephas intoned.

'So it makes no odds if they go by us,' Franklin added. 'We're well mounted and can catch them easy.'

'Get on those horses now – I ain't letting him pass an' I seem to recall what I says goes.'

'No killing,' Franklin insisted.

Jahleel stuck his weapon in his belt and grabbed the reins of his horse. 'Happen it might not be our choice, brother.'

Having been in the copse all night and most of the morning, even moving around, the wildlife had almost accepted their presence and it never occurred to men who were of the sea and not of the land that it could be otherwise. But the movement of eight horses and their riders changed that and the first pigeon broke noisily from the thick-leafed branches, an act which spooked the others. Within seconds the sky above the trees was full of flapping wings and they startled the other birds, the sight of which made Pearce feel much better. He knew that the Tollands were in that copse and he had been relying on them acting before he got abreast of it, for if they did not, things would be much harder.

If he could have heard Jahleel Tolland cursing he might have had a proper laugh; it was, of course, the fault of others not him, but he knew that very likely surprise was gone and he spurred his mount out onto the roadway without any attempt at subtlety, the rest behind him.

Pearce had already spoken in French to give instructions that his charges should stay still, brusquely dismissing the count's attempt to enquire as to why that should be, a question that became superfluous as the road ahead was filled across its width by eight properly mounted, grim-looking men all with pistols in their hands.

'Hold, Pearce,' Jahleel yelled, 'it time you paid for your folly.'

Michael, at the back, had taken out the pistols from

the wooden case, that thrown to the ground, eased back and locked the hammers, before kneeing his pony to get it to move forward until he was abreast of Pearce and could hand one over, an act remarked on by Tolland.

'It will be two pistols agin eight and no time I reckon to reload.'

'Monsieur?' the count demanded. 'What is this about?'

Pearce was brusque in the way he told the count that he had no time to explain, accompanied by the sound of Jahleel Tolland's voice again floating through the warm morning air. 'You can come on or flee, Pearce, it be up to you, but it will, in the end, make no odds.'

'What is it you want?'

That got a loud snort; it had to be to cover the distance that separated them. 'Now't much: a sound ship, a valuable cargo and, as a bonus, some of your skin, and I reckon you would do all a favour if you send off the lady and gent and allow us to have a little talk with you and your hulking mate.'

'I doubt it would do any good if I told you we made not a brass farthing from the whole escapade, that I was dunned as much as were you?'

'None at all,' Jahleel shouted, 'for we would not credit it. You'se a thieving bastard an' that be that.'

'Does the name Arthur Winston mean anything to you?'

'Never heard of him,' Jahleel spat, clearly thinking

111

what Pearce was up to. 'Now stop playing for time, that is if you don't want your lady and the gent in velvet to share your fate. Get rid of them now.'

Pearce had never thought they knew the man who called himself Arthur Winston but it was something he felt he needed confirmed; Tolland's dismissive tone implied that he had spoken the truth. As he trotted back to take station alongside Puisaye he was smiling, for he was indeed playing for time and he gave a long explanation of their predicament to both the count and Amélie.

'Monsieur, I will not explain why these men have come to seek me out, enough to tell you they mean me harm.' Amélie, close enough to hear the words, responded with such a sharp intake of breath that he addressed his next words to her. 'But I beg you not to worry, matters are in hand. Might I ask you, as I approach these men, to move over to one side of the road and get close to the trees.' Seeing the count's mouth open he added sharply, 'And please do not ask me why.'

Then he spun his pony again and, slowly, pulled out his sword, rested it on his shoulder and kicked his mount into a trot.

'He's going to do a death or glory charge,' suggested Franklin. 'He wants us to kill him.'

'Then shoot his pony,' growled Jahleel.

If they wondered what Pearce was about they were too busy looking at his face to concern themselves overmuch. Halting some twenty feet away he smiled

112

at both brothers and said. 'Gentlemen, I ask you to cast an eye over your shoulder.'

'Oldest trick in the game,' Jahleel snarled, unaware that Cole had done just that.

'Best have a look-see, Jahleel.'

'Don't be a fool . . .'

The elder Tolland had only turned to look at Cole, but he got no further, for there, in the very corner of his vision, lined up on the road, stood a party of a dozen sailors, each with a musket up and aimed at their backs. When he looked for Pearce he was no longer there; he and Michael were heading for the trees and out of the line of fire, at the same time opening enough distance to render the Tolland pistols close to ineffective.

'Hell and damnation!'

'Don't you go getting a twitch,' called Matthew Dorling, at Jahleel Tolland's cry. 'In fact, don't so much as do other than let those pistols drop to the road.'

'You reckon to do murder?' Franklin called, hoping to bluff a way of escape.

'We reckon to match what you was about, yes. We'll down you if you want, but at this range, I reckon a musket ball will tear a right hole in your flesh, enough to maim if not kill.'

'I should do as he says,' Pearce called, as he and Michael O'Hagan emerged from the copse in which the Tolland gang had been camped, to take up station halfway between his tars and the gang, but to the side to remain out of the line of fire. 'Drop the pistols, then the swords.'

'You have not the heart to kill, Pearce.'

'No, but I have the heart to put a couple of balls into your knees so that none of you will ever walk again.'

'Sure,' Michael cawed, 'I am not soft. One right in your eye will do for me.'

'It won't end here, Pearce, so happen you best let your Paddy do his worst.'

'Mother of God, the man doesn't know how close to the wind he's sailing.'

'You can, of course, send for a Justice of the Peace and perhaps explain that you are not highwaymen. I wonder if he would believe you when you are up against the word of a King's Officer, half the crew of one of his vessels, not to mention two total and foreign strangers. I think you know the penalty for highway robbery. Make quite a spectacle, and bring a huge crowd, eight men swinging at once.'

Dorling had brought his men forward in a line, so close that the musket barrels were now close to being pressed into the backs of the gang.

'Drop the weapons. Now!'

'You saying you won't hand us in?'

'To the Justice, no.'

'Murder us?'

'You can choose that course if you wish.'

'Jahleel, for the love of Christ.'

'Best listen to Cole, brother,' Franklin hissed. 'We've been right humbugged but at least we'll live to fight another day.'

Jahleel Tolland slowly let fall the hammer on his pistol and one of the sailors leapt forward to grab it from his hand, an act repeated until they were all unarmed and their weapons, swords and knives included, were gathered and made safe. Then they were obliged to dismount and once on the ground their horses were taken to be tied to the trees. The men of HMS *Larcher*, not without the odd sly and painful poke, expertly tied their hands, the whole eight then lashed to make it easy to walk in line.

'Mr Dorling, perhaps you would show our captives something, that little notion you whispered to me last night.'

'Line them up,' the master shouted, 'an' get your muskets, all of you.'

Weapons that had been laid aside were fetched, those who had stood armed and ready joining in to stand ten feet away from the Tolland gang, each musket raised and aimed, eye along the barrel, at a man's heart.

'I reckoned not to believe you,' Jahleel rasped.

'You'll hang of this, Pearce,' Franklin shouted, but if it was laced with anger there was high dose of fear included.

'Sir,' Cephas cried, 'we was only doing—'

He got no further; Jahleel headbutted him, which would have sent him reeling if he had not been tied. 'Don't beg, never beg.'

'I want you to know what kind of man I am,' Pearce replied. 'Steady yourself, lads, take good aim and now . . .' He held the suspense, saw many eyes close, but not those of Jahleel; he spat on the ground to let his executioner know what he thought of him. 'Fire.'

'Holy mother of Christ,' the one called Cole yelled, his open mouth showing his lack of teeth.

A dozen triggers were pulled, a dozen cocked hammers struck the flints to produce the necessary spark but there was no flash in the pan – the only sound was a dull click, and then the crew began to laugh. One of the gang fainted and had, like the still groggy Cephas, to be held up by the ropes that tied him. Two, judging by the pools that began to form at their feet, had soiled themselves and one was weeping. But there was one pair of eyes fixed on those of John Pearce that told him that the next part of his plan was as essential as what had just taken place.

CHAPTER EIGHT

There were matters to sort out, not least that the count and Amélie should be allowed to choose a horse to replace their ponies; they, like the carthorse, would be taken back to Buckler's Hard. Michael O'Hagan was going to be their escort to Lyndhurst, his task to get both on to the coach to Winchester, where, after a night's stay they could catch the flyer to London. The Irishman would then make his way to Lymington to where Pearce would go after and if his scheme was complete.

The old man continued to press for a more detailed explanation than Pearce was inclined to give; the men now sitting in a circle on the ground were people who meant him harm for things that had happened in the past and these were matters about which he was

117

not
∧ prepared to divulge the facts. He had underestimated the count's persistence and eventually, to fob him off, he hinted at there being a lady involved. That to a Frenchman made perfect sense; such a pity that Amélie overheard it, thus further diminishing him in her eyes; from being that young and eager lover in Paris he had, no doubt, descended to being seen as something of a satyr.

There was another argument with O'Hagan, who hated to see good money wasted. 'You can't just let the spare mounts go, John-boy, five good horses, not to mention the saddlery and harness.'

'They won't starve, Michael, we are surrounded by some of the best pasture in Britain, neither will they be lonely given the place is full of mare ponies. Who knows, they might improve the stock and, in time, some of the forest verderers will rope them in.'

'They would fetch a goodly sum of money.'

'They would also attract attention, Michael, for you will only be mounted on three. Why would such a small party have so many spare horses? No, we will let half of them go, take a fourth for the chests and if you can sell them in Lyndhurst, do so, but I have my doubts that anything equine has much value around here. In which case stable them until we can pick them up when we make our way back to London. We'll get a better price for them somewhere on that road, I'm sure, and besides, they can be got rid of one at a time, which will arouse less comment. Now I have to tell our

French friends what I have in mind for them, so fetch me that bag of coins we raided earlier.'

'The others?'

'Will go with me.'

That took time and it was obvious neither of his one-time passengers was entirely happy at the proposed arrangement, that was until Pearce produced that which he had held back, a half-full purse of gold. If Puisaye did not know how much it contained he could feel its weight and that mollified him somewhat, his only objection that without John Pearce he would struggle to make his case to the British Government.

'Monsieur, I will be in London in three days at the most. Please take the coach and make for Nerot's Hotel, where my name will aid you to get rooms. I will come to Nerot's as soon as I can and from there we will send word to Whitehall.' Then he turned to Amélie. 'I will also, from there, make contact with the French émigrés already in London, in the hope that one of them will find both you and the count a more permanent residence.'

'I have no desire to be a burden, Jean, on your conscience or your purse.' That made Pearce smart; he was having his own words thrown back in his face. 'I have my jewels to sell to support myself.'

'I do not say,' he responded coldly, 'that you will not have to consider such a sale, but not yet, not until I have seen you comfortably settled. Now, Monsieur the Count has the means to keep you until then, so if you do not mind I have matters to attend to which cannot be delayed.'

Michael had to be provided for as well, which Pearce did from his own purse, more than enough to get him to Lymington, and he took off him the satchel Michael had so that he could carry his pistols, recovered case included, and the remains of the government gold. While they were mounting up to depart, Pearce had the smugglers' saddlebags taken round so they could extract any personal items, he joking that unlike them he was not a thief and that what they took out could be rolled into their riding dusters, these tied into bundles for them by the *Larcher*'s crew. As that was happening, with much unobserved rummaging from Jahleel Tolland, he was saying a final farewell to his friend, now mounted.

'I take it, John-boy, that none of what has occurred here is to be told to Mrs Barclay?'

'God no, and forgive me if I remind you not to call her by that name. Remember its Raynesford in these parts.'

Emily Barclay knew that, waiting outside for the midday coach to make a short and prearranged stop at the King's Head – the morning one had been full – she was the object of much interest from the local population. Many women had found an excuse to promenade up and down, for her imminent departure had been passed down the parochial rumour-fed grapevine. All seemed to be in pairs, this no doubt so they could whisper to each other under their parasols and compare impressions, not one of which would be flattering.

There were a fair number of menfolk too, the idle of course, who might have been loitering anyway, but not just them. Better dressed and more well-fed creatures seemed to have found a reason to traverse Quay Street, which they did alone and, if they glanced in her direction and she caught their eye, Emily saw in that a message wholly different from that of their womenfolk – nothing short of a desire that, in better circumstances, they might have become acquainted.

Partly to damn the whole charade, she had dressed well in a gown that showed a decent amount of décolleté and done her hair so it was a crown above her head, that flattering her long and slender neck. She had also eschewed the wearing of a bonnet so that anyone who wished to gaze on her very obvious beauty could do so, that not being the reason Emily had dressed in that manner; like many very attractive women she did not see herself in that way, which would have meant indulging in the sin of vanity. Her motive was to face down their ill-informed criticism and to send the message that, for her, their opinion, especially that of the ladies of the town, carried no weight whatsoever.

There was also the fact that those well-heeled male admirers who had looked in her direction – many if not all of whom would have been hard-pressed to give a valid reason for their perambulations – would be marked, and she was in no doubt they would pay a price in local tittle-tattle for showing any interest in a person perceived as a fallen woman. Lymington, if smaller, was little different from her hometown of Frome; these were the provincial mores that were followed there and they would likewise pertain here.

The curious seemed to congregate as the four-horse coach made its way up the incline that formed the road to the harbour, its iron hoops rattling on the cobbles and the driver calling loudly to his team to put in more effort, till finally it stopped outside the front entrance. For a moment Emily thought she was going to be obliged to load her own luggage, so tardy was the man on the box to get down – no one from the inn itself was to hand – but having fixed him with a cold stare, he responded with a grunt and leapt down to do his duty.

'An' where would you be headed, lady?'

'Does it not suffice that I am leaving Lymington?'

'Curious, that's all.'

As, thought Emily, is everyone else; the whole town is dying to know where I am going, no doubt with a mind to writing if they have a close-by relative or friend to warn of what now resided in their vicinity. This was what John Pearce did not appreciate, that the act of living openly with another man out of wedlock was far from as simple as he supposed. Still, it could have been worse: she had once seen someone named as a strumpet pelted with sods of mud when being driven ignominiously out of Frome; it was to her shame now, as she took a seat in the coach, that she, a fourteen-year-old, had heartily approved of both the censure and the method of demonstrating it.

There were three other passengers in the coach and they had obviously been advised of her character; none would catch her eye.

With Michael gone in one direction and the Buckler's Hard equines in another, the time came for Pearce to gather his charges and get them moving, which took them into the forest and down a sloping track to the riverbank. Enquiries as to where they were being taken were ignored, as they joined two eight-oared ship's boats waiting in a small inlet, brought there by eight more sailors. Untied, the captives were split into two parties of four, were ushered aboard and once their restraints had been lashed to the thwarts on which they would sit, their escorts followed to take up the oars.

'What's the game, Pearce?' Franklin Tolland asked as the two boats were pushed off, the oars beginning a rhythmic dipping that took them quickly downriver.

'Peace and quiet, the latter of which you would be best served to follow, lest you want to be gagged. That goes for all of you. Stay silent and breathe easy or take a gag and struggle to get in air.'

Pearce would have loved to talk, to seek to tell them the whole story of his foolishness, to prove to them that he as a source of any information was a waste of

.fort. He probably would still not be believed and, besides, he had no desire to diminish himself in the presence of even such a benign group of tars that manned his boat. Not that his offence was extant: he had paid his price for the crime of smuggling, or rather Charlie Taverner and Rufus Dommet had done so by volunteering for the navy to get any sanction against him set aside. Smugglers, which they claimed and were believed to be, were highly prized aboard a warship, given they were already competent sailors who required no training in any aspect of sailing a ship or keeping it in good repair.

It had been a well-practised gambit for *contrabandiers* over the years to avoid being jailed or strung up for their nefarious trade: sacrifice a couple of their least competent men to the King's Navy and magistrates would set aside their convictions and see them wiped from the record. It never seemed to occur to those freeing their villains that they immediately went back to their old trade; replacing lost hands was never a problem in east-coast and Channel towns where smuggling was a near industry.

The boats moved at a steady enough pace on fresh water and a falling tide but that became less so as they exited the estuary and pulled out on to the Solent, where if there was not much of a sea it was enough to making rowing twice as hard. Pearce went down to four oars at a time and settled for the slower pace that imposed; if he wanted the business finished he had no mind that the crew of HMS *Larcher* should suffer for it.

In a busy shipping lane they occasionally came under scrutiny, in one instance close enough to a frigate for Pearce's blue coat to tell them that here were a pair of navy boats. Also the dishevelled state of their passengers, being in riding clothes clearly not tars like the men on the oars, was noticeable. The hail from the quarterdeck for information got no more than a wave; he was not about to shout out where he was going and given the frigate was heading out to sea they passed each other by in such a short space of time to not allow for repeated request.

'No need to be shy, Pearce,' Jahleel Tolland said, speaking for the first time since he had been forced aboard and lashed down. 'Don't take a sharp mind to work out what you're about, given the heading.'

'It won't last, Pearce,' Franklin spat. 'I for one will come after you till death takes my breath and there will be no more mercy in my thinking.'

'I never thought there was much anyway, and I would say this is a poor place to be sending out threats, that is unless you can swim.'

'Idle that,' Jahleel crowed. 'You ain't got the stomach to see a man die an' your hand in it.'

'So you keep telling me, which sits odd with the fellow you think I am. No, even if I can imagine what extremes you might have gone to question me, I cannot just do murder, nor condemn you to the hangman's noose. All I can assure you is a degree of discomfort that will be a daily burden on your black heart, for I have served before the mast in a King's ship.'

'You, now't but a hand.'

'More than just that, I hope, but none of your concern. Now be silent or face the gag.'

It was a long row, four on four, rarely out sight of the shore, until they raised the classical frontage of the Haslar seamen's hospital and Pearce got all the oars working. There was no mistaking the vessel he wanted, given it had three short stumps on its deck instead of tall masts. An old 100-gun ship it was now a hulk anchored offshore, the proximity to Haslar more to convenience the medical coves that needed to visit with frequency than anyone aboard.

As a vessel anchored head and stern and one that never moved, the receiving hulk HMS *York* was surrounded by its own filth — waste from both cooking, cleaning and the heads — dependent on the tide to remove the effluent, and that only ever wholly successful when there was a bit of a blow. Thus the smell easily overwhelmed the briny odour of clear water and had even Pearce's oarsmen looking uncomfortable as they swept round the stern to pull close to a gangway that led up to the barred entry port to the main deck.

If Jahleel Tolland had worked out the destination long past, half his gang had not and the sight and smell set them cursing and wailing, noises which Pearce made no attempt to stop; he had never taken pressed men aboard a vessel such as this but he had good grounds to feel that that was how they commonly behaved. Ordering the boats to be tied off he made his way up the gangway and spoke to the marine sentinel, who unlocked the gate and ushered him in. There was no ceremony here, no bosun's whistles or guard lined up, even if an admiral came calling; this was the pit of hell and indifference as far as the navy was concerned.

Nor was it a posting to attract the better class of officer, and the man in command, a Lieutenant Moyle, though he had granted himself some comfort in what had once been the captain's cabin, was very much not out of the top drawer. There were, to Pearce's mind, an excess of mirrors in the space but Moyle had a settle on which he could conduct business and a comfortable chair for his visitors or guests, for the pay and perks were good. It was a command that went to someone well connected or perhaps a fellow owed a favour by some superior officer.

His face was wide and his skin showed a trace of a bloodline not wholly British, perhaps with a Caribbean influence, for all that his eyes were blue, only truly visible when he took them from their common drooping state to wide open and that came about at any mention of money. Not that the subject came up first, for Pearce, while he was willing that the Tolland gang should be pressed and trigger a bounty, also had certain favours he wished to request, all designed to fit a policy yet to be forwarded.

'Prime hands, you say.'

'They are that, Mr Moyle, and it would not surprise me to find that they were engaged in the smuggling trade.'

'Then doubly welcome, sir. Would you care to make that assessment official?'

'No, but perhaps you could question them and ascertain the nature of their occupation.'

'There's credit to be had, Mr Pearce, for fetching in such men, and not just from the navy. The Government might issue you a reward.'

'Then, sir, let it be yours, for I am sure it will enhance your situation many times more than it will do so for my own.' That was when Pearce had to pause and look Moyle right in the eye, aware that such a statement of generosity had shocked the fellow. 'And for that perhaps you could do me a service in return?'

Moyle did not respond right away and the slight smile that came upon his face was far from reassuring; he looked to be a man too calculating to trust. 'And what would that be?'

'It is my intention to write to a certain post captain who has aboard his vessel two men I consider followers of mine.'

'You fear he will not release them?'

Now it was Pearce's turn to produce a wry smile. 'I fear we are not what you could call friends. I had in mind to offer him in their place twice the number and if they were prime hands, which I fully suspect these fellows I have fetched along to be, it would be an odd commanding officer who would hold out against such an offer.'

'You said eight volunteers in all.'

Pearce had to stop himself then; the navy called everyone they pressed a volunteer but it was pure smoke.

'Yes. I am aware that when a demand comes in for hands, a man in your position is not always able to oblige a fellow officer, even as much as you may desire to do so. I am very afraid that if these eight are sent together to one ship then that may be introducing onto the lower decks a nuisance capable of causing much dissent.'

Moyle knew what that meant: mutiny.

'So in order that such a thing should be guarded against, that is if you are unable to hold them and meet my previous request, the eight men should be split into two fours and sent to different vessels, with the added fact that two of them are brothers and should be separated. You cannot mistake them: one you will see as a natural leader—'

'He will not be that aboard my ship, sir,' Moyle barked, 'and if he tends to that, be so good as to point him out and I will see he receives special treatment to cool his spirit.'

'I believe his given name to be Jahleel and I do think a little extra discipline might do him good. The other brother is younger and seeks to appear more cultured.

He has a scar on his cheek and is easy to mark.'

'Be assured we shall take some rough sand to buff off his refinement.'

'Then I am content.'

'You are due a bounty, Mr Pearce,' Moyle said, standing from the settle and walking to his deck, pausing on the way to catch his image in one of the many mirrors, which hinted to Pearce at an excess of vanity. 'I will be happy to write the warrant that allows you to draw it from the Navy Board at your convenience.'

'Mr Moyle, I discussed with those hands I have the honour to command and we felt that since taking these men up was in the nature of being fortuitous it was felt that any bounty should go to the Greenwich Chest.' Pearce produced a false laugh. 'For none of us knows when we might be in need of a pension and with Haslar hard by it is also, in wartime, a place any one of us could end up with a wound.'

'That, sir, is very noble, indeed!' Moyle exclaimed, yet the look of cunning that crept into those narrowed eyes implied the opposite: that only a fool turns down a bounty. 'Charitable indeed.'

'Also,' Pearce said, knowing he was at the crux, 'it may well incline you towards my earlier request.'

That made Moyle sit down in his desk chair, very slowly, and it was clear his mind was working at pace and when he spoke he was obviously playing for time to continue whatever train of thought he was on. 'Your earlier request?'

'Yes, it is one that concerns me as you may have noticed. No officer likes to see his personal followers under the command of another and the officer in question is . . . how should I say . . . strict.'

'Of course.'

That was followed by several seconds of silence, in which all that could be heard was the creaking of the old hulk as it rose and fell on the swell. Then Moyle spoke, in a voice meant to be friendly, which it was not, unlike the calculation, which was clear.

'It occurs to me, sir, that if I enter these fellows as soon as they come aboard, I cannot keep them from any draft that is called for from a vessel short of hands and needing to get to sea, and that happens very frequently since every captain is short of hands.'

'To do so would risk your position, sir.'

'Sir, it would destroy it.'

'I am aware of what is at stake.'

'I have it!' Moyle cried, leaving Pearce sure he was about to articulate a thought he had arrived at long before. 'The trick is not to enter them right off, but to leave it to me to register them as volunteers when I hear from you regarding your followers.'

'Sir, that is nothing short of brilliant, but can you carry it off?'

Moyle's voice dropped, taking on an air of imparting a confidence. 'I am very much my own master here, sir. The men I command fear me, as is only right, for I can ship them off to sea as easy as any of the men we hold. And as for higher authority, well, I never see them for one month to the next. I will hold these men in an unlogged capacity and await your instructions. How would that suit?'

'It would suit me fine.'

The brow furrowed, again Pearce thought a bit theatrically.

'One problem does present itself. When the time comes to enlist them I will have to do so under my own name.'

'Yes.'

'I am happy of course to do so.'

Happy, Pearce thought, to take the bounty yourself or assign it to some relative or friend for a commission: neither the Greenwich Chest nor Haslar would see a penny.

'Sir,' Pearce cried, standing up. 'It is rare to have dealings with such an honest, and may I say perspicacious fellow. I give you my hand.'

'And I, sir, am glad to take it.' The grasp was firm, but Moyle would not look him in the eye lest it reveal his avarice. 'Now, lead me to your volunteers, so I may see them aboard, checked for vermin and settled in cells.'

CHAPTER NINE

Ship visiting was not a prerogative much extended to midshipmen, added to which HMS *Agamemnon*, for the officers of Hotham's flagship, was a destination it would be unwise to frequent, given the admiral's known dislike of Commodore Nelson. Toby Burns suffered a few frustrating days in which he could see but not touch deliverance; like many people who form a notion untested against reality, the idea that Richard Farmiloe was his route to salvation grew from a possibility to an absolute certainty. In the end it was the reverse; Nelson came visiting and brought with him his acting lieutenant, more as a courtesy to the lad than necessity – when it came to the conference being held to discuss the attack on Calvi, as far as the navy was concerned it was captains and above only.

Given his acting rank, Farmiloe was invited to the

wardroom, likewise barred to mids, and Toby had to wait until his erstwhile saviour had been wined and picked clean of news from home – so much more available in Gibraltar – mostly about the progress of the war. The twin and mutually exclusive desires of his fellow lieutenants would be exposed: the men who occupied that section of the ship wished for the nation to be triumphant but they also hoped that if victory came it would not be too soon to allow them the chance of advancement and, of course, prize money. Eventually Farmiloe came up for air and Toby could accost him.

'Gosh, Dick, it's so good to see you.'

The effusiveness of that greeting threw Farmiloe somewhat, for if he had known Toby Burns since the outbreak of war he did not consider him to be a close friend, even if, both aboard HMS *Brilliant* and at the recent siege of Bastia, he had intervened to provide cover for his manifest shortcomings. At the latter they had manned a forward battery together, trading shots with a too close enemy, the recollection of which added another stream of terror to the Burns nightmares, not least that he should have been in receipt of a wound like the man originally given command.

'How is Lieutenant Andrews?'

'Fully recovered, Toby, which I daresay you could tell by the mere use of a long glass to rake our quarterdeck.' The head gesture to *Agamemnon*, berthed within plain view, underlined the point. 'How do you fare with all your afflictions?'

That made serious the Burns countenance; his health and well-being a matter of prime concern. Yet it also presented him with an opportunity to take matters all the way back to Sheerness.

'I am in topping form, Dick, almost since the first time we met.' The Burns face took on a wistful look now. 'Do you recall that day when you first came aboard my uncle's frigate?'

'Hard to do so here, Toby, in "brilliant" sunshine.'

Farmiloe waited for the pun on the ship's name to strike; he waited in vain, for his companion was more concerned with the low cloud and scudding rains of the Medway, immediately recalled and described. 'And that was before the mids turned to unpleasant duties.'

Farmiloe laughed. 'I seem to recall that we new mids found any duty we were asked to perform congenial.'

'Some more than others, Dick. Do you recall, for instance, the night you went out pressing seamen?'

The change in Farmiloe's posture, the stiffening, was palpable. 'Not fondly.'

'You regret it?'

'I do, not that I hold any responsibility for the act, that falls to your Uncle Ralph.'

'Who faced a court martial for it.'

'And was acquitted, I seem to recall.'

There was a note in Farmiloe's voice, faint but detectable, of something like disapproval, or was it latent amazement? He had been sent off to the Bay of Biscay with John Pearce and his Pelicans, under the command of Henry Digby, a former lieutenant aboard HMS *Brilliant*, in short all the people who could have blown the testimony given at the court martial out of the water.

'Dick, I think I need to confide in you, but before I do, I would ask that you peruse this letter I received from London, I think from a lawyer fellow acting on behalf of John Pearce.'

'Named Lucknor?'

'How do you know that?'

'I had a letter too, asking me about that night.'

'They seek to embroil you?'

'No. It merely asked for information and made it perfectly plain that I was in no danger, given my rank.'

'Mine is, I think, less kindly meant. Will you read it?'

There was clear reluctance; Dick Farmiloe had been part of the gang doing the misdeed on that night and it had until recently been long buried at the back of his mind. He had not enjoyed having it dragged up by Lucknor's letter. It took no genius to deduce who the lawyer was after and on whose behalf he was working. Added to that, and despite what the lawyer had intimated, if Ralph Barclay came a cropper others would get caught up in the backwash and he might be one of them.

'Who do you think is behind it, Toby?'

'Why, John Pearce of course, he means to dish my uncle come hell or high water.'

'I reckon the same, but I apologised to Pearce for

my part and I am glad I did so, for he turned out to be a very decent fellow and damned brave at that.'

'Apologised?'

That was said so Toby Burns could cover for the hearing of an opinion at total odds with his own; Pearce decent and brave? The man was a menace. He did however press the letter on Farmiloe, who took it very reluctantly and read it very slowly. When Burns thought he had finished, the point at which his eyes flicked back to the top of the page, it was time to speak.

'Dick, I have something to tell you and, in part, it is a confession of my stupidity.'

The letter was waved. 'I have no desire to be involved in this.'

'But you are my friend, not in as deep as me, but involved nonetheless.'

Sensing Farmiloe trying to digest and rationalise that, Toby started speaking quickly, outlining how Hotham had arranged matters to ensure an acquittal.

'Anyone who knew anything germane was sent away – you and Digby, for instance. The depositions that the Pelicans made and signed, Pearce included, written out by Hotham's second clerk, were never introduced into the hearing. My uncle lied, so did his clerk Gherson and me – well, I was pressed by family obligation to come to the aid of Captain Barclay.'

That, 'family obligation', sounded so much better than the truth; Toby Burns had done as he was asked for a number of mixed emotions: downright terror of that uncle by marriage and what he could do as a post captain to a lowly midshipman. Added to that was a complete absence of backbone compounded by a visceral hatred of John Pearce. Toby Burns, very early on in HMS *Brilliant*'s commission, had received accolades for an act of conspicuous bravery; the man who truly deserved the plaudits was none other than the same John Pearce, acts which had earned him and his friends a reluctant discharge from Barclay, nothing short of a release from the navy.

Added to that was the fear that retribution would be visited upon him for obeying another instruction from his uncle; that should they, in the act of taking home a prize ship, encounter in soundings any vessel looking for hands, then the fact that the Pelicans had been released from the navy on the grounds of being landsmen need not be made plain. Toby Burns had remained silent when he could have spoken to save them from being pressed for a second time and, on many an occasion, he had uncomfortably reprised the threat that Pearce had made: that one day he would be made to pay.

'And that letter indicates what I was called upon to say.'

'Why were you called as a witness?' Farmiloe demanded. 'You never left the ship that night.'

'No, but my uncle, as far as the hearing was concerned, had me in place of you. He persuaded me to say that I made a mistake and landed the press gang in the wrong part of the river, in the Liberties of the

138

Savoy rather than just upriver of Blackfriars Bridge where anyone we found could have been taken legally. In short, the impressment became illegal by my faulty direction rather than any action by my Uncle Ralph.'

'And they believed this?'

'Dick, it was rigged from the start. Who do you think chose the captains to sit in judgement, the same man who suppressed those depositions?'

'Hotham?'

Toby held a finger to his lips; that was not a name to mention out loud on the man's own flagship, given the subject. 'Trouble is, somehow my part in the farrago has become known. The fellow who signed that might only hint at seeking information, but the questions he poses leaves me in no doubt of what he is fishing for.'

'Evidence against your uncle?'

'Damn my uncle, Dick,' Burns quietly wailed, 'he's out to get me. I lied to the court, and is it a defence to say I was coerced?'

'You want my advice?'

'Do you know that you can hang for perjury and I was under oath?'

'Do you?'

'Yes.'

'Then tell the truth now.' Seeing the shock on Toby's face, Farmiloe spoke at a more rapid speed than hitherto. 'Reply to this fellow as I did, tell him everything, the truth unvarnished, as I did and I am sure that such an admission will sit well with any court assembled to judge the case.'

'Court? You think there will be one?'

A piping voice floated from the quarterdeck. 'Mr Farmiloe, is that young Burns I see you with?'

'It is, sir.'

Nelson lifted his hat. 'Good day to you, Mr Burns, I hope I find you well.'

'You do, sir,' Burns replied, cursing the man for his intervention at this time; there was, however, the requirement of a reply. 'And you, sir, how are you?'

'Plagued as ever, Mr Burns. Farmiloe there will tell you, if there is an affliction in the air, and as you know that is full of such things, it finds Nelson first and most viciously. I swear I am naught but a medical bellwether for those with whom I serve.'

'Until a cannon goes off in anger,' Farmiloe whispered, a fond and, to Toby's mind, a mistaken note of affection in his voice. 'Then the cure is instant.'

'I fear I must tear you apart, my young friends. Mr Farmiloe, it is time you called in my barge.'

That Richard Farmiloe then bent his head to talk earnestly to Toby Burns had every other officer on the quarterdeck of HMS *Britannia* – and the conference just concluded, there were many post captains – either nonplussed, or, in one or two cases, seething with fury. Commodore Nelson had issued a precise instruction to one of his officers, a very junior one by his appearance, who then saw fit to take his time in obeying; the only person not in the least put out was Nelson himself, which only underlined to many his main failing: he might be a tiger in a fight, but he was a booby when it came to discipline!

'Write that letter, Toby, tell all and condemn yourself if need be, but do not spare anyone else either, whatever their rank.' That was plain enough: if it meant dishing Hotham along with Ralph Barclay he should do so. 'This is bound to come out if Pearce is pursuing matters and the only hope you have for your own neck is a confession.'

'Damn Pearce,' Toby said, tears pricking his eyes.

'Damn your uncle if you must, but not John Pearce, for I am sure if he were here he would forgive you.'

No he would not, Toby thought, as his hand was grasped and shaken. Why is it that I am the only one who can see Pearce for the poltroon he is? As he was ruminating on that and his own endangered future, Dick Farmiloe was shouting that the commodore's barge should make for the entry port. Soon, with much whistling and stamping of marines, the ship began to empty of all these captains and their attendants but what emerged as gossip was not anything to cheer a midshipman who wished to avoid danger; the siege of Calvi was about to begin, indeed it would proceed as soon as Lord Hood signalled it should proceed.

Alongside fellow passengers who could not even talk to each other, lest it inadvertently include her, Emily Barclay was free to peer through the gap left in the coach door blind and take stock of the sunlit New

Forest, a place to her of some attraction. Having made her statement about leaving, it had soon occurred to her that she had very few choices of where to go. The idea of going back to Frome was anathema, not least because it would require her to share her marital home with Ralph Barclay's twittering sisters, all spinsters and destined to remain so. To them their brother was the very soul of probity, brave beyond peradventure and close to saintliness in his personal habits. To tell them the truth, that he was a bully as well as an endemically dishonest satyr, would bring Emily satisfaction but it would not be believed.

Nor could she return to her old family home, for to do so would send a message to the whole town that the marriage of one of their most potent citizens was not as it should be. Never mind the rumour mill, her parents would be aghast that their comfortable life would be threatened by her actions. They would not see her case even if it were explained; selfishness and the fear of gossip would combine to bring upon her pressure to make amends with her husband, something she knew she could never do.

Nor did she have friends outside of her hometown and all of her relations lived in close proximity; from there, upon marriage, she had gone aboard her husband's frigate and if she had met other naval wives none were more than an acquaintance. How distant that seemed and not only because of the dismal February-March weather. Unlike now, there had been no money to spare then – Ralph Barclay had been on half pay for five whole years and was plagued before departure and after the wedding with impatient creditors. Keeping his wife on the ship saved him the cost of leaving her at home where she would require to run the house and incur expense; his sisters were enough of a charge upon his purse without he should add to it.

If her new husband was not passionate there had been romance in that one act, for it had only come to her afterwards that it was brought on by dearth. When first mooted it had sounded different, for Emily was told very quickly by others that for a serving naval officer to have his wife aboard was against all the rules of the service and here was her new spouse flouting them for, she supposed, proximity to her. She had found out the true reason when, in the company of other wives, she had gone shopping in the Medway for the kind of stores a naval captain needed to hold up his head afloat. Ralph Barclay had gone wild when he saw what she had spent and most of her purchases had been returned forthwith.

Would John Pearce get the note she had left, or would that innkeeper fail to hand it over on his return? Even then he should go to where she was now headed, for he had kept rooms at Nerot's Hotel and that was, at least, a place where she was known and could book into under her own name. Pearce had taken a room for her there after that unfortunate fracas with a group of men she had come to understand were smugglers. Even if he failed to get the note, given he must report back to the Government, he would come there regardless.

Pulling into Lyndhurst, Emily guessed that they would stop at the local inn for a fresh team of horses, then wondered if the passengers would change, glad that two of them appeared fidgety enough to indicate that they might alight here, that more obvious as the coachman called down to say they were approaching the Stag and that they should get ready. There was the usual creaking and sudden darkness as they swung under the arch that led to the stables and she too made ready to alight, in her case to take some refreshment and stretch her legs. Such things were the commonality of travel; the surprise was that when the coachman jumped down and opened the door, the first person Emily saw, standing with two well-dressed people, one male the other female, was Michael O'Hagan.

'Michael,' she called, leaning out of the door. 'Is John here too?'

Under his breath, as he turned, O'Hagan was cursing a God in whom he wholeheartedly believed but knew to be fickle. 'And Jesus,' he hissed to himself as he hurried to the coach door, 'Not only what is she doing here, but how do I greet her?'

'No, John-boy is on an errand.'

'But he is back from France, he must be if you are here.'

'Yes, we berthed yesterday.'

The brow furrowed as Emily demanded, 'And why did he not come to Lymington?'

144

'He had some pressing matters to attend to, like those folk you see me with. They are envoys from where we went to, come to talk to the Government, I believe, and I am to get them aboard this Winchester coach and off to London an' may the Good Lord aid them when they get there, for there is not a word of English in either of them.'

'Then I must help them, for I speak French and I too am on my way to London.'

That she thought the Irishman confused became obvious as he threw his eyes skywards. It was not that simple question that troubled him but many others, not least the notion of a pair of women John Pearce was determined should never meet sharing near two whole days of intimate coach travel.

'But were you not to wait in Lymington?'

Emily dropped her head to hide a slight blush. 'Circumstances forced a change of plan. Now best you introduce me to these people.'

'Which I will do Mrs . . . Holy Mary, what do I call you?'

'Emily will do, Michael; after all, we have seen too much together to be anything other than good friends.'

'Sure, I thank you kindly for the sentiment, but I am going to have to introduce you and I was told by John-boy to use the name Raynesford.'

'I am back to being Mrs Barclay,' she replied rather testily.

'Strikes me, Mrs Barclay, that you would be better

alighting here and going back to where John-boy expects to meet you.'

'Do not ask me to explain, Michael, but that is not possible.'

'I am to go there so I could escort you.'

'No! I will make my way to Nerot's and have left a note saying so. Are you all right Michael, you look pale?'

'Perfectly so, Mrs Barclay,' he lied, for he was feeling that if he had been standing on an insecure trapdoor it had just opened to cast him into a pit of all the snakes the saints had rid his homeland of.

'Introductions.'

'Happen, since you have their tongue, you'd be best seeing that yourself, for I am bound to falter over their names, them bein' hard to pronounce.'

'Then hand me down.'

Which he did, to lead her over to the count and Amélie, the former getting a half curtsy, the latter receiving a warm smile and a welcome to *Angleterre*. At least, Michael thought, with some relief, Emily Barclay does not recognise the Labordière name. He was not to travel with them, so if the dung did fly inside the coach he would be well out of it.

'I am going to take our guests into the inn for refreshments, Michael, would you care to join us?'

'No time, Mrs Barclay, I've got to see to certain matters that I am charged to perform for John-boy.'

'Jean-boy? *Une appellation, très jolie, n'est-ce pas?*

Amélie Labordière, having said this with a warm

146

smile, got a curious response from Emily Barclay, given it hinted at an intimacy that should not have been formed in what could only have been a few days' acquaintance. Michael watched them as they went indoors, thinking that when his friend next met Emily Barclay, there was going to be hell to pay and no pitch hot.

Sir Phillip Stephens was wondering if that bane of his life, Admiral Sir Berkley Sumners, had gone off his head, for the letter he had sent in this time made no sense at all. What was the old fool talking about with secret missions and his aiding them to fruition? And who was this Lieutenant Raynesford whom he had already told the sod was an officer who did not exist? There was a suspicion that Sumners was just making waves where none were present, but the undertone of his letter was that there was some chicanery afoot somewhere – either this Raynesford was a projector seeking to make some underhand money; the other thought, that perhaps he was a French spy, had Sir Phillip calling in a clerk.

'I need to send a note to Mr Dundas.'

CHAPTER TEN

Freed of the Tolland gang, the eight-oared cutters were much lighter, but against that the tide was still rising, which would make it a doubly long haul back to Lymington, the next destination; from there the ship's boats could be taken back the relatively short distance to Buckler's Hard at a time of year when, thankfully, there was no shortage of daylight. The option of waiting in either Gosport or Portsmouth did not appeal, so Pearce aimed for the boatbuilding seaside town of Cowes, which had the advantage, even so close to Spithead, of not being naval in any way; the only military presence resided in the forts built by Henry the Eighth to repel a French invasion and they were manned by soldiers.

Snug in the River Medina they could tie up at one

of the many jetties and proceed to a tavern to eat fresh food, albeit the instruction was to go easy in the article of drink, and it was there that John Pearce heard first of the great victory being claimed by the Channel Fleet, of which the place was abuzz, not that anyone expressed surprise; Britannia ruled the waves and if the French had ever beaten a British fleet – and it had to be admitted that had happened – then it could only be by the employment of low and despicable cunning.

Not only had the King's favourite admiral, Black Dick Howe, trounced the French battle fleet, but he had sunk – it depended on who was declaiming – anything from a hundred to five hundred merchant ships bringing grain from the Americas. Seeing one of his oarsmen about to respond and put the boaster right, Pearce intervened and ordered him to be silent. His mission had been a secret one and even here it had to remain that. The subject did not arise again until much later, when on a falling tide they were rowing south-west towards the Lymington Estuary and one of his crew raised the question.

'Savin' your presence, sir, how can that be, for we saw those very ships an' too close for comfort?'

'Simple, is it not? Rumour runs ahead of truth every time. For all we know Admiral Lord Howe has suffered a reverse and is at this very moment sitting in a boat this size wondering what happened to his ship.'

The reaction to that was amusing, so much so that Pearce had to control his features; if the people of

Britain held that their ships and men were inherently superior to the French, that was as nothing to the opinion of the men employed to sail them, which never ceased to amaze the man on the tiller. He did not know if any aboard HMS *Larcher* had been pressed, it was not an enquiry any officer made, but he did know that for every willing volunteer going to sea they were far outnumbered by those who chose to serve as an alternative to a miserable existence ashore, which could extend to downright starvation. It had always annoyed his father that such people carried within them a patriotic attachment to a form of government that served them so ill.

'But we must assume,' Pearce added, to restore his own standing as much as anything, 'that our men had trounced the sods good and proper.'

'Hear him,' came the chorus, even from those whose breath must be constrained by the need to row.

'You're sure of this, Gherson?' Ralph Barclay demanded, as he sought to digest the information that his clerk had brought back from *Queen Charlotte*, where he had gone to deliver the ship's logs and accounts.

'One of Lord Howe's fellows chose to confide in me, sir, I daresay in respect to the freemasonry of our occupation. The despatch to the Admiralty was dictated by Sir Roger Curtis in the presence of Lord Howe and it questioned the actions of several of the ship's captains as to their participation, or not, in the battle. Many, it was claimed, were tardy when it came to obeying what were clear orders. Others were praised for their application and they have been recommended for special favour.'

'Any names given?'

'Captain Molloy was particularly censured for inaction it seems, but he was not alone. The general tone of Sir Roger's communication was that too many officers dithered instead of acting promptly.'

'I meant me,' Barclay snapped, 'as you damn well know.'

'Your name was not mentioned, sir,' Gherson replied, leaving his employer in limbo.

Sitting on the cushioned casement at the rear of his cabin, injured and bandaged leg stretched out, Ralph Barclay was back in that action, examining his own behaviour and wondering if it could be interpreted as sluggish? He recalled that the flagship had ordered him to close with the enemy several times before he actually did so, but he was sure he could justify those actions on the grounds of a crew not fully worked up, with the added problem that being so close to *Queen Charlotte* as she engaged – *Semele* was the next vessel astern – he knew, as she put down her helm to close, he stood a chance of being a victim of her shot as much as the enemy; thus he had held off until that threat had diminished.

Yet he had fought hard once he met his opposite number, having let the one he was ordered to engage go by. That had come about because he had really been given no choice as their forward rigging became entangled.

Only superior gunnery, the rate of fire of his cannon, had saved HMS *Semele* from a severe mauling. After a long pounding it was *Vengeur* that had suffered and, added to that, damn it, he had taken a serious wound.

'I daresay a good dinner and a few bottles of claret could tell us more.'

That got Gherson a very cold stare; he no more trusted his clerk than the man trusted him, not that Ralph Barclay was much given to reposing faith in anyone. If he did not quite see himself as alone against a hostile world he did know that there were forces extant who seemed to have it as their aim to do him down and it had been like that since his first day of service as a midshipman. It had come home to Ralph Barclay very early in his naval career that no man got anywhere lest he had on his side someone with more weight. Thus he had always attached himself to men with power, first senior lieutenants, later captains and finally admirals, the most potent of whom had been Lord Rodney, a man who knew his responsibilities to his followers: he saw to it that if there was a plum going it went to them.

Rodney's death had been a setback compounded by the elevation of Lord Hood to the Board of Admiralty. Hood had little regard for Rodney and he had no inclination to promote those who had depended on a deceased superior, which had left Ralph Barclay, a very outspoken and loyal follower, on the beach for five whole years until the outbreak of the war, and even when he had been employed it had not matched his place on the captain's list. The likes of Nelson, one of Hood's favourites, got a ship of the line; he had been given a frigate and one that only just made its rating as a post captain's command.

'Do you wish for me to arrange to meet with the said clerk, sir?'

That brought Barclay back to the present and his original thought that Gherson probably already knew the answer to the proposed question and was just seeking to dun him for a good meal ashore. Not that he felt he had much alternative but to agree: slippery Gherson, who now had on his absurdly handsome face that knowing smile which so irritated his employer, would never let on lest he was indulged.

'Very well, but before you go I want you to read back to me that repeat letter I composed to my wife. I want to make sure it leaves her in no doubt of her choices now that circumstances have altered, then it can be sent.' The voice changed, becoming harsh. 'Which are to return to the marital home or damn well starve.'

How do I tell him, Gherson was thinking, that he is in no position to make demands? In his mind he imagined Emily Barclay reading such a letter, which would be passed on by a solicitor called Studdert she had engaged. It was not so very different from those that had preceded it except it did allude quite openly to her having nothing now with which to threaten him, which she would almost certainly know to be false. He had arranged for the solicitor's offices to be burgled by a low character called Codge but they had not found the copy of the court martial record, leaving the only possible alternative that Emily Barclay had retrieved it before the break-in.

She would thus be well aware that she had no need to pay any heed to his instructions, so much so that she had refused to even reply to the previous communication he had sent before HMS *Semele* sailed to join the Channel Fleet. Was now the time to be open and save his employer from making a fool of himself, to tell him the robbery had gone wrong? Never one to leap before it became imperative, Gherson held his tongue and went to Barclay's desk, there to retrieve and read out what had been dictated, aware of the change in his employer's demeanour each time he espoused the more threatening passages.

The knock at the door led to a command from Barclay to wait until Gherson had finished. The cry that the visitor could enter brought in a midshipman with a message from the officer of the watch to the effect that there was boat alongside with an invitation from Captain Molloy to dine, the name making Barclay frown and raising an amused Gherson eyebrow.

'My compliments to Captain Molloy and I fear my injury prevents me from acceptance.'

'Aye, aye, sir,' said the mid prior to his exit, which left the two men looking at each other, for both knew that had he so wished, Barclay was healed enough to cross to another ship and back without danger to his wound. But Molloy was under a cloud, the flagship clerk had named him, so he was not a safe person to associate with, regardless of long acquaintance.

It was impossible to invest Calvi purely from the sea; the castle which guarded the bay sat on a high and rocky promontory right above the only deep-water channel into the harbour, while the rest of the wide cove was cursed with extended shallows that precluded a ship of any draught from taking up a position to bombard the town from anything like a reasonable distance, which was in itself dangerous against shore-based fire. Likewise the coast to the east was low-lying, and while eminently suitable for landing by boats, did not put the attacker in any position to use their own artillery to subdue the defences, which would have to be completed before any actual assault could take place and even then that would be bloody.

Thus, after much discussion, it had been decided to land at a bay a little down the west coast then seek to take the high ground above the town itself, which would at least give the guns parity with the defenders, the caveat to that being the need to get the cannon off the warships and ashore, then up the steep escarpments to where the battery positions would be constructed, something the defenders might well think impossible. For all the jocularity and keen anticipation of the forthcoming battle, there was an undertow of hidden concern throughout the fleet. They would be landing on a hostile shore from boats – never easy, and if the garrison of Calvi was limited and insufficient to hold the beach they were still numerous enough to inflict heavy casualties prior to withdrawal.

Thus, with the fleet hove to and Lord Hood's permission to proceed, there was a final conference aboard HMS *Victory*, anchored off San Fiorenzo, really an excuse for a capital dinner at which the commanding admiral could praise those like Nelson whom he admired and do his very best to make sure that all knew it was not an emotion he extended to his second in command. If he and Hotham were naval rivals that extended to their politics, for Hood was a Tory and Hotham a Whig. Hood's problem was Prime Minister William Pitt's lack of a binding majority; while he could master the domestic agenda he needed the support of what were called the Portland Whigs to successfully prosecute the war. Hotham was of that faction and in constant communication with the Duke of Portland, and every letter did nothing to praise the abilities of his commanding officer, not that such an opinion was a secret.

All around the fleet, flagship included, those who could write home were composing their final letters, the ones that would be sent to their loved ones should they expire in the coming action. In reality naval letters read like a chronicle; they were often written with no knowledge of when they would be sent, for even in such a well-ordered fleet as Lord Hood's they would wait for the arrival of a packet bearing despatches and letters from home. So they tended towards a lengthy tale and most were only adding to what they had already composed and were penning sentiments that, regardless of the truth, sought to reassure their relatives of their happiness and good cheer, while inserting what should happen if anything should befall them.

Toby Burns was bent over his own letter, but it was not to his family. These were communications he found hard to compose, not being as willing as his peers to disguise his loathing of a service that had him existing on a diet of foul food, often near to rotten in the cask, in the company of people with whom he shared at best mutual disinterest, and under the command of men whose soul aim was to make his life a misery. Occasionally he summoned up the will to lie, but always he really wanted to write home to say that his only wish was to get out of the navy and back to a school he had, at one time, desired to get away from with equal passion.

Writing in reply to Lucknor was not easy and he had to remind himself that paper on which to do it was not in great supply, so he ended up with a set of corrected scrawls that would have taxed one of those coves that sought to decipher ancient languages. Toby did not want to blame himself in any way, yet even he could see that to plead outright coercion would not wash on the page, for it smacked of a weakness of personality that he did not recognise and was certainly not prepared to commit to paper even if it was designed to make him look innocent. Once again family obligation came to his rescue, and taking a fresh sheet he composed the best of what he had penned and scored out before sanding the letter, folding it and applying sealing wax, then penning the address.

'Damn me, Burns,' cawed one of his fellow midshipmen as he waved it to ensure the wax had dried, 'I reckon the time you've been at it you have told your life story.'

'At least, Myers,' Toby responded, standing and crouching, for the deck beams were low, 'I have a story to tell.'

He was out of the berth when he heard Myers answer to that. 'Am I alone in despising that admiral's bumboy?'

That led to a chorus of negatives, which infuriated him; why could they not see he had no desire to be cosseted by Admiral Hotham, no wish to be constantly put in jeopardy, which those with whom he shared his quarters mistakenly saw as an opportunity to distinguish himself? He would have gladly given those opportunities over to them, for in each one he had been granted the possibility of not surviving had been present, higher in his imagination than true, perhaps, but there nevertheless. Then there was his reputation as a hero, gained on the back of John Pearce off the Brittany coast. That it was false mattered less than the yearning he had to be shot of it, for that made everyone expect him to show reckless courage.

The letter went to the second of the admiral's two clerks, as did all those being composed, to wait for the next packet or a sloop being sent off to Gibraltar with despatches. Not an overly nosy individual the fellow nevertheless looked idly at the superscription, which was so unusual that he stared at it for some time. What was a toad like Burns doing writing a letter to the Inns of Court? The curiosity was mentioned to the senior clerk, Mr Toomey, who had been with the admiral for years and was something of a confidant – no letter went off to the Duke of Portland that he had not had dictated to, and approved by, him – so that when a seething Admiral Sir William Hotham returned from his uncomfortable dinner aboard HMS *Victory* this was mentioned, in turn, to him.

Those who knew Hotham were given to remark on what seemed to be his endemic indolence. Had he been informed of that, the man in question would have pointed out that haste in making decisions was inclined to lead to crass errors of judgement; he was a fellow who liked to weigh matters before pronouncing on them and this was no exception, even if he could immediately discern what it might portend.

'Are we at liberty to . . . ?' Hotham said eventually, not, as he often did, managing to finish the sentence. It made no odds – he was with a man who could read his mind.

'We have a responsibility, sir,' Toomey replied, 'that no communication should be permitted that would diminish the effectiveness of His Majesty's vessel of war on active service.'

If that was imparted with confidence it was all show; there was no right by anyone to interfere with the private communications of correspondents writing home.

'And the letter is available to us?' Toomey nodded, as Hotham, for once, was able to quickly construct a suitable conclusion. 'Then I fear young Mr Burns may be in some difficulties, Mr Toomey.'

'Very possibly, sir,' came the smooth reply.

'I do wish he had possessed the faith to trust to me for advice.'

'It had always been my position, sir, that lawyers are best avoided.'

'He is too young to be making judgements that he might not appreciate the consequences of, don't you think?'

'Therefore it would be best if we know the contents of his letter, either to advise him if it is serious, or to merely forward it on if it is harmless.'

'The seal?' Hotham asked, only to receive in response a look that enquired if he was being serious. 'Best fetch the damn thing, then.'

Toomey reached into his pocket. 'I took the liberty of bringing it with me, sir. With your permission I require a candle and a knife.'

Having landed at Lymington, Pearce could not say goodbye to his oarsmen without he gave them something for their trouble – if it had been a private matter they had come to his aid so willingly; and then there was the rest of the crew to consider, which led to him dipping into Michael's satchel and pushing aside his pistol case to extract a bit more of the money given to him by Dundas.

'Can I say, sir, on behalf of the crew, it has been a pleasure to serve under you.'

'Thank you, Mr Dorling, it has been equally agreeable to see what a fine body of men Mr Rackham has under his command.'

The mention of their permanent captain's name produced a commonality of responses, many frowns, a few hissed curses and one man spitting over the side, which had the effect of making Pearce feel cheap rather than glad; it was as if he was courting flattery and that was an activity he despised in others.

'You had best be off, Mr Dorling, for there is not much daylight left. Convey my regards to Mr Bird, the Kempshall twins and, of course, Mr Bellam, the cook. Who knows, one day we may meet again.'

'For which I can say they would hope, your honour.'

He stood on the quay and watched the boat row away, staying there, much as he was eager to be off, until they were out of sight and then, with a lightness in his step he knew to be keen anticipation, made his way up from the harbour to the King's Head Inn, aware that he had a physical as well as an emotional yearning for the presence of Emily Barclay. Indeed he was singing to himself as he entered the doorway to be confronted by an innkeeper who took one look at him and disappeared into the back of his establishment. Following him opened up the taproom and sitting there nursing a tankard was Michael O'Hagan. He stood up when he saw Pearce, but he did not smile and the way he said 'John-boy' while crossing himself did nothing to provide reassurance.

'What in the name of creation has happened?'

If, as he asked that, John Pearce had feared the worst, it came as no comfort to him to be told the truth. No, Emily was not harmed in any way, but at this very moment, if she did not know already, she was about to discover the one thing her lover had sought to keep from her.

'Is it too late to procure a pair of horses?'

By lantern light, Sir William Hotham, for the tenth time, was reading Toby Burns' letter to Lucknor and wondering how to deal with it. The boy had gone from being a necessary asset to get Barclay off the hook – though being a bit of a nuisance by his needy presence – to a downright threat to his position, for if he had sought to limit the damage to his own reputation in his composition he had certainly done nothing to diminish the ordure he was prepared to heap on both his uncle and Hotham himself. What had been a very necessary construct to save a gallant officer from a pernicious accusation laid by a gimcrack officer was made by the young toad's hand into a most damning conspiracy to utterly pervert the course of justice.

To confront him was not a consideration, though Hotham was sure he could browbeat the lad into continued silence. The problem was that in the future some other person might lean on him just as hard to repeat these exaggerations he had just penned, and who knew where that would lead if there was no one around to impose restraint? All being well – sea state and weather – the assault on the beach south of Calvi would be going ahead on the morrow at dawn, so he rang a bell for Toomey.

'Mr Toomey, when the orders were written for the morning, as regards our boats, where did you place Mr Burns?'

'Why sir, right at the point, hopefully in the first boat to beach. That is the position where he can garner most honour. Have you not always shown him much favour in that regard?'

'I have, many times, much to the annoyance of those with whom he shares his berth.' Looking at the letter, now on the table, Hotham growled. 'Still, he deserves no less!'

'It's not too late to make a change, sir.

'No, Toomey, leave the orders as they are.'

CHAPTER ELEVEN

Emily Barclay read French reasonably well but had rarely spoken to a native with any degree of application until she had been resident in Toulon, first with her husband as prisoner of war, then in day-to-day contact with the locals as she helped out in the shore hospital set up by her good friend and surgeon Heinrich Lutyens. Being a nurse had provided both a distraction and a reason not to reside and sleep aboard HMS *Brilliant*; indeed it had given her an excuse to initiate a separation from Ralph Barclay that she hoped would not set tongues wagging. In that Emily was being naive; when it came to gossip a fleet at sea could match a clutch of fishwives on any given day.

She had learnt the language under the tutelage of the governess from one of the local manor houses, who saw that having other girls in her class could provide a foil to aid her own charges. Seen very much as an aristocratic refinement she had attended twice-weekly sessions with a group of other aspirant girls and for the same reason: to be bilingual was to enhance the prospects of making a good marriage. The struggle to separate the divergences that existed had not been comprehensively mastered, not least the way gender was employed when referring to specific objects – but more tellingly was the need to employ the correct verb endings, and if that had been refined in Toulon, it had not been wholly conquered.

So when she began a conversation with the count and Amélie Labordière, first inside the Stag Inn at Lyndhurst, then ensconced in the coach when they departed, being drawn by fresh horses, her conversation was not entirely fluent and if she managed to make herself understood it was not without repetition allied to some confusion on the faces of those with whom she was seeking to communicate. Then came another problem: her ear was not attuned to what was being said in reply, it consisting of sounds so unfamiliar and addressed to her in an accent with which she struggled to cope, for it was nothing like that of the Mediterranean French naval port.

The Parisian accent was very different and originally her governess had learnt her French in London from a fellow Briton, so that, as well as any refinement that was Provençal in accent, rendered the conversation, if it could be called that, stilted in the extreme. This left Emily wishing she had the fluency brought on by living as a native Parisian that had been enjoyed by John Pearce. The expression '*lentement, s'il vous plaît*' was frequently employed to slow what was a too rapid exposition from two companions; one reserved, the other extremely voluble.

The Count de Puisaye was eager that this *femme anglaise* should know just how much the Revolution had impinged on him personally: the loss of his several houses as well as his estates, and naturally the rents and revenues thereof, the whole taken over by a rabble of *sans culottes* who would reduce them to a desert. The count had barely escaped with his life, but soon all would be restored to him when the British Government saw the sense of sending him back to the Vendée with the means to put the trouserless peasants back in their place. Even if Emily could only really pick up one word in three, it was noticeable from the odd barely suppressed yawn and expression of boredom that Madame Labordière found this exposition and complaint tiresome and it was with a sense of escaping what was turning into a tirade that she sought to engage more her fellow female.

'And how, Madame,' Emily asked, her voice paced and deliberate, 'did you come to be rescued and brought to England by the Royal Navy?'

Pearce had found horses in Lymington and they rode out as the sun was setting in a clear sky that would soon produce, once it had risen from its cheese-coloured position on the near horizon, a clear moon aided by strong starlight by which to proceed. He left behind him a very chastened innkeeper who had taken his tirade regarding Emily without a murmur; Pearce only realised why when they were well gone – he had forgotten to demand reimbursement for the days of non-occupation. The fellow might look cowed but he was much in profit, so being insulted was worth it.

Michael had, as requested, left horses stabled in Lyndhurst, saddles and harness included, that he could claim as his own, so there was no sparing the ones he had rented from Lymington; they were driven hard so that he could get to a change before the Lyndhurst stables closed for the night, which they would do early in a quiet country town. In his imagination Pearce reprised any number of conversations that might be taking place, none of them inducing much in the way of comfort; perhaps Amélie would smoke who she was travelling with and show discretion, but if the way she had behaved aboard HMS *Larcher* was any guide, that came under the heading of pigs might fly.

Likewise the notion that Emily would, on discovering that she was bouncing along a turnpike road with his ex-mistress, accept that the whole *affaire* was over, bordered on risible; if it was, why had he brought her to England? Many scenarios presented themselves and that continued after Lyndhurst when the pace, of necessity, had to be more measured; these horses had to get them all the way to Winchester, a distance of over twenty miles. It was a tempo that allowed him to share his worries with his friend and riding companion, not that he got much in the way of sympathy.

'How can you say I brought the whole thing on my own head, Michael?'

'For no other reason, John-boy, than it be the plain truth. Sure, I will admit you're a victim of your own soft heart, but Mary, Mother of God, it has done naught but get you into trouble since the day we met.'

The reply had a definite note of pique. 'It has led me to get you out of a few scrapes.'

'It got me into more.'

'It's all the fault of those damned Tollands. If I had not had to deal with them I could perhaps have avoided such a meeting.'

'Well, you are shot of those sods now.'

'Not entirely, but they will serve in the navy for the duration of this war, which will keep them from bothering us.'

'Did you not feel shame, pressing men after what we have been through?'

'Not a jot – they were murderous villains who deserve a flogging captain and I hope they get one. Besides, I have yet to tell you of the arrangements I have made with the fellow in command of the receiving hulk.'

As they rode, Pearce talked of his hopes in that area, which had the advantage of keeping his mind off more pressing concerns, making no attempt to sound anything other than a fellow proud of his own scheming.

'So with luck we might see ourselves joined up again with Charlie and Rufus very soon.'

In the waters off Gosport, on a creaking HMS *York*, Lieutenant John Moyle, his duties complete for the day, was considering, over an evening snack of cheese on toast washed down with some strong Gascony wine, how to play a very different game. That fellow Pearce had tried to be cunning, yet in truth he had been too open, for he had indicated to Moyle that at least two of the men he had taken up were not run-of-the-mill fellows. If he wished them to be separated that meant they were trouble together, and if they were a smuggling gang that told a mind not short of calculation that they might well be the leaders. It was not a question posed that was likely to produce a straight answer, but there were ways to ask that would get to the truth and perhaps, if his nose was leading him in the right direction, even more profit than he had got from his dealing with Pearce.

He had watched them as they were brought aboard and stripped for examination, prodded and poked for disabilities and their orifices checked for signs of disease. It had not been hard to spot the men about whom Pearce spoke, the one with the scar too obvious. Yet it was the other who was of the most interest, for where others had complained he had remained silent and that told Moyle he was likely the fellow to deal with.

Slowly, as he munched on his supper, Moyle framed his questions as well as the possible answers, then called to the man who guarded the door to his cabin to tell one of gaolers to proceed below to the very lowest deck and fetch up for him the fellow brought in this very day called Jahleel Tolland, adding a description, given he had not been listed as being aboard and had as yet no number. By the time the summons was answered – he could hear the clanking of the leg irons and chains – he had finished his food and a servant had cleared it away, but the bottle, not yet empty, was left on his table.

'Leave us,' he said to the man who had brought Tolland up from below, an individual in a short blue coat with brass buttons gone green from the rank atmosphere and white ducks that had been clean once but were grimy now. Then he added, as soon as that was obeyed and the cabin door closed, 'Would you care to sit?'

Jahleel Tolland raised his chained hands and replied in his rasping voice, 'I'd care more to have these struck off.'

Moyle smiled, which would have looked pleasant if his eyes had not narrowed at the same time. 'The wish of every prisoner, everywhere.'

'I'm not a prisoner, nor am I a volunteer to the King's Navy, which is what I reckon you have in mind for me and my company.'

'Company? That is a strange expression. Are they not mates, friends, companions?' Moyle picked up the bottle, filled his tankard, then added, 'I suggest you sit and perhaps drink some of this wine.'

Jahleel Tolland had come up from below expecting to be humiliated, on the grounds that John Pearce would have left instructions that it should be so, taking him down a peg prior to this fellow sending him to serve before the mast: there he would be, till he could find his feet, at the mercy of anyone with a rope starter. This was not like that, and if the elder Tolland was a ruffian he was no fool. He had been obliged many times in his life to deal with folk who made him appear saintly by comparison, for smuggling was a business full of violence. But it was also one in which subtlety was as necessary as a pistol and one where the need to pick up on the least hint was required for success and profit.

'I would be wanting to know if there's a price for that wine?'

Moyle smiled again. 'There is, Tolland, a price for everything.'

Tolland clanked forward and sat down, picking up the tankard. 'Then I do not mind if I partake of some, happen enough to cover what was in the purse your men filched from me when we were stripped of our clothing.'

'That is a serious allegation,' Moyle replied.

In reality the lieutenant was cursing himself for it had not occurred to him that, coming aboard as they had, these fellows might have possessions of value still upon them, the sort of things normally stolen by the press gangs long before they ever made the hulk. He sat rigid until the glass was drained, saying nothing but watching unblinking, like a cat examines an unsuspecting bird. Finished, his prisoner was in no hurry to speak either, which left the pair in mutual examination, seeking to discern from eye contact alone what could only be explained in words.

'I am told you are a smuggler?'

'By a liar, so why believe him?'

'Do I take kindly a fellow naval officer being so traduced?'

'You should have put that question to John Pearce, not I, for he's your smuggler.'

'And you?'

'A man seeking a bounty by bringing him in, which failed, for we did not know that he had a whole crew from a King's ship to prevent his being taken up.'

Moyle leant forward, his elbows on the table. 'If we are to understand each other, then I require the truth, not some made made-up tale.'

'Are we to understand each other?'

'The possibility exists, Tolland, but first I need to know to the very last detail what I am dealing with.'

What followed was another double stare, but it could only have one outcome: Jahleel Tolland had the choice of telling the truth or being taken back to his stinking cell not much above the bilge. After a few seconds he nodded and began talking to a man who had the ability to listen without in any way showing on his face either surprise or understanding. It was lengthy and the glass was refilled to wet Tolland's throat, but eventually all was explained from the very first sight of the Tolland ship sailing out of Gravelines with Pearce at the helm, to how they had come to be sent aboard HMS *York*.

'You got to admire this Pearce, have you not?'

'You can if you wish, that I will forgo.'

'I have to tell you Pearce has made the strangest request, one that has seen him "forgo" a decent bounty.' Now it was Moyle's turn to explain, which he did in short, sharp sentences, but never once letting his eyes leave his visitor's face. 'So, Tolland, what do you make of that?'

'Is it your intention to meet his wishes?'

'I must, but I have room to manoeuvre, do I not?'

The question was left hanging in the air, not that there was any doubt as to what it was. 'A better offer might change matters?'

'As of this moment none of you have been entered as having been brought aboard. I have to tell you that not to meet Pearce's primary concern is something I suspect might backfire, but that only applies to half of your . . . what did you call them? Company.'

'You could be brought to let half of us go.'

'I could be brought to let go anyone who could prove to me he was a gentleman, indeed I would be obliged by law to do so. It is not often that a press gang takes in a forty-shilling freeholder but it has been

173

known to happen. But I must have a care, for there has never been a case where a press gang has taken up four of such fellows.'

'Two?'

'Highly unusual, but possible,' Moyle replied.

Tolland picked up the empty tankard. 'And then there is the price?'

'Of course, but the other question is can you meet it?'

'I would need to know what is being asked for.'

Moyle nodded, then shouted out for a gaoler, his lips compressed in a more cynical expression. 'However, I do think a night with the rats will make you more amenable when it is discussed.' The door opened and the man who had brought Tolland up from below appeared. 'Take him back down, and tell my servant on the way to fetch another bottle of wine.'

'Aye, aye, sir.'

The destination of the Lyndhurst coach was another inn called the Wykham Arms, which, like all of Winchester was in total darkness by the time the two weary horsemen rolled up. They were required to bang hard to rouse out what passed for a night porter, in truth a fellow who, judging by his rank breath, drank too much and looked very unthreatening albeit he had a cudgel in his hand. That, originally raised in a defensive manner, dropped as he lifted his eyes to take in the height of one of the men he might be obliged to thwack – Michael O'Hagan made it look as if he would hardly reach, for the porter was short in the leg, so he undid the chain and let them into the hallway.

'The Lyndhurst coach came earlier?' That got a nod and a foul exhalation. 'Were there aboard two French folk and an English lady?'

'There were, took their bags in myself.'

'How did they seem, I mean in each other's company?'

'Weren't attending to that.'

'Did they dine together?'

'Can't rightly say, don't take much to foreign folk who don't know a coin is due for porterage and I has other work to do, any road.'

'Would that be the supping of ale?' Michael asked.

Courage came from somewhere, probably what he had consumed throughout the day. 'None of your damn business, Paddy.'

That got the fellow a grab at the front of his grubby shirt and a lift that had his feet off the floor until Pearce admonished his friend to put him down. As soon as he was released and breathing normally Pearce asked for a room they could share. For all he was in fear of the giant before him, that did not extend to rousing out the innkeeper or his wife, so both new arrivals had to settle for a bench in the taproom with Pearce moaning that he seemed to spend all his nights now on hard board instead of a comfortable cot. That fell on deaf ears; Michael O'Hagan was already snoring as through the window by John Pearce's head came the first whistle of the dawn chorus.

Toby Burns had not slept at all, but at least in that, on this occasion, he was not alone. Brave as they sounded, every fellow going ashore was prey to nerves and it was a relief to man the ship's boats and, when daylight came, head for the troop transports to load on the bullocks who would carry out the main assault. On a shore in plain view it was obvious that the French garrison had a clear idea of where to mount a defence: files of blue-coated soldiers could be seen deploying and some of them digging, their backs to the slight dune that kept storm tides at bay.

On board HMS *Britannia* the marine officers had paraded their men, for it was the Lobsters who would mount the initial landing given they were more nimble, on a swell, at getting in and out of cutters and the like and quickly engaging. In reality it was because, inured to life at sea, they were less likely to be seasick, which the soldiers would most certainly be, for the swell in a ship's boat cannot compare to that of a large capacious transport.

'You have done this before, Mr Burns, I am informed.'

Staring glumly at the shoreline through the open entry port and lost in a reverie of a life so much less dangerous, Toby started at being so addressed. Walker, the man who had posed the question, a captain of marines, had arrogance written all over him, nose high, chin in and a look in his eye that implied he was of superior mien. The captain had served on the ship all the time that Toby had been aboard, yet these were the first words he had ever addressed to the midshipman, no doubt a lowly creature in his elevated eyes. The thought of his previous experience in carrying out a by-boat assault was not a fond one and his reply was almost savage enough to be disrespectful.

'I was, sir, at San Fiorenzo, and the man who commanded my boat took a ball in the leg.' He had no idea what had happened to that naval lieutenant but he felt it deserved embellishment. 'I do believe it led to an amputation.'

'It will be hot work right enough,' the captain replied with studied calm, which had Toby cursing the man under his breath; this was not work, it was slaughter.

'Hotspur's on deck,' came a whispered alert, which referred to Hotham, whose wholly inappropriate soubriquet that was, ironic rather than complimentary. 'An' heading your way.'

The marine officer had gone rigid and Toby too was obliged to stand upright, to turn and to raise his hat. 'Well, Mr Burns, here you have another chance to distinguish yourself.'

'For which I am truly grateful, sir,' he replied. 'I was just explaining to Captain Walker how I lost my officer the last time and perhaps he would not be pleased to know that in a previous action above Bastia the fellow in command of the marine detachment was taken by a ball in the chest when we attacked a French redoubt. Come to think of it, the lieutenant who commanded our battery at the actual siege was wounded too.'

Hotham was not alone in glaring at him, for the implication was plain; Walker was too, for no man likes to be told that he is going to action in close proximity to the kind of Jonah that draws enemy fire, which was what Burns was telling him. It took some effort on the part of the admiral to recover a degree of composure.

'Then, Mr Burns, it is time that matters were altered and I am sure even if Captain Walker leads you into the thickest part of the action, you will both have tales to tell your grandchildren.' He addressed Walker directly. 'Not that he lacks for those, for did you know, captain, that this lad here was wounded at Toulon and, on his first voyage, stole back a merchant vessel that had been taken by the enemy.'

'I had heard the tale, sir.'

'"Tale", Mr Walker? I rate it more than that.'

'Time to get my men into the boats, sir.'

'Carry on, Mr Walker, and since young Burns here is something of a talisman to the fleet, I suggest you gift to him the prow of your cutter. It will inspire those who follow to see an acknowledged hero standing to lead the assault.'

CHAPTER TWELVE

The boat took time to load and when complete it was crowded like every other in the initial assault. The number of marines that shared their thwarts cramped the rowers, with their muskets upright between their legs and bayonets glistening in the morning sunlight, the only difference being that the Lobsters faced forward while the oarsmen had their back to the shore. As they set off from the side of HMS *Britannia*, they were joined by marine detachments from the remainder of the fleet. Many of them in reality were soldiers who had been drafted into naval service to raise the numbers, but that notwithstanding – the two services heartily disliked each other – they received a collective cheer of encouragement from every main deck.

As it died away, Hotham's voice could be heard

in what was, for a man of his elevated rank, a rather undignified display of being partisan, given nearly all of his flagship lieutenants and midshipmen were engaged in getting the fighting men ashore and the more senior they were, the more they resented the apparent favour being shown to one of their number.

'Good luck to you all, and I know, Mr Burns, you will not fail to show an example.'

Under so many eyes and sat on the tiller, despite Hotham's suggestion of the prow, there was little choice for Toby; he took hold of the berthing line and, wrapping it round his wrist, he stood, feet as far apart as he could, using his attachment to the body of the boat to stay upright and still able to steer, gazing into the stoical faces of those men it was his duty to command and seeing there no joy. The notion of shouting slogans of bravery, which should have accompanied such a gesture, was beyond him and Captain Walker, sat in the prow with his back to him, showed an indifference to the idea that he might do so.

The warships and transports were obliged to anchor far offshore in order to ensure a good depth of water under their keel, given the very rocky outcrops, and also they were subject to wind and the state of the tide, not much of a rise and fall in the Mediterranean but sufficient to create eddies and flows as well as choppy waves. It needed a tight grip on the line to hold his place and that lasted as they passed the bomb ketches, further inshore and firmly anchored in the soft sand of the bay, the mortars primed and ready to play upon the hastily slung up French defences.

For these fellows, given the range of their weapons left them normally too close to the defence for any comfort, it was in the nature of an exercise; the enemy had nothing with which to retaliate and that lent to their cheers as the stream of boats began to pass a less than welcome bent that implied rather you than us. Toby could see the lips of the sailors move and the marines' as well, most likely, all cursing the idle buggers in whispers and asides.

From such an elevated position and with the eyesight of his years, the youngster had a good view of the beach. He could observe that pieces of driftwood had been used to create ramparts against musket fire and in some cases sacks had been used to build up more. In his mind's eye he could only too easily imagine rushing up the tilting sand, his feet dragging and slowing him down, as several Frenchmen took aim at his heart, which had him struggling, so vivid was the vision, to hold on to his bowels.

Soon they were over the shallow waters that ran all the way to the beach, able to see the rippled bottom and to make out the swaying seaweed where it covered the bed. Also, if indistinctly, he could see the enemy, not just their uniforms but individual faces, as well as the cocksure walking to and fro of parading officers, no doubt telling their recumbent men that this was the day they would achieve glory. Down at the water's dge a single fellow stood, wearing a tricolour sash, a plumed hat and with gold frogging to his jacket that denoted superior rank. He had a small eyeglass raised and was sweeping the line of boats. Having held his position for some time he suddenly dropped the glass and slammed it closed, then turned and walked back up to join the rest of his men, which brought forth the first words from Captain Walker that he had uttered since casting off from the flagship.

'We will be in musket range soon, my lads, so make yourself small. Mr Burns, I would suggest that the position you have adopted is an unwise one and you will oblige me by not only sitting down but doing your best to use the men before you as protection against a ball.'

'But the admiral, sir—'

He got no further and the reply, in tone, was icy. 'Sir William is master on his own deck, and so it should be. But I am the ranking officer in this boat and what I wish supersedes the desires of admirals, however hungry they are for the glory of those they cherish.'

That shocked Toby; even if it was a thought many held it was not one to articulate in public and Walker turned to drive home his point. 'Get down, sir, this instant, for there will be enough futile injury on that strand of beach without we add to it by braggadocio.'

Toby obliged, easing himself down to look into a stony-faced superior, who merely gave a sharp nod, as Walker, still facing the stern, issued his orders to all.

'You, Mr Burns, will take equal cognisance of what I am saying. On the tiller you will oblige me by grounding at an angle of forty-five degrees and on my command, which will be given when we have alignment with our confrères in the other boats. My fellows, you will stand and deliver one volley of musketry. As for you tars, you may cower in the bottom if you so desire but do not get in the way. My Lobsters will then disembark on the seaward side, for the water will scarce cover their ankles.' His voice now rose and it was harsh. 'No man is to get onto the dry sand and expose themselves until I give the order and I'll break at the wheel any sod who disobeys.'

He had to pause then, the bomb ketches had opened up, sending huge balls arching towards the shore, there to land and send up great plumes of sand close to the water's edge that seemed to rest in the air before settling slowly down in the form of a cloud.

'Useless,' Walker spat. 'More of a danger to us than John Crapaud, but it is not too much to ask that perhaps they will up their range and keep down French heads. Now, we are coming in long range, so prepare to receive fire.'

Toby Burns was slightly taken aback; if Walker had previously addressed no words to him, seeming arrogant and taciturn, he was certainly employing enough now, while what he explained was in itself remarkable. Officers, both naval and doubly so marines, rarely explained anything to their men; they just drilled them and expected them to follow orders when engaged. Yet here was this fellow outlining in detail what he wanted to do, while seeking to keep them from unnecessary harm.

'Mr Burns, the men rowing at the point of disembarkation become yours to lead, the boat yours to command. Once we have ceased to use it as cover and have begun our advance it will be entirely at your discretion as to whether the oarsmen take part in seeking to secure the beach or return to bring in reinforcements. You do not have to seek my permission on how to proceed.'

'Sir.'

The voice softened, as Walker added, 'Orders which should have been issued to you by your superiors – I take it they were not?'

'No, sir.'

'Well, you have them now, so act as you see fit – and, Mr Burns, a piece of advice: valour does not come from what others wish of you but what you do yourself and unbidden.'

Toby would have replied if he had not been forced to duck into his own body as the first musket balls fizzed into the water alongside, the captain still talking.

'Steady lads, it's all chance at this range, so pray to God that he wants you spared. Now hang onto something as we strike the sand.'

Toby, looking left and right, could see others in line and seemingly setting their pace by Walker, who had just asked the oarsmen, politely, for extra effort, a request to which they responded by bending their backs. If the boat picked up a bit of speed it was, in open water, hard to tell, but the marine captain seemed satisfied and within what seemed like seconds, and still a goodly distance from the waterline, the keel grounded, bringing the cutter to a shuddering halt, at which point Walker did stand, to order his men up with him. They obeyed and with a sluggishness that amazed Toby – it was as if no one was shooting at them – they lowered their muskets as if they were in no danger, took aim and fired off a very disciplined volley at their officer's command.

'Wet your feet, lads.'

The boat dipped heavily to one side as they leapt into the water, which in truth came up to their knees, setting about the ritual of reloading as soon as they were steady on their feet. Toby, cowering down now that he was fully exposed, found the voice of Captain Walker close to his ear, as were the cracks of passing shot aimed in their direction.

'It never will do to have the men you lead in ignorance of what we are about, Mr Burns.'

'Ready, sir,' called his corporal, which had Walker ordering another volley, this as mortar balls flew over their head to land three-quarters of the way up the beach, the onshore breeze carrying the sand over the enemy defences to hide any success the marine fire might have achieved.

'Damn me,' Walker hooted, 'we are going to drive them away with the discomfort of sand down their necks.'

'Will we drive them off, sir?'

'Oh yes. Our aim is to clear the beach, not die trying to take it, though I daresay some fools, even if they know that, will earn themselves a Corsican headstone for their stupidity. The French cannot hold, they lack the numbers, and nor have they fetched out field artillery to impede us, not that we are sure they possess any. They will seek to hold us up, to make the landing as bloody as they can, then, when the situation ceases to be tenable, they will withdraw back to their citadel and outer forts where, in time, unless a relief force comes from the mainland to drive us away, we will accept their surrender.'

'They should surrender now,' Toby spat.

'Nonsense, lad, even the French are careful of their honour.'

'Main body coming in, sir,' shouted someone from along the beach, by his tone another officer, which drew all eyes to a mass of boats heading for a point where the beach ended and the hills began, mostly men in red, but also several boats full of men in white, French Royalists come to do battle with their fellow countryman.

'The Bullocks are heading for the northern section,' Walker continued, 'and once the Johnny in command of our enemies sees that they are about to succeed in securing it he will blow for the retreat to avoid being cut off from an easy withdrawal. At that point, and not before, my men and I will advance.'

'Reinforcements, sir?'

'Judging by the rate of fire I doubt we'll need any. You'll be fetching cannon ashore soon and my poor lads will be obliged to haul the damn things up that great hill you see to the north. Once over that we will then be set to filling bags for battery ramparts and a good month of looking down on our foes.'

If Walker thought it was close to a finish it could not be discerned by silence; balls cracked overhead, others thudded into the side of the cutter to embed themselves in the strakes and every so often, regardless of using the boats as cover, somewhere along the waterline a marine would spin away having been hit in the upper part of his body or his head by a lucky shot. The mortars kept up their bombardment, mostly useless on such soft ground that just sucked the balls in to dissipate the effect. The odd one did land where it was needed, the screams of those it had hit rolling down to the shoreline, until from their left came the sound of cheering as the army units came ashore to rush those who lay before them.

When, as predicted, the bugle sounded the retreat, Walker ordered his men out of cover and, after one volley and in extended order, they began to advance, this as flags waved out to sea to bring an end to the bombardment. But the French were not routed, they retired in good order, able to turn and subject those pursuing them to volley fire every so often, some of those missing and sending up founts of sand near the boats.

'Man the oars,' Toby croaked, his throat feeling as dry as sandpaper.

'We'll need bodies over the side to get us off,' a voice called. It was, no doubt, that of the senior hand aboard, keen to remind a young gentleman – useless as a breed in most sailors' eyes – of what he should have thought of for himself. That they did not respect him was in the next words addressed. 'An' since you ain't rowing, Mr Burns . . .'

There was no choice but to expose himself and as he leapt over the side two others followed, putting their shoulders to the prow and driving the cutter back till it floated. One man to his right, from being bent over suddenly became upright, then arched backwards, this before he fell forward with a moan, his hands clutching at a rowlock, the midshipman transfixed by the sight as the same gruff voice called out.

'Get Tosh inboard, for the love of Christ.' Hands dragged at the wounded man and the second sailor who had helped to free the boat secured his legs and heaved, the inert body crumpling into the bottom followed by a less than respectful shout. 'Get aboard, young sir.'

At that very moment, holes appeared in the wet sand by his boots and Toby could not move; his legs were useless even as he mentally ordered them to comply.

Was it collective or did that leading hand give another command. Whatever, the oars were dipped and the boat was moving, a voice floating back to the ears of the rock-still midshipman.

'Got to get him to the surgeon, quick.'

It took several seconds for Toby to realise that the distance between boat and shore was now too great to cover, to realise that he was stuck ashore in what was still a battle for possession of the beach. Running out of the shallows he threw himself down in the sand, praying to God to be spared.

'What are you about, Mr Burns?' called Captain Walker. 'Can you not observe that the enemy are now in full flight?'

The first boats bringing in the heavy cannon, their wooden and wheeled trunnions, as well as powder and shot, provided Toby Burns with a way back to HMS *Britannia* and he left a beach now full of men, strangers to him, constructing tripods to get them ashore with ropes and pulleys, and slatted roadways to get them across the soft sand to the base of the hills. He had declined Walker's invitation to join in the advance of the marines, shepherding the French back into their pen as he called it, on the grounds that it had to be dangerous, only to find when he came back aboard he was being praised, not too fulsomely, for staying ashore when he could have departed.

The boat crew, or whoever had taken charge of

them and had elected to leave him behind, did not tell anyone in authority that the Midshipman Burns had been abandoned, that they had sought succour for a wounded sailor above both his needs and his position of command. Instead they had reported Mr Burns as insisting on remaining where there was fighting, which left the youth – who could have seen the grating rigged for what they had done – in no position to dish them, without likewise doing the same to himself. Later a hand, taking advantage of the lack of anyone else close by, spoke behind Toby's back, to point out that it would do him no harm to drop by the sickbay and look in on the fellow who had taken a ball in his back.

'Name's Feathers, an' he's in a bad way. Might never have the use of his legs again, young sir, which you has to say is a foul jest played by a spiteful God, seeing it did not need a ball in the spine to brace your'n's rigid.'

Toby turned to remonstrate only to find himself looking at the back of a checked shirt rapidly moving away and beyond him the quarterdeck, where stood the officer of the watch and, unfortunately, Sir William Hotham, who was glaring at him. All Toby could do was touch his hat, note the flash of very apparent disgust and wonder what it was he had done to deserve it from a man who had so recently given all the impression of smiling upon him, Toby being unaware of how much of the admiral's time had been taken up thinking of a way to deal with the problem he presented.

* * *

'You see, Sir William, if you read this Lucknor fellow's letter, it is plain that he has never corresponded with Burns prior to this.'

'I do not see how that changes matters, Toomey.'

The admiral's senior clerk had on many occasions been obliged to suppress his frustrations, working as he did for a man who too often seemed incapable of seeing the obvious, and that had to be kept from his tone of voice as well, for Hotham was just as prickly of his honour.

'He has no knowledge of the lad's hand, sir, so if he was to receive another letter, penned by me in the same style but with a vastly different list of responses, how is he to know it is not genuine?'

'What if your letter and Burns are together in one place, eh?'

'The chances of that are slim, sir. This Lucknor is in London, Burns out here with us.'

'But it is possible, for that lawyer is not airing a grievance of his own, he is acting on behalf of a client.'

Toomey knew the import of that, for he had in his possession the depositions made by that fellow Pearce and the trio of sailors who were attached to him. Given they and Burns served in the same navy, who knows what might happen. Matters were bad enough and if forgery was added to his suspect court martial it could become an even steeper slope to perdition. Hotham merely wanted to suppress what Toby Burns had written – to not forward his reply – but there was strong argument against that.

The affair could not just be left to stew for, if he was not a lawyer himself, he suspected that this fellow Lucknor, in the absence of a response, would write again, and how could they be sure of the same level of interception a second time? This, slowly and tactfully, he explained to his superior.

'You said, sir, I admit in some passion, that you were damned if you could keep Burns within sight.'

'I want to swat the treacherous little toad every time I clap eyes on him and, damn me, I might lose myself one day and do it in front of the ship's officers.'

'So it is your intention to have him shift to another berth?'

'It is, and damn soon, but not before he has had a few weeks of service before the guns of Calvi. I intend to send him to the siege batteries where he can share whatever risks that popinjay Nelson affords himself. Given his stupidity that will be right with the foremost guns.'

There was no need for Hotham to elaborate on that; Burns would be put in a position of maximum danger as he had in the beach landing. That this was an act of pure vindictiveness did not trouble Toomey, his task was to serve his master and keep his own position, which was about to be much enhanced. Lord Hood could not remain in command for much longer and his admiral was in line and had the political backing to succeed him. That would take Toomey to the pinnacle of his trade; to be the senior clerk to a commanding admiral was a position from which a man could make a fortune and such a notion was just as appealing to him as the actual role was to Hotham.

'Then that gives me time, sir, to put my mind to a solution.'

'More than your mind, Toomey, I want your heart and soul engaged in this.'

The solution was not long in being presented. Toomey would write a letter of his own to Lucknor and, as he pointed out, any further immediate attempt to contact Burns would come to the flagship and could thus be intercepted, which would be rendered especially safe if the youngster was shifted to another vessel, preferably one where the captain had a strong attachment to Hotham and one who could be primed, with a made-up tale, that any correspondence that Burns undertook should be passed first to HMS *Britannia*.

'Shifting mids is not easy, Toomey, a captain likes his own choices aboard ship.'

'I am aware of that Sir William, and I point out to you that Lord Hood has called for an examination after the fall of Calvi so that the high number of midshipmen acting as lieutenants should have a chance to attain the actual rank.'

'You're not suggesting that I put up Burns?'

'I am, sir.'

'Won't work, dammit, I doubt the little bugger would pass.'

'He would if he knew what the questions were going to be and had the answers. After all, I daresay if you offered to relieve Lord Hood of the burden of arranging the examination, to which I think given his great responsibilities he would accede, the choice of captains to sit on the judging panel would be yours.'

Hotham was now toying with a nut and a pair of crackers, though one showed no sign of being placed in proximity to the other and as usual he was applying his less than rapid mental processes to the suggestion. If it was not a commonplace for an admiral to stuff the board about to test the skill of a relative it was not unknown and a hint to those sitting, no less than it had been at Barclay's court martial, that a certain result was required, was one that would be taken on board. The only difficulty came from those same captains having sons or nephews of their own; the day would come when a favour granted would be one called in.

'And what then?'

'Then he could be placed aboard another ship as the most junior lieutenant, out of your sight but still under your supervision, given there are no plans to change the make-up of the fleet.'

'That will not pertain for ever.'

'I am proposing an immediate solution to an immediate problem. No one can know the future, but if we can kill off enquires now, that argues we may choke off the whole affair.'

A gleam came into Hotham's eye then, for he thought

Burns would make a poor, indeed a terrible deck officer – the boy had no spunk in him – that would expose him to the wrath of his captain, especially if another hint from him indicated that would be permissible. What he would really like was for the sod to stuff a cannonball down his breeches and jump over the side on a dark night and at that moment he was fancying a fellow could be driven to that.

'That seems to me,' Toomey pressed, 'to be the only alternative to keeping him on the flagship. After all, we cannot send him home.'

Another long pause ensued and Toomey knew not to press; Hotham had no ideas of his own and also little choice but to accept those put to him and that eventually penetrated his thinking.

'No. Write your letter and send it off.'

'Sir.'

'And send Burns to me so I can give him news of his new appointment and his future prospects.'

CHAPTER THIRTEEN

Pearce had become accustomed to sleep being short but the same could not be said for spending the night on bare boards and his bench seemed harder than deck planking. He awoke stiff and in an ill temper, caused as much because of what he might have to face as his limbs, well aware that he felt grubby and needed, before he faced anyone, a wash and more particularly a proper shave. The inn was up and buzzing with activity, preparing for the day and at last he and Michael could retire to a room where hot water was provided, not that O'Hagan was interested: he dropped his boots on the floor and lay down to continue his slumbers, despite the loud ringing of the bells from the nearby cathedral.

A man was sent up to take Pearce's uniform coat; that to be sponged and pressed, his stock washed and ironed dry, while, razor in hand over a bowl of steaming water, looking into a less than clear mirror, he rehearsed again and again the lines he had worked to death on the way to Winchester, continually aiming to hit the right tone. It had to be firm but apologetic that no warning of what had occurred could be made. Breakfast came as well – he was assured that the other guests had yet to appear or request refreshments – added to the information that there were no places on the London Flyer until the next day; whatever was about to happen would take place here in the Wykham Arms.

After a knock, the door opened and the serving man returned with his clothing, which he handed over with a look at O'Hagan, awake but still recumbent, that promised hellfire for his being fully clothed while laying on the establishments linen. All he got in response was an exaggerated wink and the remark that, sure, soft bedding beats a hammock any day and if he had a wench handy his pleasure would be complete.

'Saving your presence, but you asked to be informed if the other guests were up and about. I am to say the ladies have called for hot water.'

'There's no justice in the world, John-boy, here's you with two paramours hard by and me bereft.'

If they, as a pair, did not already stand very high in the regard of the staff of the Wykham – no doubt the night man had described their arrival – that remark and its implications, judging by the expression on the servitor's face, took it to a new low. He exited murmuring about the world going to the dogs, with Pearce calling after him to fetch two hearty breakfasts and quickly, as well as an inkwell and paper, the latter immediately.

'I have no mind to face anyone on an empty stomach.'

'Am I allowed to be an observer, John-boy?'

'No you are not. This is serious, Michael, and the last thing I need in the background is you grinning and leering at me.'

That was what Pearce got now. 'Then you will give Mrs Barclay my compliments.'

'Would you not be better seeing if the horses are being well looked after?'

'Why, brother, are we planning a quick getaway?' O'Hagan started to laugh, his body heaving. 'Sure that would be a sight, the hero John Pearce in flight from a couple of women.'

Another knock, another glare at the bed, but the means to communicate was handed over, with Pearce carrying it to the dresser and immediately sitting down to write.

'Instead of vexing me, Michael, you would do me a service if you were to ask for a private room in which I can speak to Emily. There will be one on the ground floor, I'm sure.'

Michael dragged himself up, pulled on his boots and headed for the door. 'And here was me thinking my days of being a servant were at an end.'

The note Pearce wrote was short, simply saying that he was staying in the same inn and that he desired a word in private. The temptation to add 'to avoid a scene' he considered but put aside; Emily, if she knew the connection to Amélie Labordière, would smoke his reasons without them being spelt out. Michael returned to say the room had been reserved and where it was, just off the hallway, and that Pearce appended, as well as a time he hoped she would accept. Breakfast arrived next and the pair sat down to a couple of beefsteaks washed down with strong local cider. The plates were clean and the cider jug empty when Emily's reply came that she was at his convenience.

'At my convenience,' Pearce moaned, for it was so very formal. 'This is going to be worse than even I imagined.'

'Hell hath no fury, I am told, like a woman scorned,' Michael said, getting to his feet. 'And now, if you will forgive, I must go about my occasions, as polite folk say.'

'I have another letter to write, to Dundas, telling him I am returned and who with.'

Michael's eyes were twinkling. 'Your one-time mistress, John-boy?'

'Damn you, no, the Count de Puisaye.'

'Sure, I cannot help but think your man would prefer the former.'

Aboard HMS *York* Lieutenant Moyle was likewise examining his empty breakfast plate, washed down in his case by a bottle of claret, and ruminating on the state of his existence, which seemed as messy as the remains of the fowl he had just consumed. Like all young men he had entered the navy full of ambition and had, in his first midshipman's berth, dreamt of the glory of command in battle, of a great victory that would set him up with his richly deserved estate and carriage and four with which to go about and impress. How different it had been in reality! A struggle to maintain even employment as a midshipman, then once that had been achieved a scraped pass in the lieutenant's examination followed by years of pleading for a place afloat and, on landing one, being shown to be barely competent in the necessities of his profession.

He still occasionally shuddered to recall the very obvious mistakes he had made, added to the realisation that he was not cut out to be a seaman. It was a distant relative and MP, much badgered and eventually worn down, who had secured for him this posting, which if it was a lowly one was at least secure as long as he did not foul his own anchor. But it was also, most assuredly, not a platform to better things; to be promoted to captain, to be made post from his present position was too fanciful for words, so it was incumbent upon him to make the best he could out of what was a dead-end position.

'Tolland, sir,' said the guard, a different fellow from the previous night, through the open door.

'Let him enter and close the door behind him.' The guard obliged and Jahleel Tolland clanked forward as he had before, to stand just inside the closed door, his eyes on the breakfast remains with Moyle jesting as he observed the direction of the look. 'I daresay you did not eat as well as I.'

'You knows I did not,' Tolland growled. 'I had gruel not fit for pigswill.'

Among Moyle's less attractive traits, and he would have been pushed to admit it as true, he seeing himself as an upright soul, was his tendency to bully and the tone of the prisoner's voice irritated him enough to bring what was never far from the surface to the fore. When the nature of his task and his lack of prospects took him into a depression, which it did on many occasions, there was the saving grace of always having other people to physically take it out on.

'I could have you flogged at a whim, cur, and be assured it is not a task I delegate to others. It is my own arm I employ and my own retribution I satisfy.'

'I daresay you provide what you can,' Tolland replied, working hard to look contrite, for there was a game to be played and an angry hulk commander was not helpful.

'I do,' Moyle purred, 'and I am seen as generous.'

Outside the door, the guard who had fetched Tolland from below raised his eyes to the deck beams above his head in disbelief; with the exchange loud enough, he could hear clearly what was being said and his reaction would have been greeted by his fellow guards as correct. Moyle was a lying, thieving bastard who stole what rations he could, a tyrant and an oppressor of those beneath him, as well as an arse-licker to anyone who had the means to allow him to further line his pockets.

The last thing the guard heard was that Tolland should sit down; with the two now close the talk was too indistinct to make sense.

'I sense you have come to a proper appreciation of your situation?'

'Hard not to,' Tolland responded, holding up manacled hands that showed evidence of being bitten more than once.

'Ah yes. The ship's cats do their best, but with rodents so numerous it would take a blaze to shift them.'

'Moving up a deck would suffice some.'

'So it would, Tolland, but I am sure you have not come to see me seeking only a bit of deck elevation.'

'I want to know what would it take to get my brother and I free?'

'Not a great deal – someone to attest in writing, of course, and it would need to be a person very respectable, that you are not seamen and are, in fact, gentlemen.'

'And how would this person of standing be made aware of where we are?'

'You would have to communicate with them by letter. I take it you can write?'

'My brother has a fair hand, yet he lacks the means to do what you say, for he too had his purse swiped by your men.'

'True,' Moyle replied, with a grim smile, 'but I do not lack the means.'

Dealing with a plague of rats did not preclude thinking and Jahleel Tolland had been gifted many waking hours to do that. He had guessed that this Lieutenant Moyle had in mind to set them free and for a price, only neither of them knew what that should be. Moyle was keen to extract the maximum he could, without any knowledge of what kind of funds the Tollands had access to; Jahleel had the opposite aim, to get off this ship for as little disbursement as he could.

He had hidden the money he carried in his saddlebags in a pocket on the inside of his riding boots, unobserved by Pearce and his sailors who were not, in any case, looking to steal. That was now hidden in the filthy straw on which he and his gang had been obliged to sleep; even if rats might leave the odd mark of their teeth they could not eat gold. Having palmed a couple of guineas on being called to come to the great cabin, he moved his hand across the tabletop and left them in plain view. Eyes drawn to them, Moyle moved slowly to pick them up.

'There has to be more than this?'

'For paper and an inkwell?'

'For the right to walk free.'

'All eight?'

'Two, no more.'

If Jahleel Tolland thought about that at all, it was not for long; his other men would just have to take their chances. 'Happen the man I write to could satisfy your needs and mine but I would need to know how much that would be. I can scarce ask if I do not know.'

Moyle sat back, still playing with the coins. 'I would need ten times this and more. Judas priced Jesus at thirty pieces of silver. I am sure you value your head higher than that.'

If Jahleel Tolland was thinking, I've got you cheap you grasping sod, there was no sign of it on his face. If anything he looked worried, as if what was being requested was too steep. He had that sum hidden in the straw, but he knew this Lieutenant John Moyle was not a man to trust. He could just take what Jahleel had, then laugh in his face; better a couple of night's fighting off rats than that.

'I'd say he might go to that, but there's only one way to be certain.'

'A letter?' Tolland nodded as Moyle flipped the coins. 'Let us say this pair of beauties will cover pen and ink, shall we?'

'Does it cover a higher deck too?'

'Perhaps when your letter is written and I have seen what it says and to whom it is addressed. After all, I must make sure you do not try to dish me by some code I cannot comprehend.'

'My brother will write in front of you.'

'He will have to,' Moyle laughed.

'When?'

'The guard that takes you down can bring him up.'

'After we's had a word, so he knows what needs sayin'.'

Moyle nodded, loudly ordered Tolland taken down, then went to admire his image in one of the many mirrors that dotted the bulkheads of his cabin, thinking that if he was not as much a sailor as many of his contemporaries, he was very much their match in the means to extract profit from a situation.

Pearce was standing by an unlit fireplace when Emily entered the private room, his elbow on the mantle. He had been staring at a very poor reproduction of the kind of painting done by the leading London artists – in this case no doubt executed by a travelling limner and copyist – of men mounted on horses, their pack of hounds chasing a fox across, he assumed, the Hampshire landscape, and thinking how often in his life he had been the prey and not the hunter. Turning as the door opened, what he observed, a tight-lipped Emily Barclay, did nothing to make him feel less so and that was compounded when he walked towards her, holding out hands she declined to take, with a sharp shake of the head.

'Emily, I . . .'

The head dropped so he could not see her eyes. 'Do you not think, John, that explanations are superfluous? I assume that you have arranged the meeting for that purpose?'

'It is all coincidence, happenstance. I found Amélie to be in distressed circumstances and felt obliged to help her.'

'While providing for yourself an outlet for . . .' That obviously conjured up a word for Emily she could not use. 'How very convenient that must have seemed.'

'It was not convenient, in fact it was damned . . .'

205

Pearce threw up his hands, for to use such language with Emily was to destroy his case on its own. 'Forgive my blaspheming but can you not see that I am being judged in a light that is unfair?'

'It is not a pleasure,' Emily whispered, 'when you think you have secured someone's heart, to find you are required to share it.'

'You cannot think I would do that. Is your opinion of me so low that you can even consider such a thing?'

'You have needs, have you not?'

'I am a man, I grant you.'

'Which I seem to recall you expressed in embarrassing circumstances in Leghorn. It did not seem to affect you at all that you were the butt of the laughter of the fleet, running through the streets, pursued by an irate husband, in nothing but your smalls.'

'That was before you and I discovered our mutual regard. I cannot be blamed for red-blood prior to—'

'To what, John, my disgrace first and humiliation second?'

Her shoulders started to heave, not much but it was easy to discern her distress. Slowly, and with no pressure, he put his hands on them. 'I pledged myself to you and I do so again now.'

'So Madame Labordière means nothing to you?'

'I cannot say nothing,' he replied moving one hand to lift her chin, 'but in comparison to my feelings for you . . .' Emily allowed her head to be lifted, and as it was, the shaking of her shoulder turned from suppressed to violent and as soon as he could clearly see her face, John Pearce exclaimed, and not with joy, 'Emily, are you laughing?'

Her hand went to her mouth. 'Forgive me, I cannot help it, and only the Good Lord knows how I kept it hidden for this length of time. You looked like a lost child when I came through that door.'

John Pearce swept past her and flung open the very same door. Michael O'Hagan was standing in plain view, as so were the Count de Puisaye and Amélie, they looking at him with some curiosity.

'Michael,' Pearce barked. 'Is your hand in this?'

'Mother of God, I did you a favour, for I could not imagine the poor fist you would have made of matters had I not explained them first. Now gather yourself, for Mrs Barclay has arranged to take these poor travellers on a tour of the city and they are anxious to be on their way.'

John Pearce felt his arm taken by Emily Barclay, his mood unsure. Was he angry or glad? – it was hard to tell.

'I'm told the cathedral is especially fine, John, and as we walk we must indeed talk, for while you have been away, I cannot say that I have been comfortable regarding our future.'

'You and Amélie?'

'Have become, on a very short acquaintance, very firm friends. After all, what a boon it is to be able to talk with someone who knows all your faults and is prepared to list them, albeit I sometimes struggle with the French.'

'What faults?'

Emily smiled sweetly, then sighed. 'It is a blessing we have the whole day to discuss them.'

'I suppose you have taken the count to your bosom as well.'

The reply was an emphatic 'No'.

That was a condition the fellow in question did nothing to alleviate as he disparaged that which he was shown: Winchester Cathedral was fine, if cramped compared to Notre Dame, Chartres, Reims or the great double basilica of Bourges, proper edifices built to the glory of God, of which he was sure this English church was just a pale copy erected by poorly trained masons. Not a religious man at all and certainly disinclined to defend the unnecessary property of what he knew to be a bloated established church, John Pearce was thinking that the guillotine was too good for the old fool.

Franklin Tolland wrote his letter still chained, which did nothing to aid the fluency of the quill; indeed he could bareley recognise his own hand, a point Moyle dismissed as he picked up the sanded page and read it, nodding as he saw that the sum of forty guineas was required for release, close to a year's income for a gentleman. Added to that which he had been gifted by Pearce that would add up to a tidy sum that he could invest in government Consols, as he did with anything he could get from his benighted office.

One day he would have enough to relinquish HMS

York, enough to add to his half pay as an unemployed lieutenant, the means to purchase a cottage and a bit of land that he would see worked to his advantage, and then there was also the possibility of a woman with whom to share it. The name of the addressee he noted, to be written down later. This Denby Carruthers fellow was surely well heeled and might, at some future date, be a source of more funds.

'I will have you and your brother moved up a deck, away from the most pernicious rodents.'

'No,' Franklin barked, 'you must move us all or the others will become suspicious that we mean to ditch them.'

Moyle was halfway across his deck before Franklin finished. 'Do not use that tone of voice with me, lest you want a scar on your other cheek to balance up your looks. And for your tone you can stay where you are!'

'The letter?'

'Will be sent, never fear, but I wonder if your friend will want you and the vermin you will fetch along?' The look that crossed Franklin Tolland's face then gave Moyle the impression that this Carruthers fellow might not – that indeed he might not get what he now considered his due. 'Pray he does, cur, for I have it in me to make what you have now seem like paradise.'

CHAPTER FOURTEEN

A flurry of communications arrived in London in a very short time. Ralph Barclay's demand that his wife return to her married state the first, and this from the solicitor to whom it was originally addressed but unopened and forwarded to her last known address at Nerot's Hotel to await her anticipated return. There was one from Mr Studdert too, still trying to recover from a burglary in which every document he had stored in his strongroom had been stolen, which meant that wills had to be rewritten, copies of deeds and all sorts of other papers acquired, the sheer time taken merely to contact his clients and inform them leaving him a weary man. Added to that, to reassure his clients, Mrs Barclay included, and for future security, a cellar was being dug out under his office floor, which a steel trapdoor would cover, for he was not about to risk a repetition of the previous loss.

Pearce had written to Nerot's, bespeaking rooms for his whole party and, of course, to Henry Dundas, William Pitt's right-hand man, though the letter was delayed in actual delivery due to it having to be paid for – in all departments of the state there was a reluctance to accept private letters for that reason; government correspondence was carried out on pre-franked sheets and only a certain level of government employee could sanction a delivery sixpence. It did eventually end up on the right desk and was then shown to a minister too busy to sort out his own mail.

'Send to Nerot's,' Dundas, said. 'I shall see Pearce and this . . .' that required another perusal '. . . *Comte* de Puisaye tomorrow evening; Pearce first, then the Frenchman.' The clerk responded with a quizzical expression, which had Dundas waving the communication. 'This does not fill me with the feeling that we have on our hands something of which we can take advantage, but I need to get chapter and verse from the man who has seen the situation on the ground.'

The letter from HMS *York* was the one to produce a string of curses, given Alderman Denby Carruthers had invested a great deal of money already in buying a ship with which the Tollands could resume smuggling; had he not done so he seriously questioned whether he would accede to their request. But having got in so deep, there was no choice but to sell the ship at a loss

211

– everyone would know how short his ownership had been and would suspect he had discovered some flaw in the vessel he was trying to pass it on.

'Portsmouth, sir?'

'Yes, Lavery, or to be more precise, Gosport, which is across the water. You are to take with you this sum of money and pass it on to a Lieutenant Moyle, but only on his granting to you a pair of gentlemen wrongly taken up for the navy and to whom I owe a favour.'

'Might I enquire what kind of favour, sir?'

'No you cannot!' Carruthers barked. 'I have noted lately in you, Lavery, a tendency to ask questions that are outside your remit as my clerk.'

Being far from the first flush of youth and with a pallid countenance made more pronounced by his bulbous, purple nose, Isaac Lavery did crestfallen well. 'I seek only to be of full use to you, sir.'

'I will decide what use you are to be and, while we are at it, I would ask you to stop running errands for my wife without informing me of where they take you.'

'I felt it my duty to oblige her.'

That got the man who had replaced Cornelius Gherson a cold look, for his master was wondering if the old booby really thought he could fool the man for whom he worked; Lavery was betraying him and was being used by Catherine Carruthers to find her one time paramour, with whom, no doubt, she would take up again if he were found. Odd that Denby Carruthers knew exactly where Gherson was, what he did and for whom. Captain Barclay was a client of his brother-in-law, a partner in the Prize Agency practice of Ommanney & Druce. There was temptation to enclose a sealed note to the Tollands asking them to see to Lavery and dump his cadaver somewhere on the way back, but on reflection it was not yet time to settle matters and, in truth, he did not know them well enough to be sure they would do his bidding.

'In future, if my wife asks you to do something, you will come to me, tell me the task, and I will either approve its execution or not.'

On the way to Portsmouth in the public coach, Lavery passed a private one moving in the opposite direction, a conveyance hired by John Pearce on government money to get him and his party to London. While there was a general air of calm aboard – the count continued to drone on about his glittering prospects – all travelling had their concerns, not least the man who had hired it and the woman he loved, for even if she had not referred to it since that private meeting, and being in company on their walk round Winchester, it was obvious that they would at some time have to talk and decide their future, shared or not.

The only one who gave the impression of having no worries was Michael O'Hagan, though that was far from true; the last time he had been on the way to London, on foot with Charlie Taverner and Rufus Dommet, they had come across a poster telling the world that a fellow fitting his description, and he was quite singular in that, was wanted for theft and assault. Having no idea how close he was to the part of the country where that had been displayed he felt it wise to stay out of sight.

'You're not getting down, Michael?' Pearce asked, as they stopped for a change of horses, the three others already gone into the parlour of the busy coaching inn.

'Sure, I'm comfortable here, John-boy.'

'Damned if I know how, brother – my posterior aches.'

'You've not enough flesh on your arse and too much in your head.'

'A drink, food?' Pearce enquired, grinning.

'Can wait.'

'Michael, I cannot believe that of you. I have never known you turn down a tankard of ale.'

'Happen I'm goin' temperance.'

'And the moon is cheese.'

'Might be a tadge dangerous, John-boy, me being easy to recognise and in a part of the world where folks could be looking for me. Folks lookin' to take up bounties are the types to frequent coaching inns.'

'Sorry, never occurred to me.'

Michael had recounted the adventure in getting from Portsmouth to London overland when they had met at the Pelican, and Pearce had heard with his own ears, from an impress gang, what had happened when the Irishman had nearly been taken up by a couple of low-life crimps on the Sussex shore. He had seen to them good an' proper, but that had led to the poster offering a reward of twenty shillings for his arrest.

'So send someone out with a tankard and some bread and a bit of that moon.'

Pearce left Michael in the coach, to find when they all came out to get aboard again, on a warm sunny day, the blinds were pulled down. He was obliged to take back to the inn the tankard and plate his friend had used, and inside Michael stayed until they were safe in Nerot's Hotel.

Afforded a chance to be alone with Emily at last, Pearce went to her room and knocked – opened, he was not cheered by her attitude. 'John, this is not fitting.'

'It will have to do, Emily, so am I allowed to enter or shall we talk of matters personal with me in the hallway where the Lord knows who will overhear me?'

The look of determination on his face left her in no doubt he was not to be deterred and she stepped aside to let him pass, where he went to the unlit fireplace, turned and faced her. Pearce nearly faltered then; even in her distress she was so damned beautiful, the auburn hair framing flawless skin, saving a few entrancing freckles, and those green eyes that could flash so enticingly when she was angry. At the moment they were expressionless, which had to be deliberate.

'I cannot believe, Emily, that you are suggesting our attachment to each other should cease.'

Her reaction was odd; it was as if that had never occurred to her. Seeming deflated she sat down in an armchair. 'John, I do not know what I am suggesting for I am at a loss to know what to do. I have not had a chance to relate to you what happened in Lymington while you were gone and why I left prior to your return. I was about to do so in Winchester, but you did not allow me time and the rest of the day was spent with our French companions.'

'Then tell me now.' Which she did, leaving Pearce dumbfounded. 'I have no knowledge of this admiral of whom you speak and nor can I fathom how he knew you and I had lodged at the King's Head.'

'He did know because our arrival and names were printed in a local newspaper, and that indicates what things will be like in the future: we constantly on guard lest our unmarried state be revealed to everyone around us.'

'Then let us not lie about it.'

'What are you saying? That wherever we go I should expose myself to scandal?'

'Only here, in a nation so prurient that such a thing is considered worth remarking on.'

'Unlike France?'

'Not so! London is full of folk having affairs and it is common knowledge that the King's own sons are amongst the most active in that regard. Damn it, the Prince of Wales is openly living with a Catholic and rumours abound that they are secretly married.

William, the so-called Sailor Prince, shares a home with a woman who has borne him half a dozen children.'

'And this you approve of?'

'Actually, yes, much as I see them as wastrels and a burden on the common man, let them do as they wish.'

'And that is what you would want for us?'

'I want for us to be together.'

'And I cannot see how that can be possible without my having to defend myself each and every day from the like of Sir Berkley Sumner and his horsewhip.'

'Should I ever encounter him he will regret carrying one.'

As her head dropped he moved swiftly, in what was not a large room, and he was forceful, pulling Emily Barclay to her feet and kissing her. She sought to resist at first, seeking to push him away, yet that effort faded and her body, while not going limp, ceased to be rigid. Pearce was on fire and he knew that he had it in his power to proceed as he desired, that Emily would not, could not put up any resistance. He was edging her towards the bed when the knock at the door broke the mood, not aided by his exclamation of 'damnation'.

They had to break contact, she had to go to open the door and there stood Didcot, the hotel servant who had been both a bane and a boon to John Pearce since the first occasion on which he took up residence.

'Letters for you, Madame, two of 'em, which was left at the desk and should have been given over when you arrived, though you would wonder at some folk not doing their job proper.' The open door also revealed John Pearce and that brought to the old fellow's eye a salacious look, for he had watched this pair sparring before; he knew what Pearce was after just as he guessed what he was not getting. 'Saving your presence, Lieutenant Pearce, will you be taking supper in your room?'

The servant's gleam sharpened when Emily, having looked at the addressee on the first one, showed the unopened letter to Pearce, for he had given both a good look over before delivery and he had a nose for these things: Captain Ralph Barclay RN. HMS *Semele*; Plymouth Roads, was whom it came from, no doubt a husband often away at sea. These two were thinking on the old diddle-me-de he had no doubt, which was one to tuck away, for there was money to be made from both silence and letting on if it came to ought, given one had to be from her husband and the other had come from a lawyer.

'No!' Pearce said coldly. 'Shut the door, Emily.'

'Emily is it he calls her now?' Didcot said to himself as he lurched down the corridor. 'It were Mrs Barclay in public afore. Happen they're more hugger than I thought.'

Inside the room Emily had cracked the seal on her husband's letter, unfolded it, and as she read it her eyes widened. Finished it was handed to John Pearce who spotted very quickly what had caused her to react, a passage saying that she was no longer in a position to do him harm, this while she read the letter from Studdert.

'What can he mean by that?' Pearce asked. 'That you have nothing more with which to threaten him?'

Emily passed him the second letter, her eyes wide with what Pearce took to be wonder or surprise; it was only when he read it he knew it to be another reaction entirely, for the solicitor had only written to confirm that Emily had removed from him the single set of papers she had left in his care and there were no others, his apologies for any inconvenience, but he required to be sure in case copies must be acquired; he did not read on about the precautions being taken.

'Burgled?' Pearce said.

'And everything in his strongroom taken to the last will and testament.'

'Match it with that remark in your husband's letter.'

'Coincidence?' Emily asked.

'Too much of one. It seems there are no lengths to which your husband will not go.'

'What am I to do?'

That was asked in a spirit of enquiry, not with any sense of fear or despondency.

'I think it is time you made your husband aware that not only will you refuse to return to the marital state, but that you have other plans, and if he chooses to keep pursuing you, you will embarrass him further.'

'You and I?'

Pearce nodded.

'I might as well tell the world – place an announcement in *The Times*.'

'Emily, we cannot keep hidden what we have.'

'Have?'

'Do you not trust my advice?'

'I don't know who or what to trust.'

'I would start with your instincts, but, just in case, I have invited Heinrich Lutyens to dine with us this evening. I know you value his judgement and I ask that you allow him to exercise it.'

'Would you abide by it if it were negative?'

'No. Now come here and let us take up where we left off before that old goat Didcot knocked on the door.'

Isaac Lavery was seasick in the wherry that took him from Portsmouth to the receiving hulk and given he lacked colour anyway that gave him a greenish hue. His stomach was still troubled as he enquired at the gate after Lieutenant Moyle, giving his own name but not the purpose. Nor, once he was admitted, was his state improved by being on a larger vessel, for if HMS *York* did not move much, she did react to the incoming swell to tug at her anchors. Entering the great cabin he found Moyle adjusting his stock in one of the many mirrors, an act which imposed a period of silence until he was fully satisfied.

'Are you the person to whom the letter was addressed?'

'No, sir, I am his clerk.'

Moyle turned and pulled a face. 'A fellow of means, then?'

'Mr Carruthers is a man of business and a competent one.'

'Rich?'

Lavery did not care much for his employer; the man was a bully to him and treated his lovely young wife shamefully, so much so that she sought comfort with him, conversational comfort to be sure, nothing untoward. Yet Lavery had hopes that his ministrations of sympathy might proceed to something more tactile, for if, when Catherine Carruthers looked at him, she saw that bulbous nose on a lined face, enclosed by those big stuck-out ears, added to the age bags under watery eyes, he, if he cast a glance into one of the cabin mirrors, saw a fellow not so very long past his prime. But regard for the wife did not mean he was about to betray a trust with a total stranger, moreover a man to whom he had been instructed to pass what amounted to a ransom.

'It would not be my position to answer such a question, sir.'

'You have what was requested?'

'Do you, sir, have the gentlemen in question?'

'Gentlemen,' Moyle hooted. 'I would not be after calling them that and nor will you when you see what the rats have done to them.' The humour vanished and Moyle looked at Lavery hard. 'Show me the payment.'

221

Feeling decidedly queasy, and in any case not a brave man, Lavery nevertheless managed to hold the glare. 'I believe in such matters it is common that both sides show their assets at the same time.'

'You're a clever bugger, are you?'

'I doubt I am one and certain I am not the other.'

'Guard!' Moyle yelled, happy that it made Lavery jump. The door was opened and the order given to fetch up the Tollands from below, as the lieutenant added, 'Two smugglers for you to take away with you.'

Lavery had to bite his tongue then, for the word 'smugglers' nearly had him blurt out that they could not be anything other than gentlemen. He was aware that not everything Denby Carruthers did was above board; he, like his city contemporaries, often sailed close to the wind to ensure a profit. Downright illegality had never occurred to him but if he was getting smugglers out of trouble, why would that be? If the information did not settle Lavery's stomach, it did make him feel better; at last he might have something concrete on his employer.

When they appeared Moyle could not be faulted for his description, for they had been provided with no means to shave or stay remotely clean and they smelt high, like a pair of workhouse wastrels, even to a man well used to the dung-filled streets of London. Lavery still refused Moyle his money until the chains were struck off, at which point he handed over that and the letter claiming a high enough status to allow for their release, this necessary to cover Moyle against any retribution. With no ceremony the three left the hulk and took to the waiting wherry, which cast off immediately.

'Didn't see fit to come to our aid hisself, then?' Jahleel asked.

Lavery just leant over the side and tried to vomit from a stomach that had been voided on the way out.

'My dear, Emily, there is no such thing as untrammelled happiness, there are only degrees. Some days the world looks bright, the others it looks dark and forbidding and our souls are no different from one to the other.'

Heinrich Lutyens raised his head as he finished that peroration on the nature of existence, and if seriousness of countenance could be a mark of conviction her friend had certainly told the truth. His upturned nose was raised and his fish-like eyes, if they were incapable of flashing, had a brightness to them that accentuated the translucent nature of his skin. Having finished dinner they had taken to a couch in the foyer, away from prying ears, where they could talk of what she needed to do in the future.

'That, Heinrich, does not answer my question.'

'Do you believe that you will be judged by God?'

'I do.'

'John does not.'

'That does not make him right.'

'Can you envisage a just God that would punish a

poor soul for allowing love to triumph over a miserable duty?'

'It is not necessary for the Lord to be merciful.'

'Then you must decide to torture yourself in this life or the next.'

'Which would you choose?'

'Science demands that facts take precedence over faith. But it is not for me to choose, or, my dear, even to advise. It is such a pity we are at war with France, for if we were not I would recommend crossing the Channel to allow yourself time to think.'

'Run away,' Emily sighed. 'Leave everything behind.'

'I seem to recall you telling me that everything did not amount to much.'

Both looked up as John Pearce approached, waving yet another letter. 'From Dundas, I am to see him on the morrow.'

'And then, John?' Lutyens asked.

Pearce looked hard at Emily then. 'The freedom to choose what I do, when I do it and with whom.'

CHAPTER FIFTEEN

The Count de Puisaye, an object of much amusement to both the staff and most of the guests, stood in the foyer of Nerot's, once more bedecked with jewels on velvet, his wig re-powdered, and quite heavily, so that when he moved he left behind a slight puff of white dust. He had also acquired a long cane, which he leant on in a bored posture, acting as if he desired to embody the monarchical regime of which he had been a part, now coming up to five years in the historical dungheap. That was where John Pearce found him, having returned to fetch both the count and the satchel containing the residue of the government gold, which had spent the night locked in the hotel safe.

He had spent a trying morning doing the rounds of the groups of French émigrés, previous escapees from the Revolution, seeking some with whom Amélie Labordière could take up residence. That sorted out he had then gone on to visit his prize agent, Alexander Davidson, and Lucknor, the lawyer who had written to Toby Burns, neither visit producing much in the way of satisfaction: nothing had come back from the Mediterranean and all his prize cases were still mired in dispute, while the whole trade was agog with what would come from the victory of the Channel Fleet.

This got Davidson an irascible lecture on the fact that Lord Howe had totally missed what Pearce now knew he was supposed to be after, that damned grain convoy, but he returned to a more important matter fairly swiftly: Charlie Taverner and Rufus Dommet. Davidson was charged to establish the whereabouts of HMS *Semele* and get a letter off to Ralph Barclay, with an offer from him of four prime hands from HMS *York* to replace the two men to be released back to that hulk under Davidson's surety. His name was not used, but he had no doubt Barclay would smoke the source of the request, which left open any hopes of a swift and positive result and did nothing for his mood.

His temper was not aided by the fact that he was still suffering from the frustration of having spent the previous night alone, this due to the fact that there was no way Emily was going to consider letting him stay in her room when she was registered under her married name, which came as a great disappointment to Didcot, to whom evidence of criminal conversation

226

was a possible route to income from the cuckolded spouse. He considered passing on a bit of tittle-tattle to the Grub Street coves that wandered the London hotels looking for sleazy gossip and always willing to part with a sixpence, but decided against it; in time it might work out to be worth more.

Despite the letter telling them to call and giving a time, it did not seem to Dundas that keeping them waiting in an anteroom constituted bad manners, but for once Puisaye showed no sign of impatience; he expected powerful men to be rude and, it seemed, rated their ability to meet what was asked of them by their utter lack of consideration for others. This meant, Pearce surmised, that when the count did meet the man whom enemies and friends alike – he had more of the former than the latter – called the 'uncrowned King of Scotland', he would no doubt be impressed. Dundas controlled the entire body of Scottish Members of Parliament and used their block vote to support and sustain William Pitt's Tory administration, brushing off the continual accusations of influence peddling, and corruption, which were always attached to his name.

John Pearce had met Henry Dundas many times, the first in the company of his father, Adam – two men who, if they shared the fact of being Scottish by birth, shared nothing else, especially in terms of politics. Adam Pearce was a radical dedicated to fighting privilege, Dundas the ultimate party manager and upholder of state power. Their dislike was mutual, not aided by the very strong suspicion that the writ from which Pearce *père et fils* had been obliged to flee to France had been engineered by Dundas.

An hour passed in which neither explanation nor refreshment was offered until, finally, a rather superior clerk announced, 'Lieutenant Pearce, the minister will see you now.'

A supplicant look came from Puisaye, who knew what was about to happen; Dundas would ask for a detailed assessment of matters in the Vendée so in some sense his subsequent supplications rested in this naval lieutenant's hands. All he could say, and the Frenchman took it entirely the wrong way, was that he would tell the truth. Pearce was barely through the door, satchel in hand, when Dundas barked at him, his accent as harsh as was remembered.

'What in the name of the Devil Incarnate have you been up to?'

'Obeying your instructions,' came the sharp and not very polite, if mystified reply, this as he conjured how he was going to tell Dundas to mind his manners.

'Does the name Raynesford mean anything to you?'

That stopped Pearce cold, but he prevaricated by asking why.

'I have on my desk a request from Sir Phillip Stephens seeking to know if there is anything of a secretive nature going on in the lower parishes of Hampshire? The only thing that could possibly come to mind involved you.'

'I fail to see the connection,' Pearce insisted, though given the use of Emily's maiden name the two had to be linked.

'A certain naval officer rolls up in Lymington, leaving behind him in a certain inn a paramour who has no right to be with him at all, given he is apparently, according to the lady, on some kind of secret assignment for the Government, at sea on a mission, for all love, vital to confound the nation's enemies.'

'Ah!' Pearce responded, having heard Emily's tale it was now possible to guess at what had happened. That old admiral she had confronted had continued to poke about, obviously not satisfied with what she had told him.

'How this has come about I cannot tell, but it has and I must deal with it.' Dundas looked at his desk, picking up and reading a letter. 'You know Sir Phillip Stephens quite well, do you not?'

'I would not say we were friends,' Pearce replied, trying to be jocular with his tone and change the mood, while also to cover for a mind racing to seek an explanation. 'Quite the opposite, in fact.'

'Probably because he dislikes you and makes no secret of it, which shows he's not entirely bereft of judgement.' Tempted to get up and leave, Pearce knew he could not; Emily was involved so he let Dundas continue. 'He seeks clarification from me, given anything of a secretive nature concerning France must emanate from my department, and I am obliged to tell him I have no knowledge of what he is talking about.'

'Which should be an end to the matter.'

'And if it is not, what then?'

'Tell him and swear him to secrecy.'

Dundas had a high colour anyway, the sort that comes from an over-consumption of claret and port, which passion did nothing to diminish and to that was added his hard Scottish voice.

'He is not that kind of person, Pearce, in fact he's a tiresome auld gossip and busybody. If he finds out what you have been up to on my behalf it will be all over the town and it will certainly be known to our political opponents in a day, and I hardly need point out it will not go down well with our fair-weather Portland friends either.'

Pearce was as aware as anyone of the needs of Pitt's government, since it was never out of the newspapers and was the stuff of coffee house discussions. They kept office due to the support of the Whigs led by the Duke of Portland. Lose them and the majority in the house became paper-thin to the point of ceasing to exist. Yet from what he knew, and he had to admit that was limited, Sir Phillip Stephens was not overtly political.

'I cannot see why he would concern himself.'

Dundas picked up the note and waved it; obviously it was the communication from the Admiralty. 'Somebody's been traipsing around Hampshire calling himself Lieutenant Raynesford and no such person exists, which hints at skulduggery. That may impact on the reputation of the navy, which is very much Sir Phillip's bailiwick, so I need to know if you and this Raynesford are one and the same person. Did you, Pearce, take with you a lady, and did ye book into a Lymington inn under an assumed name as a married couple prior to sailing to the Vendée?'

Pearce was in a bind and could not answer right away, only to be made aware by the knowing look he received that he had answered in the affirmative merely by his silence. 'The lady's name must be kept out of this.'

'By which I judge that she at least is married?' Pearce nodded and Dundas slowly shook his head. 'We must nip Sir Phillip's curiosity in the bud.'

'Surely a denial from you will suffice.'

'I cannot rely on it. You travelled to and from the ship, I take it from Lymington?' Another nod. 'Say he sends someone down to investigate and that leads to a certain vessel lying at Buckler's Hard and a crew who will be only too willing to tell of a recent trip to the Vendée and back under a certain Lieutenant Pearce.'

'He might make the connection anyway, it was he who supplied to me the temporary commission for HMS *Larcher*.'

'A request that emanated from this very building, which he will find out if he pursues the matter. This will expose the fact that I have been dabbling in things that would not find favour in certain parts of the administration, and so close am I to Billy Pitt it would be bound to drag him in as well.'

'Are you planning to enquire if the mission was successful?'

'Judging by the hints in your note asking for this meeting it was not, and who, any road, is this Count de Puisaye you mentioned?'

Pearce was on safer ground here, happier to talk about what he had observed than the problem of false naval officers. He gave a detailed account of what he had found in the swamps and forests in that part of France as well as his opinion of that which he had observed as he travelled to the edge of the region.

'It seems to me that they are merely being left to wither, confined to the region, which would be difficult to penetrate and no doubt cost many casualties, so it is, in effect a stalemate.'

'And the second part of my question?'

'I thought it best to bring back a representative of the rebellion, who wishes to make a plea to you for support.'

'I'm not sure that was wise.'

'While I am sure that it was unavoidable.'

Dundas sighed, but he did not request an explanation. 'And how do you suggest I deal with him?'

'I know you will find it hard to be polite.' That got Pearce a glare, which pleased him; he liked to score off Dundas – it somehow redressed the balance of what had been said earlier. 'He wants the British Government to launch a full-scale invasion and, in company with the Vendéen rebels, to take Nantes and, from there, to march on Paris.'

'A capital notion if only we had the means.'

'He believes the country is ready to rise up and help restore the Bourbons.'

'Which is not certain to be our desired aim.'

'These are not matters with which I am concerned,' Pearce said, reaching for his satchel. 'I have here what is left of the money you gave me. Since I had to sign for the full amount, I suspect I require your signature for the residue.'

'Residue?'

'Yes, I left six of your bags with the rebels, to facilitate their activities, and since I have had to travel the Count de Puisaye, I have used your money—'

'Government money!'

Pearce shrugged. 'Call it what you will and count it if you wish, but there is at my reckoning something like three hundred and ten pounds, though I cannot be sure due to the variation in coinage.'

'You've given away and spent two-thirds of what I entrusted to you?' The tone of the Dundas voice did not require John Pearce to enquire if his actions met with approval. 'This for a rebellion you tell me is likely to get nowhere?'

'I used my judgement.'

'As you did in taking your bonny lass to Lymington! It strikes me Pearce that you have exceeded your brief somewhat and, apart from that, I have only your word that the money you say was given out to the rebels is indeed in their hands.'

'It would be a bad idea, Dundas, to judge me by your own standards.'

That struck home; rumours of his light-fingered attitude to government money were the meat and drink of London gossip, added to the conviction that if he was not lining his own pockets then he was doing so for his loyal group of Scottish MPs.

'And as for proof, there is a man outside who can confirm my endowment.'

'A fellow I have never met, representing a group, according to you, I do not need?'

'It strikes me, Dundas, that you may have to indulge him somewhat.'

'Why?'

'To keep your secret, for the last thing you want is a French émigré aristocrat bleating all over the town about being fetched over from the Vendée in a naval warship to no purpose.'

'I asked if bringing him back was wise, I now know it was not.' There was a moment when, hands resting on the edge of his desk, Dundas was lost in thought. 'Best have him in.'

Pearce raised his satchel. 'Signature?'

'Can wait till I have had it counted.'

'Then I will leave it with you.'

'You will not,' Dundas snapped. 'You will stay where you are and aid me in dealing with this Puisaye.'

* * *

'I don't often see Dundas in a good light, Emily, but the man is a politician to his toes. He dealt with our count with consummate skill, a bit of flattery, a bit of reality. Had the old buffoon eating out of his hand.'

'To the point that he has not returned to the hotel?'

Pearce topped up both their glasses with wine as he replied.

'No, and he will send for his chest. The Government will play with him for a while, I suspect, and put him up in the meantime in some comfort. But I imagine they will be wanting rid of him and will contrive a very good reason why he must go back from whence he came to prepare the ground for something that, if my assessment is right, will never arrive.'

'Michael?'

'Has gone to visit some of his old haunts and will no doubt be drinking to excess, at which point he will probably fall out with some innocent and clout him.'

'You should restrain him.'

Pearce just laughed and spooned some food towards his mouth. 'Then I would be that fool. It is a fact that he would listen to you before he would listen to me.'

'And Amélie has gone now too, she left me a note.'

'She has been invited to stay with a party of French émigrés that have a house in Spitalfields. She also thought that it was wise to take up their offer quickly and I have to say I am grateful, for while she was here in Nerot's she was a charge on my purse.'

'As am I.'

'Emily, it is not the same and you know that.'

'I will need the address, since I must write to her from time to time.'

Pearce smiled across the dinner table. 'To enquire after more bad habits?'

'I would say your worst habit, John, is not talking about that which is most pressing.'

'Do you recall the first time we dined in this room? I think it was then that I first realised how attracted I was to your person, though I seem to recall you left in a hurry and rather flustered.'

Emily frowned. 'Another bad habit is your determination, when something comes up which you wish to ignore, to change the subject in quite so obvious a fashion.'

'Perhaps I fear what will come out of not doing so, Emily.'

'You did not then question Heinrich last night?'

'I did not feel it was my place to and you seemed so deeply engaged in conversation.'

'Yet you walked part of the way home with him.'

Pearce was dying to respond with a comment about her insistence that he should come nowhere near her room, but he held his tongue; matters were proceeding to some kind of conclusion and his cause would not be aided by references to his desire to make love to her.

'You did not ask, when you must be curious?'

'Oddly enough, Emily, if I was faced with physical

danger I think I would react in a way that would smack of upright behaviour . . .'

'You have done so in the past, I have seen and admired it.'

'I do not want you to admire me for that.'

'Heinrich and I talked of happiness, or rather the impossibility of ever achieving such a state.'

'We talked of matters in France now and how many more of his perceived enemies, his one-time friends, Robespierre will guillotine. Heinrich and I share the opinion that he will one day fall to that himself. Who will take up the reins of power if he does was a subject for speculation, and if he does fall, will it bring peace?'

'And?'

'We came to the conclusion as I suspect did you and he – that is, no conclusion at all.'

'On the contrary, John.'

That surprised him but he did not speak.

'Heinrich convinced me . . . perhaps "persuaded me" would be a better expression, of how I should deal with the circumstances in which I find myself, deal with you, my husband and his threats. If indeed he did cause the offices of Mr Studdert to be broken into and burgled it argues that he will, as you say, stop at nothing to get me back.'

'It is not for love of you, Emily.'

'No, his pride is deeply wounded.'

'Hurt one man's pride or break another's heart.'

'Tomorrow I will reply to his letter and in it I will say

237

that his attempts to ensure my return will not succeed and I will allude to that theft, while adding that it was a failure and that I still have the documents that will see him in court on a charge of perjury. I will then go on to tell him that my heart is spoken for elsewhere and though I do not mean to cause him pain, he will soon, no doubt, learn that I have taken up residence with you and observe that I intend to do so openly.'

Pearce reached over and took her hand. 'I will try to make you happy.'

'That is what Heinrich said, John – that only you could do that.'

'A noble sentiment from a fellow who carries a torch for you himself.'

The rap at the door of the private dining was unwelcome, the face that appeared even more so, it being Didcot bearing a letter, which got him barked at.

'Has anyone ever told you, Didcot, that your timing is appalling?'

'Can't be helped, your honour, not when a messenger comes from the Houses of Parliament itself, and I take leave to guess what he fetched will not brook delay in the reading.'

'Leave it.'

Emily laughed. 'You might as well open it, John, we are only halfway through supper.'

'Very well, give it here.'

Handed over, Pearce was breaking the wax when he realised Didcot had not departed, which got the crook-faced servant a hard look that had him withdraw, a sour expression on his chops.

'He probably knows what it says,' Pearce whispered loudly before the door fully closed, pleased to see it jerk; then he began reading. 'My God, they have a damned cheek these politicos.'

'Am I going to have to get used to that kind of language?'

Still looking at the letter Pearce's reply had a vague quality. 'I daresay, Emily, but you would wonder at someone sending me a missive demanding my immediate presence at Westminster and at this time of the evening. Dundas can go to the devil!'

The door swung open again. 'Will you be sending a reply, your honour?'

Pearce looked at Emily as he answered Didcot. 'I will, to tell them that tonight I am otherwise engaged.'

Had she not had her back to him, Didcot would have seen her blush.

CHAPTER SIXTEEN

The shell from Fort Monteciusco could be seen and it was heading towards the redoubt set up to enfilade it from the western heights, yet no one moved or sought protection because this had been happening for weeks now, and since that included a pair of senior officers, a captain and the commodore, who stood rock still hands behind their back, it behoved everyone else to show the same indifference to potential danger. As a rule the fire from French cannon, required to elevate their guns to account for the marginally higher position of their British counterparts, landed just short, the odd one catching the rock face in the right way bouncing up to threaten the protective breastwork. This one was different; it grew and grew and did not even show any sign of dropping in its arc as it lost velocity.

'They've doubled the charge!'

That shout came from Captain Staunton, the man at present in command, and he turned to tell everyone to get down. The missile hit the top of the stone-built part of the rampart and sent the carefully arranged rocks flying in all directions, one of which, a large object, struck Staunton in the back. Others clanged into the quartet of 24-pounder cannon, dislodging one and setting off a noise like demented church bells with the others. Another rock seemed to bounce in the air before coming down to land not very far in front of Commodore Nelson, sending up from the ground a salvo of loose stones made too hot to touch by the sun, many of which struck him in the face.

From being an orderly location the battery redoubt was reduced to a place of seeming carnage. Staunton was face down and still, his hat a yard away from his outstretched hand, his back and side a mass of bright-red gore. The gunners, being the furthest forward and working the guns stripped to the waist because of the heat, had suffered badly from ricochets and a goodly number of the wounds seemed serious. A cacophony of shouts mixed with cries of distress filled the air and it was those that made Toby Burns move, but not before he had checked his body to ensure he was unscathed.

Nelson was shouting, one hand over an eye, with blood streaming through his fingers, 'Get any medical men up here, and stretchers too. Mr Farmiloe, man

241

those cannon and fire off any that are primed and ready, we do not want Calvi to know we are hurt.'

'Sir, you are wounded,' Toby said, rushing over to him.

'I am ambulant, Mr Burns, see to those more in need.'

A voice called out. 'Captain Staunton's dead, sir.'

'Poor fellow, a loss to the service,' Nelson replied, removing his hand to show a mass of nicks around his eye, which was already looking flaming red, and above that a deep and copiously bleeding cut. 'There is a bit of linen in my right-hand pocket, Mr Burns, be so good as to fetch it out and tie it over my face.'

'The major wound will need stitching, sir.'

'Which means Surgeon Roxburgh and his damned needle,' Nelson hooted. 'Now there's a man who would struggle to make a living as a seamstress.'

That was Nelson all over and it irritated Toby: how can he make jokes at a time like this? There are men groaning and badly hurt, the French have humbugged us by using a double charge, which no one expected given they were as likely to blow apart their cannon as harm us, and now we are in mortal danger of a repeat blow. These were the thoughts that ran through Toby's mind as he did as he was asked, equally aware that two of the 24-pounders had been fired as ordered and they were being reloaded, this while the last one was inspected for damage.

Farmiloe, unbidden, was allocating men to fill the

gaps and form as many complete gun crews as possible and one was short of a commander. 'Toby, take charge of one of the remaining cannon.'

The reply was automatic. 'Aye, aye, sir.'

'Dick will do, Toby, the lieutenant's exams are not yet sat and who knows, you and I may have our pass dates on the same day.'

God, Toby surmised, he's looking forward to the damned examination, which prompted an outburst of truth.

'I'm sure I am not yet ready and I cannot fathom Hotham's reasons for pushing me forward to take them. He admonished me to study hard, and I have, but nothing makes enough sense to give any confidence at all. And how can we sit for lieutenant in the midst of a siege anyway?'

'But that's the point, Toby,' Farmiloe said, when the artillery duel had ceased and, sat in the shade, they were studying the books, mainly that fount of all nautical wisdom, *The Seaman's Vade-Mecum*. 'I admit we have to study for the technical aspects of the exam but I am reliably told by Captain Nelson that every candidate is expected to know their stars, mathematics, spherical trigonometry, sail plans and knots, as well as log keeping for stores and stowage. The vital part is the emergency, how we will cope when suddenly required to act on a situation of which we have not been forewarned.'

'They were forever setting exams at the school I

attended,' Toby responded, gloomily. 'And I never did well.'

'Lord in heaven,' Farmiloe hissed, 'Captain Nelson has returned. I bet he has a corker of an eye under that bandage.'

'He's lucky he's got an eye at all, Dick, from what I saw.'

'Gentlemen, I see you about your labours.'

'Boning up, sir,' Farmiloe replied.

'Then I must ask you to bone less, for we cannot allow that battery yonder the freedom to do to us tomorrow what they did to us today.'

'An attack, sir?' Farmiloe asked, his face eager.

'To spike the cannon, not to hold the fortress, to seek to that would only invite a counter-attack we would find difficult to repel. I have asked Captain Walker to provide a party of marines for the assault but I need you two to ensure their cannon are rendered unusable.'

It was fanciful, on an early July day in the Mediterranean, to think that a chill hand had gripped the heart of Toby Burns, but that is what it felt like to him and he was back in Hotham's cabin as the old scoundrel explained to him that he was once more being sent to serve ashore under Commodore Nelson, his face as usual full of apparent concern, to mask what Toby was certain to be his insincerity.

'I admit to ulterior motive this time, Mr Burns, for it has been decided by Lord Hood, given the shortage of officers brought on by wear and tear as well as casualties, to hold a set of examinations for a lieutenant's commission. Naturally, all of those acting the rank, and there are quite a number after so much action, will sit, but so will those who have served a goodly time in the mid's berth, and you . . . well, with what I have seen despatched to other vessels you are near the top dog of that particular berth.'

He was not; in fact Toby knew he was far from admired and the cause was jealousy. 'I hardly feel I am ready, sir.'

Hotham came over avuncular, even to the point of a glistening in his pale-blue eyes, as though his memories warranted tears. 'Never met a mid who thought otherwise, but I have seen the same fellows pass with flying colours.' Then the voice became more brisk. 'Hence the transfer to *Agamemnon* for I know that when it comes to a siege Commodore Nelson will not oversee it from his deck. He will be ashore and in the thick of it and so will those who accompany him. Be assured the captains who sit in judgement on those who aspire to promotion will have in front of them the service activities of the candidates and, in your case, that can only do you good. To volunteer once is commonplace, to do so continually, as you have, is exceptional.'

For a midshipman who had never volunteered since he first set foot on a ship's deck that was a comment to which it was hard to avoid reacting, and that with plain disbelief.

245

'Mr Toomey has a letter for Commodore Nelson, so as soon as your dunnage is gathered I suggest you make haste.' That was followed by a grin Burns saw as wolfish. 'Be a damned shame if it was all done and dusted afore you arrived.'

'Sir.'

'Good day, Mr Burns, and good luck.'

He had taken the letter from Toomey as requested, wondering at the look in the clerk's eye, which seemed to contain a degree of revulsion. Of course he was Hotham's man, heart and soul, but Toby could recall no event that would have made his reaction to his presence one of personal affront.

'Mr Burns, are you with us?'

'Sorry, sir.'

'I daresay it is the heat that has your mind wandering. Did you hear what I said?'

Toby Burns had been aware of the piping voice, but lost in his own concerns and sure Nelson was talking to Dick Farmiloe he had paid insufficient heed. 'I am forced to admit I did not, sir.'

For once Nelson showed a hint of exasperation, which was not generally in his nature, no doubt brought on, Toby surmised, by the pain of his wound, which must be acute.

'Then I would ask you to concentrate, young sir, for this is important. Fort Monteciusco mounts a battery of six heavy cannon, yet I assume, given they are of an age and have been plied much these last days, that there is only a single piece that they dare double-charge and that is the vital one, which must be destroyed.'

'Surely we should spike them all, sir.'

'Bravely advanced,' Nelson replied, in a tone of voice more common to his nature, 'but I doubt that practically you will be given time to do so. As soon as the marines assault the walls there will be flares aloft to tell Calvi that their south-western fort is under threat. That will bring out the French reserves to repel the attack and we will have limited numbers to hold for any length of time.'

'How will we tell, sir, which is the one to destroy?'

'Why, Mr Burns, each cannon I have ever seen is stamped with its date of casting.'

'Hard to see in darkness, sir,' Farmiloe said.

'Failing the ability to see the date of manufacture, the best cannon will take its ball tightly, the older long-fired ones will be loose.'

'Am I allowed to say, sir, that is not very scientific?'

'You are, Mr Farmiloe, and you are right, but it is all the indication we have.'

'Will the Bullocks not support us, sir?' asked Toby.

'Not in this lifetime; I have never known a body of men who take so much time to plan an attack, never mind execute it. Were we to rely on them it would be next week before we saw any attempt to give us succour and they would want a full frontal assault, no doubt.' Feeling perhaps he had been too harsh on the soldiers, the voice softened a little. 'General Stuart is having to cope with much debilitation in their ranks also. Bullocks are never as healthy as tars.'

Overheard by the sailors manning the battery that was greeted by much growled yet wholehearted agreement about the first part of Nelson's complaint. To the men who had slaved to get these cannon into position and done so over terrain the defenders of Calvi thought impossible, the tardy behaviour of the army, who seemed to envision obstacles rather than possibilities, had been a running complaint. Officers and men alike of the fleet thought them scrimshanks and bellyachers. When he added his rider about sickness in the ranks there was none of the sympathy so evident in the commodore's tone.

Books were put aside and preparations made, blades sharpened, pistol and musket flints checked and the weapons themselves cleaned and oiled. There was no shortage of cork trees and that burnt was used to blacken the faces of those taking part; each mid would lead a party of sailors who knew their guns, while the marines dulled the shiny parts of their weapons, discarded their white webbing and removed from their person anything that might make the kind of noise when moving to alert the enemy. Night came early and noisy with insects in the Mediterranean and since every bastion, French and British, was torchlit, the exit through the besieging line had to be made from a point away from the battery position.

Toby was afraid, but felt more calm than he had

ever been going into action, almost in the mood to let whatever would happen take place, though he had a mind to wait till everyone else was over the walls opposite before he ventured to join them. That still left a risk and he accepted he had no choice. If it was not bravery it was indifference, for the man who held power over his future existence seemed determined that he should not have one. The night was hot and sticky for those crouched in the thick scrub that coated the island and everyone was looking forward to moving for one very simple reason – the breeze that would cool their perspiration-soaked clothing as they stood up. Above the sky was a carpet of stars, but the moon was new and no more than a sliver, high in the sky.

'Ready?'

The hissed demand was answered in like fashion and when Captain Walker was sure all had responded he gave the signal to move forward into the deep valley, rock and wood strewn, that separated the two batteries, leaving them unavoidably slithering downhill on scree until they reached the bottom. There Walker halted to allow the stragglers to catch up and so he could ensure that, when they moved again, they were doing so in the right direction, not easy, as surrounded by trees, there was practically no light.

That made more fiery the flash of the first musket and so disoriented were the assault party that there was no assurance it was not coming from behind rather than in front. It was Walker who shouted but he could not know if his command to get down was being obeyed because he could not see, this as an order roared out in French and a line of flashing musket pans and the flaring discharge indicated that they had perhaps walked into a trap; had the enemy suspected that an assault might be attempted to spike such a dangerous weapon?

'Mark those flashes, lads,' Walker yelled. 'Pick one out and aim for a foot below.'

Lying flat on the pine needles that covered the forest floor Toby Burns was aware, first of the musket balls cracking through the trees to eventually create a thudding sound as they embedded themselves, then of the illumination of the immediate area round him as the marines replied, then of the smell of spent powder mixing with the odour of human sweat, or was it fear? He could hear the man closest to him as he went though the mantra of reloading, which had to be slow and by touch and experience in the darkness.

'Bite charge,' that followed by a spitting sound, 'hammer back, prime the pan, ground weapon, powder in, ball in, ram home, cock the hammer, take aim, fire.'

That brought a long powder flash from the muzzle and another in the pan. Toby was crawling backwards as that was being repeated all around him, seeking to get deeper into the undergrowth so as to avoid what must surely follow, hand-to-hand fighting in the dark with bayonets, knives and clubs, combat at which he knew he would be useless. The forest was full of shouting, screaming and fusillades but he had no notion beyond that of what was happening and that went on for what seemed to his ears an age. Then it began to fade, the voices becoming, if not faint, more distant, the sound of discharged muskets beginning to echo all around rather than close, and thankfully no more balls cracking overhead.

Silence was slow to descend and he lay there, feeling the rivulet of fluid running down his spine and wondering whether it was safe now to move. About to get to his knees he heard a rustling sound and that induced near panic, for this Corsica was a strange place and who knew what demons and bloodthirsty creatures resided in these forests? To stay still was to face whatever was making the noise; to move might mean pursuit but it was the lesser evil so, on hands and knees, Toby began a slow crawl, he thought back the way he came, reassured when the ground beneath him began to slope and the treetops opened just enough for him to see the star-filled sky.

That did not show him the butt of the musket that clouted him on the top of his head; lacking a hat it might have killed him. As it was he was too stunned to react when a voice spoke a rough command and a hand grabbed his collar and sought to drag him upright. That brought forth a squeal and got him a hard slap on the face and a demand for silence. The word might be the same but the pronunciation was not; the man holding him and now shaking him ferociously was French.

* * *

'He could be out there wounded and in need of help, sir,' Farmiloe insisted. 'I do not ask that anyone else goes out, but I will.'

'I must forbid it, young man,' Walker responded.

'And I too,' Nelson added. 'We raise a truce flag when daylight comes and ask to be allowed to recover our wounded, the same to be granted to the enemy.'

'Do you think they will agree?'

'It is common practice,' Walker said, 'but it will depend, Mr Farmiloe, on their having people to search for. If they have none they may decline.'

'How long till daylight, sir?'

'A couple of hours, which you know very well,' Nelson insisted, 'so I suggest that you would be better served getting some sleep than standing around fretting and that I must make into an order.'

'Sir.'

'He's a brave young fellow,' Walker whispered as soon as Farmiloe was out of earshot.

'Aye, we ask a lot of our youngsters and in my experience they never let us down. The pity is you never got to spike the guns.'

'I cannot believe that they were forewarned, sir, though it is possible that they saw what damage their cannon did this morning and therefore anticipated that we could not leave matters be. My impression, and I admit it is only that, was that the French were as surprised as were we when we made contact. One musket going off in panic is what began the exchange.'

'Well, we came out of it relatively unscathed, did we not?'

'More scratches from the undergrowth than wounds, sir.'

'Then we are left to pray for the safety of Mr Burns.'

Sat on the cold stone floor the young man about to be the subject of their prayers was rubbing the top of his head, which was very sore and sticky with dried blood, not forgetting his other aches and pains, for he had not been gently handled by his captors as they dragged him back up the hill to Fort Monteciusco. There had been a brief and pointless conversation with an officer who did not speak English, and in failing to get much response from a groggy non-French-endowed captive the officer had ordered, Toby presumed, that he be tossed into this cell, all rough stone walls and lit by a single piece of smelly tallow.

He had shed tears at first, but pain aside it soon occurred to the youngster that he was, in this cell, which was well below the parapet onto which he had been dragged, a lot safer than being in the redoubt with his fellow Britons, given the cannon that had been used to such effect was no doubt being prepared to do so again and he was presumably to the rear of it. Then there were the thoughts based on opinions from his own side. If the French could not sortie out from Calvi and if the outer British perimeter was held, lacking relief it was only a matter of time before they would be obliged to surrender.

If that happened he would be freed and surely the French would feed him in the meantime, though they might, and this was a worry, employ torture. Yet they had showed no desire to that yet and as he ruminated on the pros and cons of being a prisoner it occurred that he would be more likely to survive in a deep cell than out on the battle area. And incarcerated he could not study for his examination, which he dreaded. Being a captive had to give him an excuse to decline to take part.

At dawn, when the request was made for a truce to recover any wounded, the French were very decent; they admitted they had as a prisoner a young officer and that although he was wounded it was superficial and he was not in any serious danger, though any notion that he should be paroled to return was declined. An English speaker was found to inform Toby Burns of this outcome and the youngster had to struggle to look crestfallen, though he was, in truth, pleased. Where he was, he felt, left him secure and safe for the first time since he had set foot aboard HMS *Brilliant* and come under the tutelage of Ralph Barclay.

'It is, Sir Roger, a travesty and an insult to my professional standing and I demand to see Lord Howe to have the matter redressed.'

'His Lordship has retired to Bath to take the waters.'

He'll need a stiff brandy when I am finished with

him, Barclay thought angrily, what was being thought upon in his head very obvious on his countenance, a fact which certainly registered with Admiral Curtis. The fog of war had cleared somewhat and it was now known for a fact that towards the closing stages of the 1st June battle that the elderly Howe, exhausted, had retired to his cabin to rest, leaving the quarterdeck of his flagship, and consequently direction of the battle, to his captain of the fleet, before whom Barclay was now sitting and demanding answers.

'For a fleet commander he seems strangely reluctant to carry out his responsibilities.'

Sir Roger Curtis had very pronounced black eyebrows, which moved up significantly at such a remark from what was a mere captain. 'I will pass on to His Lordship your opinion of his capabilities. I am sure he will appreciate it.'

'You may also pass on that I, and I am not alone, demand that some kind of despatch be sent to support the original communication to the Government which gives full praise to those officers left out, and thereby diminished, and now see their reputation in question.'

'Captains who were slow to obey orders?'

'I complied with my orders with as much alacrity as circumstances dictated.'

Curtis sat forward. 'I was on the deck of the flagship at Lord Howe's side, Captain Barclay. It was I who ordered, on his instructions, that the requisite signals be sent aloft and I can tell you from where I stood you took a damned long time to get into action, when you were quite specifically directed to close with the enemy.'

'Which I did as soon as it was prudent to do so.'

'Damn you, sir,' Curtis exploded. 'It is not your place to be prudent, it is your duty to obey and do what you are told.'

Ralph Barclay refused to be cowed. 'I waited to avoid being caught in the fire of the flagship, which would have done more damage to HMS *Semele* than that inflicted by the enemy. Or would you have my hands die under the balls of your cannon? The vessel I engaged, I would remind you, was so successfully handled that it sank. And since you are chucking around accusations of being slow, I am bound to ask why nothing was done to pursue the French fleet, which was beaten and vulnerable, which given Lord Howe was no longer directing the battle, must fall to your lack of strategic grasp.'

Curtis was on his feet before Ralph Barclay was finished. 'This interview is at an end.'

Barclay stood too. 'It may well be, Sir Roger, but I will tell you now that the matter about which I came to complain is still very much in play. It seems to me, sir, that you have heaped praise upon those who would fawn on you personally and damned by omission anyone with the audacity to stand up to you and identify your errors of judgement. Good day!'

'The man's arse is bruised with the act of being

kissed! As for Howe, I suspect he is asleep somewhere, up to his neck in Bath salts and convinced he is a hero.'

That got nods around the groaning table ashore, where Ralph Barclay had convened a meeting of those officers who shared his concerns, including Captain Molloy, whose conduct had been deemed so shameful he was close to demanding a court martial to clear his name, an option also being considered by the senior man present, Rear Admiral Caldwell, who had shared the supervision of the centre squadron of Howe's fleet, not that he had received recognition for it, and it was he who spoke.

'How are we to reverse it, Barclay? The King esteems Howe and praises him to the skies, as if a man at home on a farm conversing with his trees knows anything about fighting at sea.'

'Perhaps his great knowledge comes from his son, William,' hooted Albemarle Bertie to general amusement; the Duke of Clarence might be a post captain but he was generally held to be a useless one and that was as nothing compared to his arrogance and condescension.

'I had what I thought was a bright idea, that we set up a fund to pay for stories supporting our case. The written word will play harder on the Government than any amount of bleating by us. They are, after all, struggling to keep their majority in the house and if we can get some peers on our side . . .'

That did not need completion. 'And I also suggest

we pay for some cartoons to bring Curtis down a peg or two. With that great nose of his and those eyebrows he should be easy to caricature. In short, gentlemen, I think we should dig deep into our purse and subscribe to a campaign.'

Just outside the dining room door, Cornelius Gherson, who could clearly hear this suggestion being approved, swelled slightly, for it had been his notion. That Barclay did not credit him was not a consideration; positions reversed, he would not have ascribed it to his employer.

'Then, gentlemen,' Barclay said, standing and raising his glass. 'I shall proceed to London to get the campaign under way. To our future recognition, I say, and damn those who would do us down.'

That got the room up and drinking deep.

CHAPTER SEVENTEEN

The fellow who turned into Downing Street – a subsequent message from Dundas had been sent to tell him to attend there – had a lift in his step so jaunty that he would not have been angered to be hailed a sailor, and in truth John Pearce might even have broken into song. If not everything in his life was rosy then he could at least say that the most important aspect was; Emily Barclay was committed to him and from there all things were possible, though he asked her not to reply to her husband, telling him of her intentions, until the matter of Charlie and Rufus was resolved – any mention of his name would not aid matters.

Such a mood did not survive when he entered the door of the First Lord of the Treasury, to find a pair of weary-looking and bleary-eyed ministers.

William Pitt and Henry Dundas were seeking, with a hair-of-the-dog bottle of claret and a copious breakfast of fish, fowl and red meat, to recover from a bruising session in Parliament and the prior consumption of wine that had both preceded the night sitting and sustained them throughout the small hours.

'We have another mission for you,' Dundas said, through some heavy chewing.

'Do you, indeed?' That got a hearty nod. 'Then I must disappoint you for I will be obliged to decline.'

It was William Pitt who responded, and softly. He did not have either the Dundas high colour or the brisk Caledonian way of expressing himself; called upon for a description Pearce would have said he had lazy eyes and an almost translucent pallor to his skin hinting at a lack of robust health. But he would also have been obliged to add that here was a fellow who had risen to the highest political office at the ridiculously young age of twenty-four and had held it through many a crisis for over ten years. That suggested remarkable powers of political guile and a strength of character not replicated in his physical appearance.

'You feel you have the ability to do so, Lieutenant Pearce?'

Pearce chose to be flippant in his response. 'Is not freedom of choice the right of every true-born Briton?'

'Perhaps if we were to remind you of previous writs,' Dundas responded.

'Previous and, given my father is no longer with us, surely spent.'

'Ah, spent,' Pitt exclaimed, playing with the fish on his breakfast plate; he did not look like a trencherman. 'You seem to have a talent for that, Pearce, given what you used of the funds entrusted to you.'

'For which I have accounted.'

'We want you to take a message to Lord Hood in the Mediterranean, as you did previously.'

Pearce looked at Dundas as he said that and found himself staring at the bottom of a glass in the process of being drained. 'You make me sound like some kind of ever-at-the-ready post boy.'

Dundas replied, once he had swallowed his wine. 'I would hate to flatter you by elevation, Pearce.'

'I believe my father, even if he did not give credence to religion, often had occasion to tell you to go to hell.'

'Your father—'

Dundas got no further than that; a held-up hand from Pitt was enough to stop him.

'Please, Harry, let us not go there, to where you two will find nothing but dispute. Your father is no longer a trouble to the Government, for which I am grateful, while having said that I am bound to add he died in the most appalling fashion and we are sorry for it.'

'I can believe you might be, sir.'

Dundas just shrugged at the obvious exclusion of himself as Pitt continued. 'We are required to communicate with Lord Hood, as we did before, outside the normal channels; in short, to pass to him a letter that only he knows has been delivered.'

'Send someone else.'

'Someone we know we can trust?'

'I'm not sure I am that person.'

'We want to send you, and not on the mail packet this time but in a ship that you will command.'

'Which,' Dundas added, 'has the advantage of removing you from any chance of what you got up to in the Vendée becoming common knowledge.'

'Is that what this is really about, for if it is, my lips are sealed?'

'But not those of your one-time crew,' said Pitt. 'They could still set us a problem.'

Pearce was surprised, but he made the connection after a minimal pause. 'You want me to take *Larcher* to the Med?'

'Two birds with one stone, Pearce! You still have yet to turn in the temporary commission giving you command of HMS *Larcher*, and from what we can glean the fellow you replaced is about to go under the knife for whatever ailment it is he is suffering from, which implies at least a long convalescence.'

'You see us,' Pitt interjected, 'in the midst of one war, when in fact we are mired in two and the second one is of such duration as to have no beginning or end, for it is politics. In order to pursue the actual conflict with France, Dundas and I spend days, and as in the case of the last twenty-four hours, many hours of the night, fighting a shadow political one to keep up the struggle.'

'Do you believe,' Dundas, demanded, 'that we have to defeat the dark forces that exist across the channel?'

'Of course I do, though given I am in the presence of a very dark force indeed, I take issue with the word "we".'

'You're a serving naval officer.'

'And you know just how I feel about that!'

'So you intend to disappoint us?'

'I have other plans.'

'To do with the lady who is, like you, staying in Nerot's Hotel, perhaps the same one who was sharing your accommodation in Lymington?'

'Have you been spying on me, Dundas?'

'Don't sound so shocked, Pearce, it's what I do and the country is safer for it.'

Pitt stood and Pearce noticed that his pale cheeks had a touch of rouge. 'I will leave this to you, Harry, if that is all right.'

'Fine, Billy.' As soon as Pitt had exited Dundas spoke again. 'A delicate soul he is, not one to enjoy unpleasantness.'

'Is that what I am about to experience?'

'What did the man I send round to Nerot's learn, eh? That the place has gossipy servants, but who does not? That you have an attachment to a certain Mrs Barclay, which on further enquiry turns out to be the wife of another naval officer. Promises to be messy, I suspect.'

'You are wrong, Dundas, it is not messy, it is about to be the very opposite. Mrs Barclay has repudiated her marriage and hopes circumstances will allow her to live happily with me.'

'True love is it?' Dundas sneered.

'Something that can be given to most people, although I doubt you are aware of it without the use of a mirror.'

'Your father was wont to exercise his wit on me, laddie, and I would advise you to recall where it got him. A married woman running off with one sailor, and leaving behind to grieve another. Now that would make a tasty morsel for the morning papers, would it not?'

'I told you she had to be kept out of it.'

'So you did.'

'And I would remind you,' Pearce barked, 'that I have all the details regarding my mission to the Vendée and so am in a position to retaliate should you break that requirement.'

'Where you managed to pocket some substantial sums belonging to the Government.' Dundas reached into a coat pocket and produced a document, which he made great show of opening and reading. 'Here it is, specie to the value of a thousand guineas, signed for and dated by Lieutenant John Pearce on Buckler's Hard.'

'Monies for which I am prepared to account and I have a witness in the Count de Puisaye as to how the majority of it was employed.'

'I wonder what the count would put first – you in Newgate for debt, since I don't think you have a spare sum to make up the losses, or a promise from the Government to provide help for his rebellion? Still, you'd have Mrs Barclay to come and visit, which would be a comfort as well as food for a right good scandal.'

Dundas stood now, a wolfish grin on his rubicund face. 'I will leave you to cogitate on that, Pearce. Help yourself to some wine if you need it, but know this. I am no a man to trifle with and if old Adam were here he would tell you that too. It's a wee trip to the Mediterranean or . . . ?'

'Has anyone ever told you that you are lower than a snake?'

'Every day, Pearce,' Dundas replied from the open doorway, 'and, laddie, it is water off a duck's back.'

The mood of the earlier part of the day was gone now, to be replaced with gloomy reflection, for he had no doubt that Dundas would carry out his threat; he was not a man to make such in idle fashion. There was a moment when he wondered what could be so important that it had to be carried by hand all the way to Lord Hood, but that was not a thought on which to linger; the paramount one was the public shaming of Emily, for there was a vast difference between the likes of the *Hampshire*

Chronicle and the much more numerous papers printed in London.

She would become the butt of public disgrace, and that in newspapers that were distributed throughout the whole country, for if the people who printed them claimed high moral values they would sink to the gutter in a trice for a salacious story of marital infidelity. There would, no doubt, be some artist only too happy to do a very accurate pen and ink likeness and he would not put it past Dundas to distribute pamphlets so the chances of escaping ridicule wherever she went were slim.

The threat of Newgate he had to think was real; again, Dundas was not a bluffer and it would be his word against that of a minister in high office. Even if he talked of what he knew, the experience of the Government, which he had observed his father having to fight, was plain: when they decided to play dirty they did so very seriously indeed. Adam Pearce had never been able to get anything he wrote published in the newspapers, or make a case for his freedom of speech, the very simple reason being that men of power had no trouble making it plain to the editors and proprietors that there was a line they must tow if they wanted to be on good terms with Downing Street.

Oddly, Pearce suspected if he put the case to Emily, despite her fears, she would probably tell him to resist. It was part of what made him love her, that part of her personality that he had first observed when she had stood up to her husband over punishing him and had then, when she found out that he was a both a tyrant and a liar, caused her to move from his cabin to Heinrich Lutyens' hospital in Toulon. Emily Barclay had a rod of steel in her, added to an innate kindness to go with her outstanding beauty. In short, he was a lucky man and he would not do anything to see her unhappy, and if that meant acceding to the recent request, so be it.

Sailing to the Mediterranean was not all bad for by the time he arrived the high summer heat would have faded to something very pleasant. Toby Burns was there and so, as far as he knew, were the other people with whom Lucknor had corresponded. It was a chance for him to gather evidence of his own, facts which would further enhance his ability to silence Ralph Barclay and truly cow him, for he had in mind something he had not dared even mention to her, the notion of launching a parliamentary bill for divorce. That it was hard, going on impossible, to get such a dispensation was no reason not to try.

Turning his mind to the proposed mission he was not sure that an armed cutter like HMS *Larcher*, being cramped, was a vessel for such a long voyage. She had been built for inshore work and even the trip to the Ile de Noirmoutier had taxed her ability to carry enough stores to cover for unforeseen eventualities like being held back by foul weather. Mentally he began to calculate what would be required to facilitate a voyage to Gibraltar, where he would be able to revictual, then from there to where the papers told him Hood was, off the northern tip of Corsica.

Lord, he thought, it is so cramped too, that tiny cabin, and that set off another train of thought. It was the sound of Pearce laughing that brought Dundas back and he looked as if he thought him deranged.

'You have your post boy, Dundas, so prepare your communications and let me know when to collect them.'

'I am curious to know what made you change your mind?'

'Certainly you are, but you will never know and I suspect never guess. Now I bid you good day, I have other matters requiring my attention.'

A few miles away, in the City of London, Denby Carruthers was closeted with the Tolland brothers and demanding to know how they had got themselves into such a bind. If the explanation he received was not the entire truth, it was plain that they had put a private matter of retribution against this fellow called John Pearce ahead of what he saw as their duty, which was to get back to their trade and begin to repay his investment, a point he made forcibly.

'I will not let it rest for all time, Mr Carruthers,' Jahleel said, which had Franklin nodding too and vigorously. 'I will have that fellow's blood, but I see I must set it aside for a while until you and we are in profit and you know you have chosen well.'

'Of course I must deduct the cost of your freedom from our first transaction.' Seeing the elder Tolland's eyes narrow, Carruthers added quickly, 'Unless it imposes a burden, in which case it can wait until payment does not sting.'

'Fair enough, but one request, and I promise not to act on it without you being informed. We need an eye kept on the Pearce fellow and we need to know that when the time comes we can gift to him what he has coming his way.'

'Which is?'

It was Franklin who ran a finger over his throat, then said, 'And this time we will not stop to talk. The time for that is past.'

The alderman's next words were tentative, for he had just been informed that the notion of committing murder was not one to trouble these two before him. It had not been something about which he had harboured much doubt but there was a great deal to be said for outright confirmation.

'I do have in mind another way to settle that debt and perhaps even add to it a payment.' Denby paused for a couple of seconds then added, 'A substantial payment.'

'How so?'

'If I were to say that I have certain people who trouble me, as much as this Pearce fellow seems to trouble you, people whose removal would add to my

269

contentment, I am wondering if I could engage your services to rid me of them?'

Jahleel Tolland just shrugged.

'That is good and I will bear it in mind. Now, when can you take possession of the ship I have purchased and when can we set sail?'

'We?'

'Yes. You cannot fill its holds without you spend money, my money, and it is a habit of mine when that happens for me to be present.'

'This is not a game, Alderman, we deal with some right hard bargains and suspicious as hell with it.'

'Then I shall look to you to protect me and our investment. I ask again, when can we begin?'

'Got to gather a crew first. Can't sail a ship without we have hands to man the barky.'

Carruthers frowned. 'How long will that take?'

Jahleel laughed. 'No time at all, Mr Carruthers, the coast is teeming with those willing to do the work, men who know how to hand, reef and steer and never be taken up by the press neither.'

'A week at most,' Franklin added.

'Then I suggest today is a good day to begin looking.'

'That I agree to, but it would be best we look over what you have purchased first.'

The scraping of chairs had Isaac Lavery scooting back to his high desk and by the time the door opened he was over his quill and scratching away. He had not heard everything, only those words made plain when voices

270

had been slightly raised, which left him wondering about this John Pearce fellow, for that name when first used had been near to a shout and accompanied by a loud slapping sound – he assumed a hand on the table. The name resonated, for he had been sent weeks past to visit the Strand offices of Edward Druce, his employer's brother-in-law, to find out where that very fellow was serving.

'Lavery, you are to remain here, do you understand, until I return. No errands.'

'Certainly, sir, and can I say to where you have gone if anyone enquires?'

That got him a glare. 'No, you cannot.'

With that Carruthers followed the Tollands out of the door.

'Fishing in dangerous waters seems a strange expression to use Mr Lavery, are you sure it is the right one?'

Looking into the corn-blue eyes of Catherine Carruthers the clerk saw innocence mixed with naivety and it was to him a charming combination. This woman, trapped too young in an unsuitable marriage, could not even begin to make a true assessment of her husband's nature even if she had shared his bedchamber. She saw him in the domestic setting and if that was strained through past indiscretions on her part, it was, nevertheless, conducted in a polite way. In his business dealings Denby Carruthers was very far from that and, now it seemed, not satisfied with ne coups he regularly achieved in legitimate trade, he was about to dabble outside the law.

'He is mixing with some very strange people and of excessively low character.'

The nod, along with pursed lips, looked like sage acceptance; in truth, Catherine Carruthers could not care less what her husband got up to, outside his need to care for the upkeep of a style of living to which she had become accustomed, and if he got harmed in the process so be it. She listened to this grumbling regarding his activities only to ensnare Lavery to her true purpose, which was to find and reconnect with the man who filled her dreams, Cornelius Gherson, Lavery's predecessor and the person who had so strained that domestic harmony.

'It is good of you to keep me informed, Isaac, for it would never do that my husband should overreach himself.'

'I will seek to ensure he does not and certainly forewarn you of any risk . . .'

The sentence was plainly unfinished and there was a fear then that he might call her Catherine, but thankfully the moment passed, that being a favour which would have to wait. Her task was to play the old fool, and each step in allowing him familiarities had to be carefully graded so as to avoid anything that might force her to reject him, a game in which she was well practised. Catherine Carruthers had been a precocious beauty and learnt very young how to use her gifts to gain her ends; nothing blinded a man, even a clever one, as much as sexual desire. Lavery would be no different, and if she handled matters correctly he would do her bidding. Having softened him up she could now proceed to the real question to which she required an answer.

'How goes our search?'

'I confess, not well.'

'Then it must be stepped up, surely – widened.'

'I fear your husband has laid constricts upon my ability to act on your behalf. I must seek his permission to do so.'

'He has no idea of the nature of . . . ?'

'None.'

'Then how are we to proceed?'

It was a bold step to take her hand, and a nervous one that did so, though the charge of electricity that ran through Isaac Lavery's body was a thrill which he had never before experienced and he looked at Catherine Carruthers for a sign she had undergone the same, taking her frown as evidence that she had. Rationally explained to anyone with sense, his suit would have invoked hilarious laughter – he, of middling years, strained income and no great beauty, making love to a ravishing young woman, and a rich one? But in Lavery's imaginings all things were possible and here, running up his arm, was proof positive. He had nothing to fear from Cornelius Gherson; if the fellow had held a place in her affections once it had been replaced now.

'With caution, my dear lady, but proceed we must. I will find Gherson and deliver to him your concerns for his well-being.'

She had been tempted to withdraw her hand and show some displeasure, for which, she was sure he would react like a whipped dog. But in the end she let it rest in his fingers for, to find the man she loved meant everything, the man who would rescue her from her unhappy situation of being wife to a man far too old to understand her.

CHAPTER EIGHTEEN

'A voyage to the Mediterranean?' Emily asked, turning away so he could not see her face; was she troubled or pleased?

'And aboard HMS *Larcher*, the very same vessel that I recently commanded. The crew are in the main splendid fellows and since I must go—'

'Why must you?'

'Let us say a combination of duty and a debt.' Turning to face him she looked unconvinced as he added, 'And since I fear to leave you alone in London, I wish you to accompany me.'

'What?'

'I cannot just leave you, Emily, for at sea I cannot protect you. We have already established that your husband will stop at nothing. Well, that might include abduction and incarceration, from which no force of law would be able to release you. Justice is iniquitous in the subject of matrimony and all the rights rest with the man. He could keep you chained in his cellar and nothing could be done short of violence to free you.'

'I could go somewhere and wait.'

Not having mentioned Dundas's threat – and he did not trust the man one inch – he felt the need to press. 'Like Lymington, which is no different to any other town in the country and a damn sight better than most. A strange woman alone, you will be a subject of interest. What will you do for company, and will you be comfortable with the lies you have to tell, for people will probe?'

'You are asking me to embark on a very bold step.'

'I am asking for your companionship on voyage to and from the Mediterranean, to make life more bearable than separation, and you can depart in secrecy – no one will know you are aboard whom we do not wish to have that knowledge.'

She finally smiled; it was not acquiescence but a sign of a break in her resistance. 'Run away to sea, as boys do in tales of adventure?'

'Think of it in the nature of us getting to know each other.' Pearce produced a wide grin then as he recalled how he had come to the thought originally; it had been none other than the notion of that little cabin and the propinquity its size would force on two occupants. 'Which we will do even if disinclined, for the cabin we will occupy is so very tiny we will forever be in each other's way, from which I for one will take great pleasure.'

That got a becoming blush. 'Is it fitting, John?'

'It's a damn sight more discreet than taking a house in some out of the way place while I fret that you might be in danger.'

'And when we get there you will have duties to perform.'

'Only one, to deliver a private letter, and then it is a happy return.' He could see the flaw and so could she – her presence would be known throughout the fleet as soon as he joined, so he came close and embraced her. 'I will drop you in Leghorn, proceed on my mission, then sail back to collect you when it is complete.'

'You have such freedom.'

'I would like to see the fellow who could infringe on that.'

The knock at the door was this time anticipated and Pearce opened it to the hotel servant, who had come to grumble as well as respond to a summons.

'That big Paddy of yours is in the stables a'sleeping on hay an' snoring fit to wake Lucifer. There's not a soul in the hotel willin' to seek to rouse him, for he was threatenin' to mince them when he barrelled in last night an' he might have done them in if he had not passed out.'

'Tell them that, when sober, he is a lamb.'

'Never in life – wakin' him is a task for you, sir.'

'Very well, Didcot, I will see to it shortly. Now I wish someone to begin to pack my sea chest – Mrs Barclay's trunks and valise too – to be ready for departure either tomorrow, or I think at the latest the day after.'

'You is leaving, your honour?'

'We are.'

'An' might I ask to where you is headed?'

'I am off to sea gain, Didcot, but Mrs Barclay is going to King's Lynn in Norfolk.' The intimation that he had said too much was well performed as he dropped his voice. 'But I would be obliged if you would keep that bit of knowledge to yourself. I'm sure I can trust you.'

'Lips is sealed, your honour,' Didcot responded, mentally rubbing his hands while in fact touching his forelock. 'I shall see to it that all is clean afore it is packed away, an' all.'

'Good man,' Pearce said, slipping him a coin.

Door closed behind him Emily began to shake with laughter, Pearce with a finger to his lips to insist she should not do so out loud lest Didcot hear her.

'You are so sure he will let on?' she asked, still not fully in control.

'Near certain,' Pearce replied, again keeping the Dundas business to himself, 'and maybe I would be the same if I had his life. It may mean nothing, yet it may also send your husband on a wild goose chase if he seeks to find you. Now I must go and rouse out Michael and tell him we are off to sea again.'

* * *

If, when he woke, Michael had a sore head, he also had Celtic powers of recovery, aided by the swift despatch of a tankard of ale, so that washed and shaved he looked to have no ill effects from his nocturnal debauch; his eyes were as bright and his grin as wide as ever. The day was spent in preparation, with the Irishman acting as escort and protector when Emily went shopping, carrying a small club, not so very different from a marling spike, inside his short blue coat. Pearce received from the Admiralty, by hand messenger, not only confirmation of the extension of his commission, but also the order and flag that would see him sail under their pennant, which precluded any other officer from impeding his passage all the way up to admirals.

With his papers he went to the Victualling Board to enquire as to where he could draw supplies for HMS *Larcher*, very little of which would be available at Buckler's Hard. He departed Somerset House with a sum of money for purchases plus the written authority he required to draw on any naval stores at any dockyard en route, including Gibraltar. His last call was at Downing Street to pick up the communication he must carry and another bout of traded invective with Dundas, who seemed afire to know what he was going to do with his lassie.

'I have told you twice now, it is none of your damned business.'

The man could not help himself; he had to show off and there was a lopsided smirk to go with it. 'A nice quiet place in the county would suit, I hazard. I hear Norfolk is bonny at this time of year.' Seeing the look that got, he added, 'Oh, your secret's safe with me, Pearce, but it does mean there'll be no backsliding or finding reasons not to complete your task.'

'Don't you repose trust in *anyone*?'

'Not many and certainly no one bearing your name, so put that letter in a weighted sack and if anything should happen to make you think it might fall into the wrong hands chuck it in to the briny. Until then, guard it with your life.'

'Perhaps I will sell it to the Whigs, the proper ones, of course. I am sure Charles James Fox would excel himself in the house with sight of it.'

That got him a look of thunder, which was pleasing, for it indicated that he had hit home. Fox was a fearsome debater, but more than that he employed the kind of wit that tended to squash opponents across the floor of the house and Dundas, too often the butt, hated him with a passion.

'Do that, Pearce, and you'll spend the rest of your days in a prison hulk off the Medway Marshes! And stick to your duty, for I never met a naval officer yet that did not whore after a prize or two.'

Ralph Barclay was testing the use of a stick to support his wounded leg, this for his journey to London, a trip he had insisted to a reluctant Sir Roger Curtis was necessary for him to consult the very best physicians.

280

He was stomping to and fro when Gherson brought him Davidson's letter, the clerk exchanging a glare with his employer's so-called servant Devenow, tall enough to have his head touching the deck beams and broad with it. He now had his arm in a sling as well as a still swollen ear given to him just before the 1st June battle, though it was not as bloody and as gory as it had been right after it was inflicted. The sling at least stopped the cack-handed buffoon from trying to do any of the tasks that fell to a servant, for it was an area in which he was worse than useless.

Gherson and Devenow loathed each other as much for their differing manner as for their competition for the captain's attention. The clerk saw Barclay as a means to an end, while Devenow was slavish in his devotion, a man to follow Ralph Barclay from ship to ship and, it had to be said, into the cannon's mouth; indeed he had turned up in Sheerness to join him aboard HMS *Brilliant*, though at that time his presence had been seen as a mixed blessing. He had been welcomed but with reservations.

Not anymore; it was Devenow who had carried Ralph Barclay to Heinrich Lutyens' hospital when the captain had taken the ball that shattered his left arm, subsequently amputated. If he had not changed from what he was – a lout, a drunk and a bully – then he had risen in Barclay's estimation to become a very necessary aide, if not a confidant, and there was only a modicum of true regard. In truth, neither was Gherson a confidant, but he did handle things of a private nature, even down to arranging investments for the large sums of Barclay prize money already earned. The safe investments were in Captain Barclay's name, the very risky ones, which might go bad and lead to writs for repayment, were in the name of Devenow; Ralph Barclay reckoned the ruffian could stand a debtor's prison more easily than he.

The name on the letter Barclay recognised, for if he was represented by Ommanney & Druce, he yet knew the name and reputation of every person who traded as a prize agent for the officers of the Royal Navy, their various abilities a common subject of conversation as well as their failings when it came to settling cases; like most captains Barclay had one mired in the courts for a well-laden merchantman recaptured off Brittany in his first week at sea.

'Surely he is not soliciting my custom?' he said as he broke the seal and began to read, his head slowly beginning to shake. 'I cannot believe that a man of his standing is worried about a couple of tars.'

'Sir?' Gherson enquired and Barclay passed the letter over and after a short perusal he provided an explanation. 'I think you will find that Davidson represents John Pearce, sir.'

'Of course, damn it, I did not smoke the names.'

'Do you recall sir, that absurd soubriquet, the Pelicans?'

That got a low growl from Devenow; it was Charlie

Taverner who had split his ear and he had suffered at the hands of those Pelican sods before that, the worst being Michael O'Hagan.

'Why would he offer four prime hands, it says here they are ex-smugglers, for two such creatures?'

'They have a bond, sir, and I fear he thinks you might ill use them.'

'Give me half a chance, Gherson, and I will do so. The slightest slip on their part and I'll see them at the grating for a round dozen each.'

That had the clerk smirking at Devenow, who obviously had not told the captain the truth of his head wound – Barclay had assumed he had been drunk and fallen over. The look Gherson got back was full of bile. But soon Gherson's attention was back on Barclay and he wondered if he should tell him that between decks Charlie Taverner and Rufus Dommet had a mess that would act to protect them. Indeed he half suspected that was the root cause of Devenow's damaged ear.

'Well I'll be damned if I'll oblige Pearce.'

The letter was handed back. 'Four good hands in place of two, sir.'

Barclay waved the paper with some irritation. 'You're not suggesting I do?'

'Wouldn't be right, your honour,' Devenow snarled.

That got him a rebuke. 'This is none of your concern, man, please stay out of it.'

Gherson was strong on self-preservation and he could recall very clearly the scary tales he had been told when he too was a pressed seaman. If others eventually saw that the older hands were playing upon them, Gherson had taken to heart their tales of how easily a fellow aboard a ship at sea could come to harm – the most frightening, for a man who had been tossed by Denby Carruther's thugs into the River Thames to die, was the notion that on a dark night any unpopular cove could so easily go over the side.

Vanity, and he had a great deal of that, did not prevent Gherson from the knowledge that he was not much loved by his fellow man – he despised most of them in return and made little secret of it, the only exception being his propensity to grovel when he needed their help. Having no idea how Devenow had got his split ear it was not too far-fetched to suppose it had come from either the Pelicans or the members of their mess, and if they would attack and wound a big sod like him, what would they do to anyone else against whom they had a grudge, he being the most likely?

'I think it would be safer if they were off the ship, sir.'

'Safer?' Barclay demanded.

It's all right for you, Gherson thought, secure here in your great cabin with a marine sentry at the door and every eye on you when you go anywhere, never mind that Devenow is ever by your side. What about me? I dare not go on deck after dark, and who is to say that daylight renders me safe?

'Sir,' he said, trying to sound sage, 'they are troublemakers.'

'Not on my ship.'

'They are cut from the same cloth as John Pearce and he has caused you no end of nuisance in the past.' That being reminded did not go down well was obvious by the expression on Barclay's face – he looked like a mastiff who had swallowed a wasp. 'I am merely suggesting that it is not prudent to allow these two individuals to remain aboard when you have an opportunity to remove them and stop them from fomenting disorder.'

'It seems to me, Gherson, that you have some indication that they have been at that already.'

'I took it upon myself, sir,' Gherson lied, 'to warn them against it, but can I be sure they heeded me?'

'By damn, they'll heed me.'

'Ask Devenow how he got his ear.'

'What?' Barclay asked, turning to the man in question.

'You thought he was drunk, sir, but I know he was not, so how did he come by such a wound?'

'Well, Devenow, how did you?'

'I'd not like to say, your honour.'

'No doubt,' Gherson advanced, his tone mocking, 'because of a spirit of comradeship within the lower deck.'

'Who was it, Devenow?'

'Can't rightly say, your honour. It were dark and it came out o' the blue.'

Gherson surmised he was lying, he being reluctant to admit that he had been bested in a fight.

'Just the kind of trouble, sir,' he droned, 'that no one wants aboard a ship of war.'

It was interesting to watch Barclay ruminating, for he was fighting an internal dispute, between obliging John Pearce, which he hated to do, as against having trouble brewing under his command, which, like every officer in the Royal Navy, he dreaded. In concert with the likes of Gherson he neither sought nor needed popularity, but he did need efficiency and between decks feuds were inimical to that.

'What are they like as hands?' he asked, after a long silence.

'Mediocre, sir, I am told.' Gherson had no idea and would not have been able to give an opinion even if he had watched them; when it came to being useless in the art of sailing he was top of the class. 'You could enquire of their divisional officer.'

The response that such a notion was stupid nearly came out – no captain who valued his dignity would ask such a question of anyone but his premier, and having equal to his regard for his standing now, he made a great play of reading the letter again.

'They are of insufficient interest to me to care. If Pearce wants them so badly let him have them and we will profit by it.' Thinking perhaps that he might be giving way too easily, Barclay actually barked, 'But the replacements better be as he says, or I'll have his guts.'

Even Devenow, devoted as he was, seemed embarrassed by that idle boast.

'Detail one of our mids to rig out the pinnace and take this pair up-channel to HMS *York*. Best take a quartet of marines also; we don't want any trouble on the return journey. Now, is all in order for my journey to London?'

'Your barge is waiting, sir,' Gherson replied.

'Then let us be off.'

'I will just gather my investment portfolio, sir.'

That cheered Gherson's employer up no end; if Ralph Barclay had possessed two hands he would have rubbed them, sure as he was that the money he had put into various projects should by now be beginning to show handsome returns.

Ralph Barclay was not the only one on the move; when it came time to take a hack to Charing Cross, there ostensibly to put Emily Barclay aboard the northbound coach, the whole trio were in a joyous mood. Pearce had gone round the hotel tipping the various people who had seen to his needs, for along with Didcot there were the maids who cleaned and made up the beds, the people in the kitchen, and even the stuck-up sod who manned the front desk, the same fellow who had presented a bill that made the recipient's eyes water a little.

'I do hope you will grace us with your custom again, sir.'

'I will if I take a Spanish plate ship.'

'Which, sir, I surely hope you do and recommend us to your fellow officers.'

Pearce was tempted to say that a recommendation from him in that quarter was likely to lead to bankruptcy, but held his tongue and he went out to the waiting hack calling out loudly their destination, that being changed as soon as they were out of sight. The hack took them to the same person from whom Pearce had hired transport to take him originally to the New Forest, with Michael riding on the box seat with the driver.

'We are free, Emily,' Pearce said as they passed the Bishop's Palace at Fulham.

'For now, John.' Seeing his crestfallen face she took his arm and squeezed tightly. 'Let us enjoy it while we may.'

The crew of HMS *Larcher* were mightily pleased to see him again, and given that their previous passengers had been odd no one raised an eyebrow to the fact of a woman, and a very pretty one at that, being brought aboard. Emily, if she was surprised at the paucity of accommodation, hid it well, praising it as cosy in such a way as to win the smiles of those who overheard her, that to the accompaniment of nudges, nods and winks regarding the rakish nature of their master and commander, who was brisk about his business once she was settled.

'Mr Dorling, we will sail to Portsmouth to victual from the dockyard.'

'And then, sir?'

'Then we will sail down-channel, and when we are out of sight of land I will tell you where we are going.'

The Admiralty pennant was inside his coat; that would not be lifted to the masthead until no one could see it from the shore.

'If anyone asks in Portsmouth what we are about, tell them we are casing smugglers.'

'Could become a habit that, your honour.'

CHAPTER NINETEEN

HMS *Larcher* took on board what she could from Buckler's Hard, especially fresh provisions such as bread and greens, but there was no way they could supply salted beef and pork, as well as the quantity of peas, small beer and rum and general stores that the vessel would need for such an extended commission; that could only be found in a proper naval dockyard, likewise spare canvas and yards, which were too steep for the funds Pearce had. As soon as all was loaded that could be acquired the anchor was raised and the ship drifted down on the tide and the rudder into the Solent, where sails could be set to take advantage of the prevailing westerly wind.

The quartermaster weaved a course through the dozens of warships anchored off Spithead: 100-gun Leviathans, abundant seventy-fours as well as numerous frigates and sloops. Emily Barclay was confined to his cabin, in which he had admonished her to stay until the armed cutter was fully loaded with stores and anchored away from the shore. The surprise for John Pearce was when Michael O'Hagan approached and asked that he be allowed to stay out of sight as well, seeing he knew the intention of where to tie up.

'It was from here myself, Charlie and Rufus ran and I fear that the press gang you overheard might be based at Portsmouth too. Sight of me and they might just want to take me up on that warrant, and that does not speak for those in pursuit of the reward.'

'Which I would not let them do, and I would point out, Michael, that if they know you by your description they do not know your name.'

It was a stroke of good fortune that had the Pelicans on a vessel in which they had never been mustered; it was a frigate that had rescued them from the ocean and a ship that had caught fire and sank, leaving them drifting in an open boat.

'And since we are going to pack every spare inch of space with victuals, where would you hide?'

'I daresay Mrs Barclay would not object to my sharing your little cabin for a while.'

'No she would not, and if it makes you feel secure, so be it, but we will miss your muscle when it comes to shifting barrels.'

'Port admiral's boat approaching, your honour.'

'Best get out of sight now, then.'

It was not, of course, the admiral in charge of Portsmouth Dockyard in that launch, but one of the officers employed by him to keep in order the busiest naval base in the world. The town sat on the best and safest anchorage on the south coast and had grown from a small port to a sizeable conurbation entirely due to the presence of the fleet, replacing the Nore, once of equal importance and still a major base. When the Dutch had posed the greatest danger to the nation the mouth of the Medway had been the vital location for the fleet but for nearly a century the threat had shifted and stayed with the French. Not only did it provide ample space to anchor – the whole of several fleets could assemble here – it also, for the purposes of shore leave and a way to put a lid on discontent, abutted the Isle of Wight, which held the two satellite bases of Ryde and St Helen's. As an island it was a place that allowed for shore leave.

Portsmouth might be on the mainland, but it had an added advantage: the city stood on a series of islands, was traversed in its entirety and entered and exited by a series of bridges. Given the propensity of Jack tar to desert that meant a few well-placed marines could stop the flow – necessary, for once in open country the men of the sea were hard to catch in a nation whose sympathy extended to those perceived to be oppressed. Indeed there were many old hands who boasted they could travel the length and breadth of the country and never be taken up by those seeking deserters.

The fellow who clambered aboard was, like

Pearce, a lieutenant so the lift of the hat was to his commission in command of the ship rather than his rank, and he gave his name as Pettigrew. Under normal circumstances it would have been in order to offer him some refreshment, a glass of wine and a biscuit perhaps, as well as a period of conversation in which the hunt would be on for mutual acquaintances; that, with his fugitives occupying the cabin, was not possible and for once, and against all common custom, John Pearce did not merely introduce himself by name alone.

'You will have heard of me, I am sure, given I was assigned my rank at the insistence of King George himself.'

Pettigrew's face took on that look folk have when they are memory searching and it was not long before enlightenment replaced the furrowed brow; the case of John Pearce had rippled through the navy with most officers deciding that such an elevation, even by royal hand, was an insult to a service which prided itself on its professionalism. That a man could be made a lieutenant by a mere stroke of the pen at the base of an Order in Council flew in the face of all precedent and it was only long-serving and getting-nowhere midshipmen who saw a possible avenue to advancement.

'I would invite you to take a glass of wine with me, Mr Pettigrew, but—'

The other man cut across him. 'I would have to decline, sir, as I have too many other duties to perform.'

Since Pettigrew would not meet his eye it was probably a lie, but having achieved his aim, Pearce could allow himself to look hurt, which produced on the other man's face a hint of satisfaction; he would be able to tell his contemporaries, and quite probably his superiors, that he had put the upstart John Pearce in his place. For all he had set out to produce that result, there was still the temptation to reverse matters and that could not be put aside, which led to a very pointed and long look at the city of Portsmouth all the way down the shore to Southsea.

'A nice safe billet you have here, Mr Pettigrew, not much chance of being required to face shot and shell in a safe anchorage. Tell me, what kind of interest does it require to get you such a comfortable posting?'

'Your orders?' the man snapped, holding out his hand.

These were passed over to be examined in a manner that implied they might be forgeries, which told Pearce just how successfully he had got under Pettigrew's skin, then followed the list of stores Pearce required and that got a lift of the eyebrows.

'Where are you off to with all this?'

'I am not obliged to respond to that, sir.'

'I do think my superiors will want to know.'

'Then, sir,' Pearce said, 'I will decline to tell them.' The face changed yet again to a 'you would not dare' look. 'Now please be so good as to advise me at what point I can berth alongside the storerooms and load.'

It could only have been malice that brought the reply, as well as the sneer that accompanied it. 'I do not think an armed cutter warrants a berth at an overworked dockside where vessels are queuing to load. No, you anchor at a buoy and we will send out hoys from which you can take your stores.' Spinning round he pointed to one of the farthest from the actual shore in any direction. 'There, number forty-seven seems a likely spot.'

That angered Pearce for it would make the task for his crew ten times as hard – loading when afloat was much harder – and for those doing the supplying it would be even worse. They would not be pleased to have to get a flat-bottomed hoy loaded with supplies out so far into the anchorage. There were none so spiteful for anything that engendered effort as dockside labourers, and Pearce had heard too many tales of their ways of taking revenge on sailors to just let this pass. There was a very strong chance he would get meat long in the cask and closer to rotting than fresh, and that would be before he was supplied with short cables and poor canvas.

'Please wait there a moment.'

'Whatever for?'

That got him a held-up hand as Pearce disappeared into his cabin, a finger to his lips to induce silence and, despite his words to Dorling about secrecy, he took from a casement locker the red and gold Admiralty pennant. Back on deck he showed it to Pettigrew unfolded.

'You will find me a dockside berth, sir, for if you do not your intransigence will be reported to the very Board itself and, if I have my way, to the King. In short, consider your career, sir, and if your superiors ask why you have been so kind as to advance my place in any queue you may tell them that you were overwhelmed by my charm. What you will not do, on pain of censure, is mention this pennant.'

There was a moment, in fact several, while Pettigrew calculated the loss of self-respect in acceding but his career won out and he nodded, though he spoke through pursed lips. 'Word will be sent to you as soon as I have cleared a space.'

'Thank you, Lieutenant,' Pearce replied, lifting his hat as the man spun and went over the side.

The loading, when it took place, was done with the ship tied head and stern using shore derricks and a long gangplank, that traversed by a veritable stream of willing hands and every item checked aboard by Dorling. Pearce, having sent a couple of hands in a wherry over to HMS *York*, made his way to the Port Admiral's offices to extract from Pay Office the wages due to his crew, which had not been forthcoming for months even on home service. He demanded their money as well as his own, all listed, submitted and signed for – though not without a series of laments from the Revenue Officer doling out the coin regarding the lack of available specie – to make what he insisted upon, a cash transfer. Pearce had declined to accept chits that local traders would take as a discount.

'Have you any idea, sir, what it takes to get gold and silver enough sent down to pay the fleet?'

'I do, sir; it is the need to find enough folk to transport it without they charge a fortune for the task.'

'That sir, would be a fine contract to possess, one

and one half of a per cent of the value of the specie carried.'

Pearce could not resist it; he leant forward and whispered, 'Would you, sir, like a guaranteed way to be able to secure such a contract?'

'I most certainly would.'

'It's easy,' Pearce responded in a louder voice, 'just grease well the palm of a man called Henry Dundas and it will be yours, for that is how those who presently make a killing get their payments.' With that, his muster books and a bag of money, Pearce walked out, calling over his shoulder, 'You'll find the grasping wretch in Whitehall.'

When he returned to HMS *Larcher* it was to find an impatient Pettigrew harrying his crew and the dockies – he had a ship of the line and an irate post captain waiting for the berth. His ship lay very low in the water, so many stores loaded that some meat barrels had to be lashed to the deck under tarpaulins, and still the last item, water, was being pumped into the 'tween decks where the carpenter, Kempshall, was filling and sealing barrels – given such a small vessel did not run to a dedicated cooper – while others in the crew struggled to move and stack such heavy receptacles.

Going halfway down the companionway Pearce called out, 'Never mind that sod shouting at you on the dock, lads, take what time you need. I saw a man killed doing what we are about now and I do not want that repeated on this ship.'

Then he went to find the men he had sent on his errand,

his heart lifting when they told him the result. Next it was to Dorling to get from him a list of those men it would be safe to let ashore. 'With the caveat that I cannot afford to lose any to tardiness or an attempt to run.'

'There are one or two I would not trust, sir, but I would hazard they are such lazy sods as to be no loss.'

'I still need a boat crew.'

'There's enough men serving of a religious nature, your honour, who see Beelzebub as residing in such places as Portsmouth. They would not go ashore if offered, lest it was to a chapel.'

'Then find me a pair.'

'Word from my brother, sir, he reckons if we take on much more in the hold we'll be supping sea water.'

'Very well, Mr Kempshall, stop the pumps. Mr Dorling, I then want the men assembled for I have their pay.'

'By the mark, Mr Pearce, that will lift them.'

Pearce pulled a face. 'Since they are going ashore it is more likely to debauch them than lift them. The elevation will go to the whores of Portsmouth.'

'Only some of them, sir,' Dorling replied with a grin. 'We ain't owed that much pay.'

'Then prepare to cast off,' Pearce responded, before calling, 'Buoy number, Mr Pettigrew?'

That had the lieutenant making an over-obsessive look full of worry at the board he had in his hand. The number that came back was twenty-four, which Pearce assumed was the closest one he had free to the shore.

The lines were taken from the quayside bollards fore and aft, the gangway slipped onto the hard and sweeps used to open a gap before the boats took up the strain on the cable that, lashed to the stern of the cutter, towed the ship out to its buoy. This meant Michael could make an appearance, which he did to many a jibe about the way he had skipped the labours of the rest, by which it was time to pipe the crew to their dinner, food taken by Emily and Pearce in his cabin, with a couple of planks over his sea chest serving as a table.

'We shall raise sail at first light, Emily, and then you can come on deck. I am sorry your confinement has been so long but I fear with my reputation there might be those come down to the shore to use a long glass to espy the ogre.'

'It was not all arduous, John. I had Michael for company and he was most informative about you.'

That got her a wry smile. 'I am not sure that you should be quite so curious as to ply people for facts about me, finding out for oneself is so much to be preferred.'

'You would not say that if you had heard his paeans to your character.'

'We are fond of each other and I suspect he over-praised.'

'John, it is more than that. I do not think you know how much you have gained in respect for your never giving up in your fight for the rights of others and not just your own.'

'A burden it would be good one day to put aside.'

'I think you will never do that, for if you would scarce

admit it, you have too much of your father in you.'

'To hear you say that, were he here, would shock him. We used to argue a great deal about his notions of the way matters could be improved for the poor.'

'You must tell me all about him.'

'Not now, my dear, for we will be at sea for weeks and have ample opportunity to talk of such things, for you, likewise, must tell me of your past.'

'I'm not sure I have one of any interest.'

'You do, everyone has things that act to form them.' He leant over and kissed her on the head. 'But the very fortunate few have a future to look forward to.'

The crew had not lingered at their mess tables over dinner, but set to at dressing for going ashore. It was blue jackets, clean ducks, a striped kerseymere blouse topped off by a gaily coloured bandana and, for those who had one, a black and shiny tarpaulin hat. Pearce, who acted as purser as well as commander, was called upon to sell to his crew lengths of ribbon for their pigtails and new socks to adorn their legs, as well as blacking to get a shine on their shoes. When the last man had been seen to he went to see the cook.

'Mr Bellam, I want you to go ashore and buy enough food for six.'

The man's round face fell. 'I do not want you to do more, since I perceive you wish to visit the fleshpots of Portsmouth. So let it be a cold collation and just leave it by your coppers and I will do the serving.'

'Six hearty mouths, or six light, your honour?'

'O'Hagan will be one of the party.'

'Then I'll buy for eight, 'cause your Irishman can eat for four on his own.'

The boats plied to and fro to the shore, some hired, for once the local wherrymen spotted a ship allowing shore leave they were like flies around a honey pot. The noise and gaiety were loud, occasionally interrupted by a prayer from the holy types who seemed to want their God to make sure that no pleasure was had by their shipmates and that perdition, which surely awaited them, should be left in abeyance. Once the noise died down, John Pearce and Michael O'Hagan set off for HMS *York*, with two hands to help row. Once there, and leaving Michael on the main deck, Pearce went to see Moyle in his cabin.

'I fear your two followers think they are being sent to serve where my whim takes them, Mr Pearce.'

'You did not tell them of our arrangement?'

Moyle was shocked and his voice in reply was abrasive. 'I will tell no one, and that especially to a pair of loose-tongued men of the lower deck. I ask that of you too, tell them nothing of our arrangement!'

'Of course, it is a matter best not talked about, but did not the men who brought them here let on?'

'I doubt they had knowledge of it. The midshipman who came aboard with them asked only that I sign for their arrival. All I did was stick them in an upper deck cell with barely a how d'ye do. They asked questions, which I ignored.'

'How fare the men I brought you?'

'You were right about a pair of them needing to be taught their manners.'

'I am tempted to give them a hello, just to depress them further.'

Moyle responded so hastily he ended up tripping over his own words.

'Never fear, they are low enough and I would not want that the sight of your face should raise in them the will for a contest that will rebound on my men.' Having said that he seemed to recover somewhat his composure. 'In fact, I would have to forbid such a thing.'

'So be it.'

'So one of my men will take you to the right cell.'

John Pearce had in him a strong streak of mischief and now it came to the fore, aided by the fact that the light was fading and it was now getting dark outside; he could see lights twinkling on the shore.

'Could I ask, then, that you have your men bring them to my boat, and it would be an aid if they were a little rough and aggressive in their handling, as I mean to play a game with them.'

Moyle tried and failed to hide the fact that he was dealing with an odd sort of fellow and nodded. 'Makes no odds to me, Mr Pearce.'

'Then I will get in the boat and wrap myself in my boat cloak.'

He was huddled in that, with Michael sat in the bottom of the boat to disguise his height, when they heard the rough voices of Moyle's guards abusing the men as they brought them out to the top of the gangplank. With lots of pushing and shoving it was rough handling indeed, but truly not harmful if you excepted the spirit, that was until they were, chains struck off, virtually thrown into the boat, which produced cries, if not of pain, then of dented pride.

'Get sat down the two of you,' Pearce growled in a manufactured voice.

'Where we goin'?' demanded Charlie Taverner, always the more vocal of the two Pelicans.

Pearce replied in the same kind of disguised voice. 'To a hell ship, that's where you're going, for Barclay has seen to you good and proper, with a man in command who loves nothing more than to wield the cat with his own strong hand and nothing done to warrant it.'

'That's agin the laws of the navy,' Rufus said.

Michael, behind them, tried to disguise his voice too, though his brogue was evident. 'Bugger the laws of the navy, we are a law to ourselves.'

It was one of the other pair, the men brought to help row the boat, who broke the deception. 'Could you tell me, Mr Pearce, what in the name of our Blessed Saviour it is you're on about?'

'Pearce?' said Charlie, his tone full of mystification.

'Sure, fellow, he is our commander.'

'And I believe,' Pearce said, emerging from his cloak, 'your good and loyal friend.'

Michael heaved himself up and stuck his head

between them. 'And, sure, boyos, he's not alone in that.'

'Pinch me, Rufus, 'cause I think I'm dreamin' now.'

'Not so, Charlie; the Pelicans are reunited.'

Back on board, they ate the cold meal left by Bellam, and Emily renewed her acquaintance with Charlie and Rufus, who were shy in her presence, particularly the youngster, and somewhat at a loss to see that her relationship with John Pearce had progressed to the point of consanguinity and that they would all be sailing together to the Mediterranean. Charlie still had about him a bit of that roughish charm which had sustained him as a sharp working the Strand and Covent Garden and it was he who proposed a toast to her, with which none present could disagree.

'Ma'am, I hereby propose that you be inducted as an honorary Pelican.'

The glasses were up and drained and Emily was delighted. The last act of the night, with drunken men coming noisily back aboard in ones and twos, was for Emily to write a letter to her husband with Pearce helping, his opinion being, and she took it, that to mention him was to fuel a fire already burning heartily enough.

CHAPTER TWENTY

When HMS *Larcher* sailed over and plucked out her anchor she was not the only vessel about to put to sea; the Tolland brothers had been true to their word and had gathered a crew in no time at all – rough-looking fellows that men gave a wide berth to when out walking – bringing them up to London to man the *Percy*, the ship Denby Carruthers had purchased, and they set about getting ready for sea with all the expertise of blue-water men, reefing and roving, bending on sails and taking in the stores needed for a short voyage.

The man himself had gone to consult with his brother-in-law on an unrelated matter and in doing so had put Edward Druce in an uncomfortable position; he had previously supplied to Carruthers men to deal with Cornelius Gherson, having been told the fellow had cuckolded his employer, a couple of Impress Service toughs of much muscle and little conscience when it came to turning a coin. He had no actual idea what they had done for the alderman, only that it was unlikely to be pretty and Druce had ever since regretted putting the risk of family disgrace to the forefront of his reaction when asked for aid, really to spare his wife embarrassment, without examining the likely consequences.

In some sense he had been relieved when Gherson unexpectedly turned up in his offices in the company of his client naval officer Captain Barclay; at least it implied that he had been beaten for his sins rather than anything worse, which had been a worry. But here was his wife's brother once more sitting in an armchair, drinking his wine and seeking more help and this to find the same fellow.

'I tried to fix him with the Bow Street Runners, Edward, but he managed to wriggle out of that somehow. That matters less than the notion he will turn up to trouble my marriage once more, so I need to find him so that I can keep a watch on his movements.'

'Find him,' Druce replied, his hands arched like a church steeple.

He was prevaricating, for he had on his desk a letter from Ralph Barclay saying he was coming to town, bringing his clerk with him, and desired a meeting to discuss the state of his present investment, as well as how to proceed with the expected payments from the 1st June battle. It was a double worry that they both might turn up when Carruthers was still here, for he had lied to his brother-in-law when asked a few months past about Gherson, saying he knew nothing of the fellow, when he knew very well he was serving as the captain's clerk aboard HMS *Semele*.

His reasons were complex and tested on them he would never have admitted to the truth, which was that in Gherson he recognised a fellow keen to profit personally from his employer's ventures and willing, if asked for advice from Barclay, to advance the schemes of Ommanney & Druce. In short, he was a source of profit now and potentially much more in the future and that was the paramount concern of a firm of prize agents who made most of their returns by speculating with their clients' money.

'It could be like seeking a needle in a haystack, Denby.'

'Not quite, Edward, Gherson goes where there is money to be made.' The nod was inadvertent and quickly stopped. 'So that narrows matters, and I know he is London born and I suspect this is where he will plough his furrow, probably a felonious one, for the city is the place of opportunity to rogues like him.'

'I'm not sure I can assist, Denby.' That made his brother-in-law stiffen. 'Ask me for the whereabouts of a sailor and that I can do by a simple enquiry to the Admiralty, where we maintain strong contacts.'

'I must find him,' Carruthers snapped, his face closing up enough to tell the man at the desk just how much hatred was in the sentiment. Obviously Carruthers knew it too, realised he was being obvious in his loathing and perhaps even in his intentions, so he sat back and modulated his tone. 'To stop him visiting mischief on another as he visited them on me, of course.'

'Quite, quite, but would not a thief-taker be a better prospect?' Seeing interest Druce went on. 'You say your man is a thief—'

'And a satyr, for all his tender years and innocent looks.'

That was a barked interruption, from a man Edward Druce had always thought too strong in his passions, the kind of thing that led him to marry such an unsuitable bride. And Druce had a duty, which was to deflect his interest in Gherson and even to send him on a wild goose chase if necessary. Serving on a ship, the man was relatively safe, rarely ashore, in London only on the odd occasion, and if things went as normal HMS *Semele* would be at sea for most of the time; a warship at anchor was not a proper use of assets even for an indolent commander addicted to taking the waters of Bath such as Black Dick Howe.

'Let us stick to larceny, Denby. If you are looking for a fellow who steals money, then that is a job for a man who takes up criminals and, I might add, I know of no one who searches up and down the land for infidelity, it is more a local interest. I do have knowledge of a fellow who might take the work, for the Bow Street Runners and their successes have made his occupation less profitable than it used to be. One of his gifts is that he is well connected and seems able to use a network of people to search far and wide. He would, of course, require funds to proceed and a payment for success.'

'I am not bereft of the means to fund that.'

'No,' Druce replied with some feeling: well heeled and successful as he was, he could not hold a candle to Denby Carruthers. 'So would you like to know where to find him?'

'You find him Edward, will you?'

'Me?'

Carruthers stood up. 'Yes, I am going away for a few days, perhaps a week. Get hold of your fellow . . . what's his name?'

'Hodgeson.'

'Retain him, Edward, and I will see him on my return.'

'Where are you going?'

'People keep asking me that, as if it is any of their business.'

The manner of that rejoinder, so cold and dismissive to what was a very simple question, eased the conscience of Edward Druce; he did not like lying to his brother-in-law even if he felt it necessary. But he was not to be treated like some busybody. Lord, he might even tell Gherson that Denby was seeking him out! There was, however, no desire to let his feelings be known or have a proper falling out, certainly not with a powerful city alderman and a brother to a wife who esteemed him highly, so the response was polite.

'Well I hope it is successful, Denby.'

* * *

'Sir Phillip, I believe Lord Howe was humbugged. We chased that frigate when we should have gone in search of those American merchantmen.'

'You may well be right, Captain Barclay, but I do not see how I can bring to the Board such a supposition. And if I did I doubt they would act upon it.'

'What I am saying, sir, is that the despatch which Sir Roger Curtis wrote at Lord Howe's behest does not detail all the facts, and there are men suffering from finding their contribution to victory ignored.'

'The King was cock-a-hoop when he heard the news,' Sir Phillip Stephens said, rather wistfully. 'Felt vindicated, for you know Lord Howe only got the Channel through his insistence. Lord Hood was livid.'

Damn them both, Barclay thought, pulling out a letter written by Gherson.

'Nevertheless, I wish to lay before the Board of Admiralty that all was not as stated and that if accolades are to be given, they should be given equally to all the captains engaged.'

'Very well, Captain, I will see it is as you wish.'

Bustling out of the building, his stick rapping a tattoo on the flagstones, Ralph Barclay supposed Sir Phillip to be right. But he had achieved his aim, had laid his evidence in what was now the public domain. Time to get on with the defamation of Sir Roger Curtis, for he was easier to attack than Howe; any assault on him might be seen as a criticism of the monarchy. He made his way to Covent Garden and a coffee house where he had arranged to meet with Gherson. His clerk had been given the task of finding out what newspaper people might take a payment to promote their case as well as an artist to begin drawing Curtis in an unflattering light. It would have been nice to engage Gillray, but he was too steep in price.

Sitting down beside Gherson, Barclay could not help his nose twitching. 'God, man, you smell of the whore you have been with!'

'She was not a clean creature, that is true,' Gherson replied, unabashed, 'but she was cheap.' He then handed over a list of names, with the various coffee houses at which each could be contacted, and it was a long one; it seemed those who wrote for Grub Street were keen to accept payment and truth was not a fixation. 'I doubt you will have trouble, sir, in defaming Sir Roger, and I have it on good authority Lord Howe as well, if you so desire.'

'Not a good move for a man's career, I think, given the King esteems him. We will talk of these tonight, now we must go and find out how well I am doing.'

It was but a short walk to the Strand and the offices of Ommanney & Druce.

It was a good hour later when Edward Druce was convinced he was having what the French called *déjà vu,* and something more than that after his corpulent partner, Ommanney, having gone through the present investments and potential future ones of

311

their client while supping fine Burgundy wine, had left him alone with Ralph Barclay and Cornelius Gherson. During that hour, Barclay could not but recall a previous visit to these offices when, with a ship after five barren years, a new wife and orders to get to sea, he had sought an advance on prospective prize money from the two partners. The level of condescension they had shown then matched their fawning on him now, and to make him feel better still, he could look at the great portrait of the most famous victory of his much loved Admiral George Rodney which he watched unfold from a distance; there it was, at torn sails, bursting cannon and an angry smoke-filled sky, the Battle of the Saintes.

'An investigator, Captain Barclay?'

'Yes, to find my wife.' Seeing the look in Druce's eye, he felt constrained to explain, his voice slightly overwrought. 'My wife Emily is much younger than I and has had her head turned.'

Was that what could be said about Catherine Carruthers, Druce was thinking, that her head was turned, which made him glance at the culprit, who was watching his employer with a very slight smirk on his face. So was this another young and pretty woman who had fallen for his charms, for he was a handsome devil, with his soft skin and near white hair? What was it about the tender sex that they could not see in such corn-blue eyes as Gherson possessed that the only thing for which he had true affection was himself?

'For reasons I have yet to completely establish she has decided to desert the marital home and take up residence elsewhere. I must add that she has done that entirely on her own – there is no other party involved.'

'And if you find her?'

'I will, of course, seek to persuade her of the error of her ways, and beg that she comes back to be the dutiful wife I married and have deep affection for.'

Gherson's reaction then, the widening smirk seen out of the corner of his eye, convinced Druce that Barclay was not telling the truth, not that such a fact was any of his concern. But there was advantage in this; he could recommend Hodgeson for both tasks that had been brought to his attention this day and hope that he only succeeded in one of them. Damn me, he thought, I should charge the fellow commission.

'I do know of someone who might be able to help.'

'And how do I find him?'

'Let me do that for you. I take it you are, as usual, staying at Brown's?'

'I am, so send him to me there.'

'Actually, Captain Barclay, I think it would be best if you met in my office, with me present to introduce him and to offer, should you be at sea, to monitor his activities, a duty I am happy to undertake with no charge upon your tariff.'

'That is kind of you, sir.'

'I take it Mr Gherson will be coming by for a more thorough examination of your portfolio?'

'Tomorrow, if that suits, Mr Druce,' Gherson replied.

'Fine, I look forward to it, but I would suggest you meet Hodgeson on your own, it is after all a personal matter.'

'I agree,' Barclay said, throwing a glare at Gherson.

And, Druce was thinking, I have the whole of tonight to think how to play this game.

To be at sea was blissful; the weather was warm, the sea, albeit with a strong Atlantic swell, presented no threat and, once past the Lizard and heading due south the ship was eating up the miles with a potent westerly on its beam. With yards trimmed near fore and aft the bowsprit was the main driver and the deck was canted like a shallow roof, which made movement interesting and meant no food would stay still on any table. The crew seemed not to have changed in any way, they treated him as they always had, with respect and what looked like regard, so it took time for John Pearce to realise that the crew of HMS *Larcher* had resentments when it came to Charlie and Rufus.

New men in a settled crew always had a hard time bedding in. In what could be years of sailing together few mysteries remain as to how a man would think, never mind speak or act. A scratched nose was a signal some fellow wanted a pipe of tobacco, moods and tempers were related to the state of the moon, the crew had a vernacular of their own, based on common navy slang but subtly altered by their shared experience and the common jests that became like old friends; his Pelicans had none of that.

They had accepted Michael because he had acted as a servant; no more, he was content to be part of the lower deck and treat Pearce as what he was, the man in command, which did not allow for too much familiarity. The fact that the other two had dined with the captain and his lady as soon as they had come aboard was seen as suspicious: were they set to spy? They could not help themselves for being a bit familiar and that was before Pearce himself dented his reputation by chastising one of the crew merely for telling a vulgar tale in the hearing of Emily.

It was a problem having a woman on board in a ship with no proper heads to speak of, saving a slops bucket tossed over and washed, and it stood to reason a lady wanted to be clean, so it was rig a sail every couple of days, fill up a butt of water and let her do her necessaries to the back of that and no hands allowed aloft, though there was no way to avoid the surreptitious looks for the hope of spotting a flash of bare flesh, even an ankle. Most of the crew were under twenty-five years of age, many of them younger, and they were as red-blooded as any of their years. But unused to company of that nature, one hand forgot that he was stitching eyelets in a sail hard by where Emily was doing her ablutions and he was not quiet in his tale-telling.

'That Black Cath, mate,' he crowed, 'I ain't never seen the like. There's me so full of ale I was erect and as hard as that Indian teak, an' I reckoned I could piss a mile an' sets a challenge for a contest. Up jumps Black Cath, eyes flashin' like Lucifer's cat, and says a shilling piece that I can out piss you any time. A woman, says I, never in life!'

Other crew members, picking up that there was yarn-telling afoot, had slowed their own work to listen, which encouraged the teller to raise his voice.

'We go into the alley and I hauls out old Harry, an' by Christ did I give it length, twenty feet for certain. Well Cath has just downed a pint of mead in one, which could be counted as comin' it high in the cheating line, but gent I am, I let it pass. Over she bends, back to the target, hoicks up her shift and let's fly.'

'She a one, Black Cath,' came the shout from one of the younger crew, a noise that brought Pearce from his logs to see what was going on.

'Well,' says the sail stitcher, 'I don't know what she's got in them private regions of hers but I hope I don't get caught in there for I'll be a gelding if I am. She out pissed me by more yards than I care to count, a stream as straight as an arrow and still kicking up a foot of dust when it landed. Stronger in them parts than our barky's fire engine, I reckon.'

Pearce looked hard at the culprit and then at the screen. Emily was behind there and must have heard every word.

'Bosun, take that man's name, and I want him before me within the hour.'

'Aye, aye, Captain,' Birdy responded, without much enthusiasm. He was looking at the screen and so was

316

everyone else, that was until Emily pulled it back and, head down, made for the cabin. Suddenly they were all busy.

'I apologise for that, my dear.'

'Why?' she whispered as she slid by, 'I have no right to be here, the men have.'

The collective behaviour of his fellow humans had ever been a mystery to John Pearce; he had seen people praise and cheer every word his father uttered in a stump speech, only to throw clods of turf at him seconds after he had finished. Mobs were fickle things, but so was collective opinion and it was very obvious to a man sensitive to such things to notice that the atmosphere had changed and seemingly in a blink: the crew were discomfited and Emily thought she was the cause. He knew better, knew that his Pelicans and their relationship to him lay at the root of the problem.

'It is my fault, John, and the fellow forgot I was there.'

'No it is not and he should have remembered. Tilley's damned lucky I am no lover of a flogging or he would have had half a dozen.'

'Will you stop cursing!'

'No, I will not!'

'You should not have stopped his grog.'

'You know nothing about discipline. A captain must act to curtail poor behaviour or who knows where it will lead?'

'It will lead to you being as bad as my husband.'

'That is unfair.'

317

'I wish to apologise to the crew.'

'And I forbid you to even think of such a thing.'

If you could not have a quiet conversation on a ship, you certainly could not hide a full-blown row and with decent movement all of the crew might have heard a portion that pieced together would constitute a whole if they had not been prevented from doing so.

'Sure, boyos, you'll be coming away from the after part of the barky.' That stopped a few in their tracks and the wiser heads were already moving to get below, for if Michael was the jolly Irish giant normally, he had a face like thunder now. 'Seems to me that a man and his woman ought to be able to dispute in peace.'

'Not a soul is like to interfere.'

The ham-like fists came up, not all the way but enough. 'Happen if I stop up a few ears no one will know what is afoot.'

'Anyone not employed,' Dorling called, 'down below now.'

Odd that the voices in the cabin became muted, as though they realised even through the bulkhead that it was not proper to so loudly argue. But it was not silent and it was obvious the matter was not settled, until Pearce came on deck and ordered all hands to be assembled.

'I have several things to say to you, first about the men I fetched ashore in Portsmouth.' That had heads turning to partake of collective agreement. 'I sense you feel they are too familiar to my person, or is it the commission I hold? Many of you must have wondered at the connection and

318

I assume they have not told you of it, so I shall.'

And he did, from the Pelican Tavern to their volunteering to save his skin, finishing with this. 'I owe these men a debt of gratitude I cannot pay, for they have stuck by me as I hope I have stuck by them. Now you know this coat I wear is a fluke, for if matters had gone another way I would still be a hand, probably a poor one too, unable to tie a decent knot. They see me as one of them not a blue coat who will flog at a whim, a threat, I must tell you, they have faced more than I.'

He paused and slowly looked over the crew, seeking eye contact. 'When I say I owe them, I owe you too, for the way you have served me since I came aboard, for which I am profoundly grateful. Having a lady aboard imposes certain restrictions which I would ask you to observe, but I cannot oblige you to do so, which has been pointed out to me by the person sharing my cabin. She wanted to apologise to you for any inconvenience, when in truth it is my request for forgiveness to make. I ask of that now, and, Tilley, your grog is herewith reinstated, but I tell you, keep your voice low if you wish to keep it.'

'Three times three lads, for Mr Pearce.'

That accolade he took before diving into his cabin, glaring at Emily and snarling, 'Now I feel less a fool and ten times more a fraud.'

CHAPTER TWENTY-ONE

Hodgeson was a bear of man, not tall but with heavy shoulders and arms that even covered one knew to be strong. He was also quiet, a listener rather than a talker, a fellow of few but acute enquiries, an observer, not the man to take centre stage, and he was doing that now to Ralph Barclay, who was having some difficulty in holding back what he wanted to keep to himself, namely that his separation was due to matters not for discussion and that even someone he engaged had no right to dig too deep.

'Am I to understand, Captain, that your wife, should I find her, will not willingly return to you?'

'She may require that some truths be explained, for instance that she will be denied bed and board if she refuses, but I do not see it coming to that.'

'But you feel sure you are able to persuade her?'

'I am, just as soon as I can get her alone.'

'So once I have found out where she is residing . . . ?'

'Tell me and I will take matters into my own hands,' said Barclay, standing up. 'Mr Druce knows where I am and will communicate with me when you have fulfilled your assignment.'

They were in the coach back to Plymouth when he raised the subject with Gherson. 'I'm not sure I can repose faith in this Hodgeson fellow, he seems to lack fibre to me. I want you to think on another way to proceed; let us give him a week or two and if he finds her, well and good Then you and Devenow can do what is necessary.'

'Me, sir?'

'She's a frail woman, by damn, surely you are not afraid of that too?'

Determined to refuse when the time came, Gherson just acceded to keep the peace, as Barclay continued. 'Mind, if he fails we may need some of your low-life contact again, like that fellow who helped you burgle my wife's solicitor.'

The man was called Jonathan Codge and he was the last person Gherson wanted to ever see again, he being a man who would sell his own mother down the river for a copper coin, then want the body to sell to Surgeon's Hall.

'I think him ill-suited to such a task, sir.'

'Then think of someone else man, someone from

your black past. Now, you spent time with Druce, be so good as to tell me what he told you about my chances of profit, and spare nothing, we have a journey of some thirty hours.'

The more he thought about the prospect of ridding himself of his wife, the more it appealed to Denby Carruthers; it sustained him through the bout of seasickness that came upon him as soon as the *Percy* exited into the wide Thames Estuary and hit the North Sea swell. Likewise, having observed the crew, he was sure he had the instrument to hand that would release him from all sorts of problems, in particular a fellow called Codge who was blackmailing him – he had tried to have him arrested by the Bow Street Runners in company with Gherson, who would have been transported or strung up at Tyburn; somehow they had both talked their way out of it.

Three disappearances, and with Gherson definitely gone and he would be free to take another wife, this time one with money instead of beauty, though he would seek both – perhaps a widow with an inheritance which would become his to do with as he wished once they were wed. Druce would engage the man he had named and he, the instigator, would stay well out of it. Let his brother-in-law handle matters and, if anything went wrong, nothing could be traced back to him.

'He is not telling the truth, Mr Druce. I suspect if I find Mrs Barclay the captain will seek to take her forcibly back to their home and keep her there.'

'And this troubles you?'

'I have known these things go wrong, sir, and I have seen death be caused by it.'

'You're surely not suggesting Captain Barclay would murder his wife?'

'How to know what harm will come of trying to take her if she is not willing?'

'There must be ways, man.'

'There are methods to ensure it is quiet, and those to ensure it is successful, sir, but without wishing to imply a lack of judgement on your part, it is not the way that navy men are accustomed to behave. It requires guile, not brawn, and patience, not the bull at the gate.'

'Then I shall persuade the captain that your expertise should be employed.'

'Good, I have my description and her name, and she sounds a rare beauty, which makes matters easier. Plain ladies are much harder to locate, they being so numerous.'

'I had you listed as a thief-taker, a man who chased felons and murderers, yet you seem to know a great deal about the gentler sex?'

'It would shock you, Mr Druce, just how many of those I have pursued were women. Do not think them gentle, sir, for they are not. When it comes to cold-blooded crime they are a match for us men.'

'Good. Now I want to talk to you of another case, a fellow to find this time. He is called Cornelius

Gherson and I have here a description: dark hair, black eyes and a stooping walk. He is a money thief and too fond of women, especially those who are wedded to his employer.'

'Singular name.'

'It is,' the prize agent replied, thinking that was the one thing he dare not change. But with luck and that description Hodgeson would not get within ten miles of the man. Let him drain the Carruthers purse, for that was no concern of Edward Druce. His task was to keep Gherson alive and seek to earn both himself and the company money.

Catherine Carruthers would never have tried to follow Isaac Lavery if her husband had not been away and, in truth, she was nervous of doing so now. But he had said he was taking the opportunity, brought on by the same absence, to make a wider than normal search and talk to more of the kind of people who might know Gherson. It was odd how quickly he disappeared into a nearby coffee house, one used by city traders and not the sort of low creatures that Lavery was supposed to be questioning. Even more alarming was the time he stayed.

'Boy, come here.' The urchin obliged, for the well-dressed lady had a coin in one hand, which she pointed at the coffee house. 'For this I want you to go in yonder doorway and look for a fellow with large ears and a purple nose. He has too quite large bags under each eye and is dressed in black, I doubt you can miss him.'

'And what then, missus?'

'Just come back and tell me who he is talking to.'

The boy shrugged and ran off, to disappear through the door. He would not be allowed long, for he was grubby and not the type for such a place; they would rate him a pickpocket if they noticed him at all. As it was he was out in less than a minute.

'He's not talking to no one, missus, just sitting reading the newspaper over a pot of coffee and a dish of steak pie.'

The coin left Catherine Carruthers' hand before she even noticed it or the boy were gone, he scarpering in case she changed her mind about payment, no doubt, leaving her to ponder on what she had just been told. One thing was plain: Lavery was not doing what he was supposed to do and had he ever done so? The thought that he might have just been leading her on was hard to contemplate at first, but in truth, over weeks and much of her spare household budget, the man had not provided a single clue to where Cornelius could be. It was a sad woman who made her way home, her mind in turmoil.

When Lavery came back he was quick to find her and all flustered, relating that some of the places he had visited were so full of villainy that he had more than once feared for his life, places where people had no shoes, barely any clothes that were not rags, and where the possession of a handkerchief was considered wealth enough to get your throat cut. He had, too, acquired a cough he was sure indicated some kind of malaise he had picked up from the air he had been obliged to inhale.

'But was it fruitful?' Catherine asked.

'Alas,' came the reply and a hand reached out to touch her fingertips. 'But we must not despair, we must take the opportunity of your husband's absence to progress things properly.'

Suddenly he took a firm grip on her hand and she knew what he meant by progress, and it was a notion that made her blood boil. But she pretended to be faint to cover her confusion, vapours that Lavery took for an excess of passionate attraction. Then he was on his knees.

'You know, dear lady, that I would go to the ends of the earth for you.'

'Mr Lavery,' she gasped, in a fair imitation of a woman in distress, 'the other servants.'

'Of course,' he responded, raising himself up with a groan that testified to less than fluid joints, and his voice sounded just as weak. 'But you must understand how easy it is for me to forget such constraints.'

'Yet remembered they must be, for if my husband was to find out . . .' That did not require to be completed and the thought of what might happen rippled through Lavery's weak frame as she said feebly, 'In truth, Mr Lavery, I do not feel entirely well, perhaps that malaise you spoke of has afflicted me.'

That stymied him; having made such a play of it he could not now dismiss it.

'I feel I should retire to my room to rest, please aid me to stand.'

'My dear lady,' he said, but he did as she wished. Then his voice recovered its strength to take on a note of hope. 'Perhaps you would like me to accompany you and see you settled.'

'No, I can manage.'

And I can mange you, she swore to herself as she climbed the stairs to her room, a seething mass of hatreds, crushing disappointments and plots for revenge. But Catherine was not a fool; she knew she could not just turn on Lavery and tell him she knew she was being both cheated and led up a garden path. Who knew what mischief would fly from such an act. A better plan would have to be formed, and before it was time for the maid to bring in a candle she had the outline of one.

'Mr Lavery will ask for me, Molly, and I would like you to tell him I am weak and unable to be up and about.'

'Yes, Madam.'

'And he has agreed to undertake some errands for me. Please be so good as to pass on how happy it would make me if he carried them out.'

When Molly had departed, Catherine Carruthers began to dream if not to sleep; it was not a new one but a common one, in which she was in a sunlit meadow, reunited with Cornelius Gherson and happy to become his willing lover there and then amongst the sweet flowers.

'Gherson!'

Barclay's shout echoed though HMS *Semele*, carrying timbers and decks with ease. The man called knew what it portended for he had seen the sender's name of the letter delivered and had fretted ever since as to what it might contain; it was worse than he feared.

'She mentions the burglary, by damn, but tells me she had removed the court martial papers beforehand.'

'Please sir, your voice.'

'What?'

'The whole ship will hear you and that was a crime.'

'It was your crime, Gherson, not mine. I've a good mind to hand you over to Devenow and let him have his way with your brains.'

'If it was my crime it was at your behest, sir.'

'You dare to threaten me?'

'No, I merely point out that we are part of the same act in the eyes of the law.'

That changed Barclay's tone; his voice dropped several decibels. 'You mean she might tell a magistrate?'

'What does her letter say, sir?'

'That I am to leave her be, that she has gone off to the country and I am not to pursue or seek to find her.'

'It seems to me a too flimsy matter to trust to her

328

word. I think we must up the search and once she is found ensure that she cannot speak.'

Still nursing a limp, Barclay threw himself into a chair and put his head in his hands. 'She has the means to ditch me twice over now, thanks to you.'

The clerk took that without murmur, it mattered not that it had been his employer's idea to steal the papers, the thing now was to find a way to silence Emily Barclay, and Gherson's thinking did not rule out the notion of doing so on a permanent basis. Not that he would suggest such a course; he knew his man too well; Captain Ralph Barclay, brave as a lion on a battling quarterdeck, did not have the stomach for a quiet bit of removal.

'The search, sir, perhaps we could put more people on to it.'

'Yes, we must. And we must pray to God for deliverance from the malice of all those people who hate me.'

Just pray for you? Gherson thought, his bile rising; thank you very much, you old goat – what about me!

Denby Carruthers was both surprised and delighted that doing business in Gravelines was so easy; nominally under French control they had done nothing to interdict the trade between Flanders and England – as the Tollands said, they needed the gold. If the people he was called upon to deal with were capable of violence they also had a good grasp of how to do commerce – quickly and without fuss – and he felt, weapons apart and without the strain of menace, right at home, as if he was doing his normal day's exchanges in London.

The efficiency extended to supply and loading, and if he had a slight worry he might be cheated, both the attitude of the Tolland brothers and the speed with which his purchases were supplied laid that to rest. The wind had been fair on the crossing to Gravelines, it was less so on the return but they got within reach of Ramsgate inside a day's sailing, where a boat was lowered to take him ashore.

'Get yourself set for the night, Mr Carruthers, and take the coach back to London on the morrow.'

'I will do that, Tolland, but, you know, I am tempted to ask, should I not come with you to land the cargo?'

Jahleel Tolland's polite tone evaporated then. 'No one who is not needed to sail this ship of yours gets to see where we land, nor who we spread out the sale of the goods to. You go back to your house and wait for us and we will bring you the money we earn to the farthing.'

'Please do not think I don't trust you.'

Looking at each other in the light of a lantern, both men knew the truth: mutual trust did not exist. The only reason Denby Carruthers would not know this night, and never know on any other where they landed their cargo, was because that was the only card the Tollands still held and it tied him to them.

He took to the boat and even in oilskins he was wet through when finally it was run up in pitch black onto the Ramsgate beach.

Hodgeson the thief-taker had contacts amongst the Grub Street hacks and they, because of their trade, knew every fly-by-night character in London, Westminster and half the counties of England. A tot of brandy here, a tumbler of wine there, and when pushed to it a coin passed over, soon had the word out that he was looking for two people and news came back within forty-eight hours about a certain Mrs Barclay staying at Nerot's Hotel, now gone to Norfolk it was believed, who had been of interest to someone at the Home Department of Henry Dundas.

That took him to Nerot's but not that he enquired within its walls; there were a few taprooms around Jermyn Street to which the staff would wander when they got a chance, anything for a quiet bit of imbibing not under the eyes of their employer, and he soon established their favourite haunt, one they shared with the like-minded servitors in the St James's Street gentlemen's clubs.

To spot a man who will tell you something for a palmed coin is a skill, and a good guide is the fellow who moans incessantly and likes the world to know his grievances, yet loudly protests his honesty. So picking out Didcot was not as hard as a layman would have supposed and it took no time at all, once he knew there was payment to be had, for the hotel servant to give chapter and verse.

'You reckon Mrs Barclay has a paramour, then?'

'No doubt about it. Now I don't say he was rogering her there and then, but it was at the top of his mind, and if it hadn't yet happened she was gettin' ripe for the fall. It were in her eyes.'

'And it was this Lieutenant Pearce who let slip about her going to King's Lynn?'

'Did too, 'cause he trusted me, ye see, knew an honest man when he saw one. Why you asking, any road?'

Hodgeson slipped him a half-guinea, which was felt rather than looked at for its value. 'What do you care?'

'Don't give a toss, friend, but I'll go to another tankard afore you light out for Norfolk, 'cause you don't have to lay it that you is looking for her. Stands to reason if she's Mrs Barclay there's a Mister somewhere about, who would not be happy to see his wife – and she is a beauty, take my word – rolling in the hay with a good-looking cove like John Pearce. And he is not backward either, not when he's getting letters from Downing Street.'

'And they left together, you say?'

'Service at sea for him, I reckon, Norfolk for her.' That was followed by a wheezy laugh. 'Rumour has it they still paint their faces blue up there.'

That was the last place Hodgeson would go looking, for Didcot was an old fool who did not have a clue when he was being joshed. If Mrs Barclay was in some kind of liaison with a naval lieutenant, regardless of how far it had gone, he would be an easier person to find than a woman who could be anywhere, especially if he was serving in some capacity. And where he was she would most likely be, or close by.

As a time to interrupt Denby Carruthers his wife could not have chosen worse. He had not long arrived from Ramsgate and had a mass of papers to look through, bills, proposals for insurance and reports on some important investments. But disturb him she did, as soon as Lavery was sent out to deliver some share certificates, to tell him of the way he was being betrayed by his clerk.

'Lavery came to me with information about your affairs, husband, and I fear he did so in order to seek a way to gain my affections.'

The alderman nearly blurted out, 'At his age?' but he actually said, 'What information?'

The head went down and her hands were twisted around her embroidered handkerchief, this to demonstrate how reluctant she was to reply, while the catch in her voice was one she had used often on a very indulgent father, as well as one employed to discourage disappointed suitors prior to her marriage.

'He told me that a man had been in touch regarding a certain individual whose name, were I to mention it, would cause you upset.'

How did he know about Codge? It mattered not, Lavery did and that was that. 'It pleases me you are aware of the hurt it causes.'

'And I hope you believe I am still penitent,' she whimpered.

Catherine Carruthers' motives were, to her, quite straightforward: Lavery had failed in his task of finding Gherson and his protestations that he had tried hard were nothing but lies. But in the process of letting her down she had shown him a certain degree of encouragement which, should her husband ever realise, would be fatal to her future. She knew her beloved Cornelius to be alive and in time she would find him; until then she must have both the security of her home and her husband's income.

Lavery could not be trusted and if he let anything slip about her desire to find Cornelius then all hell would break loose and she might be cast adrift. Better he was dismissed and much better that she, having spoken first, would render any excuse he gave for his behaviour both invalid and unlikely to be believed.

'Why did Lavery do such a thing?'

She looked at her husband then, her eyes damp. 'I think he harboured thoughts inappropriate to a fellow of both is age and appearance and that made him volunteer to me things which I had no knowledge of and no desire to hear. That a man like that should have designs beggars belief, I know, but—'

She knows Gherson is alive, he thought, but enlightenment in that matter did not in any way provide the same clarity as to what he was going to do about it. Denby Carruthers was wondering if in agreeing to keep his shame secret, on advice from his brother-in-law, Druce, he had done the right thing, while deep down he knew he had been left with no choice. Still, matters were in hand for him to find Gherson and when he did . . .'

'I should leave it with me, my dear, and I will take care of it.'

'Lavery will be dismissed?'

'Not immediately, my dear, we do not want the old fool blackening your name in revenge, for he will be aware where his trouble has come from.'

'You are so wise, I don't know what I'd do if I did not have you to advise me.'

Right at that moment Denby Carruthers, though he was smiling indulgently, was thinking he had seen chucked over the parapet of London Bridge the wrong body, or perhaps there should have been two instead of one. He had been a fool to think that someone as young as Catherine could come to love him. All his experience in business told him that there comes a time to cut your losses in a failed venture. Not that he would do so suddenly, even if he thought the Tollands at hand to do the deed. As in a trading loss he would withdraw at a careful pace, hoping to pass off to some other hand the majority of the liabilities.

'My dear, it is your beauty that makes you so vulnerable to such advances, I know for I am not immune to that myself.'

'I have wounded you, I know, but I will work hard to make good that hurt.' Catherine Carruthers approached her husband and laid a soft hand on his shoulder.

'As for Lavery, humour him, but you must not worry your pretty head about the old booby again.' In using the words old booby, Denby Carruthers wondered if he was talking about himself.

CHAPTER TWENTY-TWO

They were on the latitude of Ferrol when the first dull boom came floating across the ocean; so faint it was impossible to tell if it was real. Pearce was on deck at the time and it was not only his head that became cocked as he wondered if he had heard correctly. It was also the case that no one wanted to be the first to seek to identify it in any way lest they make a fool of themselves.

'Mr Dorling, given our position would we be able to hear land-based gunnery?'

'No, sir, we are too far from shore for that.'

'Thunderstorm over the horizon, I reckon,' said one of the hands.

The next boom was not so faint, and taking his own judgement and adding it to the direction the men before him were recoding the sound, he had it nearly due south, just a few points off his bowsprit.

'Mr Dorling, let's get more sail aloft and increase our speed.'

That got a satisfied grin; Pearce had refused to crack on before and if he progressed at a reasonable rate it was also sailing easy and Dorling had been afire to test the top hamper. Soon the decks were full of men, the rigging too. He left what was set and went to the master, aware almost immediately that the heel of the deck had increased and so had the amount of white water scudding down the side. The actual effect would have to wait till the log was cast and that he would also leave to Dorling, for in the young master he had a very competent seaman, much more so than he. All he took responsibility for was the sending of a second lookout aloft so two men could more easily scan the whole horizon.

He entered his cabin to find Emily at her embroidery doing what she had done for her husband aboard HMS *Brilliant*, though she had never admitted that to Pearce – making cushions with the name of the vessel in the stitching.

'I hear the sound of padding feet, John.'

'Yes, we're increasing sail. We heard a sound like gunfire but it may just be weather.'

'Do you wish me to desist?'

'Not yet,' he replied with a smile. 'It will turn out to be nothing at all.'

Sound is one thing, pressure on the ears quite another and when another boom came, just as he stepped back onto the deck, Pearce was sure he could feel it on the drums, but also knew the power of imagination. By now Dorling had everything aloft that HMS *Larcher* could carry, without overdoing the driving sails, which would press her head down and be counterproductive by increasing the drag on the bows. But the fourth boom, when it came, left no one in any doubt: it was cannon fire and dead ahead. Calmly he re-entered the cabin and told Emily to cease her sewing.

'We will have to clear for action, which means this cabin will become a fighting space. Thank God we ate enough of the stores to free the deck. Let's hope there's enough room below for the furniture.'

'It will not require much.'

Emily was looking at what Pearce meant by 'furniture'. Most of the space was taken up by the bed they had used, for there was no pretence this time; he slept in his cabin and was awoken from there to take his turn on the watch. There was his sea chest and her trunk, the clocks and the tiny desk he used for writing up his logs.

'It suddenly occurs to me that you do not carry a surgeon, John.'

'No, that's another duty which falls to me, with aid, of course, from the cook and anyone else who can stitch.'

That had her holding up her unfinished cushion. 'Then I know where I should be, for did I not learn from Heinrich in Toulon how to look after the wounds of fighting men?'

'I hope you do not have to deal with anything like that on this ship. I have strict instructions to avoid anything that interferes with my mission, and even if there is an exchange of gunfire over the horizon I should sail on by and ignore it.'

That was when it came, not a single shot as before, but a salvo loud enough to carry and press on the senses. Pearce was on the deck in a trice. 'Gentlemen, we will clear for action.'

This had been rehearsed almost daily on the way south, well out to sea from the Bay of Biscay, and the crew had smoothed out any gremlins. Each went about his duties without being told, striking certain artefacts below, removing a couple of bulkheads, the gunner making up charges for the guns while the captains collected and affixed the flintlocks and all the while the sound of gunfire grew.

Emily had donned an apron and was directing some hands that had completed their tasks to set up a temporary sickbay by Bellam's coppers, already bubbling with useful hot water. She had also found in the holds a store of medical equipment, not least a supply of medicinal brandy. Some aboard spied her and kicked themselves for not finding it sooner; show a British sailor drink and he would consume it and never mind that one day later he would be lying on a board dying for that same drink to ease the pain of surgery.

'Gun captains, we shall not run out the cannon just yet, open ports will slow us down, but make all ready to run them in for loading. Aloft there, can you see anything yet?'

'Nothing yet, sir,' said one, this while the second man threw out a hand. 'Belay that, we can see a set of topsails three points off the starboard bow.'

'Quartermaster.'

The man nodded and eased the wheel a few points, this as Michael came up and presented him with his pistols. He would stay at his side, while Charlie and Rufus, now fully accepted, had each been given the captaincy of a cannon.

'Gun flashes, your honour.'

The sound and pressure followed hard on the heels of that shout from the masthead, which had Pearce grabbing a telescope and heading for the shrouds, to climb up and have a look for himself, now that there was something to see. As he looked aloft he saw his Admiralty pennant, which brought back to him the words of Henry Dundas.

'Sod Dundas,' he said to himself, 'there's a fight going on and it can't just be ignored.'

You never lose sight of the first time you clamber up a set of shrouds and Pearce could recall it now; the grey waters off Ramsgate, the loud voice of the bosun, Robert Sykes, who had turned out to be a decent type made cruel working for that bastard Ralph Barclay. How many times had he done it since and how much was it now so easy, when the first time he had known a real dose of fear. Near on his back he went over the main top and on up a second slimmer rope ladder to the very top, where he could sling his leg over a yard and, once steady, lifted his glass and examined the scene.

'Three ships, your honour, and we reckon one fightin' a pair.'

The gunfire and flashes were steady now, which spoke of a duel being fought at range. He swept the scene and took in the two vessels closest – the third was obscured by smoke – their flags streaming out red and gold.

'They cannot be Spaniards, they are our allies.'

'Never in life, your honour.'

'They might be French privateers under false colours.'

'And what are they attacking?'

On a fluke of wind the smoke cleared enough for Pearce to see the third ship and he had to steady his glass to get the view properly.

'My God, it's the *Lorne*, postal packet.'

'You know her, your honour?'

'Well, and her captain too, who I hope is still with us.'

'A Falmouth packet carries more metal than we do.'

Pearce nodded in agreement as he swept the scene again to register that the vessels *Lorne* was engaged against were likewise two-masted brigs of some twelve guns. They would not be as sleek as the ship on which he had sailed with Captain McGann, yet his opponents likewise were larger than *Larcher* and better armed. Here was an old friend in a fight and that meant his orders could go hang and likewise the risks. It was time to be back on deck so he grabbed a backstay and slid down, pleased to note that they had closed so much the entire action was in plain view.

'Mr Dorling, we will need to be nippy to confound these two . . . what I assume to be Frenchmen.'

'Spanish colours, sir.'

'There are not many vessels that have the legs of a Falmouth packet so I suspect a ruse to get close to a brig that could show them a clean pair heels, indeed they were designed to avoid a battle rather than engage in one.

'Spain might have declared war on Britannia since we weighed, but it makes no odds, there is a British vessel in distress and we must give her aid. Those two are between *Lorne* and us and what I aim to do is get past them and coordinate my actions with the packet. They will not want to fight if we are acting in unison, they will want to disengage and we must help them do so.'

'We should shorten sail, sir.'

'Make it so – let's get the headsails in as well as the lateen and go down to topsails. Gun captains, as soon as we have shortened sail get your cannon run out and loaded, both sides.'

'They're bigger and heavier than us, sir, they won't expect us to come on.'

'Well they are in for a surprise. I want those cannon trained right forward and the bow chaser to fire as soon as they have a range that might do some damage. Mr Dorling, keep an eye on the sods; I want to know if they alter course to impede us or come right about to give us a broadside.'

Time can seem to stand still at sea; even with all the action going on over the bow the act of closing with whosoever were the enemy seemed to take an eternity. Having loaded and run out both sides he had split the men needed to fire them and he also had to make sure they did not all go off at once in case the ship's timbers could not bear it. The only way to control that was to take charge himself and he went to the bow, talking to each man as he passed him, giving reassurance.

'You all right, Charlie?'

'Never better.'

He turned to ask Rufus the same question, to be met by a steely look in a man who had, when he first met him, been so much of a callow boy. There was no need to question him, and that applied to the majority of the crew, because this was what they trained for. Then, of course, there was a tradition of victory at sea: Britannia Ruled the Waves, so they expected victory almost as a right. The one person Pearce had not considered was himself and he realised that he too had blood coursing through his veins, had eyesight seemingly more acute than normal along with the knowledge that he was actually looking forward to a fight.

'Enemy to starboard has put down his helm, sir, and is turning to meet us.'

'He's too late,' Pearce replied, wondering how he could be sure, but he was.

The swinging ship had held his course too long thinking that a smaller fighting ship would not attack but, more likely, only seek to bluff in order to get him to draw off from the packet. Now he had realised he was wrong and he was acting to prevent it. Pearce could see men rushing across the deck to run in and load guns which had not yet been employed, and that became crucial. Could they get them into use before he could rake them? If he won the race the first bout was his, if not this deck would be a mass of bloody broken flesh in less than a minute of mayhem.

'Bow chaser, see if you can slow their loading.'

The starboard cannon spoke almost before he had finished giving the order and he kicked himself for not loading it with grape. Yet it had an effect, called down from the masthead for he could see nothing for smoke. The enemy had shied way from their guns, probably because they expected a mass of small metal balls to sweep across their deck. As it was, the round shot hit the bulwarks and broke off a serious amount of wooden splinters.

The man in command obviously realised that he was going to lose the contest to load, but then he compounded his original error. To seek to escape by turning to port proved to be the worst choice of all, for he had only two cannon – stern chasers – with which to meet a full rolling broadside from HMS *Larcher*. If that was not much compared to a ship of the line his adversary was still presenting the most vulnerable part of his ship to his enemy.

'You've got him, your honour,' Dorling shouted.

There was a scene of panic on the enemy deck; they knew what was coming just as they knew there was nowhere to hide, for on the up roll *Larcher*'s cannons could rake the deck, on the down roll she would put her round shot right in through the stern lights and they would run the length of the brig killing anyone in their path, and that said nothing regarding the damage to the hull and her internal construction. The crack of musket balls whizzing past his ear reminded Pearce he had forgotten about that. Luckily Michael O'Hagan had not: he and a quartet of others let fly to keep down the heads of their opposite numbers, now trying to reload.

'Number one. Fire!' Pearce took three steps as the ship dipped into the swell. 'Number two. Fire! He kept walking; if he had stopped to look he would have seen the transom of the enemy brig disintegrate on the second ball, with a great crashing sound as it went through the flimsy wood, huge flying splinters following in its wake. Even over the sound of guns, the screams could be clearly heard of those who worked on the lower deck, but he was soon disabused of an easy success.

HMS *Larcher* shuddered as though she had hit a wall. It was not return fire, but a broadside from the second enemy vessel, which had ceased now to bother *Lorne* and directed her attention to saving her consort, which had suffered so badly her head had fallen off and she looked to be rudderless; cannon number four had seen to that part of her steerage gear. Aboard *Larcher* thuds and cracks indicated some of her scantlings were stove in, but a quick check got the message from below that there was no water entering to flood the lower decks or gaps so wide that daylight could enter.

'*Lorne* is attacking, Mr Pearce, sir.'

Pearce looked to where a finger pointed and there he could see that the packet had raised a tad more sail to close with the enemy and he was not alone in the observation; the fellow who had just delivered that broadside and was preparing another saw it too, to realise that if he did not move swiftly he would be trapped between two fires. That he was a good sailor became immediately obvious as he abandoned his cannon in favour of canvas, getting enough aloft, and quickly, to outmanoeuvre those trying to close with him under scraps of topsail.

Better still than that, he swept round *Larcher*'s stern and had a cable ready to take his consort in tow, at which point the packet gave up on the fight and that had to apply to the armed cutter, she being too small to continue alone. But the fight was over and the cheering started – so loud was that, it seemed it might be heard in England.

'I always thought you'd make a fighting tar, John Pearce, and by the Good Lord I was right.'

McGann, small, bright-eyed and with ginger hair, was indeed still in command and there were many other familiar faces to greet and shake hands with. But *Lorne* was Falmouth bound and carrying both mail and specie, so to linger was not possible; speed for the post was of the essence. Unusually, Captain McGann took an on-board drink to toast their victory, for he was abstemious at sea and the opposite on land. He also had fulsome compliments for Emily Barclay and a wink for John Pearce to tell him what a rogue he was, and too soon they parted company to the sound of repairs being made to *Larcher*'s damaged hull.

'I am glad he is going north, Emily. The last time I was with him in Gibraltar McGann started a brawl. In drink he is convinced that he is an object of uncontrollable desire for any woman on whom his eyes alight.'

'What, that nice old gentleman?'

'You should observe him in drink, he makes Michael look saintly.'

'Which I am to the toes, your honour,' his friend said, right by his shoulder.

'Mr Dorling, let's get our sails set again and resume our course.'

There was no more than a touch at Gibraltar to top up the water casks and to allow Brad Kempsall to make more serious repairs to the hull than had been possible at sea. Then it was a cruise in an ocean now controlled by Britannia and Spain. Blue skies met blue waters, the sun shone in the day, sometimes too hot, but the nights were comfortable enough for Pearce and Emily to sit up late on deck and have him identify for her the stars. Then the day came when he had to ask Dorling a favour.

'You are the only other person on the ship who keeps a log?'

'I am, sir.'

'Well, I want to go to Leghorn and drop off my lady and I don't intend to write up my course to there and back to Corsica. It is no great distance and the stores consumed will not tell anyone I have gone astray.'

'And you wish me to do the same?'

'I can ask, but you know you have no obligation to comply.'

'Makes no odds to me, sir, if it is discovered they will break you and I will say you threatened me with a loaded pistol.'

Having said that with a grave countenance, and seeing Pearce react in a like manner, Dorling suddenly grinned. 'I believe I had you there, sir?'

'I believe you did.'

There were a mass of British vessels in Leghorn, a few navy, but mostly privateers, for this was the base for the wolves of the Mediterranean Sea who went out only for profit and justified their activities as aiding the war effort as Letters of Marque by their interdiction of trade. Through a shore-based naval officer they found a house where Emily could stay and to which Pearce promised to be back in a few days. Having been together and so close for weeks their parting was difficult and all the old anxieties, put aside for the voyage, resurfaced for Emily Barclay, for if they had talked much they had tended to avoid the most serious subject.

'I will not be long and let us think to talk when I come back, and instead of doing that which we have – skirt round it – let us move on from speculation to a proper plan for our future.'

Pearce was not the only sad face when they sailed for San Fiorenzo, where Lord Hood was anchored. Emily had grown on the whole crew – even those superstitious coves who had predicted disaster if they took a woman on board were sad that she was no longer with them, for she had been kind to all, with a ready smile and a willing ear for a tale of a life too hard to bear, or a wife and bairns back home who lived on the meagre pay the navy allowed.

Sighting HMS *Victory* lifted Pearce's spirits; all he had to do was deliver his letter, then up anchor for Leghorn again, to collect Emily and set off on what would be a less than speedy voyage back home. Life was at that moment as sweet as it could be.

Look out for the next book in the John Pearce series

A DIVIDED COMMAND

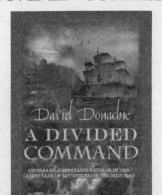

1794. The Mediterranean is proving dangerous waters for John Pearce. His lover Emily Barclay leaves while he is conveying private letters for Horatio Nelson. Learning of Emily's departure, Pearce sets off in pursuit and has to take on the superior force of Barbary Corsairs who have targeted the merchant ship Emily is travelling on, the Sandown Castle.

And another threat looms on the horizon; Ralph Barclay has learned of his wife's desertion and is on his way to recapture her.

To discover more great fiction and to
place an order visit our website at
www.allisonandbusby.com
or call us on
020 7580 1080